He-Said-She-Said

He-Said-She-Said

Talk as Social Organization among Black Children

BY
MARJORIE HARNESS GOODWIN

Indiana University Press
BLOOMINGTON AND INDIANAPOLIS

The paper used in this publication meets the minimum requirements of American
National Standard for Information Sciences—Permanence of Paper for Printed
Library Materials, ANSI Z39.48-1984.

⊗™

Manufactured in the United States of America

Library of Congress Cataloging-in-Publication Data

Goodwin, Marjorie Harness.
    He-said-she-said : talk as social organization among Black children
/ Marjorie Harness Goodwin.
      p.   cm.
    Includes bibliographical references.
    ISBN 0-253-32603-6 (alk. paper). — ISBN 0-253-20618-9 (pbk. : alk. paper)
    1. Black English—Social aspects.   2. Afro-American children—
Language.   3. Afro-American children—Social life and customs.
4. English language—Spoken English—United States.   5. Language and
culture—United States.   6. Social structure—United States.
7. Urban dialects—United States.   I. Title.
PE3102.N42G66   1990
306.4′4′08996073—dc20
                                         89-46343
                                           CIP

1 2 3 4 5 94 93 92 91 90

For Chuck
with love and appreciation

I think that, in discussing the function of Speech in mere sociabilities, we come to one of the bedrock aspects of man's nature in society.

Bronislaw Malinowski, "The Problem of
Meaning in Primitive Languages"

All great civilization is built on loitering.

Jean Renoir, quoted in his obituary
in *The New York Times*

The same-sex socialization, to borrow a phrase, that goes on between the ages of 8 or so and 11 and 12 tends to get passed over, particularly with little girls, as not very important. But when you talk to real women and ask them how important it was to them, you get a different answer.

Margaret Atwood,
The New York Times Book Review

Contents

ACKNOWLEDGMENTS   ix

1 Talk as Social Action   1
2 Fieldwork   18

Section 1 The Neighborhood and Children's Groups

3 The Maple Street Children's Group and Their
Neighborhood   29

Section 2 Directive/Response Sequences and Social Organization   63

4 Research on Directives   65
5 "Man, don't come down *in* here where I *am*"
Directive Use in a Boys' Task Activity   75
6 Task Activity and Pretend Play among Girls   109

Section 3 Disputes and Gossip   141

7 Building Opposition in Children's Argument   143
8 He-Said-She-Said   190

Section 4 Stories within Dispute Processes

9 Perspectives on Stories   229
10 Stories as Participation Structures   239
11 Instigating   258

Section 5 Conclusion

12 Conclusion   283

Appendix A The Children   289
Appendix B Ritual Insult Sequence   291

Contents

Appendix C Boys' Dispute Stories   295
Appendix D Girls' Instigating Stories   299

NOTES   307
REFERENCES CITED   329
NAME INDEX   361
SUBJECT INDEX   366

Photographs follow page 54

Acknowledgments

This book builds on work begun as a Ph.D. dissertation at the University of Pennsylvania. I owe tremendous debts to those who taught me, and stimulated me to investigate both theoretically and empirically the detailed structure of actual face-to-face encounters. Ward Goodenough provided a vision of the importance of *activities* as the locus for the analysis of culture. Erving Goffman's insistence on the primacy of mundane *focused interaction* in structuring human social experience was crucial in shaping the theoretical focus of my work, and led me to look for a research site where interactive activities could be studied exhaustively and in detail. His seminars provided a laboratory for exploring notions of frame, alignment, and participation structure—concepts which are all central to the analysis in this book. At the time I was beginning my research, William Labov's studies of Black English Vernacular were proving of major importance in changing teachers' attitudes towards their black students. His finding that the peer group is a powerful force shaping language behavior, and his demonstration of just how important it is to analyze language use in indigenous, vernacular settings, strongly influenced my decision to study a children's neighborhood peer group. Kenny Goldstein gave me invaluable advice when I was beginning fieldwork.

As readers of the book will see, my exposure to conversation analysis was crucial for the development of the methods and a theoretical framework for analyzing the spontaneous talk produced by the children. I first learned about the work of Sacks and his colleagues after I had already been collecting data for several months and had begun to study how children got from utterance to utterance in their conversation. The lectures of Harvey Sacks were a revelation and crucial to the analysis of the structural principles underlying children's talk. Gail Jefferson arrived at the University of Pennsylvania just as I was beginning to read Sacks's lectures. Those of us who have had the privilege of studying with Gail have experienced the inspiration she provides in seminars and know how extraordinary she is as a teacher, providing pages and hours of detailed commentary on our manuscripts.

I am very grateful to the Center of Urban Ethnography, and in particular to Erving Goffman and John Szwed, for sponsoring my research through a grant from NIMH (17216-01). Chuck Goodwin assisted in formatting transcript, text, and diagrams on the computer.

I owe a great debt to colleagues who have read various parts of this book. In particular I would like to thank Michel de Fornel, Linda Hughes, Manny Schegloff, Deborah Tannen, Sam Vuchinich, Norm Whitten, and Malcah Yaeger. Both Barrie Thorne and Donna Eder provided a careful reading of the entire book, and made invaluable suggestions for improving

it. Their extensive, insightful comments and supportive criticism helped
to clarify many ideas, greatly improved the readability of the book, and
enabled me to see the relevance of my analysis for a variety of disciplines.
Barrie's work on gender and interaction serves as continual inspiration for
researchers engaged in relating the details of everyday experience to larger
issues in both feminist theory and the sociology of childhood. Finally, this
book could not possibly have been completed without the constant love,
assistance, and encouragement of Chuck Goodwin. Chuck worked with
me at every stage in the evolution of this manuscript, and was enormously
generous in giving both his time and his intellect to this project. His suggestions for revision contributed substantially to the book, and I greatly
acknowledge his coparticipation in the interactive process of analysis.

I am deeply indebted to the children of Maple Street for making acces-
sible to me the actual events of their lives. The children accepted my role
as an observer and recorder of their activities and permitted me to tag along
wherever their adventures led. I believe that one of the strengths of this
study is that the children speak in their own voices of things that matter
to them. I hope that this book will help adults, especially those who have
power over children's lives, to appreciate their competence and creativity.

He-Said-She-Said

CHAPTER ONE

Talk as Social Action

This book is about how talk is used to build social organization within face-to-face interaction. It describes in detail structures and procedures used by a group of urban black[1] children to constitute their social world in the midst of moment-to-moment talk as they played on the street. Such research is part of a larger project to describe rigorously, systematically, and empirically the resources utilized by participants to build both their ongoing social organization and the phenomenal world they inhabit as the situated product of interactive practices.

The study of human interaction is typically not treated as a core component of anthropological studies in the way that, for example, kinship, ritual, and economic systems are. One of the things that I hope to demonstrate in this book is that such benign neglect is a serious error. Consider first the central place that interaction occupies in the organization of human social behavior. From an ethological perspective, Cullen (1972:101) has argued that "all social life in animals depends on the coordination of interactions between them." Human beings are not exempt. Thus according to Simmel (1950:21–22), "if society is conceived as interaction among individuals, the description of the forms of this interaction is the task of the science of society in its strictest and most essential sense." From a slightly different perspective, face-to-face interaction is the most pervasive type of social arrangement in which human beings participate. Were an ethologist from Mars to take a preliminary look at the dominant animal on this planet, he would be immediately struck by how much of its behavior, within a rather extraordinary array of situations and settings (from camps in the tropical rain forest to meetings in Manhattan skyscrapers), was organized through face-to-face interaction with other members of its species. The analysis of how such events are accomplished would clearly be a central task in the study of this animal's social organization.

Second, interaction is central to the organization of culture as well as social organization. In order to coordinate their behavior with that of their coparticipants, human beings must display to each other what they are doing and how they expect others to participate in the activity of the moment (cf. Garfinkel 1967). Interaction thus constitutes a central place where members of a society collaboratively establish how relevant events are to be interpreted, and moreover use such displays of meaningfulness as a constitutive feature of the activities in which they engage.

Third, face-to-face interaction provides the primary environment for use of the ability that sets human beings apart from all other animals: language. The talk that characteristically occurs within vernacular face-to-face interaction is typically glossed as *conversation*.[2] Talk within interaction provides the central locus for the analysis of human language production: "Conversation is clearly the prototypical kind of language usage, the form in which we are all first exposed to language—the matrix for language acquisition" (Levinson 1983:284). Moreover, it is not the case that talk and social organization are two separate types of phenomena that merely happen to cooccur within interaction but which can nonetheless be analyzed in isolation from each other. Instead, as this book will demonstrate in some detail, talk is itself a form of social action, so that any rigorous account of human interaction must pay close attention to the detailed structure of the talk that occurs within it.

In brief, the analysis of face-to-face interaction provides an opportunity to study language, culture, and social organization from an integrated perspective. Instead of conceptualizing each of these domains as a separate field of study, one can look in detail at how they articulate with each other in the production of situated human action.

1.1 NEGLECT OF TALK-IN-INTERACTION

A major perspective for the study of face-to-face interaction can be found in the work of Erving Goffman (1953, 1959, 1961a, 1961b, 1963, 1967, 1971, 1974, 1981, 1983). Despite Goffman's (1964) early call for systematic investigation of talk-in-interaction, however, the analysis of face-to-face interaction remains a neglected subject. The importance of the phenomena constituted through interaction, and their theoretical relevance, raises the question of why the field of face-to-face interaction has been so extensively ignored as a central locus for research by anthropology, and indeed the social sciences in general.

One reason can be found in the way in which phenomena and theoretical issues were partitioned among the various social sciences as they were shaped into distinct disciplines by their founders. The scope of human behavior was segmented in such a way that the integrated character of the phenomena constituted through interaction fell between the cracks, while simultaneously each discipline treated actual interactive practices as epiphenomena, or formulated basic theory in such a way as to entirely exclude interaction from the realm of what could legitimately be studied. Thus sociology left the study of language to linguistics. However, the processes of interaction within which talk is characteristically embedded were systematically excluded from study *within* linguistics by the way in which Saussure formulated the langue/parole distinction. In his quest to define langue as a "self contained whole," he located the social character of language in a shared grammatical system (Saussure 1985:29–33) rather than in interaction between speakers and hearers (and indeed from his perspective, speaking is not a social act but an individual one). For Saussure the great virtue of defining the social character of language in this way was precisely that the linguist did not have to be concerned with phenomena such as social interaction: "Language, unlike speaking, is something that we can study separately" (ibid.:33).

Saussure's focus on the study of language as an autonomous formal system to be investigated in isolation from other social processes implicated in the act of speaking set the agenda for modern linguistics, and was in fact intensified by Chomsky (for example, his programmatic argument [1965:3–4] that actual talk is so flawed and degenerate that the linguist interested in competence should ignore it). Sociologists were interested in developing their own formal models of encompassing social systems, and in these models the details of what happened in face-to-face interaction were typically assigned little importance (cf. Heritage 1984a). Similar developments occurred within psychology (Lave 1988) and British social anthropology (LaFontaine 1986). The effect of all this was a division of labor in which sociology abdicated to linguistics (at least until the work of Sacks and his colleagues) analysis of the details of language production, while for its part linguistics systematically excluded from the scope of its inquiry the processes of interaction within which language is embedded.

Anthropology, with its emphasis on holism and the fact that it encompasses the subject matter of both linguistics and sociology, might have seemed to be in a position to provide a more integrated perspective on the range of phenomena found within interaction. Indeed, movements such as Cognitive Anthropology and the Ethnography of Speaking continued the earlier holistic perspective of Boas, Sapir, and their students, and tried to establish bridges between the analysis of culture and the study of language. However, within anthropology the notion that language should be analyzed as an autonomous system held sway to such an extent that linguists left the umbrella of the American Anthropological Association to found their own association, the Linguistic Society of America. British social anthropologists reciprocated the views of linguists by arguing that the study of language had little to contribute to analysis of social organization. Thus, Radcliffe-Brown (1973:310) was of the opinion that while there may be "certain indirect interactions between social structure and language . . . these would seem to be of minor importance." The data and phenomena to be explored in this book provide evidence that challenges this assertion.

In noting the problems that arise when formal linguistics is assigned exclusive dominion over the study of language within the social sciences, I am not in any way trying to call into question the validity or appropriateness of the strategy pursued *within* linguistics of analyzing language as a formal system. The properties of language that linguistics has taken as its subject matter are absolutely central, and the gains in our understanding about the human mind that have resulted from this approach are extraordinary. My point is rather that members of other disciplines cannot abdicate to linguistics the study of language as a constitutive feature of social action (indeed, linguistics has systematically excluded the interactive organization of talk from the domain of what it will study), or even assume that the perspectives and theories developed within linguistics are the appropriate way to investigate talk in their research. Instead, analysts of social behavior must look seriously at how the detailed organization of talk is relevant to the phenomena they are investigating and develop methods of analysis appropriate to such inquiry. As this book, as well as work in conversation analysis, demonstrates, structure in talk (including details such as the syntactic shape of utterances, the intonation contour that begins an argumentative move, the way in which possessive forms are used in directives, transformations of another's talk in a return move, etc.) provides human beings with a primary resource for the dynamic organization of their social life. Such phenomena, no matter how minute and apparently "linguistic" in character, must be investigated as forms of social action and not simply as manifestations of underlying grammatical machinery.

When social scientists take talk for granted instead of treating it as part of the phenomena it is their task to investigate, a range of rather serious problems arises. Natural language is deeply implicated in the production of most of the data used by social scientists: consider, for example, practices such as survey questions, instructions to experimental subjects, anthropological interviews with informants, elicitation of myths and kinship terminology, coding schemes for observed behavior, questions to natives about subjects as diverse as crop yields, household composition, and voting behavior, etc. If natural language is treated as a transparent medium for gathering information, as it usually is, then the researcher is making use of an unexamined methodology that can shape the data being collected in unknown ways (see Sacks 1963 for more extensive discussion of these issues).

1.2 CONVERSATION ANALYSIS

One approach to the study of social order that does accord primary importance to the analysis of talk itself as a body of situated social practices can be found in the field of conversation analysis established by the late Harvey Sacks and his colleagues, and in the ethnomethodological tradition from which this work emerged. The central place that language occupies in the organization of human social phenomena is recognized by Garfinkel and Sacks (1970:342) when they equate the basic social actor with *mastery of natural language*. Such mastery includes the ability to understand more than is explicitly said within a strip of talk by situating it within both indigenous frameworks of commonsense knowledge and the practical circumstances and particular activities in which parties to the talk are engaged. Analysis thus shifts from the isolated sentence that is the focus of study within linguistics to the utterance embedded within a *context*:

> A speaker's action is *context-shaped* in that its contribution to an on-going sequence of actions cannot adequately be understood except by reference to the context—including, especially, the immediately preceding configuration of actions—in which it participates. This contextualization of utterances is a major, and unavoidable, procedure which hearers use and rely on to interpret conversational contributions and it is also something which speakers pervasively attend to in the design of what they say. (Heritage 1984a:242)

Indeed, the production of talk is *doubly contextual* (ibid.:242) in that not only does a subsequent utterance rely upon existing context for its production and interpretation, but that utterance is in its own right an event that shapes a new context for the action that will follow it. Consider, for example, the way in which a *question* makes producing an answer to that question the appropriate thing to do next. As a mode of action, an utterance invokes for its interpretation the social field from which it emerges while simultaneously creating a new arena for subsequent action.[3]

Such a perspective approaches the analysis of talk as a mode of action embedded within human interaction. Conversation analysts seek to describe the procedures used by participants in conversation to produce and understand that behavior.[4] In essence, the question is not *why* some particular action is performed but *how* conversational events are accomplished as the systematic products of orderly procedures. The stance taken is in some ways similar to that adopted by linguists toward language. Rather than evaluating a sentence in aesthetic terms (as is done, for example, in rhetoric and literature) or using it as a transparent window to gain access to some "meaning," linguists focus their inquiry on how it is possible to construct objects such as sentences in the first place. Similarly, conversation analysts seek to make explicit the procedures participants employ to construct and make intelligible their talk, and the events that occur within it (Sacks 1984:24–25). Conversation analysis differs from linguistics, of course, in that what is being investigated is not language per se but rather the systematic organization of human interaction, and the units being studied are not isolated sentences but sequences of action embedded within interaction.

Such an approach to the study of face-to-face behavior has much to contribute to a range of theoretical and methodological issues of interest to social anthropologists (a point also demonstrated in Moerman 1988). For example, a key issue that has long been of central concern in ethnographic theory and practice is moving beyond the analyst's interpretation of what is happening to capture in some sense how members of the social group themselves interpret and constitute the events being studied. Sacks and his colleagues note that displaying the orderliness of talk is not simply, or even primarily, an analytic problem for the researcher, but rather one of the central tasks that participants themselves face in producing conversation:

> We have proceeded under the assumption (an assumption borne out by our research) that insofar as the materials we worked with exhibited orderliness, they did so not only for us, indeed not in the first place for us, but for the co-participants who had produced them. If the materials (records of natural conversations) were orderly, they were so because they had been methodically produced by members of the society for one another, and it was a feature of the conversation that we treated as data that they were produced as to allow the display by the co-participants to each other of their orderliness, and to allow the participants to display to each other their analysis, appreciation, and use of that orderliness. (Schegloff and Sacks 1973:290)

Moreover, the sequential organization of conversation provides built-in resources for elucidating how the *participants themselves* are interpreting the talk in which they are engaged; within conversation, subsequent utterances display participants' analysis of prior talk:

> It is a systematic consequence of the turn-talking organization of conversation that it obliges its participants to display to each other, in a turn's talk, their understanding of other turns' talk. . . .
> But while understandings of other turns' talk are displayed to coparticipants, they are available as well to professional analysts, who are thereby provided a proof criterion (and a search procedure) for the analysis of what a turn's talk is occupied with. Since it is the parties' understandings of prior turns' talk that is relevant to their construction of next turns, it is *their* understandings that are wanted for analysis. The display of those understandings in the talk in subsequent turns affords a resource for the analysis of prior turns, and a proof procedure for professional analyses of prior turns, resources intrinsic to the data themselves. (Sacks, Schegloff, and Jefferson 1974:728–729)

In brief, participants in conversation have the job of providing next moves to ongoing talk which demonstrate what sense they make of that talk. It therefore is possible to see how group members themselves *interpret* the interaction they are engaged in without having to rely on accounts they pass on to anthropologists through interviews or an analyst's rendition of speaker's intentions. Moreover, this indigenous process of interpretation links cultural and social phenomena; the analysis participants are engaged in is itself a constitutive element of the social organization achieved and manifested through interactive talk. Conversational structure thus provides a powerful proof procedure that is quite relevant to some of the major theoretical issues that have long been the focus of ethnographic theory.

The data provided by conversation are also relevant to important methodological questions posed in the process of ethnographic description. For example, one of the major goals of cognitive anthropology was enhancing the rigor of ethnographic description. To remedy the situation of having to take on faith an anthropologist's description of how he or she observed cultural events in a society, Goodenough (1964, 1981) sought to develop methods with which cultural anthropologists could present to their peers detailed examples of the phenomena they were analyzing so that their analysis could be checked by others. Tape recordings of conversations and transcripts provide data records that can be (1) replayed extensively and (2) independently scrutinized by other researchers (Sacks 1984:26).

Ironically, it is not at all uncommon for anthropologists investigating activities constructed through talk—whether informal or rhetorical—to omit texts from their analysis.[5] Thus, while gossip is constituted by what people say to one another, in only a few instances (Bergmann 1987; Besnier 1989, in press; Brenneis 1984; Eder and Enke 1988; Haviland 1977; Shuman 1986) have researchers described how people gossip by providing transcripts of naturally occurring gossip.[6] Unfortunately, Malinowski's (1959:126) early critique that "there is hardly any record in which the majority of statements are given as they occur in actuality and not as they should or are said to occur" is still applicable to the ways in which anthropologists present their findings. For example, Goldman (1986:405), reviewing a volume on language use in the Pacific, notes that many anthropologists report their personal reactions to speech phenomena rather than providing transcripts of transactions which others may inspect for rival interpretations. He notes that "as interesting as these remarks are, we are nevertheless unable to assess how far what informants say they say is different or the same as what they actually do say, or what the anthropologist says they say." In the present study, detailed transcripts of what the children I observed actually said to each other are presented throughout. This makes it possible for others to check my analysis and provides public access to such records for comparative research.

Finally, the underlying goals of conversation analysis are quite relevant to traditional questions posed in the analysis of culture:

> The central goal of conversation analytic research is the description and explication of the competencies that ordinary speakers use and rely on in participating in intelligible, socially organized interaction. At its most basic, this objective is one of describing the procedures by which conversationalists produce their own behavior and understand and deal with the behavior of others. (Heritage and Atkinson 1984:1)

Despite important differences in the phenomena being examined and the stress given interactive processes as opposed to underlying cognitive frameworks, such an approach is quite compatible with Goodenough's conception of a society's culture as what "one has to know or believe in order to operate in a manner acceptable to its members" (Goodenough 1964:36). In short, the analysis of conversation is quite relevant to a range of theoretical and methodological issues that have long been of central concern to cultural and social anthropology.

1.3 ACTIVITIES AS A BASIC UNIT OF ANALYSIS

As Saussure observed, face-to-face interaction encompasses many different types of behavior. This raises the question of how the range of phenomena found within interaction are to be integrated analytically. Close study of activities permits systematic description and analysis of how human beings construct the events found within interaction.

> It is possible that detailed study of small phenomena may give an enormous understanding of the way humans do things and the kinds of objects they use to construct and order their affairs. . . . We would want to name those objects and see how they work, as we know how verbs and adjectives and sentences work. Thereby we can come to see how an activity is assembled, as we see a sentence assembled with a verb, a predicate, and so on. Ideally, of course, we would have a formally describable method, as the assembling of a sentence is formally describable. And grammar, of course, is the model of routinely observable, closely ordered social activities. (Sacks 1984:24–25)

Indeed, scholars in a number of different disciplines have independently advocated the central relevance of activities to the study of a range of interactive phenomena, including the acquisition of language in its sociocultural matrix (Ochs 1988:14–17), the analysis of discourse (Levinson 1979), the study of language acquisition and learning processes from a Vygotskian perspective (Wertsch 1981, 1985b), and the analysis of cognition as a situated process (Lave 1988). Within the field of face-to-face interaction, Goffman (1961b:96) proposed that a basic unit of study should be the "situated activity system": a "somewhat closed, self-compensating, self-terminating circuit of interdependent actions." Such a framework has close affinity with Gumperz's (1972:16–17) sociolinguistic notion of "speech event," an interactive unit above the level of speech act "which is to the analysis of verbal interaction what the sentence is to grammar." Both Goffman and Gumperz formulate a unit of analysis which emphasizes the interactive meshing of the actions of separate participants into joint social projects.[7]

The analysis of activities is also relevant to general theoretical issues posed in the anthropological study of culture. Goodenough (1981:102–103) has argued that the proper locus for the study of culture is not a society but rather situated activities. For Goodenough, culture consists of an underlying body of structures, practices, and procedures, much like the grammar of a language. From such a perspective, people are not "members" of a culture any more than they are "members" of a language. Moreover, the structures members of a society use to build appropriate events change in different activities. Individuals thus have access to a variety of different operating cultures. Insofar as this is the case, the notion of describing the culture of a group as a monolithic entity (e.g., black culture or American culture) is a chimera that distorts ethnographic practice more than it helps it. Rather, Goodenough argued, the proper locus for the study of culture is the local *activities* within which appropriate cultural structures are situated. Thus he notes with concern that

> in practice, anthropologists have rarely considered simple clusters associated with one or only a few activities as the units with which to associate the phenomenon of culture. . . . Culture has been so strongly associated with social groups and communities—as distinct from activities—in anthropological practice that one often reads about people as being "members of a culture," a truly nonsensical idea. (ibid.:102–103)

Viewing activities rather than societies as the relevant unit for the analysis of culture sheds light on some of the findings that this book will report about ties between gender and speech forms. Research on women's speech has argued that it is different from the talk of males, and indeed I found that when playing by themselves, the girls on Maple Street used talk to build types of social organization that systematically differed from those of the boys. However, in cross-sex interaction the girls not only used the same speech forms as the boys but frequently outperformed the boys in verbal contests. Moreover, in certain activities within their own group, such as playing house, the girls built elaborate hierarchies similar to those found in the boys' group. Stereotypes about women's speech thus fall apart when talk in a range of activities is examined; in order to construct social personae appropriate to the events of the moment, the same individuals articulate talk and gender differently as they move from one activity to another (see also Ochs 1989). The relevant unit for the analysis of cultural phenomena, including gender, is thus not the group as a whole, or the individual, but rather situated activities.

1.4 PARTICIPANT FRAMEWORKS

Activities that I will analyze in this book include *directives* (talk designed to get someone else to do something), *argument*, *"he-said-she-said"* (a gossip-dispute process of the Maple Street girls), *instigating* (a way of promoting he-said-she-said confrontations), and *stories*, with special attention to how the structure and internal organization of a story are shaped by the way in which its telling is embedded within larger activities such as disputes.

In investigating all of these activities, one of the things that I will pay special attention to is the range of participant frameworks implicated in their organization. I use this term to encompass two slightly different types of phenomena. First, activities align participants toward each other in specific ways (for example, the activity of constructing a turn at talk differentiates participants into speaker and hearer[s]), and this process is central to the way in which activities provide resources for constituting social organization within face-to-face interaction. Indeed, an important theme in recent research investigating the interactive organization of talk has been the analysis of *participation status* (see, for example, Erickson 1982; Goffman 1981; C. Goodwin 1981, 1984; Hanks in press(b); Heath 1986; Kendon 1985; Levinson 1986; and the special 1986 issue of *Text* edited by Duranti and Brenneis on "The Audience as Co-author"). Second, in addition to being positioned vis-à-vis each other by the activity, relevant parties are frequently characterized or depicted in some fashion, for example, animated (Goffman 1974, 1981) as figures or characters within talk. I am using the term "participant framework" as a gloss to cover both types of processes.

Although conceptually distinct, in practice processes through which participants are aligned toward each other and the way in which they are depicted are frequently intertwined. The he-said-she-said, to be examined in Chapter 8 of this book, provides an example. Maple Street girls initiate confrontations with statements that depict participants in a specific way: speaker reports that she has learned from a third party that addressee was talking about her behind her back. The utterances used to make such statements provide multiply embedded animations of *addressee, speaker,* and *third party*; indeed, a separate biography for each character as a relevant past culminating in the present accusation unfolds. He-said-she-said accusations thus provide an example of a participant framework that explicitly depicts relevant parties. However, the way in which relevant parties are depicted simultaneously provides grounds for positioning speaker as *accuser* and addressee as *defendant* in the activity of the moment. Methods of portraying participants thus also provide structures for aligning them.

Resources for positioning participants within an activity are not restricted to processes of explicit description. For example, a he-said-she-said accusation, by virtue of the way in which it selects a small subset of those present as protagonists, thus also aligns those who were not explicitly depicted in a specific way: as *audience* to the confrontation. One of the reasons that I am especially interested in participant frameworks is that they integrate participants, actions, and events, and thus constitute key resources for accomplishing social organization within face-to-face interaction. In short, the organization of activities provides a range of resources both for explicitly depicting participants and for situating those present in relation to each other in ways that are relevant to what is happening at the moment.

1.5 THE PEER GROUP AS A LOCUS FOR THE STUDY OF SOCIAL AND LINGUISTIC PROCESSES

Because I wanted to observe closely how humans coordinate interaction in activities indigenous to their life situation, I needed to select a site where I could observe repetitive sequences of talk without my becoming a major participant in that very talk. A children's peer group provided such a possibility. Children on Maple Street played together without adult interference after school and on weekends. In that the children were more concerned about their dealings with one another than their interactions with an adult ethnographer, I could observe them unobtrusively as they went about their play.

The neighborhood peer group, a small society virtually unstudied by anthropologists (LaFontaine 1986:13–15),[8] provides what has been argued to be the most appropriate of all settings for investigating the fullest elaboration of social processes among children (Piaget 1965:396). Anthropologists and sociolinguists have long recognized that the peer group is an important institution for the learning of language and culture:

> In many communities we find that the child passes through a period of almost complete detachment from home, running around, playing about, and engaging in early activities with his playmates and contemporaries. In such activities strict teaching in tribal law is enforced more directly and poignantly than in the parental home. (Malinowski 1973:283)

Similarly, Labov (1970:34) in his work on linguistic change has emphasized that the peer group[9] has more influence than the family in shaping speech patterns:

> Most parents are not aware of how systematically their children's speech differs from that of their own; if they do inquire, they will be surprised to find that there is no fixed relation between their own rules and those of their children. Instead, it is the local group of their children's peers which determines this generation's speech pattern.

Although Labov's work dealt primarily with sound properties of speech, his analysis appears to be equally applicable to larger discourse units. For example, Ervin-Tripp and Mitchell-Kernan (1977:7) find that "many of the speech events in which children engage typically occur among children apart from adults, and they are explicitly taught, in many cases, by children." However, "developmental studies in the child language literature rarely consider peer interaction as a major source of norms."[10] When peer groups have been studied, the focus has been almost exclusively on males (McRobbie and Garber 1976:209; Savin-Williams 1980:344).

Despite the wealth of literature on child language, the language that children use *with other children* has rarely been systematically investigated. When the language and interaction of children above the age of four have been studied, research has typically been carried out in a particular environment: the classroom.[11] Groundbreaking studies of classroom interaction include Mehan's (1979) and McDermott's (1976) detailed explication of the interactive organization of the classroom, Erickson's (1979) and McDermott and Gospodinoff's (1979) analysis of political and ethnic conflicts shaping children in our society within moment-to-moment interaction, and the work of Cook-Gumperz (1986b). Another crucial contribution of this research is the way in which it addresses such important questions as how institutions function and how schools make it possible for children to systematically fail in them.

School settings constrain the interaction of children more than neighborhood environments. Whereas in the neighborhood children play with each other over extended stretches of time, in the school talk with other children is largely limited to lunchroom periods (Shuman 1986:5). Moreover, in the school setting children commonly interact exclusively with children of the same age/gender group. A multiage peer group furnishes social experiences not found in same-age groups (Hartup 1978:132–134; Konner 1975; Sutton-Smith 1982:67). For example, mixed-age peer interaction provides opportunities for older children to direct social activity and for younger children to imitate more competent partners (Pepler, Corter, and Abramovitch 1982:216; Dunn 1986):

> Social adaptation requires skills in both seeking help (dependency) and giving it (nurturance); being passive and being sociable; being able to attack others (aggression) and being able to contain one's hostility; being intimate and being self-reliant. Since there is a greater likelihood that some of these behaviors will occur in interaction with younger children than with older children (e.g. aggression), and some in interaction with older children rather than younger children (e.g. dependency) mixed-age social contacts would seem to serve children in ways that same-age contacts cannot. (Hartup 1978:132–133)

On Maple Street, girls are provided experience with not only a mixed-age group but also a cross-gender one. Such participation possibilities are important in that they give girls and boys the opportunity to interact in easeful relationships as friends rather than merely as potential romantic partners (as reportedly occurs in white middle-class groups).

Studies of language acquisition, with some exceptions (Keenan 1983, 1974, 1977; Keenan and Klein 1975; Schieffelin 1981, Watson-Gegeo and Gegeo 1989), generally deal only with children below the age of four, and typically focus on the relationship between the child and adult caretakers rather than among equals.[12] Researchers seem to assume that children above the age of four have already acquired all the essential rules of language that are worth studying.[13] Such a perspective on language acquisition parallels the general lack of studies by developmental psychologists of social development during childhood. According to La Gaipa (1981:161) a result of this is "the firmly held, but empirically unsupported, prejudgment that the preschool period is a more central transitional period for various aspects of cognitive development."

The present research differs from traditional studies of both socialization and language acquisition in that it focuses on *children in the peer group*. Such a perspective does not see socialization as restricted to interaction occurring in early childhood, but rather as "the whole process by which an individual develops through transaction with other people, his specific patterns of socially relevant behavior and experiences" (Zigler and Child 1969:474). In contrast to the traditional social science view of the child's world as a defective version of the adult world into which s/he will eventually be socialized, this study examines children's interactions with one another as "autonomous social worlds . . . which are not precursors of the adult social world at all, or perhaps only in a strictly limited way" (Harré 1974:245).[14] A primary focus of the present study is the way in which in the midst of peer interaction children are able to create and recreate for themselves their own socially organized world of meaning.[15]

1.6 PSYCHOLOGICAL RESEARCH ON DEVELOPMENT, SOCIAL AND EVERYDAY COGNITION

In its focus on the competencies and activities of an age group of children that has rarely been studied in natural settings, the present research has a clear relevance to the analysis of child development. It does not, however, use developmental issues as a framework for the organization of its analysis; yet the ethnographic methodology used addresses a number of concerns that have recently been raised by psychologists studying the social world of the child.

One very important current in psychological research that ties cognitive development to social activity is built upon the ideas originating in the work of the Russian psychologist Vygotsky (1978). Unlike Piaget, who used the individual as his point of reference for the analysis of ontogenesis, Vygotsky (1962:29) argues that "the true direction of the development of thinking is not from the individual to the socialized but from the social to the individual." Vygotsky (1981) proposed that all higher psychological functions originate from interactions between human individuals; every function appears first at the social or interpsychological plane and only later emerges at the individual or intrapsychological plane. In addition, within Vygotsky's framework, language and semiotics play a crucial role; sign systems are used by human beings both in processes of self-regulation and to mediate the coordination of effort with others (Wertsch 1981:24).

Soviet psycholinguistics also emphasizes the role that *activity* plays in psychological development, arguing that only by interacting with the material world and with other humans can people develop a knowledge of reality (Wertsch 1981:11, Leont'ev 1981).

Soviet ideas about activity have been important in developing the relatively new field of *everyday cognition* in America. According to Rogoff (1984:4),

> Central to the everyday contexts in which cognitive activity occurs is interaction with other people and use of socially provided tools and schemas for solving problems. Cognitive activity is socially defined, interpreted and supported. People, usually in conjunction with each other and always guided by social norms, set goals, negotiate appropriate means to reach the goals and assist each other in implementing the means and resetting the goals as activities evolve.

Rogoff (ibid.:2–3) stresses the importance of including context in the analysis of cognitive processes.[16] In an important recent study, Lave (1988) has demonstrated how the analysis of cognitive phenomena must move from the laboratory into the domain of everyday life in order to analyze cognition as a dialectic between persons involved in action and the settings in which their activity is constituted. The field of everyday cognition shares with Soviet psycholinguistics the notion that cognitive processes must be analyzed with reference to the social, cultural, and interactive events within which they are embedded.

The tradition of research initiated by Vygotsky thus emphasizes how individuals are constituted through social processes in which sign systems such as language play a crucial role. Such a perspective has a deep affinity with the approach to the relationship between language and social organization that is adopted in the present study. For clarity, however, it is important to note a number of ways in which the research in this study differs from that conducted within the Vygotskian tradition. First, a developmental framework, which is central to Vygotsky's approach (Wertsch 1985a), is not employed here. Second, in large part because of the importance of a developmental framework in Vygotskian research, analysis stemming from it usually focuses on a situation in which someone more skilled in a particular process (such as an adult or older child) interacts with someone who is learning that process. By way of contrast, the present study focuses on peer interaction. Third, while both Vygotsky and those currently working within his tradition have undertaken comparative analysis of phenomena in different cultures, the methodology they use is experimental rather than ethnographic.[17] Rather than focusing on developmental issues, this book seeks to describe and analyze the interactive organization of the natural activities within which the children's talk is embedded. Despite such differences in approach, the very real relevance of the issues addressed within the Vygotskian tradition is clearly recognized. Moreover, it seems quite possible that looking in detail at the interactive organization of the activities children engage in will make real contributions to understanding the social organization and development of their cognitive activities. Thus some of the phenomena to be investigated here, for example, the organization of language within argumentative sequences, provide a rich arena for the interactive use and development of complex cognitive processes.

The field of *social cognition* also investigates social phenomena relevant to this study. According to Damon (1983:103–104),

> approaches to social-cognitive study have considered social cognition as the process by which persons apprehend one another's meaning in the course of communication. Studies within this approach have observed persons during actual social interaction and have inferred from such observations children's early abilities to engage in reciprocal exchange, perspective taking, and referential communication with others.

Unlike research in the Vygotskian tradition, which conceptualizes individual cognition as something created and shaped through social praxis, research in social cognition has typically investigated how the individual organizes his or her knowledge of social phenomena. The emphasis is thus on the content of the cognitive domain being explored (e.g., ideas about social phenomena) rather than on how cognition itself is socially organized.

Research in social cognition has recently begun to focus more on the dynamics of social interaction. Thus Shantz (1983:501) argues that "the way to reveal explicit and tacit social knowledge and reasoning is to observe social interaction, that is, the child not as a knower *about* the social world but as an actor *in* it." Arguing in favor of an interactionist perspective and against the use of more static psychological approaches in which " 'summarized' social events [are] presented in stories and pictures," Shantz (ibid.:497) states that

> the emergence of this relatively new approach to social cognition among developmentalists in part reflects the premise shared by some that all knowledge is basically social in nature, that the proper focus of study is on the knowledge and processes of social *relations* as made manifest in actual social interactions of the child with others, and that many experimental paradigms used heretofore do not allow for, or are poor analogs of, actual social interactions and meaningful social contexts.

Within such an approach, researchers such as Newman (1978) recognize the relevance of the perspective of Goffman and Garfinkel in analyzing interactional episodes. Thus according to Newman (ibid.:238), "the illustration of social organization as an ongoing accomplishment argues for viewing language use as . . . a constitutive element in the production of organization." Similarly, Shields (1981:150) notes that

> the child's development of a cognitive model of persons and their interpersonal activities has only recently begun to receive attention. . . . As the exchange of meaning becomes more complex, it becomes increasingly necessary to call on work in pragmatics and sociolinguistics where the examination of turn-taking, semantic cohesion, cohesion of adjacent speech acts, shared presupposition and intersubjectivity have emerged form the study of interactional episodes (Speier 1973; Sacks, Schegloff, and Jefferson 1974; Labov and Fanshel 1977).

More traditional studies of cognition tended to describe knowledge with reference to static structural models "representing abstract categorical knowledge" (Nelson 1981:98). According to Bearison (1982:200), "the presentation of others as social agents in the vast majority of studies of social cognition has been in the form of hypothetical people engaging in hypothetical social acts apart from a social context that has any subjective meaning for the knower." Bearison (ibid.) further notes that "very little is presently known about how children's reflective knowledge in socially isolated contexts is related to their social reasoning and behavior in naturally occurring interactive settings." Psychological studies typically have failed to account for the fact that "our knowledge of the social world is acquired through participation in ongoing dynamic interactive activities" (Nelson 1981:97). Moreover,

> One might well expect that there would be a good deal of information relating the child's understanding of other people to his actual social behavior, but there is not. . . . In fact the relation between social cognition and interpersonal behavior may be one of the largest unexplored areas in developmental psychology today. (Shantz 1975:151)

Some of the key issues that have been raised in social cognitive studies are addressed in this book. Thus it investigates a range of social and linguistic competencies[18] children use in naturally occurring interactive settings and examines the "social skills" or "wide range of techniques for establishing and managing social interaction and relationships" (Rubin 1980:4) which children must have in order to be able to operate within their peer group.

The methodology used in my analysis is quite different from that currently used by most American developmental psychologists. However it appears to be precisely the type of methodology *advocated* by critics of the discipline who adopt an interactionist perspective. In view of this I will discuss in greater detail how my research is relevant to some of the methodological issues that have been raised recently within the field of social cognition.

The current study is based on actual field observation of naturally oc-curring interaction rather than on interviews, laboratory experiments, or idealized versions of interaction obtained through elicited scripts (Nelson 1981), puppet enactment (Andersen 1978), or role play (Brenneis and Lein 1977; Lein and Brenneis 1978; Mitchell-Kernan and Kernan 1977).[19] Most psychologists and sociologists choose not to study directly the talk which children produce. For example, social psychologists concerned with com-munication between peers focus their attention not on the details of chil-dren's interaction but rather on phenomena such as (1) *relationships* (McCall 1970; Omark, Strayer, and Freedman 1980; Shields 1981), as opposed to the machinery for building interaction through which relationships become visible, or (2) *friendship* (Berndt 1988; Damon 1977; La Gaipa 1981; Selman 1980, 1981; Youniss 1978; Youniss and Volpe 1978), rather than investigating interaction in actual settings.

Within psychology, studies of friendship typically study the *content* rather than the structure of friendship. They rely on statements by children in response to interviews, problem situations, and story-completion tasks (e.g., Selman 1981; Youniss and Volpe 1978)[20] and present observational data as rates or relative frequencies of specific coding categories, thereby losing a sense of the sequencing of children's interaction patterns. Gottman and Parkhurst (1980:199) note that a major problem of interview procedures is "inferring that what children say in response to social-cognitive interview procedures is what they think about during social interaction." From a slightly different perspective, Shantz (1983:541) notes that "most research has been focused on the child's thinking and reasoning about his or her social world and not much attention has been given to the *social world reasoned about*" (emphasis mine). Inherent weaknesses of the experimental paradigm itself are noted by Damon (1983:61), who states that "the more we structure a setting for the purposes of systematic observation, the more we risk losing the richness, complexity and spontaneity of natural child interactions." However, while psychologists realize the importance of eth-nographic research with children, studies that would actually do this are generally dismissed as either too time-consuming or unscientific: "Still, some methodological structure is inevitable, since we cannot send re-searchers out all day looking for appropriate incidents; and even if we could it would be impossible to analyze incidents in a comparable manner from a variety of real-life settings" (ibid.).

In sum, although psychologists recognize the value of studying social and cognitive processes in real life settings, they are reluctant to move outside their paradigms, which call for a controlled, experimental ap-proach.[21] By way of contrast, I agree with Lave (1988) that studies of both social and cognitive phenomena must move outside the laboratory into the world of everyday life.

CHAPTER TWO

Fieldwork

I first encountered the Maple Street children during a walk near my home in Southwest Philadelphia in 1970. Seeing a group of girls jumping rope, I asked if I could watch them, and informed them that I was interested in observing them over a long time period, as I was doing a study on the everyday activities of children. I told them I wanted as accurate a record of what went on as possible and would therefore bring a tape recorder after two months. Although I initially felt that I would study only girls' activities, when the boys insisted that their activities were equally as interesting, I decided to include both boys and girls in my study. The parents of each child were visited and told about my purposes on the street. I observed the children for a total of eighteen months.

2.1 RESEARCH STRATEGY

At the time I began my fieldwork, Labov's study of the structure of the Black English Vernacular (Labov, Cohen, Robins, and Lewis 1968) had already proved to be of major importance in altering teachers' traditional view of this dialect as "an imperfect copy of standard English, marred by a number of careless and ignorant errors" (Labov 1970:1). Although I was interested in the larger play activities carried out through talk rather than BEV itself, I felt my study could eventually be of value to teachers in understanding the complex ways in which children interact with one another. In talking with the parents of the children I observed, I told them about the possible implications of my study.

In selecting the Maple Street neighborhood as my research site, I drew upon considerable prior experience as an ethnographer in black communities. I had previously done three years of fieldwork as an anthropologist employed by the Philadelphia Child Guidance Clinic. My work consisted of studying in depth the daily lives of several extended poor black families in both North and South Philadelphia. The reports I wrote of how people coped with everyday situations were utilized by psychiatrists, medical doctors, social workers, and other health professionals attempting to understand the culture and social organization of poor blacks in the inner city in order to improve the general level of health care of that community. I maintained contact with some of these families while I was conducting my fieldwork on Maple Street. I was also well acquainted with the Philadelphia school system, where I had worked as a substitute teacher for two years. In addition, I had had experience with other urban black peer groups. For six months before going to Maple Street, I conducted participant observation among two girls' peer groups in West Philadelphia. Finally, as I was beginning my fieldwork, Charles Goodwin and I spent a month observing and filming children's interaction on a playground near Maple Street.

When I began my fieldwork with the children, I was interested in their interaction in general and had no intention of focusing specifically on their talk. I originally thought that the main topic of my research would be the games of the children. As my fieldwork progressed, however, a number of factors led me to pay more and more attention to the organization of their conversation. First, I found that their primary activity was not games but talk. This was especially true for the girls, who played few games but rather spent most of their time on the street talking to each other. I thus became very interested in the question of how the children organized their social life through talk; indeed, it seemed as if their speech activities constituted forms of "situated activity systems," in Goffman's (1961b:96) terms. Second, because of the technology I used to gather data I found that the most accurate and detailed records I had of the children's actions were the tapes I was recording. Clearly, one of the weaknesses of the tapes is that they do not provide a visual record of what the children were doing. I well recognize the importance of visual phenomena in the organization of interaction, and indeed this topic has been a major focus of some of my other research (M. H. Goodwin 1980b, 1985a, M. H. Goodwin and C. Goodwin 1986, C. Goodwin and M. H. Goodwin 1987; see also C. Goodwin 1981). However, when I tried to take a camera to Maple Street I found that it was quite intrusive; when it was on, the children spent most of their time mugging for it, something that they did not do with the tape recorder. Moreover, the technology I then had available did not permit me to record sound synchronously with images. In this respect our project of filming at the playground, which was carried out simultaneously with the beginning of the Maple Street fieldwork, was quite instructive. In comparing the two field situations, I found that while the silent films provided a wealth of information about the visual phenomena, the absence of sound made systematic analysis of the basic parameters of the interaction, as well as its internal ebb and flow, difficult. The information provided by the audio tapes was far more central, and with it I could track in fine detail a range of interactive phenomena. I therefore decided that I could obtain the best record of the children's interaction with the least intrusion by relying on the cassette recorder.

My initial plan was to document and analyze the children's own activities, focusing on their play. Although the children interacted with many people other than those in their immediate play group and were actors in many other settings, school, for example, I decided to focus on a single setting which was not controlled by adults: the peer group in the neighborhood. The advantages of such a project were several. By confining myself to a specific locale where I was known by everybody, my presence as an observer was relatively unobtrusive. Moreover, the children's interaction was public and achieved in large part through language so that a record of it could be obtained. Neither my presence during their activities nor my purposes in recording them were considered objectionable by the Maple Street community; the interaction I was recording only rarely involved adults on the street, so that I avoided being caught up in domestic intrigues. By not observing the children at school and limiting my conversation with adults, I avoided being seen by the children as an informer on their affairs, and maintained consistent relationships with them. Also, rather than participating in an institution such as school, administered by adults, where adult intervention in children's activities is quite common, I was able to observe activities controlled entirely by children.

The Maple Street group differs from many others in that it constitutes a comparatively self-contained social unit. Many urban anthropologists have focused on the diverse interrelationships of personal networks of individuals scattered about a city (Mitchell 1966, 1974).[1] In contrast, I chose to closely document the activities of a particular natural group which formed as children on one city block played with one another. Within the Maple Street peer group, positions are achieved through the ways children handle themselves in social encounters and make use of speech events; by comparison, factors external to the group (i.e., father's occupation or family's economic position) are of only minimal significance in determining social alignments or group dynamics.

The Maple Street group is by no means representative of all children's peer situations. Like every social institution it is shaped by the historic, economic, and social conditions within which it is embedded. Thus the temporal boundaries of the group's existence, e.g., the fact that it would meet on afternoons and vacations, arise in large part through interaction between the economic situation of the families on Maple Street and the way in which work and schooling are constituted in our society. The adults on Maple Street worked away from their homes. It is not considered appropriate for children to work as their parents do (although child labor was common in this same society a century ago). For idiosyncratic historical reasons, the school day ends much earlier than the work day; the disjunction between these two institutions creates the block of "free time" that the children on Maple Street filled with their peer activities. Had these same children lived in a middle-class suburb, it is quite possible that they would not have filled this time playing on the street with neighbors, but would have been chauffeured to activities and play with friends outside the immediate neighborhood.

The way in which the particular families who lived on Maple Street shaped the social environment inhabited by their children was also very important. At the time I did my fieldwork, gangs were rampant in Philadelphia. However, parents on Maple Street actively prevented gang members from entering the street, sometimes at considerable physical risk to the mothers who stood up to the encroaching gangs. In short, the cultural constitution of "adults" and "children" in our society, interaction between relevant institutions within it, the economic activities of the families on Maple Street, and their very active concern for the welfare of their children created the space within which the peer group that I observed was able to flourish. Quite clearly, alternative social forces will create different types of peer groups. In many parts of the world, circumstances such as purdah (Schildkrout 1978), extreme poverty (Barrios de Chungara 1978; de Castro 1988; Moshin 1988), hazardous living conditions, such as living on a Bangkok construction site (Suthinee 1988), apartheid (Burman and Reynolds 1986; Reynolds 1988), or political violence (Burgos-Debray 1984; Women for Guatemala 1987) influence children's daily activities and severely affect their lives. For example, the conditions described by Suthinee (1988) were so harsh that children as young as four were responsible for preparing their own meals and protecting younger siblings from the extreme danger in their environment (the children lived in the midst of a construction site where heavy metal objects fell randomly). One effect was that the gender differentiation that is so characteristic of most peer groups (including that of Maple Street) completely fell apart. I very much look forward to detailed studies of peer groups shaped by social circumstances quite different from those I found on Maple Street.

In choosing the neighborhood as my research site, I observed a significant yet partial portion of the Maple Street children's world. Children participate in a family culture (Dunn 1986) as well as nonfamilial cultures beginning from parents' personal-social network (Ladd, Hart, Wadsworth, and Golter 1988:61) and the school. The neighborhood, however, is perhaps the richest setting for their interaction; there a range of different categories of children—younger and older, girls and boys—are copresent while they participate in a number of diverse activities (i.e., chores and babysitting) which intersect with play.

By way of contrast, children in American schools generally play in same-age groups. Indeed, cross-cultural studies have argued that the North American school environment, the site most often picked for study of peers (ibid.:62), with its characteristic large groups of same-age children, is atypical of peer groups world-wide (Harkness and Super 1985). In addition, investigations conducted in the school setting (primarily among middle-class white groups) find a degree of gender separation in children's groups—influenced by both children's own preferences (Ellis, Rogoff, and Cromer 1981; Maccoby 1986:263; Maccoby and Jacklin 1987) and teachers' interference (Thorne 1986)—that far exceeds what I will report for Maple Street.

2.2 FIELDWORK METHODS

My actual method of working consisted of traveling with the children as they went about their activities while I had a Sony TC110 cassette recorder with an internal microphone over my shoulder. I began recording two months after I started fieldwork and continued for sixteen months. The children knew they were being taped, but talked directly to the machine only in the early days of recording. Because I used only the internal microphone, I never had to actively point something at the children in order to record them but could get good records of their conversations simply by staying with them. Indeed, the recorder became a natural part of my appearance, almost like a purse. Strapped over my shoulder in its black case, often over my black trenchcoat, it was seldom commented upon after the first weeks of use.

Field notes were typed each day when I returned home from the street. On days in which an event I was particularly interested in, such as a he-said-she-said dispute, occurred or when conditions facilitated especially good sound quality, I tried to make a transcript as soon as possible. Encounters that led to especially good recording included sitting on the stoop talking, jumping rope, telling stories, making slingshots, practicing dance steps, hunting for turtles in a city creek, and composing songs. I excluded from consideration days when children were watching television, playing alone, or engaging in activities not confined to a bounded spatial locale, which would have prevented me from obtaining good sound: i.e., playing football, riding bikes, flying kites, playing tag. I attempted to divide my time equally between the girls and the boys.

In my fieldwork I made no effort to systematically elicit any particular speech genre, but instead tried to record as accurately as possible whatever talk the children produced, no matter how banal or uninteresting it might initially seem.[2] In this respect my field methods were quite similar to those used by Goffman (1953:3) in his study of Shetland Islanders:

> While in the field, I tried to record happenings between persons regardless of how uninteresting and picayune these events seemed to be. The assumption was that all interaction between persons took place in accordance with certain patterns, and hence, with certain exceptions, there was no *prima facie* reason to think that one event was a better or worse expression of this patterning than any other event.

These same concerns led me to reject as a point of departure for my research the study of "events that are culturally encoded as lexemes of the language" (Agar 1975:43). Researchers within the tradition of the ethnography of speaking (Gumperz and Hymes 1972) frequently argue that "one good ethnographic technique for getting at speech events, as at other categories, is through words which name them" (Hymes 1974:198).[3] However, many of the forms of action used by Maple Street children (or members of any group, for that matter) to organize their behavior do not have specific names, although they are oriented toward by participants in much the same way that the unnamed distinctions of a language are attended to. Indeed, even when labels do exist, they might not provide any straightforward insight into the phenomena they name. As Gumperz (1981:12) notes,

> One might be tempted . . . to argue that the study of conversation must begin by describing and listing these broader interactional units and then go on to state how and under what conditions they are used and what styles of speaking they require. This type of description presents no serious problem in the case of the bounded event, such as ritual performances, formal lectures, courtroom scenes, or even staged experimental classroom lessons, such as have usually been studied. But everyday conversation never takes the form of such set routines. The very labels we use are often quite different from what we really intend to do.

In order to disturb as little as possible the activities I was studying, I attempted to minimize my interaction with the children while I was observing them. In this respect my role was quite different from that of other ethnographers of children (see, for example, Corsaro 1981, 1985:1–50), and indeed most anthropologists, in that I was more an observer of their activities than a participant observer. The phenomena that were being examined in my fieldwork, the ways in which the children used language, would have been especially sensitive to intrusion on my part. As research in conversation analysis has demonstrated, talk, rather than being performed by an abstract, isolated speaker, emerges within particular speaker/hearer relationships and indeed can be modified by interaction between speaker and recipient even as the talk is emerging (C. Goodwin 1981; Schegloff 1968). If I had acted as a principal recipient of the children's talk, I would necessarily have influenced that talk. Early in my fieldwork I recognized that talk explicitly addressed to me was more formal than talk to peers. Consider the correction Tony makes of my speech in the following example:

(1)   MHG: Hi. Is it, is it all right if I watch
                       you make your slingshots?
          Tony: They're not slingshots. They're *sling shooters.*

Given the fact that speakers design their talk taking into account their particular recipient of the moment, I chose to ask as few questions as possible. I was more concerned with the indigenous organization of children's talk and activities than with accounts of their activities to an outsider.

The children's perception of me as an observer rather than a participant was frequently apparent in the way that they talked about me. In the following, Malcolm notes that I will not intervene in an argument since, as he puts it, the ethnographer is "just here studying us. Watchin' what we do":

(2)   *In the middle of a playful wrestling*
                             match between Ruby and Malcolm, Ruby
                             complains about my not coming to her
                             assistance.

    Ruby: And you not even gonna help me.
                             What kind of woman are you.
    MHG: Eh heh!
    Malcolm: She just here studying us.
                             Watchin' what we do.

Much the same point is made by Vincent with regard to keeping a secret:

(3)   Vincent: Candy won't wanna tell
                   because like when we playin' coolie,
                   Candy don't start to tell-
                   like to get in our arguments.=Right?

While the children are playing house, Annette enacts a mother greeting an ethnographer who has come to ask permission to watch children play games:

(4)   *Annette, as "mother" in "house,"*
                             addresses the ethnographer.

    Annette: I know you uh, working and you would
                             like to see my children play.=Right?
                             And you came in.=Right?
                             My house.=Right?
                             Just gotta get it straight
                             and you can come any time you want to.
                             Hello my name is Mrs. Murray
                             I try to get you groups
                             and you can see them play games.

The methodology I used, maintaining the stance of as unobtrusive an observer as possible, permitted me to make extensive records of interaction of children with other children.

2.3 TRANSCRIPTION

This study draws on a collection of transcripts of over two hundred hours of conversation. Texts of actual instances of the phenomenon discussed are provided so that others might inspect the records which form the basis for my analysis.

Data are transcribed according to the system developed by Jefferson and described in Sacks, Schegloff, and Jefferson (1974:731–733). The following are the features most relevant to the present analysis:[4]

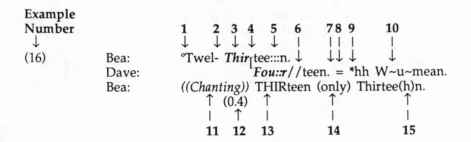

1. **Low Volume:** A degree sign indicates that talk it precedes is low in volume.
2. **Cut-off:** A dash marks a sudden cut-off of the current sound. Here, instead of bringing the word "twelve" to completion, Bea interrupts it in mid-course.
3. **Bold Italics:** Italics indicate some form of emphasis, which may be signaled by changes in pitch and/or amplitude.
4. **Overlap Bracket:** A left bracket marks the point at which the current talk is overlapped by other talk. Thus Dave's "*Thir*teen" begins during the last syllable of Bea's "*Four*teen." Two speakers beginning to speak simultaneously are shown by a left bracket at the beginning of a line.
5. **Lengthening:** Colons indicate that the sound immediately preceding has been noticeably lengthened.
6. **Overlap Slashes:** Double slashes provide an alternative method of marking overlap. When they are used the overlapping talk is not indented to the point of overlap. Here Bea's last line begins just after the "*Four*" in Dave's "*Four*teen."
7. **Intonation:** Punctuation symbols are used to mark intonation changes rather than as grammatical symbols:

   • A period indicates a falling contour.
   • A question mark indicates a rising contour.
   • A comma indicates a falling-rising contour.

8. **Latching:** The equal signs indicate "latching"; there is no interval between the end of a prior turn and the start of a next piece of talk.
9. **Inbreath:** A series of *h*'s preceded by an asterisk marks an inbreath. Without the asterisk the *h*'s mark an outbreath.
10. **Rapid Speech:** Tildes indicate that speech is slurred together because it is spoken rapidly.
11. **Comments:** Double parentheses enclose material that is not part of the talk being transcribed, for example, a comment by the transcriber if the talk was spoken in some special way.
12. **Silence:** Numbers in parentheses mark silences in seconds and tenths of seconds.
13. **Increased Volume:** Capitals indicate increased volume.
14. **Problematic Hearing:** Material in parentheses indicates a hearing that the transcriber was uncertain about.
15. **Breathiness, Laughter:** An *h* in parentheses indicates plosive aspiration, which could result from events such as breathiness, laughter, or crying.

Section 1

The Neighborhood and Children's Groups

CHAPTER THREE

The Maple Street Children's Group and Their Neighborhood

The site of my fieldwork was a street I will call Maple, a wide residential tree-lined street in a black working-class neighborhood in Southwest Philadelphia. In the late sixties and seventies when white families began migrating from Southwest Philadelphia to the Greater Northeast of the city and the suburbs of Delaware County, government-subsidized housing became available for low-income people. Families from poorer, predominantly black neighborhoods in West, North, and South Philadelphia then began to move onto Maple Street. At the time of the study, 1970–71, black families had lived in the area for from one to five years. The three white families that remained on the street were either very poor or elderly.

3.1 SOCIAL DIMENSIONS OF THE NEIGHBORHOOD

Families on Maple Street were members of the working class rather than the underclass (Lemann 1986); their values could be considered "mainstream," using Hannerz's (1969:38–42) classification. The children on Maple Street did not belong to gangs, although less than two blocks away stood the territory of one street gang.[1] One mother belonged to a city gang control committee and would physically put herself in the midst of encroaching gang members when they came within a block of the street, telling them to leave and stating emphatically, "We do not have gangs on Maple Street." Parents helped create an environment where children could play without fear from outside intrusion; during the after-school hours until parents came home from work, children elaborated their own neighborhood culture and social organization. The children spoke Black English Vernacular, although they lived in a working-class neighborhood; analyzing the language of Maple Street children, Labov (1972a:184) found it similar to that of black speakers in Harlem.[2]

None of the parents received public assistance money.[3] In single-parent households (roughly one-fourth of the families), mothers worked; in two-

parent households, slightly over half of the mothers worked at either a full-
or a part-time job. Women worked at occupations such as hospital cashier,
factory seamstress, cafeteria worker, teacher's aide, traffic guard, school
bus attendant, dry cleaner's store attendant, and nurse's aide, while men
worked at jobs such as hardware store manager, public transportation
driver, policeman, preacher, and independent handyman. Maple Street
parents valued education; indeed, all the Maple Street children completed
high school, and five attended college. In 1986 most of the boys I had
observed in 1970–71 held blue-collar jobs similar to those of their fathers;
they worked in occupations such as construction worker, handyman, pipe
fitter, air conditioning installer, restaurant cook, car mechanic, plant
worker, and T-shirt printer. Malcolm, who was by far the most adept in
the use of language of verbal play, has a white-collar job and works for a
prominent computer firm in Philadelphia. A few of the children are on
drugs and unemployed. In 1986, most of the girls I observed were married,
had young children, and did not have to work. Those who were working
tended to be in social service jobs or nursing. Kerry, a girl endlessly taunted
for her exceptional scholastic record in junior high school, graduated from
Temple University and holds a job as accountant for a major hotel; her
younger sister Jolyn attends Spelman College and is planning to go to
medical school.

In household composition, the families in the neighborhood differed
from those in poorer neighborhoods of Philadelphia, where three genera-
tions might live together.[4] Generally a household on Maple Street consisted
of adults in their twenties to forties and their children, ranging in age from
infant through teenager. Grandparents of children did not live in the same
household, and none of the adolescents had borne their own children. In
roughly three-fourths of the group (twenty-three households), fathers or
partners were living in the same dwelling as mothers and children;[5] fathers
who lived apart from children gave them money, toys, and clothes and
visited with them weekly. The average number of children per household
was two to three, although in two cases there were five children in a family.
In one case a childless woman fostered a friend's child for four months.
The organization of space in the neighborhood is diagrammed in Figure 1.
Children in each household are marked.[6] This diagram will help orient the
reader both to sibling relationships of children and to the proximity of
children to one another.

Although there was no formal block organization, neighbors met informally for activities such as Saturday street cleaning, street picnics on
Memorial Day and the Fourth of July, and projects such as painting a
"Caution Children at Play" warning at the intersection of Maple and Tulip
streets, stringing Christmas lights in the neighborhood, and electing someone to be in charge of the wrench that would open and close the "water
plug" in summer.

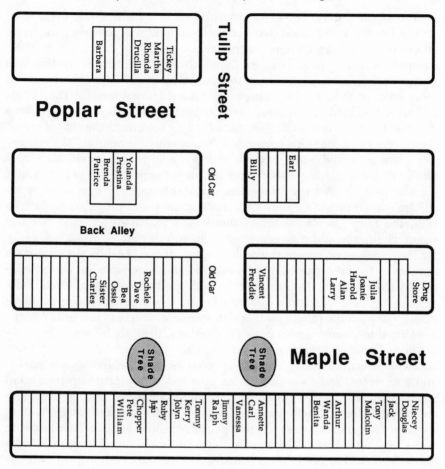

Figure 1

3.2 PHYSICAL FEATURES OF HOMES AND NEIGHBORHOOD

The ten-thousand-dollar row homes on Maple Street bore little resemblance to the rented spaces or housing projects that families had lived in previously. Homes on Maple were similar to those in white working-class Italian-American neighborhoods of South Philadelphia; they not only were more spacious but also were in considerably better physical condition than those of poor blacks among whom I did fieldwork in West, South, and North Philadelphia. Unlike the houses described by Binzen (1971) for another part of the city, these homes were not part of a "vast dreary industrial landscape."[7]

The single-family, two-story row houses in which people lived, constructed of brick and wood, were connected in lines of fourteen, spanning an entire block to its corners. People complained that they could hear arguments occurring in an adjacent family dwelling because of the thinness of the walls separating the row houses. In contrast to neighborhoods in other areas of Philadelphia, there were no abandoned houses. The homes on Maple had landscaped front-yard gardens and two flights of steps from the street to the front door. A cement landing separated the sets of steps. On the edges of the steps there were frequently iron railings. The cement step areas of two adjoining houses provided a large area for children to sit while talking or playing. When it rained, they might still sit outside, under a metal awning. A large shade tree on Maple made it cool enough for children to sit outside even on the hottest days and provided protection from the rain. On Poplar Street there were expansive covered porches where children could play protected from sun or rain.

The interiors of homes resembled closely those of white working-class families in the city, particularly those of Italian-Americans in South Philadelphia. They contrasted dramatically with the homes of poor black Philadelphia families, who could not afford to have furniture constitute a high-priority item in the family budget. For example, whereas linoleum "rugs" were used in poorer homes as floor coverings, the only linoleum in working-class families' homes was in the kitchen or bathroom. Many houses had wall-to-wall carpeting and living room "suites," matching coffee table and end tables, and chairs and sofas guarded with plastic slipcovers. On some living room walls hung elaborate patterned glass mirrors, enlarging the sense of space; family pictures adorned both walls and tables. Dining rooms were generally reserved for special occasions such as Thanksgiving and Christmas dinners. Most social activity, including eating inside the house, centered in the kitchen (usually well stocked with Tupperware) or in a small front glass-enclosed or screened-in porch. In one home a plastic footrunner led from the front door to the kitchen, signaling the place where children were allowed to walk.

3.3 THE SPATIAL ORGANIZATION OF THE NEIGHBORHOOD

Maple Street was a relatively quiet, residential street by comparison with other, more traveled streets of Philadelphia. Although it intersected a street on which there were several small stores that served the area, it was not a major through street connecting business or shopping areas of town. However, it was expected that a game of football, dead blocks, or jump rope would be interrupted many times during its course by cars. The part of Maple Street on which children lived included both a hill and flat street. Children thus could enjoy skating, bicycle riding, and go-cart racing on the incline of their street in addition to games more suited to a flat surface.

The second major street on which children played was Poplar, a much smaller and less-traveled street parallel to Maple. Connecting these streets was Tulip, a street with two abandoned cars. The back yards and garages of corner houses bordered Tulip; and a small, one-person-wide cement alleyway separated the dirt or cement back yards of Maple and Poplar and intersected with Tulip. At one corner of Maple was an elementary school and playground; an expansive city park with a creek stood three blocks from the neighborhood. The map in Figure 2 provides an overview of the neighborhood and includes the location of households of children who occasionally played with the children of the Maple Street group.

Children regularly played on the street after school, on weekends, and daily when school was not in session (which happened frequently during my fieldwork because of frequent school strikes). During these times, the street was principally a stage for children's rather than adults' interactions. In poorer Philadelphia communities, adults as well as children are constantly in one another's midst (see, for example, Rose 1987). However, Maple Street was a working-class neighborhood, and most adults were away at their jobs during the day. Those at home used their screened-in porches rather than their front stoops if they wanted to view happenings on the street. Although it was quite common in North or South Philadelphia for adults to sit outside eating or talking, such activities were conducted much more privately on Maple Street.

In contrast to patterns of play reported for middle-class white children,[8] most of girls' as well as boys' activities took place outside their homes. Parents imposed constraints regarding where play should occur. Except for special activities such as practicing dance steps to music, playing instruments, or having a club meeting, the inside of the house was generally offlimits to children.[9] In some cases parents did not return home from their jobs until late in the afternoon and did not want children to play unattended in the house with friends. In addition, some parents were afraid of potential damage to costly furnishings.[10]

Children on Maple Street also preferred to play outside among a group of friends rather than indoors with store-bought toys. In this they differed from middle-class children (Sutton-Smith 1985) but were like other black children's play groups.[11] The pattern of limited access to inside space in conjunction with children's own preference for being outside and the availability of a large pool of friends nearby made possible a rich environment for peer learning.[12]

3.4 AN OVERVIEW OF THE MAPLE STREET GROUP

In general terms, the children divided themselves into four separate clusters, differentiated by the age and sex of the participants in each;[13] members of each cluster interacted more with each other than with outsiders:[14]

Younger Girls	Ages 4–10	8 children
Younger Boys	Ages 5–6	3 children
Older Girls	Ages 10–13	15 children
Older Boys	Ages 9–14	23 children

Despite these divisions, girls and boys of the same age group were frequently in close proximity and talked with each other. On Maple Street

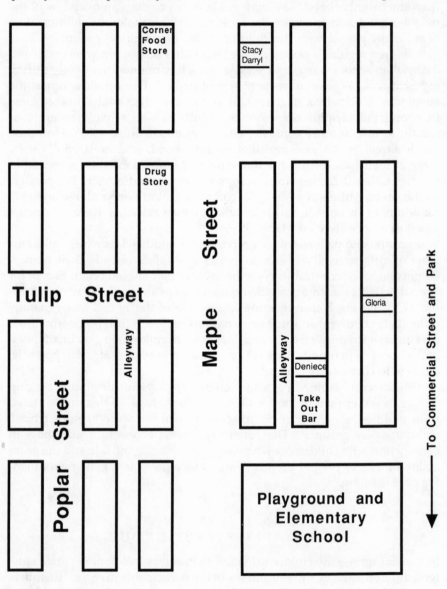

Figure 2

the children attended approximately ten different schools, where they also formed friendship groups. In addition, they maintained ties with cousins and occasionally friends from former neighborhoods in other parts of the city.

Clear age boundaries delimited the peer group that played on the street from both very young children and adolescents. Children younger than four were usually under their mother's or a caretaker's supervision inside the home or on a screened-in porch and did not play on the street.[15] Children fourteen and older generally interacted in couples and not necessarily with children from the local neighborhood; friends were chosen because they shared similar interests rather than because they lived nearby. Adolescents were frequently visiting in other neighborhoods, playing sports, working (generally at a local store), or sitting on the steps holding private conversations with friends of the opposite sex. Because children younger than four and older than fourteen were generally inaccessible for observation, the study dealt with children between those ages. I spent more time with children in the older (9–14) age groups, and far greater attention is given to the interactions of older children in this book.

Although occasionally relatives or friends from other neighborhoods came to visit, among the four- to fourteen-year-olds, most of the time the children's playmates lived within a block's distance. Whereas in upper-middle-class neighborhoods children are commonly chauffeured to play with friends they select on the basis of common interests or values (Medrich, Roizen, Rubin, and Buckley 1982:40), on Maple Street as in other urban black communities best friendships are formed on the basis of proximity (Medrich, Roizen, Rubin, and Buckley 1982).[16] Children recognized their "hundred block" as a unit distinct from others:

(1)   *Pointing to another block of Maple Street*

      Kerry: You know why that street is so noisy,
                    Because *them* kids get a*long* nice.
                    Ain't nobody gonna *t*ease somebody.
                    That's why they get along so *n*ice.
      Bea: I wish I lived down in *that* hundred block.

3.5 THE SPATIAL ORGANIZATION OF CHILDREN'S ACTIVITIES

Both girls and boys traveled to school by bus, sometimes in another area of the city. For example, some fourth- through sixth-grade children were attending an experimental school several miles away at the Franklin Institute in Center City. Generally boys spent more time away from the neighborhood than girls;[17] their activities might require them to travel several blocks. Some of the members of the older boys' group belonged to the basketball and football teams organized at a recreational center eight blocks away. Neighborhood athletic events, such as basketball or football games, and jobs such as paper routes and corner store clerks' helpers provided legitimate reasons for boys ten and older to be away from the street; not infrequently boys twelve and older spent time at a neighborhood pool hall. Girls of an equivalent age to boys did not have steady jobs outside the neighborhood; they often "went to the store" (either for groceries or to the cleaners) for parents or neighbors, receiving for their services a quarter or the change from the order; however, girls seldom traveled more than three blocks while performing such chores. Exceptions to the general practice of staying near home occurred when children visited relatives in another part of the city or when on weekends children went to a major shopping district or to the movies, fifteen long blocks away. A constraint on the girls' mobility was that they, much more frequently than boys, were responsible for "watching" younger siblings and neighbors' children and for performing household chores such as washing dishes, ironing and folding clothes, preparing lunch for siblings, and straightening up the house.[18] Boys had relatively few jobs to do in the house and often complained boisterously when asked to do work outside, such as mowing the lawn or cutting shrubbery.[19]

With the exception of jump rope, many of the girls' activities took place on the shaded steps of their row houses, where boys often played as well. From this location the girls were in range of most of the boys' activities, which were characteristically conducted on the steps, sidewalk, and street. Only on occasion did boys make use of back yards (as an area for making things such as go-carts or slingshots) or parks (for flying kites, sledding, and conducting acorn or slingshot fights). Although a school play yard stood only a block away and had a basketball hoop, children very seldom played there.[20]

3.6 SUBGROUPS AND THEIR PLAY PREFERENCES

Children of the four age/sex groups differed with respect to their play preferences. Particularly striking were the marked differences in the play of older girls and older boys. Older girls participated in activities which required a wide range of types of social organization as well as language skills. These most frequently included jump rope (usually "double dutch") and dramatic play such as "house" and "school." In addition, girls liked to practice original dance steps, make things (i.e., crocheted and knitted scarfs and hats, glass rings from bottle rims) and food (such as cake, pizza, and water ice to sell), and on occasion conduct expeditions in the park, for example, to hunt for turtles.[21] Girls clearly participated in a wider variety of activities than boys.[22] In general, however, preadolescent girls played fewer games and participated little in team sports, although one fourteen-year-old girl was on the school track team. Girls spent a greater proportion of their time talking than they did in play activity of any type.[23]

A major activity of the girls was planning club meetings and activities. This activity was enjoyed as much for the evaluation of other girls with regard to their suitability as members as for the actual execution of club functions. Many times in 1970 the older girls attempted to form a club with regular meetings and social events, which would include boys. Although they were unsuccessful,[24] the girls nonetheless talked at great length both about what activities they could conduct, and about other girls:[25]

(2)   Kerry: Stacey got a clu:b, and they club is
                    *be*tter than our club. *h
                    They having a dance where they got tickets
                    being sold out already.
                    And *we* ain't even did *no*thin'.
        Bea: Nope. And they got fourteen people in there.
                    Fourteen people in they club.

In 1971 a few of the older girls in the ninth grade and friends from high school were successful in organizing a club (members of which were called "club sisters") which included a president, secretary, and "social ambassador" as well as an elaborate set of rules and sanctions. The club sponsored several "socials," informal parties that included dancing with boys.

The older boys I studied spent most of their time playing. In this they differed from other male adolescent groups whose primary organizational unit is an "extended primary group" (Savin-Williams 1980:344) or "gang" (Keiser 1969; Suttles 1968; Whyte 1943), and indeed from boys in many other Philadelphia neighborhoods (i.e., Berentzen in press). While in comparison to girls boys participated in fewer different *types* of play activities— i.e., they rarely participated in dramatic play—their repertoire of pastimes and games was far more extensive. Organized sports such as football and basketball were played year round, while other activities involved elaborated cycles (Sutton-Smith 1953), usually lasting three weeks, of different games and pastimes such as yoyos, walking on hands, coolie or dead blocks (a game which for a successful "win" involves the moving of a token made of a bottle cap or glass bottle rim filled with tar through squares of a grid drawn in chalk on the street),[26] half-ball, pitching pennies, flying kites, making and riding homemade go-carts, flying model airplanes, shooting marbles, practicing original dance steps, playing musical instruments in a small group, etc. For example, flying kites might be popular for a while until someone bought a yoyo and began to practice tricks with it. In differentiating themselves from the girls, boys in their same-sex peer group contended that their changing repertoire of games was superior to that of girls:

(3)   Malcolm: The girls do the same thing all the time.
                      Play rope.
         Ossie: That's why Bea always go in the-
                      my house and wanna play with my top.
         Malcolm: Different times of year
                      we do the different things.
         Ossie: Boys' games *bet*ter than girls'.

In a mixed-group setting, older boys and girls on occasion would participate together in activities such as playing cards, skating, riding bikes,
yoyoing, jumping rope, or holding dance competitions. When older boys
and girls played house together, they did not enact scenes of domestic life
as did younger children, but rather elaborated verbal fantasies about male/
female relationships through a narrative format which employed elements
of verbal dueling. Younger girls and boys played together more frequently
than older girls and boys. This may in part be accounted for by the small
size of the younger boys' group (3 members) and the low number of
younger children in total (11). Another possible explanation is that greater
sexual differentiation occurs with age (Hartup 1978:144).[27] Younger girls
and boys played house together and enjoyed similar games such as "dumb
school," "Mother may I," "hot and cold butter beans," hopscotch, "hide
the belt," "red light/green light," and an acting and pretending game (Opie
and Opie 1969:304) called "Old Mommy Witch."[28] However, these games
were far less popular on Maple Street than they were among children with
whom I conducted fieldwork in poorer neighborhoods of West, South, and
North Philadelphia. Indeed, the Maple Street children had all but forgotten
the verses for acting or dialogue games. Singing games reported in other
urban environments, such as "Pizza Pizza Daddy-O" or "This Little Lady
Gonna Boogaloo" (Brady and Eckhardt 1975), and "handclap songs,"
which are among the most popular games for rural black girls (Heath
1983:99–103), were played infrequently.[29]

Younger girls and boys differed with respect to how much they played
with older children of their own sex. Younger girls enjoyed less elaborated
versions of the activities that were popular with older girls. By way of
contrast, younger boys rarely participated in the games or pastimes which
older boys enjoyed. Instead they liked dramatic play—imitating soldiers,
milkmen, doctors, traveling salesmen, monsters, Batman, cowboys—and
rough-and-tumble activities such as sliding down steep banks, climbing
trees, and tag,[30] activities largely abandoned by boys over the age of ten.

The differences in play preferences between girls and boys affected how
younger children participated in older children's activities, and thus the
social organization of play more generally. There was far greater age het-
erogeneity in the older girls' group. While older boys rarely had child-care
responsibilities, older girls frequently had their younger siblings, cousins,
or neighbor children in their charge.[31] For the most part girls played in

relatively small, three- to five-person groups.[32] However, they relished having greater numbers of players to make the activity more diversified. Because younger girls enjoyed activities similar to those of older girls,[33] they were considered suitable—even desirable[34]—players in rope, and especially in house and school. By way of contrast, older boys had a sufficiently large pool of people (in total twenty-three, although generally five to ten boys played together at any one time) from which to gather the appropriate number of players for any game; they did not need to recruit boys younger than they to obtain an adequate number of players. This differs from the situation for middle-class children studied by Lever (1974, 1976, 1978), where boys joined their nonpeers in play because of the restricted availability of players in the neighborhood for team sports (Lever 1974:151).[35]

In contrast to the middle-class situation, in which boys are reported to interact more frequently in age-heterogeneous groups than girls (Eifermann 1968; Eder and Hallinan 1978; Waldrop and Halverson 1975), Maple Street younger girls had greater access to interaction with children of the older age group than did younger boys. Such a situation may provide certain advantages for girls in that, as noted by Konner (1975) and Hartup (1978:132–134), multiage groups protect younger children and provide them with broader social experiences.[36] Hartup (ibid.:132–133), after reviewing ethnographic studies of mixed-aged groups, concludes that "mixed-age social contacts would seem to serve children in ways that same-age contacts cannot" and that "overall, the evidence suggests that social development is facilitated both by interaction with agemates and with nonagemates."

3.7 COMPARISONS WITHIN GENDER GROUPS

The differences in play preferences among the four clusters are consequential for another major activity observed among Maple Street children: evaluating themselves or others through verbal statements or bodily displays. Such activities occurred frequently when children were gathered together talking. In a group where individuals share similar types of living conditions and have parents with roughly the same income, and within which there is no fixed status hierarchy or division into specialized roles,[37] making comparisons is one of the ways that group members can differentiate themselves from one another.[38] Important differences can be seen in how comparisons are made within age- and sex-differentiated clusters.[39]

3.7.1 COMPARISONS IN THE BOYS' GROUP

The structuring of boys' games and the ways in which boys choose to organize various activities result in a form of social organization which is hierarchical. Scoring points is a central feature of many boys' games such as marbles, pitching pennies, football, and basketball. One consequence is that the structure of boys' games establishes clearly who is a winner and who is a loser. Moreover, boys turn many activities which could be pursued as individual pastimes into contests. For example, on Maple Street yoyoing was played to see who could execute the greatest number of difficult tricks, such as "walking the dog," keeping the yoyo in play while it remained momentarily motionless on the end of the string. Boys developed elaborate contests to see who could "walk" on their hands the farthest without falling down. Although the making of go-carts allowed the boys to display individual skill in craftsmanship, go-carts, like bikes, were primarily important for their use in racing to establish who was the fastest. In addition, they were used for making comparisons at a group level, as boys compared the design and racing skills of different go-cart pit crews in the neighborhood.

Older boys discussed ranking in terms of skill displayed in games and contests.[40] In contrast to middle-class American adults, who minimize self-praise (Goffman 1971:63–64; Pomerantz 1978), within the peer group "bragging" or self-complimenting[41] was frequent:[42]

(4)   *While playing with yoyos*

    Carl: I do it experience!
                             I do it *be*tter than *Os*sie.
                             Watch. I'll win again!

(5)   *Discussing whose slings are better*

    Vincent: All mines is better than y'alls.

(6)   William: I could walk on my hands better
                             than *a*nybody out here. Except him.
                             And Freddie. *Thom*as can't walk.

(7)   *Practicing original dance steps*

    Jimmy: I'm the best what you call,
                             best step maker *out* here.

(8)   *While making paper model airplanes*

    Freddie: Ossie I'm a show you a *b*ad plane boy.
                             Bad plane. Bad plane.
                             It go- it glides anywhere.
                             It's *better* *than* any airplane you know.

The children of Maple Street labeled the activity of positively assessing some aspect of self "bragging." Indeed they had a special term, "Woo," that was used to explicitly mark self-compliments (for example, about one's new clothes) or brags about skill in a game:

(9)   William: He had his knit on, out there braggin'!
                       Out there saying "WOOO:."
                       "Got my knit on. New!"

(10)   *While playing the game of coolie or dead*
                       blocks Malcolm propels his opponent's token
                       into the "cooler" as he completes a cycle
                       of moving his own token through the grid.

         Malcolm: WOO! In the pocket. AH::: HA HA *h
                       ((smile)) I beat three games.

Rather than having a single overall status hierarchy, the boys used a wide range of criteria to rank themselves in a changing fashion against each other. Thus in the data examined above, they assessed each other in terms of skill in making things (#5 and #8), their artistic ability (#7), and their success at winning a game (#10) or contest (#4 and #6). Moreover, the boys displayed considerable subtlety in the ranks they constructed, noting many different grades within a ranking system. For example, in #6 William noted two boys who were better than he and one who couldn't perform the activity at all. Indeed, in their dealings with one another, the boys talked incessantly and explicitly about the details of their relative positions in various activities. For example, in the following they discuss who gets first, second, and third claim to racing a go-cart they have constructed:[43]

(11)   *Discussing ranking of go-cart members*

         Malcolm: I'm the *dri*ver.
         Tony: He's the driver.//You know he drives it.
         Malcolm: I know what//that-
                       Ossie can't *dri*ve that good.
         Ossie: See- I'm number *three* driver.
                       I'm number *three* driver.
         Malcolm: And *Dave* can't drive that good,=
         Tony: I'm number//*two* driver.
         Ossie: I'm number *three* driver.

Being the first to initiate a sport also constituted a valued status among the boys, and the order in which a particular sport was adopted could be used to rank boys relative to each other:

(12)   *Comparing who was first on Maple Street*
                             to make slingshots

> Tony: The first people who ever knew about this stuff
>   was my brother me and I around this neighborhood.
>   Then // Jimmy.
> Ossie: Who was next. Chopper I think.
>   ┌Chopper long before them.
> Tony: └Yep Chopper. And then after Chopper,
>   ┌You.
> Ossie: └Me.
> Tony: Him- Ossie. And then today.
>   Then came up today with the rest of y'all.

(13)   *Discussing who was first in making*
                             yoyos popular this season

> Jimmy: I'm the one who started it up again!
>   I was first- one day I came outside on the step
>   and I- and the next day Carl and Billy got one,
>   then Dave- everybody had one.

Note how different sports provided the opportunity to construct different rankings. More generally, the continuous cycle of boys' activities created arenas for evaluating expertise that were constantly changing. For example in #4–#8 alternative activities ranked the boys in different orders. This had important consequences for the social organization of the group. The way in which rankings changed as activities changed resulted in fluid rather than stable hierarchies, with no one boy monopolizing a position of authority.

3.7.2 COMPARISONS IN THE GIRLS' GROUP

The literature on girls' play (for example Lever 1976; Savasta and Sutton-Smith 1979; Sutton-Smith 1979) has emphasized its cooperative, noncompetitive features. While girls' activities do not result in the extensive ranking of individuals that boys' do,[44] girls do organize some of their play in ways that make distinctions between participants. For example (as will be more fully explicated in Chapter 6), Maple Street girls structured playing house so that those in the role of mother exerted considerably more decision-making power than other girls, effectively defining for the rest of the group the boundaries of play. Girls affirmed alliances and delineated relative social ranking by excluding certain girls from valued positions in "house." Jump rope is another game which, although not inherently competitive,[45] allows for clear distinctions among group members. In describing jump rope, most researchers have emphasized the importance of traditional rhymes (e.g., Abrahams 1963). However, the jump rope chant most enjoyed by Maple Street girls, "One Two Three Footsies," was not constructed out of rhyming verses; rather, it counted by tens how many successful jumps a girl made. It thus allowed for clear designations of who was more successful in any one round of jump rope, and permitted the relative ranking of players for one cycle of the game. Girls strove to be the best jumper in any one round since this permitted them to be first in the next cycle and also to evaluate individual style. Nonetheless, the game was not accompanied by the boasting and talk about how each party ranked vis-à-vis the others that occurred in the boys' games.[46] Instead the girls rationalized a loss in the present round by noting that each new cycle of jumping had the potential to create a new ordering of players:

(14)   *While jumping rope Drucilla beats*
                        Bea in a round.

    Rochele: She beat you. She makin' me mad.
    Bea: Well I don't care if she beat.
    Drucilla: You might win this one.
    Bea: I know. Cuz you can't beat everybody.
                        Can't win them all.

Among white middle-class (Best 1983:102; Hartup 1983:127–130; Hughes personal communication 1984) and working-class girls (Coleman 1961; Eder 1985; Eder and Sanford 1986), physical attractiveness with respect to body type constitutes a major criterion in the selection of friends.[47] Girls on Maple Street, however, used criteria for evaluation along the continuum of "tomboys" and "girly girls" (Thorne 1987b). The most popular girl the second year of my fieldwork was Ruby, who was considerably overweight but who was quite adept at verbal repartees. While Ruby bragged about the battle scars she had received from rough-and-tumble activities including play fighting with boys, another girl (Julia) achieved notoriety through the way in which she provocatively displayed her figure and was attractive to boys.

Maple Street girls tended to focus on the types of relationships they could be seen as maintaining with others (both peers and adults).[48] For example:

(15)   *On seeing Jimmy's mother*

    Julia: Hi Miss Benton! That's my mother-in-law.

(16)   Kerry: And Jimmy gave me his phone number
                        when I first moved around here?
                        He done *gave* 'em to me.

(17)   *Julia points to her earrings.*

Julia: These are my *m*other earrings.

Within girls' peer groups, statements such as these may be heard in a special way: i.e., not simply as descriptions but rather as attempts by speaker to show herself superior to others. As can be seen below, recipients frequently counter such claims with insult/admonishments (#18), statements that prior speaker in fact is not different from others (#19), or disparaging comments on the relationship that speaker is attempting to portray as privileged (#20):

(18)   *On seeing Jimmy's mother*

Julia: Hi Miss Benton! That's my mother-in-law.
Kerry: Ah shut up!

(19)   Kerry: And Jimmy gave me his phone number
                          when I first moved around here?
                          He done *gave* 'em to me.
        Julia: He gave me his phone number *too*.

(20)   *Julia points to her earrings.*

Julia: These are my *m*other earrings.
Bea: She let you wear your- her stuff now.
                          She don't hit you no more. First-
                          first she didn't hit Joanie no more
                          and now she don't hit you no more.
                          And now she just hittin' Derrick and them.
                          =Right?

Girls differ from boys not only in terms of the criteria they employ for making comparisons but also in their attitudes toward the activity of ranking itself. Boys seem to openly encourage statements about relative rank in pastimes (although they of course may argue about them). However, a girl who positively assesses herself or explicitly compares herself with others may be seen as showing character and attitudes that the other girls find offensive.

Girls constantly monitor each other's behavior for displays that might be interpreted as showing that a girl is trying to differentiate herself from the others in the peer group. For example, although Maple Street girls generally wore long pants to play, Julia appeared one day with a relatively short skirt over her gym clothes. Her choice of clothing was interpreted by Kerry as an attempt to show off her figure[49] (which by comparison with those of the other girls was mature and shapely):

(21)   *Julia is wearing a short skirt*
                                  over her gym suit.

    Kerry: Tch! You ain't showin' nothin' Julia.
    Julia: I'm showin' my pretty legs!

Similarly, on another occasion Benita said that Annette was "showing off" simply because Annette was wearing a particular blouse. In the following the girls talk explicitly about why they can't be friends with a girl who tries to be "different" and whose mother wants her to "have everything best":

(22)   *Complaining about Annette's mother*

    Martha: She don't want us playin' with Annette
                                  so why sh- she try to be so different.
                                  She want Annette to have everything best.
                                  That's why Annette ain't gonna have no friends.
                                  She try to be so selfish.

Boys compare themselves with each other in terms of skill within pastimes and in general adopt a set of values expressive of the larger capitalistic society they live in. When they brag about an object they possess, they comment on its newness (see, for example, #9) or stylishness (e.g., silk and wool pants in 1970).[50] Demonstrating how speaker is different from those around him is considered appropriate behavior for the boys. Here, however, Martha interprets such behavior as "selfish" and says that because of it "Annette ain't gonna have no friends."[51]

Girls, in contrast to boys, emphasize the ways in which objects to which they have access tie them to larger social networks (as Julia in example #20 talked about how she was wearing her mother's earrings). Girls define their social personae not only by referencing relationships to adults and boys, but also by the types of friendship alliances they maintain at any particular time:

(23)   *Discussing Martha's friendship with*
                                  Bea and Yolanda

    Kerry: Bea the first one.=Right?
    Martha: Both of them are the first one.
    Kerry: How both of 'em gonna be the first one.
    Martha: Cuz they y'all two best friends.=That's all.

Girls seem more attuned than boys to intergenerational ties (to those younger as well as older than they). Friendships with adults as well as those with peers are felt to constitute points of comparison. However, girls who openly flaunt a relationship they maintain with a particular person are said to think themselves superior to others:

(24)   Kerry: Julia going around tellin' everybody that that
                        Bea- that Bea mother like her more than anybody
                        else.
                        She said she think she so big just because um,
                        Miss Smith let her work in the kitchen for her
                        one time.

An interesting parallel to how Maple Street children made comparisons in their gender groups is found in Berentzen's study of Norwegian nursery school children. He finds that "the girls' cultural premises and criteria of rank lead to their constantly denying each other's rank, whilst those of the boys lead to their allowing each other's rank and acting with reference to it" (Berentzen 1984:108).

In contrast to the comparative rankings that are found in the boys' group, the girls thus monitor for, and sanction, actions that might be seen as proposing that one girl is superior to the others. Among upper-middle-class girls, Best (1983:93) notes a similar situation. She reports that while "self-congratulation about achievement was acceptable in the boys' world," it was not among the girls. She notes an incident in which a girl who bragged about praise she had received from her teacher for a story she had written became the victim of ostracism; it was said of this girl, "she acts so smart all the time." Similar findings are noted by Eder (1985), who reports that working-class sixth-through-eighth-grade white girls describe self-congratulation as being "conceited" or "stuck-up."

3.8 ALLIANCE FORMATION AND EXCLUSION

The monitoring of behavior that girls undertake has consequences for the type of social organization that is displayed within the group. Girls compare each other with respect to physical appearance and friendship alliances. However, while the actions of the boys make visible a hierarchy, the girls' actions display an orientation less toward explicit ranking than toward similarity among group members. Indeed, some of the means they use to achieve this are quite similar to structures that anthropologists have found in societies with an egalitarian ethos. Lee, for example, reports that a successful hunter among the !Kung Bushmen "must not come home and announce like a braggart 'I have killed a big one in the bush!' " (Lee 1986:19). Others in the camp disparage the quality of the meat he returns with, no matter how good it is. The !Kung state explicitly that such customs are designed to prevent arrogance and ensure that one party does not see himself as superior to the others in the group:

> When a young man kills much meat he comes to think of himself as a chief or a big man, and he thinks of the rest of us as his servants or inferiors. We can't accept this. We refuse one who boasts, for someday his pride will make him kill somebody. So we always speak of his meat as worthless. This way we cool his heart and make him gentle. (ibid.:20)

Several features of this process deserve additional comment. First, while on Maple Street the egalitarian girls' group contrasted with the hierarchical boys' group, among the !Kung, bragging and attempts to display one's self as superior are discouraged among the *men*. It would thus be incorrect to say that structures such as these are found only in women's groups. Second, both on Maple Street and among the !Kung, creating a group in which one member was not marked as superior to others was accomplished only by systematic, ongoing work by the members of the group. The egalitarian structure is in no sense more "basic" or "natural" than the hierarchical one. Indeed, the fact that members of the group work actively to prevent displays of superiority provides evidence that the materials for hierarchical differentiation are recognized as being already present within the group.

Using terms such as "egalitarian" to describe a group might seem to suggest that it is more "idyllic" or harmonious than a group in which some parties try to display themselves as superior to others. However, as field-work in egalitarian groups has amply demonstrated, nonhierarchical groups have their own dynamics of coalition formation and shifting alliances that can provide considerable conflict. Indeed, the egalitarian Swat Pathans studied by Barth (1959) have sometimes been compared to the Mafia. Within the girls' group, there were continuous processes of coalition formation as the girls vied with each other over who would be friends with whom, and who would be excluded from such friendship arrangements. For example, in the following, Martha talks about why she can no longer play with Annette, noting among other things that she would betray her friendship with Bea if she played with her:

(25)   Martha: Annette's mother told us the other day
                          to get off her pavement.
                          And Annette's mother told Bea that-
                          "Don't play with Annette no more."
                          And Annette mad at me so why should I play
                          with her.
                          And plus Bea cannot play with her no more.
                          That's why we ain't friends with her.
                          Cuz I play with Bea.

The girls talked extensively about other girls behind their backs, and he-said-she-said disputes that emerged from this were more elaborate and more extended than any of the disputes that occurred among the boys. Moreover, the girls imposed far more powerful sanctions on parties they judged to be offenders than the boys ever did. For example, they ostracized Annette from the play group for a month and a half, a situation that led her mother to consider moving from the street.

The processes of alliance formation found within the girls' group have been talked about both by the girls themselves and by social psychologists (Caplow 1968; Vinacke and Arkoff 1957; Simmel 1902:45–46) as coalitions of "two against one." Such a form of social organization, based on what has been called "exclusiveness" and a set of close friends rather than a large group, is reportedly more characteristic of girls' groups than of boys' (Douvan and Adelson 1966:200–202; Eder and Hallinan 1978; Feshbach and Sones 1971; Lever 1976; Savasta and Sutton-Smith 1979; Savin-Williams 1980:348). Savin-Williams (ibid.:348), for example, proposes that females prefer "intense personal friendships with single other females over larger more 'extensive' relationship patterns." It may well be that in attempting to find distinctions in gender groups, differences in social processes have been exaggerated. On Maple Street exclusiveness occurred in the ways both boys and girls organized their groups. For example, during a slingshot-making session, a series of insulting acts directed by the group to Tommy eventually forced him to leave the group for the day. When asked why he was leaving, he summarized the impact of the pejorative talk about him, stating, "Nobody want me to play with them."

Among younger children interacting in mixed-sex groups, exclusion is also employed as a strategy for distinguishing insiders from outsiders. The following occurs in the midst of an elaborate comparison between Larry and others:

(26)   Arthur: You gonna have- you- you gonna have a party,
         Larry: Yeah. (0.7) You can't come.

Although exclusiveness occurs in girls' relationships, it is very important to realize that such relationships are not intrinsically dyadic in structure, as has sometimes been suggested in the literature. Waldrop and Halverson (1975:19), for example, contrast boys' groups with three or more members, which center largely around games, with dyadic relationships among girls, in which there is "more expression of intense feelings, more involvement with another, and more sharing of experiences and fantasies." While it is true that Maple Street girls' groups did tend to be smaller than boys' (see #23 above), girls' friendships often involve more intricate arrangements than simple dyadic ones.[52] As will be seen in Chapters 6, 8, and 11, the structuring of girls' activities characteristically involves groups of three or more in complex alignment arrangements.[53] While games are not neces-sarily the primary focus of girls' attention, other forms of play (house, for example) as well as social projects involving gossip result in elaborated forms of social structure, often involving groups of six or more.

3.9 INTERACTION BETWEEN BOYS AND GIRLS

Other studies of cross-sex interaction among preadolescents have reported that male and female interaction is governed by distinctive gender-specific cultural norms (Edelman and Omark 1973; Eder and Hallinan 1978; Dweck 1981; Gilligan 1982; Hallinan 1979, 1980; Hartup 1978:144; Lever 1976, 1978; Maccoby and Jacklin 1974; Thorne and Luria 1986; Whiting and Edwards 1973) which prevent easy conversational interaction across the sexes (Best 1983:139–140; Schofield 1981:72; Hartup 1983:110). Schofield (1981:72), for example, reports that at the school where she studied preadolescent chil-dren, "boys' and girls' awareness of each other as possible romantic and sexual partners, concern about rejection in such relationships, and strong sex-typing of interests and activities result in a great deal of informal seg-regation of the sexes and rather ritualized and constricted types of behavior when cross-sex interaction does occur." According to Schofield, the lack of relaxed, extended social interaction prevented girls and boys from ex-ploring mutual interests which would lay the foundation for a friendship. In a similar vein, Hartup (1983:110) has argued that "no observer would question the fact that children avoid the opposite sex in middle childhood and adolescence."

The situation on Maple Street was quite different. Given children's pref-erences for playing near their own houses, older girls' frequent child-care responsibilities, and younger children's obligations not to wander too far from home, girls and boys were frequently in one another's presence and had ample occasion to talk with one another. The ecology of the street facilitated relaxed and extended types of interaction between the sexes;[54] friendships among members of the opposite sex in the same age group were common.[55] The relationships between boys and girls on Maple Street were characterized by a type of "arrangement between the sexes" (Goffman 1977) which involved an alternation between joining with and separating from each other for various activities.[56]

Among Maple Street children, far greater attention was devoted to com-parison within one's own same-age/same-sex group than to comparing groups with each other or marking boundaries *between* groups (Thorne and Luria 1986). However, when girls attempted activities which boys perceived to be within their own domain, they were challenged by the boys. In the following, the girls are criticized for searching for turtles in a city creek with the argument that they are trying to do "boys' stuff":

(27)   *Bea has just returned from hunting*
                             for turtles in a city creek.

    Bea: Ruby felled in the water.=
                             Her *sneak*ers flew all way over there!
                             Eh-heh-heh!
    Chopper: Girls doin' boys' stuff.
    Sister: Girls doin'//*boys'* stuff,
    Sister: Like *wh*at.
    Chopper: Goin' down the park. Gettin' in that water.
                             Collectin' *rocks!*

Arguing that such activities are exclusively male undertakings constitutes one way in which the boys attempt to critique girls. Girls, on the
other hand, emphasize differences between the two gender groups by commenting on boys' demeanor ("ungentlemanly" behavior such as chasing
and pestering girls—for example, knocking them down while skating) and
unkempt appearance:

(28)   Kerry: Y'all boys have some *dir*ty *h*ands.
         Vincent: We walks on our hands *ba*by and we plays *coo*lie.
                     And knees cannot help *that!*

On Maple Street, children ages ten to fourteen did not date. However,
girls said they "stayed close to" particular boys they enjoyed talking with
more than others and who would come to their assistance if necessary:[57]

(29)   Kerry: We stay close to the person that we like.
                     Now Bea stays close to um Jimmy sometimes.
                     And Ruby stays close to Ossie
                     and I stay close to Malcolm.
                     Juju got mad cuz Bea not playin' with him.

When children of the opposite sex were said to "like" or "go with" each
other, a relationship of boyfriend/girlfriend occurred.

(30)   *Jolyn, age 4, talks about Rickey.*

    Jolyn: I can beat Rickey.
    Annette: *R*ickey, Who Rickey.
    Jolyn: Some boy in my class. Who I like.
    Annette: You like him? He go with you?
    Jolyn: Yeah!

Such relationships occurred among children as young as four, and at this age included extensive playing together, fighting, and private intimate touching. For children nine and ten who were said to "go with each other," symbolic distance seemed more important; for example, "love letters" were exchanged through female intermediaries.

While girls enjoyed the relationships they maintained with boys, at puberty they also realized their need to provide a united front in the face of sexual advances from them. Preadolescent girls talked with one another about the fact that when they started menstruating they needed to be careful that boys didn't try to "get" them, and they discussed various strategies for dealing with boys' advances:

(31)   Kerry: But you know- but you know what?
                     It's good to be able to talk about that
                     with your girlfriends.
         Martha: And if you like it that's why they keep comin'.
                     If you don't like it
                     And you tell 'em right away they stop.
         Kerry: They don't care if you don't like it.=
                     You know that?

In addition, girls acted together when they attempted activities boys critiqued as intruding into their own sphere of activities, such as hunting for frogs or making objects; during such ventures girls kept secrets from boys and tricked them.

The upper boundary of the older children's group was fourteen. After that age children cultivated more exclusive friendships with members of the opposite sex and began to distance themselves from the play group, for example, making fun of the "childish" activities that those in the group engaged in. In the following, a seventeen-year-old girl named Niecey tells Martha that playing house is for "little girls."

(32)   Martha: My mother say I can play house long as
                     I want. We play house the grown-up way.
         Niecey: No. That's that's for sissies.
                     And little girls.

Teenagers who "went with each other" frequently sat together, talking or listening to the radio, apart from other children; such a pattern was replicated even by children ages four and five, who often considered others who entered their space intruders. Preadolescent boys and girls (children 10–13) who were close friends, however, did not separate themselves from the play group. The ways in which children in paired friendships marked their relationship spatially thus changed at different ages.

During early adolescence, cross-sex relationships were characterized by physical teasing, chasing, playing husband/wife roles in "house," and by girls' making things (such as crocheted arm bands or knitted hats) for boyfriends. More frequently, however, paired relationships were not clearly defined among preadolescent members of the neighborhood group. Rather, boys and girls participated together as a group in a wide range of speech activities—including stories, arguing, playing house, and ritual insult—frequently within a contest framework. The children they talked about "going with" were generally from another neighborhood. A boy who participated in sustained joking dialogue, such as ritual insult, with a Maple Street girl could be subject to mild ridicule from other boys; such attentiveness to a particular girl was grounds for accusing a boy of wanting to "go with" someone.[58] Among girls, when someone at the upper limits of their age group spent more time in a couple relationship than as a member of the larger play group, she could be criticized by the older girls:

(33)   *Talking about Rhonda, age 14, who*
                            frequently sits on the steps with Ralph

        Martha: That's what's the matter with Rhonda.
                            She *al*ways wanna be around *b*oys.

It was felt that girls' primary allegiance should be with the girls' group.[59] Girls teased more physically developed members of their group, such as Julia (age 12), who actively pursued exclusive boyfriend/girlfriend relationships. For example, in the following the girls tell Julia they are going to shoot her unless she chooses among the many boys she likes:

(34)   *Julia has just joined the girls after squealing and*
                            running after a boy visiting the neighborhood.

        Martha: Gonna be shot shot shot shot shot shot shot!
        Julia: I said- so, so, what y'all want me to do!
        Martha: Kill! You go over there and *p*ick one.
        Julia: Pick one *what.*
        Martha: Pick one *b*oy.
        Julia: I don't like no boys from here.
        Martha: *You* do so.
        Julia: *I* don't like Jimmy no more.
        Martha: I gotta tell you how she married a couple a men.
        Kerry: Ah hah hah!
        Bea: Heh heh!
        Kerry: She will. Marry a couple of men.

Given the frequent interaction among boys' and girls' groups, it would appear that a major failing of recent reviews of gender and language (for example, Maltz and Borker 1983) and social-cognitive processes in children's friendships (Dweck 1981:325–326) has been acceptance of a "separate worlds" model of social relations, which as Thorne (1986:168) argues "has eclipsed a full, contextual understanding of gender and social relations among children." Subsequent chapters will detail the form of interactions in same- and mixed-sex groups. It will be seen that as important as the differences between groups are the interactional structures they share in common.

Maple Street row houses

Multiple activities, including play, child care, and homework, on front steps

Girls playing a hand-clap game

Boys standing on hands

Boys playing dead blocks on Tulip Street

Racing on Maple Street incline with supermarket cart go-cart

Girls and boys playing cards

Girls' and boys' horseplay

Younger girls playing Chinese jump rope

Younger boys enacting mountain climbers

Girls scraping glass bottle rims to make rings on a manhole cover

Boys practicing with slingshots

Section 2

Directive/Response Sequences and Social Organization

Directive/Response Sequences and
Social Organization

Central to the organization of any group is the way in which its members differentiate themselves from each other. One method for accomplishing this has already been examined: boys on Maple Street used *comparisons* to state explicitly how one member of the group was proposed to differ from another ("I could walk on my hands better than *a*nybody out here"). However, the process of differentiating group members through talk is not restricted to explicit statements found in the content of what is being said. Participants can also distinguish themselves through the types of actions they perform toward each other, and the way in which they respond to the actions of others. Social differentiation on the level of action not only is far more common than content differentiation, but also has far more consequences for the ongoing social organization of the group. Indeed, it provides one key arena for exploring how the local organization of a group can be constituted through its talk.

Directives are speech actions that try to get another to do something (Austin 1962).[1] Alternative ways in which (1) speakers format their directives and (2) recipients sequence next turns to them make possible a variety of social arrangements between participants. Some directive/response sequences function like comparisons, and show how participants differ. They propose that speaker and hearer stand in an asymmetrical relationship to each other. In contrast, other ways of building directive sequences minimize distinctions between participants and result in more egalitarian or symmetrical arrangements of social relationships. On Maple Street, boys typically used directives that emphasized the disparity in status between speaker and recipient, while girls used forms that minimized such differences. By examining directives, we will therefore also be able to investigate some of the systematic differences between the girls' and boys' groups. Investigating the details of how participants use syntax and formulate explanations to build turns at talk enables us to study how boys and girls construct two very different types of social order.

To make such a comparison, it is necessary to examine equivalent events that occurred in both the girls' and the boys' groups. One place where directives are not only common but also central to carrying out what the participants are doing is *task activities*. Analysis will therefore focus on the use of directives in two situations in which the children worked together to manufacture something: (1) making slingshots from wire coat hangers in the boy's group, and (2) making glass rings from the rims of soda bottles in the girls' group. Boys' activity will be examined in Chapter 5 and girls' in Chapter 6.

Girls and boys encounter similar decisions when faced with the task of manufacturing objects. Both must work out procedures for obtaining the necessary resources, allocating them, and then performing jobs relevant to the manufacturing process. The ways in which girls and boys use the directive system they share in common to organize a task reflect systematic differences in the cultures of the two groups.

- Boys establish differences between participants while performing a task. Moreover, this type of social organization permeates other aspects of their peer activities.
- On the other hand, girls engaging in a task with other girls organize their actions in ways that display equality rather than differentiation, and emphasize cooperation during task activities.

Comparison of directive use in a particular domain of action, the organization of a task, thus demonstrates differences not only in language use, but also in the types of social organization that girls and boys build through their talk. It would be a mistake, however, to apply this finding too generally, for example, to propose that girls always talk in this way, are intrinsically polite and cooperative, and lack the ability to skillfully use actions which are baldly formatted. In order to explore the girls' speech further, their talk in a number of other activities is also investigated. Situations examined include answering aggravated actions in cross-sex interaction, regulating the flow of activity in games, cautioning peers when in a potentially dangerous situation, instructing peers, caring for younger children, and playing house. Examining directives in these domains, we find in several contexts other than task activity girls using the prototypical directives which boys give to each other. The forms of social organization which girls select to carry out their play vary widely across different play activities. Rather than being intrinsically more polite, and using a single speech register that is characteristically female, girls may build differentiated speech actions that are appropriate to the situation of the moment, and speak in a *range* of "different voices."

CHAPTER FOUR

Research on Directives

One key speech resource utilized to coordinate the action of separate individuals is what will be called a *directive*, an utterance designed to get someone else to do something. As used in this chapter, the term "directive" is similar to Becker's (1982:1) notion of *request*: "an utterance that is intended to indicate the speaker's desire to regulate the behavior of the listener—that is, to get the listener to do something (e.g., provide information, give permission, perform an action)." Directives are positioned right at the interface between language and social action; although built through speech, they are designed to make things happen in the larger world of social action within which talk is embedded. Indeed, they provide a prototypical locus for study of the problem noted by Austin (1962) of "how to do things with words." According to Labov and Fanshel (1977:86), speakers "necessarily must give more attention to the proper handling of requests than to any other form of face-to-face interaction." From a slightly different perspective, Bruner has argued that "learning to make a request is, in its way, a microcosm of socialization into a linguistic community and into the culture" (Bruner, Roy, and Ratner 1982:3). In view of this, it is not surprising that directives have been the object of intensive study by scholars from a number of different fields. Before turning to analysis of how the Maple Street children built and used directives, let us briefly review some of the major themes that have guided earlier research.

4.1 INTERPRETING AN UTTERANCE AS A DIRECTIVE

The surface form of utterances that in fact function as directives frequently lacks any explicit directive content. For example, a speaker can get someone else to open a window by saying "It's hot in here," a statement that lacks the explicit imperative structure of "Open that window." This has led analysts to argue that in such circumstances "there appears to be a discrepancy . . . between what is said and what is done" (Becker 1982:15). The analytic problem posed is how an indirect request can be interpreted as a directive, or in more general terms, how does one move from the surface structure of an utterance to interpretation of the words spoken as a particular type of action?

Such a question lies at the heart of many attempts in speech act theory and pragmatics to extend traditional linguistic analysis beyond the boundaries of the sentence into pragmatics and discourse. Linguists and philosophers working on this problem used as resources for approaching it not only Austin's (1962) classic work on performatives but also Grice's (1975) theory of implicature and his maxims of conversation. This led to considerable analysis of both speech acts and the presuppositions underlying them (see, for example, Gordon and Lakoff 1971; Labov and Fanshel 1977;[1] Lakoff 1977; Searle 1969).[2] Within this tradition, indirect speech acts (for example an indirect request such as "It's hot in here") emerged as objects of special interest because of the way in which they posed with particular clarity the necessity of going beyond what was actually said in order to interpret language as action.

One problem with much of this work is that analysis typically focuses on isolated single utterances. In view of the antecedents of this work in an existing linguistic and philosophic tradition in which the sentence (and its subcomponents) is treated as the basic unit of analysis, such a perspective is quite understandable. However, there are other approaches to discourse, such as conversation analysis, which begin with an interest in *interaction* rather than the sentence as a unit in its own right. Such a perspective provides a very different solution to the question of how an utterance is to be interpreted as a particular type of action. Instead of focusing on features of the utterance in isolation, conversation analysts argue that the primary resource used to interpret talk as action is the placement of the utterance within an ongoing sequence of action, i.e., its *sequential placement*. Thus Schegloff (1984:34) has argued that whether an imperative will be interpreted as a directive or as some other type of action is governed more by its positioning than by its overt form. Similarly, Ervin-Tripp (1976:59) observes that "the work of the hearer need not begin with the utterance . . . the set or priming of the hearer can be so great that a nod is a directive."

Recent work has focused more and more attention on the importance of analyzing requests as components of sequences (see, for example, Becker 1982:25; Dore 1978; McTear 1980; Wootton 1981, 1984). In an important reexamination of the whole question of indirect speech acts, Levinson (1983:356–364) has argued persuasively that such an action and its response can best be analyzed as a contracted version of a basic four-part sequence in which the "indirect" request is interpreted as initiating a recognizable *pre-sequence* (a type of organization that conversation analysts have demonstrated to be quite pervasive in conversation). A range of systematic constraints on the production of action (for example, a preference for offers over requests) leads to elimination of the middle two moves in the sequence (recipient's answer to the pre-request and speaker's production of the actual request), with the effect that the action being requested immediately follows the pre-request rather than the request itself. What is at issue for the recipients of such an action is not decipherment of opaque surface structure but rather recognition of the type of sequence that has been initiated.

In brief, two very different solutions to the question of how an utterance is interpreted as a directive have been proposed: one describes discourse maxims and underlying constitutive rules for building speech acts, while the other focuses on the placement of an utterance within a larger sequence of action.

4.2 SYNTACTIC SHAPE AND SOCIAL IMPOSITION

A second major theme in the analysis of directives focuses on ties between the shape of directives and the amount of control they propose that speaker can exert over addressee. Directives are designed to get someone else to do something. There are many different ways that an action of this type can be performed, however. Some directive formats suggest that addressee has complete control over whether the requested action will in fact be performed (e.g., "Would it be possible to give me a match?"), while others propose that speaker is leaving addressee no choice but to perform the action being demanded (e.g., "Give me a match, punk, or I'll break your arm"). Such differences have strong relevance for the analysis of directives. Indeed, Labov and Fanshel (1977:84) argue that "in all discussions of discourse, analysts take into account the subject's desire to mitigate or modify his expression to avoid creating offense." They then describe in detail how different ways of making a request display varying degrees of aggravation or mitigation. For example, the following forms (ibid.:85) are ranked according to a scale of increasing aggravation:

Will you please dust this room?
Will you dust this room?
Please dust the room!
Dust the room!
Dust the goddamn room!

As this scale demonstrates, there are very interesting ties between the syntactic shape of the directive and the amount of control it appears to propose. Direct imperative forms are ranked as most aggravated, while indirect forms display different levels of mitigation.

Once again we find a contrast between direct and indirect ways of constructing a directive. Here, however, this distinction is being used not simply to pose the question of how an utterance is interpreted as a directive (although that is an issue to which Labov and Fanshel 1977 devote considerable attention) but also to demonstrate that the way in which a directive is formatted makes strong social proposals. One reason directives have proven to be such an attractive and fruitful topic for research is precisely that they provide a rich set of alternative linguistic forms tied to important social phenomena.

A slightly different ranking of directives is offered by Ervin-Tripp. She provides the following typology for directives "ordered approximately according to the relative power of speaker and addressee in conventional usage and the obviousness of the directive" (1976:29):

Need statements, such as "I need a match."

Imperatives, such as "Gimme a match" and elliptical forms like "a match."

Imbedded imperatives, such as "Could you gimme a match?" In these cases, agent, action, object, and often beneficiary are as explicit as in direct imperatives, though they are imbedded in a frame with other syntactic and semantic properties.

Permission directives, such as "May I have a match?" Bringing about the condition stated requires an action by the hearer other than merely granting permission.

Question directives, like "Gotta match?" which do not specify the desired act.

Hints, such as "The matches are all gone."

Although this typology differs from the one offered by Labov and Fanshel, we once again find links between the shape of a directive and the amount of social control that speaker is proposing to exert over addressee. Indeed, these links have been argued to be the driving force leading to the proliferation of alternative directive formats. Building on the classic work of Brown and Levinson (1978) on ties between politeness and language structure, Blum-Kulka and Olshtain (1984:201) note that "requests are by definition face-threatening acts . . . by making a request, the speaker impinges on the hearer's claim to freedom of action and freedom from imposition." They then argue that "the variety of direct and indirect ways for making requests seemingly available to speakers in all languages is probably socially motivated by the need to minimize the imposition involved in the act itself."

Indeed, a great deal of research explicitly links alternative directive formats to issues of social control. For example, aggravated forms of directives have been analyzed by a number of researchers of children's interaction as displaying control vis-à-vis the recipient (Andersen 1978; Becker 1982, 1984; Cazden, Cox, Dickerson, Steinberg, and Stone 1979; Cook-Gumperz and Corsaro 1977; Corsaro 1979; Ervin-Tripp 1982b; Garvey 1975; James 1975; Mitchell-Kernan and Kernan 1977; Wood and Gardner 1980).[3] Becker (1982, 1984), Ervin-Tripp (1982b), and Mitchell-Kernan and Kernan (1977) argue that children use imperatives less to get something done than to test and make assertions about relative positions among participants.

The contrast between aggravated and mitigated formats for making a directive has shaped research in other ways as well. Far more attention has been paid to strategies of mitigation, and indirect forms in general, than to actions built with direct imperatives. Researchers have noted that in most of the texts studied by sociolinguists, mitigated actions are far more common than aggravated actions (Labov and Fanshel 1977:84). Moreover, it is argued that strategies for mitigation are more numerous and more elaborated than those for aggravation (ibid.:84). An interest in ties between utterance shape and social control thus leads to greater study of indirect requests. Moreover, research focusing on how utterances can be interpreted as directives (i.e., the research discussed in 4.1) shares the same bias since indirect forms pose the issue of interpretation with the greatest clarity. In brief, there has been far more research on indirect forms than on direct ones. However, as noted by Pomerantz (1987:1), "When people talk about being direct or indirect, they sometimes assume that there is one way of being direct and there are many ways of being indirect. They assume that being direct is simple and straight-forward in contrast to the complex and varied ways of being indirect." In Pomerantz's view, there are very good reasons to challenge these assumptions: "all methods of information seeking are worth studying, including those that look so simple that it would appear that nothing much can be said about them." She then demonstrates this point with extensive analysis of direct requests.

Syntactic elaboration is thus tied to two related but conceptually distinct domains of analysis: (1) the issue of interpreting a strip of talk as a directive (where forms other than explicit imperatives can be argued to pose special interpretive problems), and (2) strategies for mitigating imposition on an addressee. Failure to keep these issues clear can lead to confusion. Thus it is frequently said that indirect syntactic forms are more mitigated and more polite than direct imperatives, and indeed the terms "indirect" and "mitigated" are sometimes treated almost as synonyms. There are, however, serious problems with such a proposal as a general statement about the social organization of directives, and indeed it constitutes a gross over-simplification of the research being discussed here:

- An indirect speech act such as "I need the pliers" may in fact be quite aggravated. Indeed, Ervin-Tripp, in the category scheme described above, ranked such "need statements" *above* explicit imperatives.
- Ervin-Tripp (1976:60) also notes that "the forms do not lie along a scale of increasing politeness for all social conditions" (see also Becker 1982:21).
- Direct imperatives certainly do not always constitute degrading actions to a recipient. In appropriate circumstances, such as task activities between peers in a work setting, an imperative can be heard as far more polite than an indirect form: "An imbedded imperative in

an office implies that the addressee is either new and unfamiliar, or separated from the speaker by age or rank. To address a familiar peer as a non-peer is to be cold and distancing" (Ervin-Tripp 1976:63).

• In many cases the situation of the moment itself warrants the use of directive formats that in other circumstances would be seen as aggravated (Brown and Levinson 1978:100–101). For example, in the midst of a game of jump rope it is quite appropriate for someone to yell "Watch out!" as a car comes, or "Go ahead, Ruby!" to urge a player to take her turn. The local environment and/or the demands of the game itself warrant such action, with the effect that no explanations for why the imperative should be heeded are necessary.

• It is also well known that indirect "polite" forms ("Could I trouble you to take out the garbage, Joseph McAllister?") provide one of the classic resources for making a sarcastic statement when an expected action has not been performed (Ervin-Tripp 1976:61).

In brief, syntactic shape alone cannot be used to measure aggravation; a direct imperative form need not be heard as a social imposition, while an indirect form can in fact constitute a quite aggravated action. As noted by Yaeger-Dror and Sister (1987:1134; see also Becker 1982:14, 21), "while many researchers use terms which imply that the directness hierarchy is equivalent to politeness, no such equivalence can be inferred." I will therefore use the terms "aggravated" and "mitigated" when speaking about social imposition. In using these terms, I recognize that they provide only a shorthand gloss for comparing the social imposition displayed by different utterance formats, and that there will in fact be far more subtle and varied distinctions than these polar terms indicate. Moreover, whether a specific strip of talk is to be heard as aggravated or mitigated is something that must be demonstrated within the data being investigated, and cannot be claimed simply on the basis of the syntactic shape of the utterance.

4.3 SOCIAL FRAMES THAT ENCOMPASS THE DIRECTIVE

One of the reasons that directives have proved so interesting to researchers is that they provide such a clear case of rich (indeed almost baroque) structural variety in linguistic form tied to social phenomena. Insofar as the same action (a request to open a window, for example) can be performed in many different ways, the question quite naturally arises how to account for the selection of one of these alternatives to the exclusion of others. Posing this question focuses on directives as a research site where one can investigate in an especially clear way ties between the details of linguistic structure and an encompassing cultural world of social action.

The research discussed in the last section, which investigated how alternative directive formats display different levels of social imposition, is representative of one approach to this question. A second will now be briefly examined. Here the emphasis is on how an encompassing social field constrains the choice of directives within it. Among the phenomena that have been investigated from this perspective are the influence of *status, power relationships,* and *situations* on directive choice.

Such phenomena might seem to overlap with phenomena examined in the last section. Thus, the way in which alternative directive formats display different amounts of deference toward, or control over, their addressee seems intimately tied to the distribution of directive formats in status and power relationships (e.g., in many situations bosses use aggravated directives while subordinates mitigate their requests). However, despite such very close ties between these two approaches, they can be distinguished from each other by their analytical point of departure.

- The research discussed in the last section starts with the utterance and works outward to features of participants or situations. Thus it looks at phenomena such as how the form of the directive displays whether or not its addressee is being imposed on.
- The work presently being examined starts from the social situation (or particular social relationships) and moves from there inward to conduct an inventory of the types of directives that occur in that particular situation. For example, such research might make statements about how the directives used by doctors differ from those used by nurses. Note that this approach uses existing social categories and identity relationships (e.g., doctor ↔ nurse) as a point of departure for analysis. In addition, a coding scheme is frequently used to classify directives into a limited range of types so that statements about frequency and distribution can be made.

These two approaches are quite clearly complementary to each other, and many research projects make use of both, often without clearly distinguishing between the two.

In brief, it is possible to approach the study of directives from at least two different directions, one that starts with the shape of a directive and moves outward to social phenomena, and another that starts with an existing typology of social phenomena and moves from there inward to look at the directives that occur within particular situations. Many studies combine both approaches, often beginning with an intensive look at directive formats which are then employed as a typology to contrast directive use in a variety of situations.

A most important contribution of Ervin-Tripp's (1976) initial study was its investigation of directive use in a range of situations, from Marine boot camp to Berkeley communal groups, including such central social settings as offices, laboratories, and small shops. Variation in how directives are structured in different situations was not only extensive but also subtle.

Indeed, the way in which directives are precisely fitted to the particular situations in which they occur vividly demonstrates the need for extensive fine-grained ethnographic study of directive use in specific settings, something that I attempted to accomplish in my fieldwork with the Maple Street children. Since Ervin-Tripp's pioneering work, many other studies contrasting the structure of directives in a variety of settings and cultures have appeared (see, for example, Becker 1982, 1984; Blum-Kulka, Danet, and Gerson 1985; Blum-Kulka and Olshtain 1984; Bogoch and Danet 1980, 1984; Ervin-Tripp 1982a; Ervin-Tripp, O'Connor, and Rosenberg 1984; Fraser and Nolen 1981; Hollos and Beeman 1978; House and Kasper 1981; Kirsh 1983; Milan 1976; Rintell 1981; Schiffrin 1984; Tannen 1981, 1984; Walters 1980; Wierzbicka 1985; Wood and Gardner 1980; Yaeger-Dror and Sister 1987). An excellent review of this research can be found in Yaeger-Dror and Sister (1987).

When statements are made about the distribution of different types of directives in different types of social situations, complex questions are raised about the nature of these relationships. Is the relationship purely descriptive and statistical, or is it appropriate to argue that the participants orient to the situation and treat it as something that in fact constrains directive choice? On the other hand, could one sometimes argue that the choice of a particular directive format in fact invokes the social relationship thus made visible (i.e., by giving someone an aggravated order, a speaker proposes that he or she is someone in a position of authority over addressee)? To what extent do directive choices in fact *constitute* the relationship/situation being analyzed?[4] Noting ties between social situations and directive use raises a range of difficult but important theoretical issues about the nature of observed correlations.

4.4 CONTEXT AND DIRECTIVE USE ON MAPLE STREET

The research described above raises a number of important questions about how directives are interpreted and utilized socially. Growing recognition of the importance of an encompassing social field that one might loosely gloss as "context" has challenged assumptions about directive force that were based largely on the shape of utterances examined in isolation from the environments in which directives are in fact used (cf. Ervin-Tripp, Strage, Lampert, and Bell 1987).[5] Long-term ethnographic observation of talk and other action occurring in a specific setting, such as that I did on Maple Street, has much to contribute to research into such issues. Moreover, while my research focused on a single setting, it provided the opportunity for comparative study since the boys and girls on Maple Street divided themselves into separate play groups and made use of directives in markedly different ways within each group.

The influence of context on directive use and interpretation is extraordinarily complex.[6] There has been increasing recognition that taking contextual features into account does not mean simply making correlations between a gloss of the setting or encompassing relationship and a frequency distribution of alternative directive formats. For example, after describing a range of important contextual influences on directive choice (including setting, activity in progress, and relationship between speaker and addressee), Ervin-Tripp (1976:59) notes that "context is not simply the factors mentioned above (and the many others in the studies in the ethnography of communication). It is also the prior exchanges of posture and language which can negotiate rank between strangers, mood, key, and the task." Major analysis of context on this level of organization has been undertaken by conversation analysts who focus on how the placement of an utterance within an ongoing sequence of action is utilized by participants as a primary resource for its interpretation. As Heritage and Atkinson (1984:6) note,

> No empirically occurring utterance ever occurs outside, or external to, some specific sequence. Whatever is said will be said in some sequential context, and its illocutionary force will be determined by reference to what it accomplishes in relation to some sequentially prior utterance or set of utterances. As long as a state of talk prevails, there will be no escape or timeout from these considerations. And, insofar as unfolding sequences and their constituent turns are unavoidable analytic concerns for interactants, they provide a powerful and readily accessible point of entry in the unavoidable contextedness of actual talk.

The nature of my data collection (long-term audio recording of extended sequences of talk) and the theoretical interests that motivated my study permit me to examine in detail how directives function within indigenous sequences of action. Chapters 5 and 6 will thus explore the interrelationship between directive structure and context on several different levels, investigating both how directives are used in specific environments in order to make visible particular types of social organization, and some of the ways in which sequential organization provides a resource for the interpretation and deployment of directives.

In brief, I will attempt to demonstrate that directives are best understood as actions embedded within a larger field of social activity. On the one hand, recipients utilize that field as a key resource for interpreting an utterance as a particular type of action, and on the other hand, directives provide participants with powerful resources for making public displays about how those present take up a position or "footing" (Goffman 1981) vis-à-vis each other—how they "align" themselves in ways relevant to the activities they are collaboratively pursuing. Central to the analysis which will be developed is the notion of "alignment." By this I do not mean "alliance," as one might talk about two parties being aligned against a third. Instead I will use the term in a more general way, roughly equivalent to Goffman's (1981) notion of "stance." Thus a speaker can display an alignment toward her *own* talk or actions or toward other parties and the events in progress. Several different dimensions of how directives operate within a larger social field will be examined, including their *sequential organization, participation frameworks,* and encompassing *activity structures.*

Such an approach to the analysis of directives requires close examination of specific activities in which they occur. Chapter 5 will focus on directive use in a particular task activity of the boys, making slingshots, and Chapter 6 will examine a task activity in the girls' group.

"Man, don't come down *in* here where I *am*" Directive Use in a Boys' Task Activity

Play for the boys on Maple Street involved moving from one activity to another. They would become engrossed in a particular game (yoyos, go-carts, marbles, etc.) for a brief period and focus most of their attention on it. Interest in that activity would then wane, and the boys would move to another. In this they differed quite markedly from the girls, whose play revolved around repetitive, long-term engagement in a few basic games such as jump rope.[1] Since different boys excelled in different activities, relative rankings in the group changed as new pastimes were introduced. The boys' group was therefore characterized by a fluid rather than a fixed hierarchy.

5.1 MAKING SLINGSHOTS

One of the activities the boys became interested in was playing with slingshots. Slingshots are usually made from a tree branch with a Y-shaped fork in it. An elastic band is tied between the Y, and projectiles such as stones are shot by seating them on the elastic and stretching it. However, the boys on Maple Street were city children, and instead of using wood and stones they constructed their slingshots from materials available in an urban environment. Both the slingshot and the projectiles (which the boys called "slings") were made from wire coat hangers. To make the sling shooter, a piece of coat hanger was cut and then bent into an appropriate Y with the wire bent double to reinforce it. Rubber bands were stretched between the ends of the Y. Since the rubber bands were quite narrow, the boys did not use stones or other found materials as projectiles. Instead they cut off a small section of coat hanger, bent it into a ⊃ shape, and fired it by putting the notch in the ⊃ over the rubber band. Manufacturing the slingshots and ammunition thus required specific raw materials (wire coat hangers and rubber bands) and tools (pliers to cut and bend the wire) and involved a set of recognizable manufacturing operations (cutting the wire, bending it into different shapes, attaching the rubber bands, etc.).

A pastime such as this could be organized in a variety of different ways. Since the slingshot is an instrument that can be used and manufactured by a single person, play with it could be construed as an individual activity in which all participants fend for themselves. The only preparation necessary is that each player bend wire coat hangers with pliers to make a slingshot and have an adequate supply of "slings." Among the boys of Maple Street, however, the activity of making and using slingshots became organized into a competition between two separate "sides," with a division of labor among participants in each group. Such an organization has parallels to football or basketball, popular games among boys of this age.[2]

My analysis will focus on interaction that occurred on a single afternoon. The boys had divided themselves into two groups, each of which was making slingshots and ammunition for an upcoming battle. Almost all aspects of this process were the subject of extensive negotiation. For example, early in the afternoon Chopper had arrived with a bunch of hangers and argued that the activity should take place in his yard. However, Malcolm challenged him and got others to agree that the boys would make their slingshots in Malcolm's yard. Eventually Malcolm and his older brother Tony were acknowledged to be the leaders of the two competing teams. Of the two brothers, Malcolm emerged as (1) the person intensely concerned with working out the details of how the game was to be conducted, and (2) the person with whom most of the boys preferred to be allied. By way of contrast Tony, although older and stronger than any of the others present, expressed relatively little interest in defining aspects of the game except for the requirements for being a member of his team.[3]

While making their slingshots, the boys divided themselves into two groups that roughly reflected team membership.

Malcolm's Group	Tony's Group
Ossie	Jack
Tokay	Pete
Chopper	William
	Dave

Tony's group was working under a back stairway, and Malcolm's was working on a landing above them.

Despite the spatial division of the boys into two work groups, team membership was not fixed. Indeed, it was the subject of repetitive, ongoing negotiation.[4] Not only did lower-ranking members of the group (William and Dave, for example) try to get one of the leaders to accept them on a team, but in addition there was dispute about how many players would be permitted on each team, and thus who would be allowed to play. When sides were eventually chosen, Dave was excluded.

The fact that the activity occurred in Malcolm and Tony's yard provided them with a number of resources that could be deployed during negotiation about the game. For example, either brother could argue that others should move where he wanted them to, or do what he requested, because they were on his property. However, while this provided both Malcolm and Tony with significant strategic resources, it would be wrong to assume that this material or territorial substratum was decisive in shaping either interaction or social structure. Chopper also provided important material resources (a supply of wire hangers) but within interaction with Malcolm was unable to enforce demands that the activity take place on his property.[5] From a slightly different perspective, Chopper was later able to counter demands from Tony that he leave Tony's yard by using a story to transform the arena of dispute into events occurring at a different time and place (this process will be examined in more detail in Chapter 10). In brief, control over the territory where the activity was occurring was a resource that could be deployed within the interaction, but also one that could be effectively challenged.

5.2 DIRECTIVES AS SITUATED ACTION

The rest of this chapter will be devoted to detailed analysis of the boys' directives. The principal phenomenon that I want to investigate is the boys' use of directives to build, and display to each other within the details of their talk, a distinctive type of social organization, one in which participants are pictured as aligned toward each other in an asymmetrical, "hierarchical" fashion. Pursuit of this topic will provide an opportunity to investigate a range of phenomena relevant to the organization of directives, including

- Sequential resources that participants employ to understand directives and build next actions to them;
- Structures used to animate speaker and addressee as characters within talk performing directives;
- How these characters are embedded within larger scenes of action, and tied to specific features of those scenes;
- Procedures for transforming such scenes and the character structures they contain in order to build appropriate next actions;
- How the social proposals contained in a single speaker's talk can be ratified or challenged in subsequent talk;
- The interactive organization of specific social arrangements, such as hierarchy, within the group.

Analysis will initially focus on a single example. Looking in detail at a single series of events will permit us to explore in an integrated way a number of phenomena relevant to the organization and interpretation of directives, including the way in which participants analyze them as embedded within larger activity structures, and how images of participants are deployed within directives. Analysis will then turn to examination of a range of structures used to depict participants within directives, and tie these characters to features of a relevant context. Finally, the social consequences of alternative responses to directives will be examined.

5.2.1 DISPLAYING SOCIAL IMPOSITION

In the following, Tony issues a straightforward directive:

(1)   *Addressed to William*

　　　Tony: Go downstairs.

What is said here is phrased as a bald imperative. Such a structure is handled clearly and explicitly by all theories that focus on directives. First, with a surface structure that states quite unambiguously "Do X," it provides a prototypical example of a directive, and is thus not treated as raising the interpretive problems posed by indirect speech acts. Instead it is assumed that the interpretation of such an utterance is quite straightforward. Second, all scales ranking directives in terms of power differences and social imposition place explicit imperatives like this strongly on the asymmetrical side of the scale. Thus it is the second most salient form on both Ervin-Tripp's (1976:29) ordering in terms of "relative power of speaker and addressee . . . and . . . obviousness of the directive" and Labov and Fanshel's (1977:85) scale of increasing aggravation.

Questions have been raised, however, as to whether it is proper to judge aggravation on the basis of syntactic shape alone. As was noted above, in some circumstances a direct imperative provides the most appropriate way to accomplish a particular action. More generally, using observations about the shape of a directive to make judgments about phenomena such as social imposition, degree of aggravation, and relative power involves an interpretive leap on the part of the analyst. There is a marked gap between the language structures actually being analyzed and the social phenomena being imputed to those structures. The practice of making judgments of this type is clearly derived from linguistic methodology, in which native speakers (including the analyst) rely on their intuition to decide whether a particular arrangement of language forms is or is not grammatical. There are important differences between these two situations, however. Intuitions about social imposition go beyond the string of language forms itself to an encompassing social environment. Moreover, that environment has been systematically hidden from view and made inaccessible to informed judgment by the way in which the language being analyzed has been extracted from the interactive circumstances in which it in fact functions. Looking more carefully at how directives are shaped and utilized in the midst of interaction provides one way of attempting to come to terms with such issues. If features such as asymmetry and social imposition are indeed relevant to participants, one can expect that they will in fact display such features to each other, and orient to them in the production and interpretation of their action.

The events surrounding this utterance will now be examined, beginning with talk by the speaker that accompanied the directive:

(1)   *Addressed to William*

    Tony: Go downstairs. I don't care ***what*** you say
                     you aren't- you ain't no good so go down***stairs***.

In the second line of this fragment, Tony repeats his initial imperative but now makes it the dependent clause of a larger sentence:

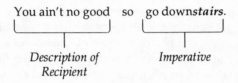

Embedding the imperative within this larger structure displays to recipient (and thus also to analysts) a reason for demanding that the action requested in the directive be carried out. More precisely, by linking the first clause of the sentence to the directive clause with "so" (which here has the sense of "therefore"), speaker formulates what is said in the first part of the sentence as grounds for the directive. Looking at this section of speaker's talk, we can see that it contains a pejorative description of recipient: "You ain't no good." In these data speaker thus explicitly tells recipient that he is ordering him to do something *because of* recipient's degraded status.

By looking beyond the imperative form itself to the environment in which it occurs, we are able to investigate the aggravated character of this imperative as something that speaker specifically orients to and explicitly displays to recipient. It is entirely possible, of course, that in other circumstances a similar imperative could be formulated in quite different ways.

In brief, there is much to be gained by expanding the scope of analysis to include more than the directive itself. Rather than relying on global judgments about the aggravated character of different types of directives, we can empirically investigate how the participants themselves deal with such issues.

5.2.2 DEPICTING PARTICIPANTS

What happens in these data raises a more general issue. Quite frequently the talk used to produce a directive not only states the action to be performed but also explicitly portrays parties involved in the action, especially speaker and addressee, and on occasion other parties as well (see, for example, Ervin-Tripp's [1976:31–32] discussion of directives made on behalf of a beneficiary). In the data presently being examined a particular technique is used to accomplish this. In saying "You ain't no good," Tony uses the pronoun "you" to animate William as a character in his talk (Goffman 1974, 1981) and then attaches pejorative attributes to the character he has constructed ("ain't no good"). Of crucial importance to what occurs here is that speaker does not simply cite addressee in his talk but simultaneously comments on the cited character and formulates him in a particular way, a process given considerable attention by both Goffman (1974, 1981) and Vološinov (1973).

In the sentence being examined, "You ain't no good," only addressee appears as a character. There is, however, at least the shadow of a very active second character in the scene portrayed through the utterance: speaker himself. The sentence is an assessment, a type of action that displays an experiencing agent performing an evaluation of something.[6] Here speaker is making an evaluation of recipient. The explicit animation of recipient thus contains an implicit portrayal of speaker as well.

Support for the active presence of speaker in this field of action is found when we examine the rest of the talk in this turn. Between the initial directive and the assessment, speaker explicitly animates himself as a character:

(1)   *Addressed to William*

    Tony: Go downstairs.
  →   I don't care *what* you say
                  you aren't- you ain't no good
                  so go down*stairs*.

Speaker thus portrays himself not only as someone entitled to judge recipient, but also as a character who "doesn't care" what recipient says, that is, as someone who is in a position to disregard and treat as irrelevant actions made by recipient. The two characters are thus linked to each other in an asymmetrical fashion, with recipient being depicted as "no good" while speaker proposes that he has the competence, rights, etc., to judge the performance of his addressee in this way.

It was noted above that making judgments about degree of aggravation on the basis of the syntactic shape of utterances extracted from the contexts in which they were in fact spoken involves an interpretive leap that is not always warranted: i.e., in many circumstances direct imperatives are the most appropriate way to perform a particular action. This does not, however, mean that the social weight that directives carry cannot be investigated. If phenomena such as aggravation and social asymmetry are indeed relevant to what participants are doing when they issue directives, then we might expect them to display this to each other. The present data have revealed one way in which this can be done: a speaker can animate his addressee as a cited figure in the talk of the moment and portray him in a particular way, and also do the same with himself, so that an alignment of speaker toward addressee is explicitly displayed. Here recipient is portrayed in a pejorative fashion, and the relationship between speaker and addressee is depicted as asymmetrical. However, the resources being used to make these displays are quite general, and one would therefore expect that many other configurations are also possible.

5.2.3 SITUATING DIRECTIVES WITHIN ACTIVITIES

The way in which speaker here focuses not only on the action being requested but also on attributes of participants implicated in that action begins to give us some sense of how participants are attending to a dynamic field of action as they organize their directives. However, important characteristics of that field have not yet been considered. Most crucially, directives are designed to do something, and are thus situated within a larger framework of activity. Levinson (1979) has called attention to the gains that can be made by focusing on how an embedding activity is utilized by participants for the interpretation of certain kinds of utterances. He notes that by adopting such a perspective, the analyst can begin to take into account Wittgenstein's (1958) insights into the organization of language within specific "language games," i.e., "having a grasp of the meaning of utterances, involves knowing the nature of the activity in which the utterances play a role" (Levinson 1979:365), something that traditional speech act theory cannot handle (ibid.:366). Directives are characteristically linked to larger projects in which participants are engaged, and indeed are a primary resource used to coordinate the action of separate individuals in such projects. They thus seem to constitute a most appropriate place to investigate how talk might make use of an encompassing activity for its production and interpretation.

How do participants interpret "you ain't no good so go down*stairs*"? For the analyst looking at the utterance in isolation, a puzzle arises. What is said in the first part of the utterance is explicitly offered as the reason why the action requested in the second part of the utterance should be performed. But why should being "no good" mean that one should move to a particular place: "downstairs"? How are these two propositions linked to each other such that one provides the warrant for the other?

An answer to this question is found when we stop focusing on the utterance as an isolated, self-contained object and instead treat it as something embedded within a larger sequence of activity. Here is the talk that led up to this utterance:[7]

(2) 1	Ossie:	Which side you on, Pete?
2	Pete:	I don't know yet.
3	Tony:	You don't know who side you on?
4	Chopper:	He on your, he on your side.
5	Tony:	If you up here, you on my side.
6	Tommy:	If you down there you on Ossie's.
7	Tony:	Get downstairs.
8	Malcolm:	Everybody down here right now
9		is on my side.
10	Ossie:	I'm down here.
11	Chopper:	Us, us four.
12	Malcolm:	So you better pick four people.
13	( ):	All right, all right.
14 →	Tony:	Go downstairs.
15 →		I don't care *what* you say you aren't-
16 →		you ain't no good so go down*stairs*.
17	Malcolm:	Don't come in here cuz you ain't on my side.
18		You come down here you get shot.
19	Ossie:	Here he come.
20	Malcolm:	⌈Shoot him.
21	Pete:	⌊Get outa my way.
22	Ossie:	I ain't got none loaded.
23	Malcolm:	Somebody shoot that boy.

In this sequence the participants establish and collaboratively recognize a link between spatial position and team membership: being in a specific place counts as belonging to a particular team. As was noted above, the boys are making slingshots and ammunition in the vicinity of the stairs in back of the house that belongs to Malcolm and Tony's family. One group is working under Tony's direction on a landing halfway up the stairs, while Malcolm's group is working under the stairs. In lines 1–4 the question arises which team Pete belongs to. In line 5 Tony, by saying "If you up here, you on my side," explicitly ties being in a specific place to membership on a particular team; and in line 6 Tommy elaborates this to include the other team as well by saying "If you down there you on Ossie's." Immediately after this Tony tells William for the first time to "get downstairs."

As conversation analysts have long pointed out (Sacks 1978; Schegloff 1968; Schegloff and Sacks 1973), a major resource utilized by participants to interpret and understand an utterance is its sequential environment, and in particular the talk that immediately precedes it. The sequence that has just unfolded provides a framework to be utilized to interpret "Get downstairs" such that it is heard not simply as a command to move to a certain place, but rather as a statement that Tony will not permit William to belong to his team. Specifically, insofar as Tony in line 5 has stated that those who are "up here" are on his side, a statement a moment later telling someone to leave that space can be heard as excluding that person from his team.

The sequence also further specifies what "Get downstairs" means. While "up here" has been identified with Tony's team, "down there" has been specifically identified with Malcolm's (for example, in line 6 Ossie is someone in Malcolm's work group). With his talk in line 7, Tony is thus telling William to go to the place that Tony and Tommy have just proposed as establishing membership on Malcolm's team.

Malcolm's talk in line 8, "Everybody down here right now is on my side," provides evidence that "Get downstairs" has indeed been heard in just this way. Malcolm replicates what Tony did in line 5 by defining his team as those "down here." However, by adding the words "right now" to his version of the definition, he formulates it so as to exclude the addressee of line 7 (who is being told to "Get downstairs" and is thus not already there). The talk in line 8 thus explicitly deals with the possibility that someone not now in Malcolm's teamspace might move there and thereby claim membership on the team, precisely the interpretation of line 7 made available by the talk that preceded it (i.e., William is being told to leave Tony's teamspace and move to a space defined as constituting membership on Malcolm's). This interpretation is made completely explicit in line 17 when Malcolm says "Don't come in here cuz you ain't on my side."

If Tony is treating William as an undesirable, Malcolm is not about to accept him on his team. When taken together, the actions of both Tony and Malcolm put William in a very difficult position. Not only is he being denied membership on either team, but Tony is demanding that he leave his teamspace while Malcolm is threatening to shoot him if he attempts to move downstairs.

It was noted earlier that "you ain't no good so go down*stairs*" (line 16) poses an interpretive puzzle: why should being "no good" constitute a reason for demanding that someone move to a particular place? Such a problem arises only when the utterance is divorced from its interactive context and treated as an isolated, self-contained unit of meaning. By bringing to bear the sequence within which this utterance is embedded, participants can unproblematically see the demand to leave a particular place as excluding addressee from speaker's team.[8] Being "no good" is one of the best reasons possible for not wanting someone on your team.

Most research on directives has treated explicit imperatives such as "Go downstairs" as obvious, and has therefore focused study of interpretive processes on indirect requests. The present data raise questions about such assumptions. Understanding the direct imperative spoken here is by no means straightforward but instead involves interpretive work similar or identical to that which would be required to make sense out of an indirect request; i.e., in order to find out what Tony is demanding, recipients must place what is actually said within a larger framework of action and background understandings, here shaped and displayed within the local sequential organization of the talk of the moment. In brief, direct imperatives require as much interpretive work as indirect actions, and certainly do not constitute a privileged "neutral" site where issues of understanding are simplified or held at bay.

5.3 STRUCTURES USED TO DEPICT PARTICIPANTS

The data which were just examined revealed that one of the things that Maple Street boys can do when they issue a directive is portray characters implicated in it, and in particular the addressee of the directive and the party issuing it. When figures are animated (Goffman 1974, 1981) in this way, they are frequently evaluated in some fashion. This process captures in a nutshell some of the more general features of the boys' directives, which typically (1) individuate participants involved in the directive, (2) evaluate them, and (3) portray these participants as aligned toward each other in an asymmetrical fashion. By way of contrast, as will be seen in Chapter 6, the directives Maple Street girls issue to each other do not individuate participants or portray one girl as superior to another. The participant structure of a directive thus provides an arena within which a range of interesting and important social phenomena relevant to the organization of directives can be investigated. Some of the structures used by Maple Street boys to depict participants, their machinery for animating and evaluating characters, will now be investigated.

5.3.1 ADDRESS TERMS

One of the simplest techniques available for depicting another participant is an address term. Moreover, choice of a pejorative address term provides a clear, concise way to evaluate the party being addressed:

(3)   *Regarding a hanger which Ossie is*
                 cutting with pliers

   Malcolm: Put your foot on it Stupid.
                 You afraid?

(4)   *Regarding coat hangers*

   Malcolm: Gimme the *th*ings *d*ummies.
                 If you expect me to *b*end 'em.
                 Y'all act *d*umb.

(5)   Douglas: Get outa here s:ucker.

(6)   Chopper: You sh:ut up you big lips.

(7)   Pete: Dag. Stop boy. Should be mindin' your business.

Several observations can be made about the use of address terms in these data. First, the denigrating description of recipient found in the address term is sometimes elaborated in surrounding talk. Thus in #4, a short time after Malcolm appends "*d*ummies" to his directive, he devotes a whole sentence to this evaluation: "Y'all act *d*umb." Moreover, the address term is not just a general term of degradation but rather an evaluation of recipients based specifically on their performance in the activity of the moment. In Malcolm's reading of the scene, his recipients expect him to bend their coat hangers without having transferred them to him, and therefore they are "dumb." Similarly, in #3 recipient is characterized as "stupid" because of the way he is performing his current task, and a possible reason for this is elaborated in an additional sentence that expands the pejorative description of recipient: "You afraid?" While not all address terms are tied to the task of the moment in this way (cf. #5, #7), the way in which they can be provides some demonstration of how directives and characterizations of participants are not separate, independent phenomena but rather aspects of a larger field of action.

Second, although frequently only the addressee is explicitly depicted within the utterance, the speaker is often a strong shadow character. Thus in #3, #4, and #7, speaker depicts himself as someone in a position to judge the performance of his addressee, and in #4 he proposes that recipients depend on him in order to complete the task in which they are engaged. The characters are thus linked to each other in a complementary alignment.

Third, terms such as this which are used to degrade recipients are clearly relevant to the analysis of how honorifics are organized within particular languages. From this perspective it is interesting to note that the boys do not use address terms that honor the addressee. While honorifics exist in their language and are used by these boys in other settings (e.g., school, home) to address adults, the boys do not address each other with them. One thus finds here an example of markedly skewed honorific use, with many terms employed to degrade addressees but none to honor them.

Within such a pattern of honorific use, neutral terms of address become especially interesting. Two forms of neutral address, personal names and the term "man," will now briefly be examined.

In a system that lacks explicit honorifics, one might expect neutral terms to be used in situations that might otherwise call for honorifics, for example, when making requests to one being treated as "superior," in the sense that addressee has the power to determine whether the request will be granted.[9]

Maple Street boys frequently employ personal names to address each other in such requests:

(8)   Chopper: Could I held yours now Ossie?

(9)   Pete: My brother got my hanger to make a slingshot. Ossie can I have one?

(10)   Tokay: Chopper can I have one?

Thus, in situations where speaker is acting as a suppliant, the slot where honorific address might occur can be filled with a neutral mode of address such as a personal name. However, the boys' use of personal names in this way is truly neutral in that personal names can also be used in situations where speaker is proposing that he has the power to order addressee to do something:

(11)   Malcolm: All right. Give me your hanger Tokay.

(12)   Malcolm: Get *out* of here Tony.

Finally, it must be recognized that personal names are used within directives to accomplish a range of tasks, most important specifying a particular other participant as the designated addressee of the directive:

(13)   Malcolm: Whose hangers in my way.
        Chopper: They ain't mine.
   →   Malcolm: Pick 'em up Tokay.

Here Malcolm uses a personal name to select one particular addressee from a larger pool of potential recipients. Needless to say, the ability to select an addressee in this way provides speakers with strategic resources that they can employ in a variety of ways. For example, in the following Tommy addresses his bid to join a team to Ossie, one of the members of Malcolm's team, rather than to Malcolm himself, who has already rejected a previous bid:

(14)   Tommy: May I be on your side Ossie?

In sum, personal names provide Maple Street boys with resources for designating the recipient of a directive without making further comments about addressee's elevated or degraded status.

"Man" is another address term that the boys frequently include in their directives. For example:

(15)   Malcolm: Give it to me man.

(16)   Malcolm: Man back out. I don't need y'all *in* here
                      I keep tellin' ya.

(17)   Malcolm: Man you not *ch*oppin' fast enough.

"Man" and personal names are used in different ways in the talk of the Maple Street boys. In part this follows from the fact that these alternative address forms are capable of doing different things. For example, unlike "man," personal names can select and designate specific addressees. In #18 Malcolm first designates an addressee with a personal name and then, in the very next word, addresses him again with "man." Similarly, in #19 recipient is addressed with "man" after being summoned with a personal name:

(18)   Malcolm: Come on Ossie.=Ma:n you wastin' *t*ime.

(19)   Malcolm: Hey Ossie hurry up man. You waitin'.

"Man" can thus be used as an address term in environments where the addressee of the current talk has already been specified. Indeed, it is rarely if ever used to select a particular addressee.

If an address term is not doing the job of designating an addressee, why is it included within the turn? One possibility might be that it is being used to comment on addressee, and indeed derogatory address terms such as those examined in #3–#7 provide excellent examples of just such use. However, semantically "man" (unlike "boy") is not a term of degradation.

Restricting focus to the semantic content of a particular term may not be the best way to uncover how that term is being used. Instead the term might obtain its affective valence from the way in which it is embedded within a larger field of action. In my data, "man" was almost always used to address someone being treated as a subordinate.[10] Indeed, when we examine utterances in which "man" is used, we find that typically speaker and recipient are depicted as aligned toward each other in an asymmetrical fashion with speaker proposing that he can tell recipient what to do. Consider #15–#19 as well as the following:

(20)   Malcolm: No man. I gotta show you how to do it.

The larger framework of the surrounding talk individuates the participants from each other and places addressee in a subordinate, inferior position vis-à-vis speaker. Within such a framework an address term such as "man" focuses special attention on addressee. Although semantically neutral in its own right, by virtue of the way in which it functions as an *addressee intensifier*, "man" can become colored by the disrespect visible in the participant structure of the talk that encompasses it.

Finally, one other feature that might shed light on the emphatic use of a semantically neutral address term is the rhythm and a sense of prosodic completeness. Exposition of such issues is beyond the scope of the present analysis (for detailed analysis of the interactive organization of rhythm, see Erickson 1982). However, to get some flavor of what is involved here, try reading the data provided with and without "man."

Address terms have been given little attention in most studies of directives. This may be because they are *optional* elements of the *sentences* used to perform directives. For example, one need not consider the address term in "Give it to me man" in order to investigate how the utterance embodies a directive of a particular type; the core syntactic formulation of the directive is found in "Give it to me." If, however, we choose not to use syntactic shape as a point of departure for the classification and analysis of directives, and instead view performing a directive as a small activity or task that speaker is engaged in, it becomes possible to view the talk that embodies the directive from a different perspective. Directives function to coordinate the behavior of separate individuals and thus involve some notion of participants as an essential element of their structure. Moreover, Maple Street boys typically build their directives so that they depict participants aligned toward each other in an asymmetrical fashion. In building a directive, a Maple Street boy is thus faced with the task not only of specifying the action to be performed, but also of individuating the parties linked by the directive and explicitly displaying their differential standing. Address terms provide one very effective tool for accomplishing such tasks. From this perspective a directive is not an utterance but rather a small activity that participants accomplish by deploying a range of resources, including alternative syntactic structures for specifying the action to be performed, address terms, intonation, body movement, sequential organization, etc. While address terms are *optional* syntactic elements, they provide *crucial* resources for delineating participants, something *central to the activity in progress*.

5.3.2 CHARACTER TIES

In building their directives, Maple Street boys also make use of resources that enable them to establish links between a particular character in the directive and some aspect of the surrounding scene. I will call such structures *character ties*. Possessives provide a clear and simple example. Consider the following:

(21)   Tony: Get off my steps.

With the possessive "my," speaker ties himself but not recipient[11] to a feature of the scene that is relevant to the action specified in the directive.

A larger social framework of rights over property is embedded within the talk of the moment. Such ties between speaker and the space that recipient is told to leave provide a warrant for the directive by establishing grounds for this particular speaker demanding that recipient perform this specific action; by virtue of the fact that they are "his" steps, Tony is claiming the right to demand that his addressee leave them. Character ties thus enable speakers to formulate participants and aspects of context as linked to each other in ways that establish the appropriateness of the directive.

Several features of this process require additional comment. First, it might be proposed that the possessive employed here is simply redundant with existing contextual information. All present know that they are working on property that belongs to Malcolm and Tony's family. Tony is thus not telling his recipient anything that recipient doesn't already know.

A perspective such as this would be quite wrong. The space in which participants are situated can be formulated in many different ways. The sequence examined in #2 demonstrated how these same boys defined this same space in terms of *team membership*, a framework for organization that had nothing whatsoever to do with ownership of this land by a particular family. By using the possessive, Tony makes one feature of the setting visible and relevant at the moment to the exclusion of others. Describing things in the way that he does is a political act, a formulation of events designed to further speaker's goals at the expense of recipient.

In building this action, Tony makes use of existing features of the scene that are differentially distributed among those present (e.g., only Tony and Malcolm can claim property rights over this space). The choices available to participants for making their arguments about rights are shaped and constrained by sometimes dense standing features of the scenes, social arrangements and activities within which they find themselves embedded. However, within such constraints choice cannot be avoided. As Schegloff (1972) has demonstrated, any procedure for formulating space and linking participants to it in a specific way involves selection from a larger set of alternatives, with the effect that any such description is a creative act tied to the particulars of what is occurring at the moment. The space surrounding their activities is not something static to which participants have continuous, unchanging access. It is instead a dynamic field of action that is shaped into relevant phenomenal units by the very talk (or other action) that it helps to organize and make comprehensible (see also Hanks in press[a]).

Second, Tony's use of "my" here is in some ways quite similar to Goffman's (1974, 1981) analysis of how speakers animate figures. By using the possessive, Tony is able to interject an aspect of his social persona, his status as someone with claims over specific property, into his talk. An image of speaker is thus deployed within the utterance. However, the version of speaker that appears seems something less than what Goffman analyzed as a cited figure. While cited figures *do* things, speak, for example, a character indexed by a possessive does not engage in any activity. Rather than animating a full-fledged character, the possessive merely indexes those limited properties of a social being that are relevant to actions of the moment. While the shadow of a participant appears, that shadow is not put on stage as a character in its own right.

Nonetheless, some of the essential features of Goffman's analysis appear valid for possessives as well. Most relevant, such a perspective offers insight into how Tony the speaker is able to depict Tony the property owner within this talk, and the very real differences between these two entities. It thus seems appropriate to expand Goffman's analysis beyond the situation in which figures appear as full-fledged characters to include the ability of speakers to animate attributes of participants in more limited ways.

In developing the notion of animation, Goffman, following Vološinov (1973), focused on quotation and other forms of *reported speech* as the prototypical example of the process he was describing. Within such a framework, a character (either current speaker or a cited figure within an embedded frame) is tied to an action of some type, typically speaking:

Character   ← **Tie** →   **Talk (or other action)**

Thus in the sentence "I told you John said he would be late," the phrase "he would be late" is tied to "John" through use of the *laminator verb* "said," and this whole strip of talk is tied to "I" through use of the laminator verb "told."

Character	← **Tie** →	**Talk (or other action)**
John	said	he would be late
I	told you	John said he would be late.

This structure can be expanded and generalized in a very straightforward way by permitting characters to be tied to phenomena other than talk and action. Thus possessives can be used to establish links between characters and objects or features of the local scene:

Character	← **Tie** →	**Feature of scene, social attributes, etc.**
Tony	Possessive	Steps that Chopper is standing on

Invoking a character in talk and then tying that character to something else is as central to the organization of possessives as it is to reported speech. Character ties are an essential component of both processes. Expanding Goffman's analysis of animation in this way permits us to see how speakers use a variety of resources to create scenes within which images of participants are deployed in ways relevant to the tasks at hand.

5.3.3 SCENES AND THEIR TRANSFORMATIONS

The phenomena just examined suggest that what is involved in even as basic a directive as "Get off my steps" is not simply an imperative or request that some action be performed, but rather a small dramaturgical structure encompassing a scene, characters, and action. The question arises whether participants do in fact orient to such utterances in this way. To explore this, let us look at how Chopper replies to Tony:

(22)   Tony: Get off my steps.
   → Chopper: *No.* You get on *my* steps.
                  I get on *y*ours.

Chopper's answer is constructed by systematically transforming the event described by Tony. Thus Tony's utterance depicts a scene in which there is a specific bit of property, steps, tied to two characters: (1) a party depicted as the possessor of that property, Tony, and (2) another party who is on the property but does not possess it, Chopper. Chopper builds his reply by using this basic structure of property, possessor, and nonpossessor as a template, while interchanging the characters who occupy the position of possessor and nonpossessor. Chopper now becomes the owner of the steps, and Tony is depicted as the outsider standing on them:

Speaker	Property	Possessor	Outsider
Tony	Steps	Tony	Chopper
Chopper	Steps	Chopper	Tony

What happens here provides evidence that Chopper does in fact analyze Tony's directive as an utterance with storylike features, including a framework of characters linked to a surrounding scene in specific ways. Indeed, the types of operations he performs to build a reply to it are quite similar to those that Sacks (1970) describes as involved in the production of "second stories." An underlying continuity of action and theme is maintained, while character structure is transformed so that an animated version of subsequent speaker assumes a position analogous to that occupied by prior speaker in the first story. To perform this transformation, Chopper must shift the narrative scene from the present (i.e., the steps he is standing on) to a nonpresent, hypothetical domain of action (Chopper's steps, not at a specific, defined moment in time, but rather as a place where Tony habitually positions himself). Consistent with the analysis of Hanks (in press[b]), Chopper uses the current scene, and in particular the way in which it has been formulated in the talk to which he is replying, as the raw material for building his hypothetical scene. Reuse of the material in prior talk permits a subsequent speaker to build a reciprocal counter that is precisely shaped to the talk that is being opposed. For this reason, such *format tying* occurs quite frequently in argument, and it will be discussed in more detail later in this book.

Further evidence that orientation to an integrated scene is in fact organizing Chopper's analysis and interpretation is provided by what he says next:

(23)

1	Tony:	Get off my steps.
2	Chopper:	*No.* You get on *my* steps.
3 →		I get on *yours.*
4	Tony:	I haven't been on your steps.

In line 3 Chopper returns from the hypothetical scene on his property to the current scene, where he again describes himself as standing on Tony's steps, only now as someone with legitimate rights to perform the action objected to in Tony's original directive. The characters that were rearranged in line 2 are now shifted back to their original positions.[12]

The scene that Chopper constructs in line 2 depicting Tony on *his* steps warrants Chopper's refusal to comply with Tony's directive. In his response in line 4, Tony challenges the facts portrayed in that scene by arguing that he hasn't been on Chopper's steps. Thus immediately after Chopper returns to the present, Tony switches back to debate events in the hypothetical scene that has emerged. Tony's initial directive in line 1, through the way in which it ties figures of participants to features of an encompassing scene, creates an organized phenomenal field that is capable of serving as a template for systematic transformation, and the protagonists end up zigzagging between the scenes it generates as they pursue their dispute.

In the following, a similar process of frame transformation occurs:

(24)   Tony: You better stop hoppin' on this thing.
    → Ossie: I'll hop on it. He always hoppin' on my banister.

Here Ossie is told to stop hopping on someone's property. He counters this directive by transforming the scene that it contains into a new scene in which activity is held constant but characters switch position: the initial property owner is pictured as performing the action being objected to, only now on Ossie's property.

Looking at these data from a slightly different perspective, one thing that is going on in these sequences is a debate about the *right* of one party to issue a certain directive to another. Speaker's right to issue a directive to addressee is frequently listed as one of the preconditions that underlie a valid directive (cf. Labov and Fanshel 1977). These data certainly support the notion that participants do in fact attend to such rights in interpreting and responding to directives. However, glossing the details of their talk in terms of an overriding concept such as "right" hides the intricate cognitive and interactive work they are performing. Thus, to establish his claim to order Chopper to do something, Tony uses a possessive to embed some of his relevant social attributes within the directive. The notion of a right as something to be made visible to addressee thus has detailed consequences for how even a very simple directive is constructed.

Similarly, in order to build a response that challenges Tony's claim, Chopper first analyzes Tony's talk as providing a structured, coherent scene that links features of the setting, participants, and action to each other in a particular way, and then systematically transforms that framework to build a new, hypothetical scene that supports *his* claim rather than Tony's. Such cognitive operations, which appear to be quite general (cf. Sacks's [1970] discussion of second stories), provide a more detailed and dynamic view of the work recipients are engaged in when they reply to a directive than would simply noting that speaker's right to issue the directive is being challenged. These processes are also quite relevant to the analysis of the cognitive work involved in establishing a reciprocity of perspectives. In brief, while rights are certainly quite relevant to the organization of directives, the cognitive and interactive work that participants perform to show each other that claims about rights are being made, and to counter the claims made by others, is important and worth study in its own terms.

The processes of scene transformation which have been examined here are relevant to one final issue. Because Goffman and Vološinov focused their study on single speakers animating others in quoted speech, there is a tendency to see the talk of the individual as providing a natural home for the study of processes of frame transformation (for example, the multiple embedding of frames that occurs in reported speech). In these data, however, we find a subsequent speaker building a reply by transforming the scene provided by prior speaker (or the scene in front of him). Indeed, one of the general tasks that subsequent speakers face is using prior speaker's talk as a point of departure for transformations that will further what subsequent speaker is trying to do. The sequential work involved in using prior talk to build an appropriate next utterance, rather than the cognitive operations of an isolated speaker, might therefore provide a primary environment for analysis of the work involved in transforming strips of talk.

Scene transformations can be used in other ways as well. Consider the following:

(25)

1	Dave:	Hey Malcolm.
2		*Th*ey *d*oin' what we did down in the park?
3		(1.5)
4	Malcolm:	You ain't on our side.
5		You ain't *play*in' *n*either!

In line 2 Dave asks if the activity in progress is similar to another event: "what we did down in the park." In lines 4 and 5 Malcolm analyzes Dave's talk as a bid to join his team. What Dave says can thus be seen as a type of directive, a request to join the activity in progress.

What features of Dave's talk enable Malcolm to interpret it in this way? Note that by including the pronoun "we" in his description, Dave portrays not only Malcolm but also himself as a participant in the earlier activity. Indeed, the phrasing here is somewhat awkward and seems designed precisely to set up speaker as a participant in the hypothetical frame being created. Once Dave is specified as a character in this scene, the description can be seen as making a proposal about his standing in the current activity: (1) if speaker was a participant in the prior event, and (2) current event is another instance of prior event, then (3) speaker is entitled to participate in the current activity as he did in the initial activity. The possibility that the talk might contain such an argument is reinforced by other features of Dave's turn, including the way in which it is addressed specifically to someone who can be seen as a team leader, Malcolm (line 1), and ends with rising intonation, which might be heard as marking what is being said as a request. It is precisely a proposal of this type that is identified and countered by Malcolm.

What happens here provides some demonstration of how describing something in a particular way is not a neutral rendering of activity, but rather a political act: a way of formulating events in progress and giving the current scene a texture of intelligibility that is congruent with the goals that the party making the description is trying to pursue.

5.3.4 ALTERNATIVE POSSESSIVE STRUCTURES

Possessives provide very powerful tools for depicting participants within directives, and embedding characters within scenes in ways relevant to the current activity. First, use of a possessive can partition those present into at least two relevant subsets: those included within the scope of the directive and those excluded by it. Thus, when "my" is used, current speaker differentiates himself from all others present because he is the only one included by the directive. A possessive such as "ours" can display wider membership and partition participants differently. This ability to subdivide those present into reciprocal sets can be especially useful to participants, such as the Maple Street boys, who emphasize asymmetry in their directives. Second, a possessive is a very concise technique for embedding claims about rights, social standing in an encompassing world, etc., within a directive (for example, the status of speaker as someone with claims over certain space or other resources) and making these participant attributes a visible part of the scene of the moment. In view of the way in which a possessive enables a speaker to differentiate himself from his addressee, it is not surprising that the Maple Street boys made frequent use of possessives in their directives. Some of the different ways in which they employed directives will now be briefly noted.

First, possessives that identify speaker as the possessor can be used to make claims about speaker's rights to demand that his addressee perform a particular action. Since this process has been well demonstrated in the data already examined, it will not be explored further.

Second, possessives that locate addressee as the possessor are frequently used by suppliants asking for goods that another controls:

(26)   Chopper: Tony can I have one of your slings?

(27)   Tommy: Malcolm could I be on your side?

(28)   *Requesting use of the pliers*

         Chopper: Could I hold yours now Ossie?

Addressee possessives display that speaker recognizes another's rights over the property in question as legitimate. Such a display is quite congruent with other features of these directives, such as the modal construction which grants addressee the right to decide whether or not the request will be granted.

In a variety of different ways, directives structured in this fashion are reciprocals of the ones examined earlier. "Get off my steps" demanded that addressee do something, while in these data speaker is making a request that may or may not be granted. Both types of directives display asymmetry. However, in the data currently being examined, speaker is depicted as someone petitioning a more powerful addressee, while the structure of the directives examined earlier portrayed speaker as someone entitled to tell addressee what to do. Different language resources are used to build these alternative types of directives (for example, modal constructions and interrogatives vs. imperatives), and indeed such differences form the basis for the various typologies of directives that have been proposed.

The presence of both types of directives is quite important to the social organization of a group, such as the Maple Street boys, characterized by asymmetry and hierarchical displays. If they had access only to one type of directive, reciprocal protestations of asymmetry would not be possible; there would be all leaders and no followers. A group such as this thus provides an arena for studying both 'aggravated' and 'mitigated' directives as reciprocal, interconnected components of larger patterns of action.

Possessives can be used to make yet a third type of display about the standing of speaker and hearer in relation to each other. Once again possessives that recognize the addressee's legitimate rights to the goods in question are employed, only now speaker demands those goods:

(29)   Malcolm: All right. Give me your hanger Tokay.

(30)   Malcolm: Gimme your other hangers.
                      I'm a bend them all.

In these directives speaker portrays himself as someone able to control goods that legitimately belong to addressee. Thus in #29, while explicitly recognizing through his use of "your" that the hanger is in fact Tokay's, Malcolm demands that Tokay give it to him.

The way in which addressee possessives are used here contrasts quite markedly with the data examined earlier where speaker depicted himself as a suppliant petitioning addressee for access to addressee's goods. In both cases possessives are used to demonstrate that addressee has valid claims over property that speaker wants. However, embedding that basic structure within different types of directives produces markedly different proposals about the alignment of speaker and hearer toward each other. In one case speaker shows that his action is constrained by addressee's rights, while in the other he displays himself as someone able to demand what he wants despite addressee's prior claims over the goods in question (claims which speaker recognizes as valid by employing the possessive). The ability of possessives to index social information about participants thus provides speakers with resources that they can manipulate in a variety of ways to construct directives that make complex proposals about the standing of speaker toward hearer.

5.3.5 EXPLOITING PARTICIPATION FRAMEWORKS

Parties making a request frequently use an address term to designate the target of the request. A participation framework linking speaker and a specific individual within an action structure is thus created. Moreover, this participation framework has sequential consequences: the addressee of the directive has the right (and obligation) to respond to it. He is expected to be next speaker. The framework of relevance thus established creates an environment that someone wishing to display his ability to arbitrarily control the actions of others can exploit to his own advantage. In the following, Tokay asks Chopper for one of his hangers:

(31)   *Chopper is carrying hangers.*

        Tokay: Chopper can I have one?
    → Malcolm: No boy. He givin' them to me.

Here Malcolm not only makes claims about his ability to control resources that properly belong to another (cf. #29 and #30 above), but he also violates the sequencing conventions that govern the talk of others by usurping a turn addressed to Chopper. Within that turn he animates Chopper as a figure who will give the hangers in question to Malcolm.

Chopper is deprived of the right to control his hangers. In addition, he is not even given the opportunity to reply to Tokay. What happens here is not challenged by Chopper. Malcolm is thus able to exploit the participation framework of a directive, and the sequential organization it invokes, to make very powerful claims about his position within the group.

In a number of ways, then, Malcolm selects acts which bypass expected displays of deference. He ignores the patterns of sequencing and formulating utterances which constrain the talk of others, differentiating himself by flaunting his ability to defy conventional conversational practices. The status of someone as a "team leader" is thus a phenomenon that is collaboratively constructed through systematic choice and action within the details of moment-to-moment interaction.

5.3.6 DESCRIPTION

While possessives and address terms enable speakers to depict features of participants in a very concise fashion within directives, descriptions provide an opportunity for more elaborate exposition of both the relative attributes of participants and the reasons for insisting that a particular action be carried out. Analysis of such phenomena will also provide us with an opportunity to investigate in more detail how leaders in the Maple Street group set themselves off from their followers through the way in which they organized their talk. In the slingshot session being examined here, one boy, Malcolm, gave a particularly virtuoso performance as a leader. Indeed, I had the sense that Malcolm was almost playing with the structures available to him. The leader of the other team, Malcolm's brother Tony, although older and larger, did not engage in this type of verbal pyrotechnics. Much of the data used to illustrate how a speaker can portray himself as a leader is therefore drawn from Malcolm's talk. In the following, speaker first interprets recipient's behavior in a pejorative fashion, and then compares that behavior with his own:

(32)   Malcolm: Come on Ossie.=Ma:n you wastin' *t*ime.
                    Look at all them things I got down there bent
                    and you *j*ust st:artin' on that.

(33)   Malcolm: Man you not *ch*oppin' fast enough.
                    Cuz I'm sittin' up here waiting.

In these data speaker portrays himself as competent and addressee as incompetent. An explicit, indeed vivid, comparison is made between speaker and hearer. Moreover, speaker anchors the description around himself, depicting his activities as the reference point for what everyone else is doing. The incompetent behavior of others is consequential because it requires *him* to wait. Speaker and his comfort become the point of reference for judging what everyone else is doing and the current progress of the activity. This extreme egocentrism, which is found frequently in the directives of boys portraying themselves as leaders but not in the talk of subordinates, is well illustrated in the following:

(34)   Malcolm: PL:IERS. I WANT THE PLIERS!

(35)   Malcolm: Everybody. Now I don't need all y'all
                           down here in this *little* ***space***.
                           Get back *up* there. Get *up* there. *N*ow.
                           *G*et back *u*p there please.

Here the only reason Malcolm offers for why the action demanded should be performed is his own needs and desires.[13] Others are expected to cater to his arbitrary whims.

However, in task activities it is possible to account for directives by referencing not the whims of an individual but rather the demands of the activity itself. Note the different types of accounts offered by Malcolm and Ossie in the following sequence:

(36)   *Asking for pliers*

  1   Malcolm: Gimme the thing.
  2   Ossie: Wait a minute. I gotta chop it.
  3   Malcolm: Come on.
  4   Ossie: I gotta chop it.
  5   Malcolm: Come on Ossie.
  6   You gonna be with them?
  7   Give it to me.
  8   I'll show you.
  9   Ossie: I already had it before you.
10   Malcolm: So? I brought them out here.
11   They mine.
12   So I use 'em when I feel like it.

In lines 2 and 4 Ossie counters Malcolm's demand for the pliers by noting that they are necessary for the completion of the task in which he is engaged. In line 9 he switches to a different explanation, one that stresses his legitimate rights to the pliers. By way of contrast, Malcolm provides no account whatsoever for his initial demand in line 1. His later accounts emphasize his position as controller of resources, team membership, and territory. In lines 5–8 Malcolm attempts to enforce his demand, not by describing why the tool is needed but rather with an implicit threat to throw Ossie off his team ("You gonna be with them?") followed by a statement about his superior skill with the tool ("I'll show you"). Ossie's claim that he is entitled to the pliers because he had them first is answered in lines

10–12 by Malcolm's statement that he is their owner, a status that justifies his using them "when I feel like it." The accounts that Malcolm uses differ markedly from those used by Ossie in that Malcolm justifies his actions in terms of his own needs or superior position, while Ossie accounts for his refusals in terms of either the demands of the larger activity or a legitimate claim on the object in question.

5.3.7 COMBINING THESE RESOURCES

For clarity, different structures available for depicting participants within a directive have been investigated separately. However, in building an actual directive, a speaker may employ a variety of resources. The following directive encapsulates in a short utterance many of the structures that we have been examining:

(37)   Malcolm: Man, don't come down *in* here where I *am*.

Malcolm's directive begins with "Man," an address term that is semantically neutral but which intensifies focus on addressee, contributes to the individuation of participants, and can heighten the sense in which the directive is placing addressee in a subordinate, inferior position vis-à-vis speaker. Moreover, the inclusion of this term gives the directive a distinctive rhythm that is in fact characteristic of many directives in which speaker portrays himself as telling others what to do. Second, speaker is tied to a particular place ("down *in* here where I *am*") through a description. Although an explicit possessive is not used, the description does much the same work by displaying speaker's claims over the property in question. Third, the only reason provided for excluding addressee from this space is speaker's mere presence. Speaker thus portrays himself as someone whose whims must be catered to, and who does not have to justify his actions to others. Finally, the utterance explicitly depicts both addressee ("Man") and speaker ("I"), separates them from each other, and portrays these characters as aligned in an asymmetrical fashion.

5.3.8 INSTRUCTING OTHERS

It was noted above that leaders frequently construct directives in which they display themselves as competent and addressee as incompetent. These proposals can become reified within a subgenre of directives: *teaching* or *instructing*. Speaker assumes the position of an expert telling less competent others how to perform the activity in progress:

(38)   Malcolm: No man. I gotta show you how to do it.
                           I'm a do it *my* way.

(39)   Malcolm: See this how we gonna do ours.
                    It's a lot better and faster.
                    Bend that side and then
                    we bend this side too.

(40)   Malcolm: Look I wanna show you how to do it
                    so when you get the things
                    you gonna know how to do it.

Instruction such as this implies an asymmetrical relationship of participants, with the teacher providing actions such as getting the attention of
subordinates, giving them information, and criticizing them (Cazden, Cox,
Dickerson, Steinberg, and Stone 1979:210). Note also that by performing
actions such as this, a party is not simply making abstract claims about his
superior status but rather proposing that he is an expert in the very things
that are being done at the moment, and that the others present are not.
The status being claimed is tied to and situated within the activity of the
moment.

Such claims about the superiority of speaker are only proposals, of
course, speaker's version of how he stands vis-à-vis his addressee. Recipients can choose to actively dispute such claims:

(41)   Malcolm: No man. I gotta show you // how to do it.
        Ossie: Cut ₍the thing.
        Malcolm: I'm a do it *my* way.
   →   Chopper: *I* know how to make the slings.
   →   *I* could make the slingshot.
   →   *I* know how to make the slings.

(42)   Malcolm: Wait wait wait.
                        Now what do you wanna make first.
                        You wanna slingshot.=Right?
        William: Yeah.
        Malcolm: What do you want.
   →   William: *I* know how to make one.
   →   Ossie: I know how to make both of 'em.
        Malcolm: Man I told you it's gettin' a little
                        crowded up here.

The insistence with which Chopper in #41 objects to Malcolm's assuming
the position of an expert telling him what to do provides evidence that
recipients do, in fact, interpret such instructing as treating them as incom-

petent with reference to speaker. In brief, although boys in the position of leader attempt to define for others various aspects of the activity in progress, those in a subordinate position do not unquestionably go along with their plans. Such disputes demonstrate the interactive character of the proposals about the alignment of speaker and addressee contained in directives.

However, if such proposals can be challenged, they can also be ratified:

(43)

1	Malcolm:	Now. Re*mem*ber what I sai:d.
2		And don't try to shoot till
3	Tokay:	Like- like they in sight?
4	Malcolm:	That's right.
5	Tokay:	What if they ain't.
6	Malcolm:	But if they- if they hidin' in some bushes,
7		don't you shoot.=
8		=You let them waste theirs.
9		Count for the man how many he waste.
10		Then after he waste as many as you got
11		you let him shoot his.
12		But then you let him waste some more.

The interactive character of Malcolm's role as both instructor and leader is particularly clear in these data. Not only does Malcolm specify how the activity should proceed, but Tokay, beginning in line 3, actively acknowledges Malcolm's right to issue such actions.[14] In line 5 Tokay requests additional information which further ratifies Malcolm as the party in control of knowledge about slingshot fights. In response to Tokay's requests, Malcolm (lines 6–12) displays his expertise with an extended account of appropriate battle maneuvers.

Throughout the slingshot-making session, differentiation between participants is displayed through the types of actions which are initiated toward leaders such as Malcolm. Because Malcolm is felt to be in control of knowledge regarding the craft, his opinion and assistance are summoned repetitively in the form of requests for information (#44 and #45) as well as requests for protection (#46) and assistance (#47):

(44)   *Illustrating bending and cutting coat hangers*

	Malcolm:	You bend it over like that and when-
		when you finish I'll show you how to
		just do these.
→	Tokay:	After it break, stomp down?

| | Malcolm: | Just clap 'em. |

(45)	Malcolm:	After I cut these up
→	Ossie:	Who turn is it.
	Chopper:	Mine. Mine *Uh* uh.
		Ain't it my turn Malcolm,
	Malcolm:	((*nods yes*))
	Chopper:	See?

| (46) | Chopper: | Hey Malcolm. Tony shot me! |

(47)

1	→ Chopper:	I want- 'Member it was a lot more-
2		Kay I want some more like you-
3		like the one you had for me before.
4	Malcolm:	It's small.//It's all right.
5	Chopper:	But you had fixed it before.
6		It was good and small.
7	Malcolm:	I *will*. I *will*. And boy you keep
8		*l*ettin' me//see your head.
9	Ossie:	They- they don't know how to//do it.
10		That's why they ask Malcolm so much.
11	Chopper:	My boy Malcolm'll do it.
12	Malcolm:	Yeah yeah yeah yeah.
13	Chopper:	Malcolm can you-
14	Malcolm:	Man I'm *d*oin' it already.

Vaughn and Waters (1980:361, discussing research by Chance and Jolly 1970) have argued that "the *structure of attention* within a group, rather than aggressive or agonistic interactions, priority access to food, objects, mates, and so forth," should be "used to draw the outlines of social organization." *Visual* attention was the form of attention investigated in the ethological studies reviewed in Vaughn and Waters (1980:361–362); as can be seen in these data, attention through asking questions is directed toward the party acting as instructor of the play activity in progress. As Ossie (lines 9–10) asserts, the boys' asking Malcolm to make the slings for them ratifies their definition of Malcolm as the party most knowledgeable about making slings.

Malcolm plays the roles of both instructor and leader or controller of the activity. The range of mitigated requests directed to Malcolm, as well as the imperatives and aggravated counters delivered by him, display and construct a form of social organization in which actions by others are generally offered in a mitigated form, while his own actions are designed to display control relative to others.

5.4 ESTABLISHING ROLE DIFFERENTIATION THROUGH THE INTERACTION IN DIRECTIVE SEQUENCES

The types of directives we have examined thus far provide some indication of how boys such as Malcolm and Tony attempt to establish their role as leader through the actions they initiate to others. As the data in the last section demonstrated, the success of such attempts depends not only on the actions of the putative leader, but also on the responses that others make to these actions. Most studies of directives consider only initial moves in a social control sequence and omit consideration of their sequential organization, and in particular the responses which follow them.[15] However, positions of leadership are maintained not simply by issuing social control acts or directives of a particular shape. They are also constituted through the way in which requests from others are responded to, either ratifying or challenging the stance taken by a boy proposing to act as leader. As ethologically oriented researchers of children's dominance hierarchies have observed, a crucial feature of social conflict is its interactional nature,[16] which "requires that equal attention be given to the activity of both participants in the aggressive social exchange. This approach implicitly assumes that dominance between two individuals is established by a *mutual agreement* symbolized by the submissive response" (Strayer and Strayer 1980:154 [emphasis added]).

Following the delivery of a directive, a range of responses is possible. Some directives are answered with compliance—a nonvocal carrying out of the requested action and/or signals of vocal agreement as in the examples below:

(48)   Malcolm: *All* right. Gimme some rubber bands.
     → Chopper: *((giving rubber bands))* Oh.

(49)   Malcolm: PL:IERS. I WANT THE PLIERS! (0.6)
                                 Man y'all gonna have to get y'all own
                                 wire cutters//if this the way y'all gonna be.
     → Pete: Okay. Okay.

(50)   *Regarding coat hanger wire*

      Malcolm: Give it to me man. Where's yours at.
                                 Throw that piece of shit *out*.
     → Chopper: *((gives Malcolm his cut-off piece of*
                                 hanger)) Now I got some of 'em.

(51)   Tony: Go downstairs. I don't care *what* you
                     say you aren't- you ain't no good so go
                     down*stairs*.
→ Dave: ((*moves down the steps*))

(52)   *Instructing how to use pliers to cut wire*

        Malcolm: Put it on the ground and jump on it.
→ Ossie: Aye::::. ((*jumping on pliers*))

Alternatively, next moves may reject the activity being proposed by providing a justification for noncompliance:

(53)   Malcolm: *Gi*mme your rubberband. Bands.
        Tony: No.
        Malcolm: Two bands.
→ Tony: I'm not *fi*nish.
                     I got some more hangers to go.

(54)   Malcolm: Move all those hangers back.
                     ...
        Malcolm: *Who*se hangers in my way.
→ Chopper: They ain't mine.
        Malcolm: Pick 'em *up* Tokay.
→ Tokay: I'm waitin' so you can chop 'em.

Such actions, while rejecting prior requests, accept the validity and relevance of the prior action. Justifications specify conditions within the framework of the activity which make compliance difficult.

Other more aggravated types of return actions, however, refuse the directive by providing justifications which deal with the right of recipient to reject the directive given equivalent offenses by first speaker:

(55)   *Chopper moves up the steps to where*
                     Tony is seated.

        Tony: Get off my steps.
→ Chopper: No. You get on *my* steps.
                     I get on yours.

(56)   Tony: You better not-
                     You better *stop* hoppin' on this thing.
→ Ossie: I'll hop on it. *He* always hoppin' on my banister.

A yet more aggravated form of response to a directive can refuse the action put forward by flatly rejecting it. In the following, the refusal is intensified through multiple forms of negation:

(57)   Malcolm: Get *out* of here Tony.
 →   Tony: I'm not gettin' out of *no*where.

Next moves to directives can alternatively be countermoves, actions which do not reject prior actions but attempt to discount them. For example, a recipient may respond to a prior imperative by answering "Shut up," an action which challenges the activity of delivering an imperative. Insult terms (as in example #59) or explanations which allude to speaker's ultimate control (as in example #60) may accompany "shut up":

(58)   Malcolm: Man back out. I don't need y'all *in* here
                          I keep//tellin' ya.
 →   Chopper: You better shut up. I'll tell you that.

(59)   Tony: *G*imme the *things*.
 →   Chopper: You sh:ut up you big lips.

(60)   Chopper: Keep on callin' my name I'm gonna chop
                          you again like I did before.
 →   Malcolm: Ah shut up. I don't need you *in* here
                          I keep tellin' you.

As a rejoinder, "Shut up" has certain features which distinguish it from other comebacks. "Shut up" responses deal neither with the rights of speaker to make the request nor the obligation of hearer to comply with it. Although they counter prior actions with a derogatory return, they do not address the specific content of the directive; they thus do not explicitly deal with the issue of complying with or refusing the directive.

Recipients thus have available a large repertoire of optional actions for building responses that address the prior action. Example #59 demonstrated that next moves not only may counter prior ones but also can interpret the prior move as insulting. As Mitchell-Kernan and Kernan (1977) have argued, children may be more concerned with manipulating social face than with the specific outcomes of their actions. Refusing a directive constitutes a challenge on the respondent's part to the (implicit) claims of the party issuing the command.

The data just examined demonstrate that recipient does not have to obey the command of the speaker, and that either party can format his talk to the other in a relatively aggravated or a mitigated form. From such a perspective, cases such as examples #48–#52, in which aggravated commands are indeed obeyed, become more interesting. In such cases, the actions of both participants ratify a claim by one party to be able to do something ritually offensive to the other with the other's acceptance of the offense. A view of the parties as having asymmetrical rights and duties with respect to each other is thus collaboratively displayed. Ways of building directives constitute part of the currency through which status and leadership are negotiated. Viewed in this way, alternative forms of social control acts are not merely stylistic variants of a speech act but crucial elements of the process through which the social organization of the group is achieved and displayed.

Directives need not be formatted in baldly stated imperative forms. They may also be stated as a question, or a request for permission (Ervin-Tripp 1982b:35) or information. Gordon and Ervin-Tripp (1984:308) argue that "conventional polite requests, with few exceptions, are interrogatives that appear to offer the hearer options in responding. . . . Conventional polite forms . . . avoid the appearance of trying to control or impose on another."

Respondents to directives formatted as requests may answer the directive in a variety of ways. One possibility is that the second speaker may provide a reason for why the requested action cannot be carried out at present:

(61)   *Requesting use of the pliers*

      Chopper: Could I hold yours now Ossie?
      Ossie: No. I didn't even get five yet.

(62) Pete: My brother got my hanger to make a slingshot.
                  Ossie can I have one?
      Ossie: I gotta come make some more slings.

In these justifications which reject prior directives, recipients describe factors making it difficult or inappropriate for them to perform the requested action; such factors deal with the situation at hand rather than with the personal whims of speaker. These next actions attempt to match the politeness in the first action and avoid imposition upon the prior speaker.

Different affective alignments can be displayed with other types of responses. Next speaker may baldly display opposition to prior speaker (#63), or sanction prior speaker by delivering a return imperative (examples #64 and #65). The following occurs as Tommy, a newcomer to the activity, makes a bid to join Malcolm's team:

(63) Tommy: Could Pete be on your side,
                  and I be on Malcolm's side?
                  Malcolm could I be on your side?
      Malcolm: ⌈*Heck* no!
      Ossie: ⌊*Heck* no!

(64)   *Taking a hanger*

          Tokay: Can I have some hangers?
          Malcolm: Put that thing back!

(65)   Tokay: Anybody wanna buy any rubber bands?
          Malcolm: Put 'em in your pocket. Cuz you gonna pop 'em.

In #63–#65 speakers do more than simply refuse or counter prior requests. They also take up a position with regard to the prior move and provide justifications for their responses. The slot for a justification in a counter-move provides an important locus for the negotiation of social relationships. For example, it permits current speaker to assert a definition of the situation opposing that put forward by prior speaker.

The data we have examined here demonstrate how a division of labor develops with respect to the distribution of various types of actions. Boys other than Malcolm and Tony do not initiate new phases of the activity through giving bald imperatives; instead they use more mitigated forms, requests for information, when proposing a course of action. Most of the requests for information concerning various phases of the activity, as well as requests for objects and pleas for protection, are posed explicitly to those recognized as leaders. These requests are not responded to in a mitigated way, as in #61 or #62 with reasons for refusing the command, but instead with counters and direct contradictions. It can be observed that in this particular sling-making session, the person who most often produces aggravated directives as well as responses is Malcolm;[17] his actions in countering mitigated requests seem to be substantial elements in the process through which his position as "leader" in the group is interactively achieved. His position in the group is displayed and validated in a number of different ways: through issuing direct commands while receiving indirect requests, through contradicting proposals and requests of others while expecting and getting compliance to his own, and through usurping the turn space of others. Malcolm's role, however, is complemented by the attention he gives others in his role of instructor.

5.5 PROCEDURES FOR DIFFERENTIATION USING DIRECTIVES

The examination of sequences of directives and their responses illustrates how differentiation between participants may be achieved through talk. Here we have seen how directives can invoke a participant structure that individuates speaker and addressee and portrays them as aligned in a particular way. Thus both directives and their returns can be formulated to either enhance or minimize displays of deference to the other speaker. Ways in which directives are shaped make proposals about the standing of speaker to hearer. A range of resources are used to accomplish this, including animation of participants as characters within a coherent scene of action, possessives, address terms, comparisons, accounts, and justifications (which alternatively display either the demands of the activity or the needs, whims, or alleged rights of speaker), and challenges to, or ratifications of, such proposals in subsequent talk.

Rather than being simply a speech act designed to get something done, directives constitute a complex speech genre, one that is capable of encompassing a wide variety of speech forms and action (imperatives, assessments, descriptions, etc.) and turning them to its own purposes. Moreover, directives both depict a particular alignment of participants and rely upon being embedded within larger sequential structures and encompassing activities for their proper understanding. They thus have a Janus-like quality, on the one hand looking outward as they link what is happening at the moment to larger frameworks of meaning and action, and on the other looking inward as they invoke coherent scenes, self-sufficient worlds within which images of participants are animated. Crucial to the processes that have been examined within this chapter is how speakers can portray parties relevant to the directive in ways that individuate them, mark differences between them, and display asymmetrical alignments. In the next chapter we will see that the girls on Maple Street make very different proposals about participants in their directives.

CHAPTER SIX

Task Activity and Pretend Play among Girls

In this chapter I will analyze girls' social organization by investigating (1) how girls go about organizing a task activity which is comparable to that of the boys—making rings from glass bottle rims, and (2) pretend play. In making rings, girls carefully scrape bottle rims over metal manhole covers or other rough surfaces so that the rims break evenly, leaving as few jagged edges as possible. The jobs faced by girls in making their objects do not substantially differ from those faced by boys; they involve procuring and allocating resources and establishing techniques for the objects' manufacture. Thus, in making rings the girls must decide where they will get the bottles necessary to make the rings, how many bottles are needed, who should break the bottles, how precisely the rims of bottles should be broken over metal manhole covers, how used bottles should be disposed of, and how the rings should be decorated.

6.1 THE FORMATTING OF DIRECTIVES AND ACCOUNTS IN GIRLS' TASK ACTIVITY

As we saw in Chapter 5, boys characteristically use a hierarchical social organization to coordinate their activities within a task. With the exception of the domain of pretend play, this type of organization is uncommon in girls' play. In accomplishing a task activity, girls participate jointly in decision making with minimal negotiation of status. Such "egalitarian" social organization is accomplished in part through the selection of syntactic formats for the production of directives that differ quite markedly from those of the boys. The following provide examples of the types of directives typically found among the girls:

(1)   *Girls are searching for bottles from*
           which to make rings.

    Kerry: Well let's go- let's go around the corner-
           Let's let's go around the corner
           where whatchacallem.

(2)   *Girls are looking for bottles.*

       Kerry: Let's go. There may be some more on
                             Sixty-Ninth Street.
       Martha: Come on. Let's turn back y'all
                             so we can safe keep 'em. Come on.
                             Let's go get some.

(3)   *Girls are looking for bottles.*

       Martha: Let's go around Subs and Suds.
       Bea: Let's ask her "Do you have any bottles."

(4)   *Talking about bottles girls are*
                             picking out of the trash can

       Kerry: Hey y'all. Let's use these first and
                             then come back and get the rest
                             cuz it's too *many* of 'em.

(5)   *Planning strategy to keep ring making*
                             secret from the boys

       Martha: If the boys try to follow us here,
                             let's tell 'em-
                             let's act just like we don't even know.
                             *h Just say "N:o."
                             You know.

(6)   *Planning what to do with broken*
                             bottles from which rings were made

       Kerry: Let's move **these** out **first**.

(7)   Bea: Okay. Let's go in the other **two** trashes.

     Whereas boys' directives, especially those issued by leaders, are typi-
cally shaped as a command that an action should be undertaken immediately, girls' directives are constructed as suggestions for action in the
future.[1] Syntactically, the forms utilized by the boys generally differentiate
speaker and hearer. One party is either ordering another to do something
or, alternatively, requesting action from some other party. By way of contrast, the term used by the girls, "let's," lumps speaker and addressee
together rather than differentiating them, with the effect that neither party
is depicted as exerting control over the other.[2] "Let's" signals a proposal

rather than either a command or a request, and as such shows neither special deference toward the other party (as a request does) nor claims about special rights over the other (as a command does). Thus, through the way in which they format their directives, the girls make visible an undifferentiated, "egalitarian" relationship between speaker and addressee(s) that differs quite markedly from the hierarchical relationship displayed in boys' directives.[3]

The same format is used by the girls to coordinate action in other task activities as well. In the following the girls are playing jacks (#8), jumping rope to a particular rhyme called "One Two Three Footsies" (#9), and hunting for turtles (#10 and #11):

(8)   Annette: Let's play some more jacks.

(9)   Bea: Let's play "One Two Three Footsies."
                     First!

(10)   *Searching for turtles*

          Bea: Let's look around. See what we can find.

(11)   *At end of turtle hunt*

          Bea: When we get home let's say we found somp'm.
                     =Okay?

Another syntactic form utilized by the girls to format a directive as a suggestion also merges speaker and addressee with a plural subject but uses the modal verb "can" or "could" with the verb form.[4]

(12)   Bea: We could go around lookin for more bottles.

(13)   *Discussing where to break bottle rims*

          Martha: We *could* use a sewer.

(14)   Martha: Uh we could um, (2.4) shell*ac* 'em.

(15)   *Discussing keeping the activity secret from boys*

          Kerry: We can *l*imp back so nobody know where
                     we *g*ettin' them from.

In some cases the overt tentativeness of the modal is further intensified through the use of terms such as "maybe":

(16)   Kerry: Maybe we can slice *them* like that.

(17)   *About getting bottles*

        Martha: Hey maybe tomorrow we can come up here
                       and see if they got some *more*.

Finally and less frequently, girls' suggestions for future action may use the form "we gotta":

(18)   Bea: We gotta do 'em on the ground.

(19)   Bea: We gotta find some more bottles.

(20)   Bea: We gotta wash these off.

The form "gotta" has a more nearly imperative force than the other terms examined thus far. However, by using "we" as its subject, the girls group speaker and hearer(s) together as equal agents/recipients of the proposed directive. Thus, the directive does not construct a command, as would happen, for example, if only the hearer were the subject of the utterance. Notice how different the last set of examples would be if "we" were changed to "you."

(21)   Bea: You gotta do 'em on the ground.
          Bea: You gotta find some more bottles.
          Bea: You gotta wash these off.

These actions resemble commands. Shifting the person of the pronoun thus creates very strong differences in social and pragmatic meaning. The utterances with "we" treat the reasons for performing the action as coming out of the requirements of the task at hand, while utterances constructed with "you" differentiate speaker and hearer and index obligations of the recipient.[5]

When directives are formatted to place demands on recipient, they may also contain an account providing explicit reasons for why an action should be undertaken. Characteristically, such accounts consider the benefits which would accrue to all members of the group:

(22)   Martha: Bea you know what we could do, (0.5)
                       We gotta *clean* 'em first, We gotta
                       clean 'em.
        Bea: Huh,
        Martha: We gotta *clean* 'em first. // You know,

Bea:	I know.
→	⌜Cuz they got germs.
Martha:	Wash 'em and stuff cuz just in case they
→	got germs on 'em.
	⌜And then you clean em,
Bea:	I got some paints.
	(3.5)
Martha:	Clean 'em, and then we *clean* 'em and we
	gotta be careful with 'em before we get
	the glass cutters. You know we gotta
→	be careful with 'em cuz it cuts easy.

The types of accounts accompanying girls' directives contrast markedly with the accounts accompanying boys' commands. While boys' directives commonly display no obvious reason for why an action should be undertaken, aside from speaker's personal desires, girls' accounts frequently deal with requirements of the current activity.

6.2 AVOIDING DIFFERENTIATION IN INTERACTION WITHIN DIRECTIVE SEQUENCES

It was noted earlier that asymmetry among the boys was displayed not only in the formatting of particular directives but also in the differential usage of both directives and responses to them. In the boys' group, generally only specific boys acting as leaders issued the directives prescribing actions for others, and they responded to others' directives with refutations. In the girls' group, however, proposals for certain courses of action could be made by many different participants, and the girls generally agreed to the suggestions of others. For example:

| (23) | Martha: | We gonna paint 'em and stuff. |
| | Kerry: | Yep. |

(24)	Martha:	Hey maybe to*morrow* we can come up here
		and see if they got some *more*.
	Kerry:	=Yep.

(25)	Kerry:	Hey let's go in there and ask do they
		have some *cases*.
	Martha:	Yep. Okay? Yep. Let's go and ask them.

| (26) | Martha: | You can get people to *cut* this though, |
| | Bea: | Yep. |

(27)   Kerry: Wanna sweep 'em out?
         Martha: Yeah.
         Bea: Okay.

(28)   Kerry: Hey y'all. Let's use these first and
                    then come back and get the rest cuz
                    it's too *many* of 'em.
         Martha: That *right*.
         Kerry: We can *l*imp back so nobody knows where
                    we *g*ettin' them from.
                         (0.8)
         Martha: That's right.
         Kerry: And w- and wash our hands.
                    And wash your hands when you get *f*inish now.
         Martha: If the boys try to follow us
                    we don't know. Okay?
         Kerry: Yep.

Thus in terms of both how directives are constructed and the way in which others respond to them, the girls' system of directive use displays similarity and equality rather than differentiation among group members.

It has been seen that when initiating a new activity, rather than signaling new phases of an activity with a command, girls issue proposals about future courses of action. An even less coercive way of moving into a new phase can be accomplished through simply making a statement about one's own future plans and waiting to see how others will react. For example in the next fragment, in which the girls plan a turtle-hunting expedition, Ruby (in line 1) states what she is going to do. Others subsequently offer their reactions to the idea. Bea (line 2) is in agreement, while Jolyn (line 7) (who is too young to go off the street anyway) and Sister (line 10) reject the invitation.

(29)
1   Ruby: I'm gonna catch me a turtle at Cobbs Creek.
2   Bea: Me too. I'm gonna catch//me a turtle.
3   Ruby: You goin' over there with me?
4   Bea: Yeah. Wanna go now?
5   Ruby: Yeah.
6   (1.8)
7   Jolyn: I don't wanna.
8   Bea: Wanna go?
9   (1.0)
10   Sister: I done caught one.
11   (2.0)

12	Ruby:	Well *we* done it- *we* didn't caught one yet.
13		You goin'?
14	Bea:	Wanna go with us?
15	MHG:	Mm yeah!
16	Bea:	I'm gonna catch *me* a *tur*tle.
17		Well where we gonna put him at. Could-
18		could- could- could- could we find a thing?
19		(1.6)
20	Ruby:	I get me a little plastic bag from somewhere.

In this sequence we find that both Ruby and Bea have an equivalent say in setting up the expedition. Although Ruby first suggested the activity, Bea rather than Ruby explicitly asks first Sister (line 8) and then the ethnographer (line 14) whether or not they wish to go. In line 4, when Bea proposes the time for undertaking the activity, it is agreed to by Ruby. Potential participants in the activity are free to choose whether or not they want to join it. When Jolyn and Sister state that they do not want to go (lines 7 and 10), they are not coerced. In responding to actions as well as in initiating courses of action, girls avoid establishing a differentiation of power between one another. When Bea (lines 17–18) brings up a potential problem, how the girls are going to carry their turtles home, Ruby mentions what *for her* constitutes a possible solution, without obliging Bea to do the same.

Throughout the turtle-hunting expedition, plans are discussed in terms of what individual girls wish to do, without any forcible defining for others what their course of action need entail. For example, in the following, after Ruby states what type of rocks she wants, Bea does not disagree, but instead contrasts the type of rocks she would like to have with that type proposed by Ruby:

(30)	Ruby:	I want me the kind of rocks
		like in the front of my garden?
	Bea:	I'm a get *me* some *lit*tle rocks hon,
		little rocks.

In the organization of this activity, all are invited to participate, and there is little differentiation into specialized roles. Girls do distinguish themselves from each other by stating personal preferences that contrast with those of other girls (i.e., the different kinds of rocks that Ruby and Bea desire in #30). However, participants do not enforce their version of what the activity should be, but instead provide *descriptions* of their own courses of action to be reacted to by others. Such a situation is consistent with the less coercive nature of the girls' directives as well as the relative infrequency with which the girls use the imperative form during task activities.

Although girls do not characteristically respond to directives in ways that show one party superior to another, they do counter one another's proposals for action. In fact, argumentation is as common an activity in the girls' group as it is among boys or in mixed-sex groups. The following is an example of a directive/counter sequence:[6]

(31)   *On reaching a city creek while turtle hunting*

1	Bea:	Y'all gonna walk in it?
2	Ruby:	*Walk* in it, You know where
3		that water come from? The toilet.
4	Bea:	So, I'm a walk in it in my dirty feet.
5		I'm a walk in it and I don't care if it do come.=
6		You could//easy wash your feet.
7	Ruby:	((*to ethnographer*)) Gonna walk us across?
8		Yeah I'll show y'all where you can come.

In this example, negotiations occur with regard to issuing and responding to directives. The directive initially posed by Bea in line 1 ("Y'all gonna walk in it?") is countered by Ruby (lines 2–3); Bea then opposes Ruby's counter (lines 4–6). During Bea's turn (line 6), Ruby interrupts to reinstate Bea's initial request and issue a second directive offering to show others how to cross the creek. Upon completion of this fragment, each of the major parties to the conversation has both given a directive and countered the other's action. The form of the argumentation, however, has not attempted to affirm the relative superiority of one party with respect to the other. The directives in lines 1 and 7 are requests for information, and in line 6 the directive is framed as a proposal using a modal verb. Moreover, the counters do not refuse prior actions; instead they provide first an argument against the appropriateness of the suggested action (lines 2–3), and second an argument against the consequentiality of the suggested action (line 4). The directive/counter sequences do not result in the formation of a hierarchy, in that counters to proposals are themselves considered counterable, and a proposal initiated by one party may be reinstated subsequently by another.

6.3 COMPARING GIRLS' AND BOYS' DIRECTIVE USE

Both boys and girls make use of directives to coordinate behavior in task activities. However, they construct these actions in quite different ways. By selecting alternative ways of formatting directive moves and responding to them, and by distributing rights to perform directives differently, the two groups build alternative forms of social organization. Boys' directives are formatted as imperatives from superordinate to subordinate, or as requests, generally upward in rank. They differentiate hearer from speaker not only through their syntactic form but also through the ways in which characters are articulated through address terms, pronoun selection, comparisons, accounts, and depictions of scenes. Alternative directive shapes, such as requests and imperatives, are differentially distributed among members of the boys' group.

Among the girls, however, all participants use the same actions reciprocally with each other. The party issuing the directive includes herself as one of the agents in the action to be performed, and avoids using strategies which would differentiate herself from others.[7] Girls characteristically phrase their directives as proposals for future activity and frequently mitigate even these proposals with a term such as "maybe." They tend to leave somewhat open the time at which the action being proposed should be performed, while a boy in a position of leadership states that he wants an action completed *right now*. Whereas the accounts which accompany boys' directives may specify either personal desires of the speaker or demands of the activity, girls' accounts characteristically deal with concern for the well-being of recipient. Thus the details of how participants build their directives make relevant two contrasting modes of interaction: hierarchical ones in which players are differentiated and a more egalitarian one in which parties have reciprocal rights toward each other. In short, boys' directives display distinctions between participants and stress issues of individual rights; by way of contrast, girls' directives stress the connectedness of girls to each other and their caretaking concerns, a theme elaborated in Gilligan's (1982, 1987) formulation of a morality of care and responsibility.

Within task activities, the girls thus build a form of social organization which minimizes differentiation between participants.[8] Such constructive play, however, constitutes but one of the many types of activities in which they engage. In other circumstances girls can select forms which create greater disparity between speaker and hearer and construct quite different forms of social organization.

6.4 GIRLS' USE OF BALD DIRECTIVES

Two focal ideas that have emerged from work on women's speech are that women are more polite (Brown 1976; Kramarae 1981; Lakoff 1975; Thorne and Henley 1975; Thorne, Kramarae, and Henley 1983) and that in cross-sex situations women are dominated by men (West 1979). The way in which girls play out an egalitarian social structure during the organization of tasks might seem to be compatible with such a notion. I therefore want to emphasize that the girls have full competence with bald or aggravated forms of action and also systematically use them in appropriate circumstances. Indeed, in some circumstances, such as playing house, they create hierarchies similar to those of the boys.

Girls on Maple Street distinguish between various types of directives and degrees of mitigation, as is apparent from the ways in which they talk about alternative polite and impolite forms:

(32)   *Concerning a 4-year-old girl, Jolyn*

     Ruby: Jolyn wanted to come in the house.
                           I said "You say 'ex*cuse* me.'
                           =Not '*m*o:ve.' "

(33)   Bea: I s'd *I* said "You c'd *roll* your eyes
                           all you *want* to. Cuz I'm *t*ellin' you.
                           (0.5) *T*ellin'- I'm not *ask*in' you."
                           And I ain't say no plea:se *ei*ther.

Delivering orders to someone is considered a form of insulting talk referred to as "basing":

(34)   Kerry: GET OUTA MY STREET GIRL! (3.0)
                           HEY GIRL GET OUTA MY STREET!
  → Rhonda: Now don't come basin' at me!

Delivering direct commands to another girl is identifiable as a particular speech form by the girls, while for boys such forms would rarely be commented upon. In that girls seldom use imperatives in their talk with each other these structures can be employed to sanction behavior they consider deviant. For example, the following imperative was directed to a girl during a period when she was being ostracized by the girls' group.

(35)   *Annette, who is being ostracized, is*
                            walking up her steps.

     Bea: GIRL YOU MADE- BETTER GO BACK-
                         BETTER GO BACK IN THE *H*OUSE!

Unprovoked bald commands thus constitute a marked form which can be used to make a statement about the social relationships obtaining between girls.

6.4.1 SITUATIONS WARRANTING THE USE OF IMPERATIVES

Although imperatives are used infrequently in girls' routine interactions with one another, there are a number of circumstances in which they are considered perfectly appropriate. Two contexts in which they occur are (1) in response to clear violations, and (2) during play when advancing the activity or attending to the welfare of others has a clear priority.

    In the following, girls respond to infractions committed by others with imperatives:

(36)		*Freddie starts drinking water from Kerry's spout.*
	Kerry:	You act so **gr**eedy. Go **ho**me if you want some water.

(37)		*Boy steps on Ruby's lawn.*
	Ruby:	Get out the way offa that- get off that *la*wn!

(38)		*Tommy is hitting Kerry.*
	Kerry:	Tommy, stop playin' around. STOP. Quit playin' around. STOP!

(39)	Chopper:	Get outa here you wench. You better get outa here.
→	Bea:	No! You don't tell *me* to get out.

(40)		*Ruby bounces on top of Bea.*
	Bea:	Ouch girl. Stop. That hurt!

(41)		*Ruby is sitting on top of Kerry.*
	Kerry:	Get off Ruby.

(42)		*Bea's cousin Lisa starts picking flowers.*
	Bea:	You better stop pickin' those flowers.

Note how these imperatives are directed to both boys #36–#39 and other girls #40–#42, and indeed when an offense is felt to merit retributive action, girls are as skilled as boys at countering another party.

Even four-year-old girls give commands to boys who step out of bounds. In the following, Jolyn (age 4) gives an imperative to Larry (age 6) as he begins to paint Jolyn's lawn furniture:

(43)	Jolyn:	***Don't*** play with the um table.
	Larry:	Let me just paint.
	Jolyn:	No. ***Don't*** paint that table. ***Don't*** put all that paint on that thing. That chair.

For a number of reasons the realm of play constitutes another domain of action in which imperatives systematically occur. First, imperatives can be used to promote the game's onward development or critique the style in which it is being played:

(44)   *Jumping rope*

        Bea: Go ahead Rochele.

(45)   *Jumping rope*

        Drucilla: No jumping in singles.

(46)   *Jumping rope*

        Drucilla: You gotta get your other jump.

(47)   *About rope-turning style*

        Martha: Put some life in it!

Second, imperatives provide a way of quickly and efficiently warning others about problems that can occur in the midst of play. As Brown and Levinson (1978:100–101) argue, "where maximum efficiency is very important . . . no face redress is necessary," and "in cases of great urgency or desperation, redress would actually decrease the communicated urgency."

(48)   *A car comes during jumping rope.*

        Bea: Watch out!

(49)   *During jump rope*

        Bea: Don't play in the water.

(50)   *Bea has cut herself with glass while*
                        making rings from bottle rims.

        Martha: Bea don't you lick your own blood.
                        That way it gonna go right back there
                        through your body.

(51)   *Collecting bottles while making glass rings*

        Bea: Don't pick the ones that are **bro**ken.

When issues of safety arise, imperatives are used quite frequently, as is evident from the following more extended sequence in which Kerry and Martha try to care for Bea's cut finger.[9] In preparation for putting mercurochrome on it, the girls issue commands to Bea to remove her finger from under the water spigot (lines 1, 15, 19, 36, 39) or commands related to this activity (lines 24, 26, 34). In response, Bea gives refusals rather than agreements, which lead to an extension of the directive sequence. Kerry and Martha respond to Bea's refusals with reasons why she should undertake the action they propose (lines 3–6), counters to the objections she brings up (lines 10–11, 13, 20, 22), and warnings which speak of impending consequences for her failure to carry out their directives (lines 15–16, 28–29).

(52)		*Bea has her cut finger under Kerry's water spigot.*
1	Kerry:	Take it out now Bea.
2	Bea:	No I'm not.
3	Kerry:	Get- it ain't gonna hurt you girl.
4		You got- and you want to get your hand
5		infected and they take-
6		they take the hand taken off?
7		(0.9)
8	Bea:	Yeah but it gonna bur:n!
9	Martha:	Uh uh oh!
10	Kerry:	It's not gonna burn you.
11		You run cold water over it.
12	Bea:	Yeah but it's still gonna burn.
13	Kerry:	That takes the sting. Oh shut up.
14	Bea:	It's still gonna burn.= Ain't // it.
15	Kerry:	You better get out or I'll make you eat
16		[that.
17	Bea:	Ain't it's gonna burn,
18		(1.2)
19	Martha:	Go ahead. Go ahead.
20	Kerry:	It not gonna burn.
21	Bea:	It is!
22	Martha:	Anyway it only pain!
23	Bea:	So?
24	Kerry:	Stop.
25	Bea:	But it-
26	Kerry:	Look Bea:!
27		(1.4)
28	Kerry:	Now you- you want me to take you
29		to the bathroom?
30	Bea:	Wait!
31		(2.0)
32	Bea:	I'm gettin' ready- I do it my*self*.
33		heh heh! heh heh heh!
34	Kerry:	Come on Bea. Stop playin' now!
35	Bea:	I'm tellin' you I do it // myself.
36	Kerry:	Come on. Oh put it back.

37	Bea:	Heh heh.
38	Martha:	Ha ha ha ha ha ha ha!
39	Kerry:	Come on. Put it- Come on Bea!
40	Bea:	Eh you know I'm tryin' to.
41	Kerry:	Now you see you big glup!

Thus, despite the relative infrequency of imperatives used in organizing girls' task activities, there are circumstances when imperatives constitute the most appropriate form of directive. The reasons which girls offer to support their imperatives during task activities contrast markedly with the justifications accompanying the commands of leaders in the boys' group. Rather than arguing that an action should be performed because of one party's personal desires, girls' imperatives deal with the requirements of the current activity.

6.4.2 INSTRUCTING OTHERS

It was seen in Chapter 5 that the right to instruct others was unevenly distributed among the boys. Indeed, instructing others provided a way for leaders to interactively establish their claims about special expertise and standing in the activity at hand. By way of contrast, girls actively negotiate who has the right to address others with imperatives, and modify their behavior when challenged. The following occurred while the girls were demonstrating how to break the glass rim of a bottle. Here it is not assumed that any one party has exclusive rights to instruct another. When Bea takes over the job of teaching in lines 10–17, she uses a range of paralinguistic cues to frame her talk (Goffman 1974) and contextualize (Gumperz 1982) it in a particular way. Thus she speaks with singsong intonation, caricaturing a teacher (lines 13–17), and colors what she says with laughter.

(53)

1	Bea:	Get that one. Here! Yeah give it to her.
2		(2.0)
3	Martha:	This won't know the difference.
4	Bea:	Get outa the street.
5		(0.8)
6		See you gotta do it real hard.
7	Martha:	Gimme this. I wanna do it. You're cracked.
8		I wanna show you how to do it.
9		I know how to do it *Bea*!
10	Bea:	*I* know. I ju- So you won't have to
11		break it. Like y'know. Do it like

((as she demonstrates, scraping it
against a metal manhole cover, the
correct angle for getting a smooth
bottle rim))

12	Martha:		Yeah.
13	Bea:	⌈	((*singsong instructing voice*)) But when
14			you get at the *end* you do it **hard**
15			so the thing would break **right**. Eh heh heh!
16			((*laughing at style of teaching*))
17		⌊	Harder!
18	Martha:		Do it **hard**er.
19	Bea:		Eh heh heh! // Oh:.

The negotiation which takes place here has features of what developmental psychologists describe as a considerably advanced form of "social negotiation strategy" (Stone and Selman 1982:169–179). In the "collaboration" stage of negotiation, children make use of various paralinguistic expressions to "communicate multiple, often ironic, meanings" (ibid.:175), employing "a contrast between the form they use and the form generally used in peer interaction." Here, while instructing others, Bea gives them orders in lines 1, 4, and 6; Martha in lines 7–9 counters that she wants to do it herself and does not need any instruction from Bea. Such active objection to letting another issue orders is congruent with the ways that the girls in other contexts actively monitor each other for actions that could be seen as claiming that one girl is setting herself above the others. In line 10 Bea agrees that Martha does know how to do it. When Bea again resumes instruction, she changes the intonation of her voice (lines 13–17); by adopting a singsong lilt, she mocks the way she is delivering her instructions to the group. Through this caricaturing of the talk of an instructor, Bea distances (Goffman 1961b:120–132) herself from the teaching role she is currently enacting, thereby making herself a more equal partner in the play.

6.4.3 MOTHER/CHILD AND CARETAKER INTERACTION

Another major circumstance in which girls make use of aggravated directives is when taking care of younger children and enacting such roles in a favorite pastime, playing house. The forms of directives which girls typically utilize with younger children are modeled after the more aggravated forms used by mothers to children.[10] Therefore some examples of mother/child directive sequences will be presented before we discuss girls' use of imperatives while performing and enacting (in the game of "house") the caretaker role.

An important component of the process through which mothers discipline children consists of giving directives. These frequently take the shape of direct imperatives:

(54)   *Pete is trimming bushes rather than*
            doing his assigned task, cutting grass.

    Mrs. N.:   Hey Pete. Leave the hedges alone!

Following an initial request, children may respond with an excuse or complaint which counters mother's initial action rather than with compliance. When directives are countered, mother in turn responds with return commands (#55), return counters (example #56), or actions which combine both (example #57).

(55)		*Chopper is playing with water from a hose.*
	Mrs. N.:	You better ***stop*** playin' with that water. You know it cost money.
	Chopper:	I'm not playing.
→	Mrs. N.:	Turn that water off.

(56)		*Chopper is shirking his obligation to cut the grass.*
	Mrs. N.:	Cut that grass.
	Chopper:	Carl wanted to do it.
	Mrs. N.:	Ah he don't. He didn't want to do it. He tryin' to help you and you were gonna-
→		You- You just tryin' to take advantage.

(57)		*William neglects his babysitting duties with his younger brother*
	Mrs. N.:	William come back here. You just walked away 'cuz you thought-
	William:	I always gotta watch him.
→	Mrs. N.:	Well where you goin'. Ain't nobody up there. You sit on the steps.

Various trajectories of directive forms may occur. More mitigated forms are used when mothers address a group which includes neighborhood children as well as their own.[11] In the following, the imperative form in lines 1–2 first directs the children to take account of the current scene, as if asking them to find for themselves what in their current actions is in need of change. Then in lines 5–9 imperatives are accompanied by a warning explaining why the proposed action should be undertaken:

(58)			*Boys are making slings on a neighbor's steps adjoining Mrs. D.'s house.*
	1	Mrs. D.:	((*falsetto*)) Take a look at what y'all
	2		doing on this step here.
	3	Carl:	I know. These not my nails.
	4		Freddie got them before.

5	Mrs. D.:	Y'all take that shit and put it on y'*all* step.
6		Cuz you- if you drill that hole
7		in that cement, with that lady next door
8		you gonna *pay* for that.
9		Get that stuff off that pavement!

The frequent use of imperative forms in mother/child interaction observed in my data stands in striking contrast to the findings of other research of parent/child discourse, such as Bellinger and Gleason (1982) and Gleason and Greif (1983), among white middle-class families. Both studies state that the mothers they observed from "traditional" families (ones "in which there is a division of labor by sex: a mother at home who does the bulk of child care, and a father employed outside the home" [Gleason and Greif 1983:142]) tended to use indirect polite requests (ibid.:146) and "to couch their directive intent in question form" (ibid.:148). Citing Lakoff (1973), these researchers argue that "avoidance of direct imperatives appears to be a general feature of women's language in our society" (ibid.:148).[12] Such a generalization is certainly not applicable to the data just examined. Directive use on Maple Street is consistent with research on the child-rearing practices of black (Bartz and Levin 1978; Baumrind 1972) and Chicano parents (Bartz and Levin 1978). Although not dealing explicitly with directive use, these studies report "a pattern of increased strictness, high control, and high support (nurturance) among African American parents" (Mc-Loyd, Ray, and Etter-Lewis 1985:40). The discrepancy between my data and those of the Gleason and Greif (1983) and Bellinger and Gleason (1982) studies might in part be related to the difference in ethnic/class groups investigated. Gleason and Greif (1983:148) report that fathers are frequently cast into or assume the role of disciplinarian.[13] Among the Maple Street group during the hours (after school and weekends) in which I did fieldwork, such roles were primarily played by women.

The forms of directives which mothers give their children are used by Maple Street girls in a number of circumstances, including disciplining younger children and playing "house." When girls give directives to younger children in their charge, whether cousins (examples #59 and #62), neighbors (examples #60 and #61), or siblings (#63–#65), they frequently use bald forms or imperatives.[14] Such actions may be accompanied by explanations; these may explicitly describe a benefit (such as safety) for the recipient of the imperative (as in example #61):

(59)   Martha: Stay out of the street now man.
                     Come on punk. Hurry up Glen.

(60)   Julia: Douglas you better get in there
                     and get on them *c*oat boy.
                     ...

Julia: Douglas. I'm a tell your *mother.
          Now you wait. Get off that railing.
          Get *off* there.

(61)   *Martha cautions Jolyn to stand away*
          from girls making glass rings.

Martha: Jolyn you get back cuz I don't want
          nothin fallin' in your eyes or in your face.
          Get back. Get back.

(62)   *Glen is playing in the street.*

Martha: Here go- here come a car.
          You better stay away//from it.
Bea: Sit on the steps.

(63)   *Jolyn puts down the hood of her*
          jacket on a windy day.

Kerry: *Don't* put that down. Put that back *up*!
          It's sup*posed* to be that way.

(64)   *Martha has prepared lunch for her*
          sister who has returned from school.

Martha: Go on in. Your lunch is waiting for you.

(65) Julia: Get in there! ((to brothers))
                ┌Get in there.
      Alan: Every time I look out here.
      Julia: Get in there. Don't you holler at *me*!

Directives which mothers give neighbor children differ in form from those
they give their own children. However, children in caretaking roles use
aggravated directive forms across various role relationships. In essence,
they pick the most salient form to vividly construct the activity.

6.5 PLAYING HOUSE

One of the girls' most popular games was playing house. In this activity
they built a hierarchy similar to the boys' through use of bald imperatives
and other directive formats. A specific episode of playing house will now
be investigated. Play takes place on Poplar Street at the house of Patrice
and Brenda, who live across from Martha. The most highly valued role,

mother, is played by Patrice (age 10) and Martha (12); these girls, who enact
"sisters" playing "mothers," establish two separate households at the onset
of this session.[15] A diagram of these dramatized kinship relationships will
facilitate subsequent discussion of the interaction that occurred during this
session of pretend play:

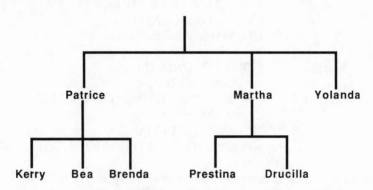

As this diagram shows, Yolanda (10) enacts the part of a childless sister
of Patrice and Martha. At the onset of play, Bea (12), Brenda (8), and Kerry
(12) (who during a large part of this session assumes the role of parental
child)[16] take the role of Patrice's children. However, during the session
Kerry negotiates a position as sister of Patrice, Martha, and Yolanda. Drucilla (7) and Prestina (5) are Martha's children.

6.5.1 THE STRUCTURE OF DIRECTIVES AND ACCOUNTS IN HOUSE

When playing house, girls enacting the role of mother address directives
to their "children" that are very similar in structure to those that their own
mothers use. They deliver imperatives loudly with emphatic stress. Such
patterning is consistent with other research on role playing among children's groups (Andersen 1978:89; Corsaro 1985:82; Ervin-Tripp 1982b:36;
Garvey 1974, 1977; Mitchell-Kernan and Kernan 1977:201–207; Sachs 1987),
which has demonstrated that directives constitute the principal means
through which children realize positions of dominance and submission
between characters such as those in the mother/child relationship:

(66)   Patrice: Hurry up and go to bed!

(67)   Martha: BRING THOSE CARDS BACK,
                      BRING THAT BOOK IN THE HOUSE
                      AND C:OME HOME!
                      Don't *climb* over that way.
                      You climb over the **right** way.

(68)   Martha: Drucilla, BRENDA, Prestina, GET IN THE CAR!
                     Get in the car.
                     Prestina and Brenda, and all y'all get in the
                     car.=
                     Where Drucilla at. GET IN THE CAR.
                     YOU GOIN' OVER *MY* HOUSE.
                     GO ON OVER AND GET-
                     UH- WHERE'S DRUCILLA AT.

(69)   Martha: COME ON *DRU*CILLA,
         Drucilla: We playin' *cards*,
         Martha: I DON'T CARE *WHAT* YOU PLAYIN'.=
                     COME ON.=
                     IT'S TIME TO GO *IN*.
                     =YOU GOTTA GO TO *SCHOOL* TOMORROW!

Accounts which accompany directives (such as "IT'S TIME TO GO *IN*.=YOU GOTTA GO TO *SCHOOL* TOMORROW!") not only supply warrants for the imperatives; in addition, they provide the primary ways that participants playing house develop domestic roles. They introduce culturally sanctioned reasons why activities should be done in specific ways, and also constitute a crucial resource for the introduction of expressively produced and topically appropriate new information into the ongoing action. Consequently, the accounts within "house" may be more elaborated than those that occur in actual interaction between caretakers and their charges:

(70)   Patrice: Well if you don't want to go to sleep,
                     don't go.
         →   But don't disturb your sisters.
                     Just because *you* don't wanna go.
                           (2.8)
                     Maybe *they* wanna go to sleep.
                     You don't know:: that.
                           (3.6)
                     That goes for *all* a you.
                     Whether you not my- children or not.
                     You *too*.
                           (2.2)
                     Don't let this happen again.

Girls playing mother talk about measures that must be heeded for the safety and well-being of members of a group (such as not disturbing one's sisters in the example above). The concerns which get voiced by girls in accounts accompanying directives thus include some which are similar to those that are expressed during girls' task activities.

The positions of those in control in house (as in the boys' slingshot episode) are manifested not simply through the issuing of directives which maintain a particular format but also through the *receipt* of various forms of action from others. The actions enacted by those playing smaller children are largely requests for permission, actions which imply an asymmetry of role relationships:[17]

(71)   Brenda: Mommy can um Yolanda play with our baby
                     brother?

(72)   Prestina: Can I hold your book?

(73)   Brenda: Mommy may *we* go out and play,

Requests are also addressed to the girls managing the activity, for example, when someone steps out of the role she is playing to ask for more information about it:

(74)   Bea: How old am *I*.

A form of asymmetry is thus built into the enacted behavior of mother and children which closely models that in caretaker/child interaction as well as leader/follower interaction among the boys during task activities.

Although Maple Street girls playing the roles of subordinates in "house" display deference through their requests for information, in contrast to the middle-class children studied by Corsaro (1985:83) they do not always display deference through their *responses* to imperatives. Rather, they follow the pattern used in responding to their own mothers or caretakers discussed earlier. Excuses rather than agreements are provided in the examples that follow in lines 2, 6, and 8 of #75 and line 4 of #76; a counteraccusation occurs in line 7 of #76:

(75)
1	Martha:	COME ON *DRU*CILLA.
2 →	Dru:	We playin' cards.
3	Martha:	I DON'T CARE *WHAT* YOU PLAYIN'.=
		COME ON.=
4		IT'S TIME TO GO *IN*.
5		=YOU GOTTA GO TO *SCHOOL* TOMORROW!
6 →	Dru:	Prestina TOOK THE CARDS,
7	Martha:	Prestina!
8 →	Dru:	Prestina took//some a the cards.

9	Martha:	BRING THOSE CARDS BACK, BRING THAT BOOK
10		IN THE HOUSE AND C:OME *HOME*!
11		Don't *climb* over that way.
12		You climb over the *right* way.

(76)

1	Brenda:	Maanaa. I want some *pea*nuts.
2	Kerry:	Well you ain't gettin' none.
3	Patrice:	Hurry up and go to bed!
4 →	Brenda:	((whining)) I was *just* eating a *pea*nut.
5	Patrice:	GO TO *BED!* YOU SUPPOSED- YOU SUPPOSED TO GET YOURS IN
6		THE MORNINGTIME.
7 →	Brenda:	((whining)) Well *you* eating them all *u:*p.
8	Patrice:	Do you want me to tell her to go- uhm
9		make you go to bed?

In #75 and #76 Patrice and Martha, the girls playing mothers, persist over several turns in their attempts to get their children Brenda and Drucilla to comply with directives. Mothers' imperatives are repetitively answered by children's counters as children negotiate their roles with respect to their caretakers.

6.5.2 DIFFERENTIATION IN PLAYING HOUSE ROLES

Symmetrical types of exchanges take place within "house" when siblings exchange equivalent argumentative forms.[18] By comparison with task activities, however, there is a minimum of egalitarianism in decision making. Insofar as those acting as children play subordinate roles, there is differentiation built into the activity itself. In addition, girls who play the role of mother act in the capacity of stage manager. As overseers of the unfolding drama, both Martha (mother #1) and Patrice (mother #2) monitor the actions of participants, commenting on them in utterances such as "Hey Brenda you supposed to be sleep!" or "Drucilla you can't hear them." For example, in the following, Patrice and Martha, as commenters on Brenda's actions, tell her how she should act as a child (line 1) and warn her of her precarious tenure in the play through a negative categorization of her behavior ("NOT EVEN *PLAYIN'* RIGHT") (lines 4–5), through commands (lines 6 and 8), and through an explanation/warning, "THAT'S WHY NOBODY WANT YOU FOR A CHILD" (line 7):

(77)

1	Patrice:	HEY BRENDA YOU OUGHTTA//be sleep!
2	Kerry:	I can't even get her in the bed.
3	Patrice:	I know.

4	Patrice:	SHE'S NOT//EVEN PLAYIN' RIGHT.
5		SHE NOT EVEN *PLAYIN'* RIGHT.
6	Martha:	BRENDA PLAY RIGHT.
7		THAT'S WHY NOBODY WANT YOU FOR A CHILD.
8	Patrice:	GET IN THERE AND GO TO SLEEP!

Girls playing mother can thus dictate for others dimensions of the activity *outside* the frame of play as well as within it. They can control not only who has rights to play what roles but also who can be members of the group.

Girls in the role of mother distinguish themselves from each other through the way they formulate stage directions. When Patrice complains about her daughter Brenda's behavior, she does not directly confront Brenda but instead talks *about her* using *third-person reference*: "SHE'S NOT EVEN PLAYIN' RIGHT." Martha, by way of contrast, delivers an imperative directly to Brenda: "BRENDA PLAY RIGHT." As the party who takes control of the duties of stage management, Martha (mother #1) and not Patrice (mother #2) assumes the right to issue commands to players not her own children.

Asymmetry with respect to roles is extended to other aspects of the activity as well. While one might expect a certain equality among two girls who play mother, only one of them characteristically makes decisions for the group.[19] In the present case, Martha assumes the right to change frame through "pretend" directives, and in general it is she who plays the role of stage manager:

(78)	Martha:	Hey y'all.=Pretend it's a- like- it's about twelve o'clock.=Okay?
	Patrice:	It's twelve o'clock in the afternoon so y'all should settle down.
	Martha:	Don't be too late.
	Kerry:	I'll fix their lunch!
(79)	Martha:	Come on.=Pretend it's two o'clock in the morning.
	Patrice:	OH: I'm goin' to *bed*.
(80)	Martha:	Pretend it's gettin' night time.=
	Kerry:	*Good* night child*ren*!

Responses to pretend directives are not randomly distributed among participants. Generally the person responding to a request to pretend is another girl situated in an equivalent role and not someone playing child. In these examples Patrice, a household head, and Kerry, an older child performing caretaking responsibilities, are the ones who reply to Martha's overt proposals for shifts in activity. Their talk elaborates the relevance of the directives for current and future activities. While not all initiations of frame shifts are begun by girls in the "mother" role, those who pass final judgment on proffered frame switches do tend to occupy that position. Thus while playing house girls display distinctions in their role relationships.

Positions of subordination and superordination between Patrice and Martha are evident in other ways as well. Patrice repetitively displays deference to Martha. In the following, for example, Kerry, a girl living with Patrice, initiates a "let's pretend" directive. Rather than respond to it herself, Patrice instead relays Kerry's proposal to Martha:

(81)	Kerry:	Okay. Pretend it's just about
		seven o'clock in the morning
→	Patrice:	What time is it Martha, (1.8)
		What time is it Martha.
		(0.6) *Mar*tha what time is it.
	Martha:	Seven o'*clock*.
	Patrice:	In the morning.

Meanwhile Martha asserts her position above Patrice in other ways as well, for example by issuing imperatives to her:

| (82) | Martha: | Where Patrice go. |
| | | You better get your children in the *house*. |

(83)	Martha:	Hey- you should beat your children cuz-
		You let her do her hair when she
		supposed to be in bed.

Repetitively Martha's definition of the situation is asserted above Patrice's. In the following, after Martha states that she has to fix dinner (lines 1–2), Patrice (line 3) offers an alternative plan of action using a modal verb: "*They* could eat dinner with us." This suggestion is flatly opposed in a next turn by Martha (line 4), and subsequently the group follows up on Martha's plan.

(84)		
1	Martha:	Don't sit over here or stand over here
2		cuz I gotta fix dinner.
3	Patrice:	*They* could eat dinner with *us*,
4	Martha:	No *uh* uh I'm fixin'- I brought all this
5		food out here and they gonna eat over here.

Not only do girls establish hierarchical arrangements among members of their groups, but they also differentiate themselves and establish implicit rankings by forming coalitions against particular girls. Among the Maple Street girls, as occurs among other girls' groups (i.e., Berentzen 1984; Eder and Hallinan 1978; Lever 1976; Thorne and Luria 1986), negotiating who is to be included within the most valued roles is an important feature of social organization. Within task activities, girls were positioned in equivalent identities. Greater social differentiation is possible while playing house as the division into families and households provides for the playing of alternative roles. The position of sibling to the party playing principal decision maker is a highly coveted position; girls can display alliances by excluding others from this desirable role. In the particular session of playing house being examined, Martha's best friend, Yolanda, had no difficulty acquiring the identity of sibling sister. However, considerable negotiation took place before Kerry established herself in a similar slot. In the following, the girls conspire to exclude Kerry from enacting the role of Martha's sister:[20]

(85)

1	Kerry:	I'm not your daughter.=All right? Um,
2		I'm- I'm her sister.
3	Patrice:	N:OO! // You-
4	Martha:	YOU CAN'T BE STAYIN' WITH ME!
5	Kerry:	I know.=I'm stayin' with *her*! But I
6		⌜can-
7	Patrice:	YOU- Uh *uh*! You- you *my* daughter.
8	Kerry:	Mm *mm*.
9	Patrice:	Uh *huh*. // Until Bea get back.
10	Kerry:	*Bea* your daughter.
11	Patrice:	⌜I know.=I-
12	Martha:	WELL HOW CAN YOU BE HER SISTER,
13	Patrice:	UH *HUH* BECAUSE *WE S*://ISTERS, HOW CAN
14		YOU BE *HER* sister.
15	Martha:	NOW HOW CAN YOU BE *MY* sister,
16	Patrice:	How can you be my // sister.
17	Yolanda:	That's r- that's right.
18		(0.8)
19	Yolanda:	We all three *sisters*.
20	Martha:	I *know*.
21	Yolanda:	Well how come you don't wanna be
22		⌜her daughter.
23	Brenda:	THERE Martha, Yolanda // AND
24	Kerry:	I'm another *sister*.
25	Brenda:	⌜There Martha and Yolanda is her-
26	Martha:	N:O.
27	Brenda:	Is your- and // she-
28	Martha:	WELL *YOU* STAY HERE WITH *HER*.

The dispute about Kerry's position in playing house begins in lines 1–2, where Kerry proposes that she enact the role of Patrice's sister rather than her daughter. This proposal is first objected to by Patrice (line 3) with "N:OO!" and then by Martha (line 4): "YOU CAN'T BE STAYIN' WITH ME!" Patrice counters Kerry again in line 7, arguing that Kerry is her "daughter" rather than sister. The dispute becomes more intense when Martha (lines 12, 15, 20), Patrice (lines 9, 13–14, 16), and Yolanda (lines 17, 19) argue that they are the only ones who can be sisters in playing house. The argument nears closure when Kerry (line 24) states, "I'm another sister." Subsequently Martha (line 28) concedes that she can be a sister under the condition that she live with Patrice. In this way Martha terminates the dispute while distancing herself from Kerry. Thus in the midst of dramatic play, as in other interaction, girls take considerable care to delineate their friendship alliances. Although an issue which is highly charged is debated, the girls continue playing together for nearly an hour after this dispute.

It has traditionally been argued that girls' play does not afford them opportunities to participate in a range of activities with varying kinds of role differentiation. According to Piaget (1965:77), Lever (1976:482), and Gilligan (1982:9–20) the lack of complex rule structure and forms of direct competitiveness in girls' games (as for example are found in boys' marbles [Piaget 1965] and team sports [Lever 1976]) limits their opportunities for practicing negotiational skills. As the argument goes, because girls do not participate in team sports (which have a large number of highly interdependent players, role differentiation, rule specificity, and competitiveness) as frequently as boys, they are less able than boys to develop ways of interacting which prepare one for "successful performance in a wide range of work settings in large, formal organizations" (Lever 1974:240–241). Making use of interview rather than ethnographic data, Lever (1976:482) argues that while playing games, girls are incapable of handling conflict without disruption of the ongoing activity.

Such findings are based on research which fails to take into account the wide range of female interactional competencies. Detailed ethnographic study of girls in play situations (M. H. Goodwin 1985b; Hughes in press[b]) presents a very different view of their abilities. Here I have shown that the forms of social organization which girls use to organize their play vary widely across different kinds of situations. While some activities are conducted with what appears to be minimal disagreement or competition, others provide for extensive negotiation and displays of status difference. As can be seen from the data on playing house, an activity which has traditionally been treated as unstructured play with few explicit rules, an incipient hierarchy emerges. Parties assume differentiated roles, both as characters in the pretend world and as participants interactively sustaining that world. Decisions regarding how the play is to proceed must be made from moment to moment; this allows for the emergence of the role of manager of the activity. Although a number of girls can give directives to children in the play frame (e.g., both "mothers" and "parental children"), one girl in particular emerges as the party who controls the staging of the activity. She makes frequent use of imperatives in her talk, and in general uses aggravated speech forms to oversee aspects of the activity. Concurrently, those in positions subordinate to the principal character (as both characters in the drama and actors in the dramatic play) display their deference vis-à-vis those in a position of authority, thereby constructing a complementarity of roles. Within dramatic play, girls further create a differentiation of participants through the ways in which they criticize certain girls or exclude them from valued positions. Alliances of girls against particular individuals are played out in a fashion which resembles alliance formation in a gossip event called "he-said-she-said" to be investigated in Chapter 8.[21]

6.6 ACHIEVING SOCIAL ORGANIZATION THROUGH SELECTIVE DIRECTIVE USE

Girls and boys make use of alternative forms of directives in a particular domain, while conducting their task activities. Girls perform directives in a variety of other contexts as well. Very different types of social organization may be built depending upon the forms of directives used to organize tasks and the division of labor which evolves in the process. In the boys' group, a differentiation among participants emerges as some boys explicitly formulate their directives to emphasize the degraded position of recipients through various types of insult terms and explanations, while others utilize mitigated actions and ratify the claims made by leaders. In brief, the boys structure their directives to emphasize differences between group members. Girls, on the other hand, share in decision making during task activities and formulate their directives as proposals which include themselves as parties who are obligated to perform the action at issue. Their directive system during task activities tends to minimize differentiation among group members. Nevertheless, in other forms of activities, differences in rank may be displayed through the way in which directive sequences are played out. Girls may also express alliances through the ways in which they form coalitions to exclude some members from valued positions.

My general findings regarding how gender groups on Maple Street (aged 9–14) organize their activities are remarkably similar to those of Berentzen (1984) for the Norwegian nursery school group of children (aged 5–7) he studied. The games and contests that boys engage in provide objective criteria for making evaluations among group members; by comparing their skill in a range of competitive endeavors, boys can establish a rank ordering, albeit one that changes from activity to activity. Berentzen (ibid.:131) argues that "boys attach primary value to material objects, while the girls attach it to each other." Because of the importance of objects for boys, *rank* becomes significant because it determines who gets support in controlling the resources they use in their games (ibid.:132). Girls, in contrast, do not utilize unambiguous criteria for differentiating members. The resources that girls on Maple Street and in Norway make use of are not rankings in competitive games but rather relationships with other girls. They display relative positionings by formulating alliances, which shift with new activities. The game of house provides a particularly apt idiom for elaboration of such alliance displays.

In an attempt to characterize women as speaking "in a different voice," recent research on female interaction patterns has tended to examine those features of female communication which are clearly different from those of males, to the exclusion of those which females and males share in common. For example, cooperative aspects of female language usage have been studied (e.g., Brown 1980; Maltz and Borker 1983), while ways in which disagreement may be expressed have been largely ignored. Here we have seen that although girls utilize mitigated directives and avoid differentiation among participants while engaging in play involving tasks, in other situations they use direct imperative forms. For example, imperatives are used to regulate the flow of game activity, warn play-group members of impending dangers, and respond to infractions committed by others. Girls also use aggravated forms while caring for younger children and enacting the role of mother in "house." Although they assume roles of superordination over those in their charge, girls support their directives with explanations which justify their use, frequently in terms of benefits to the addressee. Girls also employ explicit directive forms when instructing others. This case is of special interest because of the ways in which a girl playing instructor will attempt to distance herself from a role which places her in a superordinate position with respect to others. Although she gives explicit imperatives, she colors her talk with a range of paralinguistic cues, such as exaggerated professorial intonation, which provide ironic commentary on her talk.

Thus girls exhibit a range of different types of social organization in their activities. Many studies of gender differences tend, as Thorne (1986:168) argues, to promote the notion of "separate worlds" of males and females—"to abstract gender from social context, to assume males and females are qualitatively and permanently different." Here I have attempted to show that some features of girls' activities are similar to how boys hierarchically structure their play. A girl acting as a stage manager directs others in much the way that a boys' leader makes decisions for his group. However, the explanations that such a girl provides to support her imperatives speak to female rather than male concerns.

The findings reported here would thus seem to counter many of the prevalent notions about girls' social organization. Typically girls are seen as less competent than boys in maintaining social order and resolving disputes in the midst of play activities (Gilligan 1982; Lever 1976; Sutton-Smith 1979). Lever (1974:165), for example, argues that boys are more adept at managing disputes because (1) they have had the opportunity to observe the model set by older boys during age-mixed games, and (2) their "greater involvement in rule-bounded games gives them the experience with rule interpretation and adjudication that can help them resolve their quarrels without creating much ill-feeling among players." On Maple Street, however, girls are far more likely to be involved in age-mixed activities than boys, as girls are given the responsibility of caring for younger children, and older and younger boys' groups seldom play together. In addition, as was seen regarding playing house, girls devote considerable attention to negotiating the rules of their play activity. Moreover, such negotiation takes place without disruption of the ongoing activity or a breach in social relationships as is frequently argued to occur among girls (Gilligan 1982:9–10; Lever 1976:482). Finally, the differentiated social organization within a large group that girls evolve when playing house defies the often cited typifications of girls as interacting within small groups or friendship pairs (Eder and Hallinan 1978; Maltz and Borker 1983; Waldrop and Halverson 1975).

In patterning their directives, children may select from a range of different types of actions which construct widely different forms of social organization. In a number of specifiable contexts girls not only have access to but also make use of aggravated forms. This heightens one's appreciation of the fact that the structure of talk girls use among themselves constitutes not a limited repertoire or a kind of "restricted code," but rather systematic procedures through which a particular type of social organization can be created. The fact that their social organization varies substantially across different domains makes it imperative that studies of girls' play or interaction be grounded in detailed analysis of specific contexts of use.

Section 3

Disputes and Gossip

Disputes and Gossip

Displaying deference to others present is implicated in the organization of a range of behavior that occurs in human interaction (Goffman 1967:47–95, 1971). This is accomplished in part through watchful concern that potential discord not emerge as an explicit event in encounters. Looking at talk from such a perspective has provided a focus for much research on the pragmatic organization of politeness (and in particular forms of politeness in female conversation);[1] phenomena such as how disagreements between participants might be stated while preserving the face of each have received extensive investigation. For example, Brown and Levinson have studied how a speaker in conversation avoids the extreme of acting "baldly without redress" (1978:74) and assumes an orientation toward both positive and negative politeness. Such an orientation characterizes a range of speech actions, including the "hedged request," reported for American English speakers by Lakoff (1973:56)—"Won't you please close the door?"—and Labov and Fanshel (1977:85)—"This room is going to be dusted, isn't it?"—and for Tzeltal by Brown (1980:120)—"You don't, perhaps, have any chickens, it is said."

Far less attention has been given to how people manage opposition.[2] As Shantz (1987a:284), in a review of literature on children's adversative talk, has recently argued:

> Most of the theories that address fundamental issues in cognitive and social development posit conflict as an essential impetus to change, adaptation and development. Yet for all this theoretical emphasis on conflict, little research has been addressed to it—its basic features and effects.

It may be that researchers avoid studying conflict because it is negatively valued. Shantz (1987a:284) notes that in the psychological literature conflict frequently is equated with aggression; behaviors that are agonistic, assertive, aversive, coercive, conflictual, or disruptive are lumped together. Other research posits a similar depiction of argument among adults. For example, McLaughlin (1984:180) describes argument as a "troublesome" conversational event. Similarly, Allen and Guy (1974:239) characterize conflict as a form of "deficiency" within conversation, marking "the failure of social relations." However, when Maple Street children's disputes are examined in detail, it will be found that rather than being disorderly, arguing provides children with a rich arena for the development of proficiency in language, syntax, and social organization.

The opposition moves of Maple Street children are built in ways that contrast with actions designed to display deference to another. The children frequently seek opportunities to test or realign the current arrangement of social identities among their peers; opposition provides an effective way to accomplish this.[3] When the actions of another are construed as a violation, the offended party can take action to remedy such an affront. Opposition moves also provide the opportunity to register one's affective alignment toward the other and in so doing to display character. Thus, instead of attesting to "the actor's current willingness to accept the status quo" (Goffman 1967:254), the children create miniature versions of what Goffman (ibid.:237–258) has termed "character contests"—"moments of action [during which] the individual has the risk and opportunity of displaying to himself and sometimes to others his style of conduct" (ibid.:237). In brief, rather than organizing their talk so as to display deference to others, the children frequently seek opportunities to display character and realign the social organization of the moment through opposition. Thus the data reported here are consistent with Kochman's (1981:30) observations that "black cultural events typically encourage and even require individuals to behave in an assertive/expressive manner." As poetically put by Rose (1987:36) in his ethnography of black American street life, "the world of the street was a theater of continuous fiction where the least movement, the least gesture was a work of theatrical care and improvisation."

The present analysis will investigate how children *with other children* construct argumentative talk, and how that talk is used to build their local social world. Much previous work in anthropology and sociology has investigated disputes by theorizing about how they might function in larger social processes, while paying little attention to the procedures and competencies employed to build the dispute as a coherent, culturally appropriate object in the first place. By way of contrast, analysis in Chapter 7 will investigate the basic structures that the children use to build argumentative sequences. Two phenomena in particular will be focused on in some detail: (1) ways in which opposition can be displayed within a turn at talk and sustained across several turns; and (2) how subsequent argumentative moves tie in detail to prior ones by reusing materials in the earlier talk (a phenomenon I will call *format tying*).

Using this analysis as a point of departure, I will then examine how the specific ways of formulating talk are related to the functions they serve in the immediate interaction. First (in Chapter 8) I will look at how girls construct a type of gossip dispute activity that they call *he-said-she-said*. This speech event is among the most significant of the girls' political activities; through it they are able to realign their social organization. In Chapters 10–11 I will look at how a particular genre, stories, functions within dispute processes. Stories provide participants with arenas for interpreting events and structuring talk in ways that are relevant to larger social projects. By examining the different ways that girls and boys make use of stories within their disputes, it will be possible to specify some gender differences in the use of similar speech events.

CHAPTER SEVEN

Building Opposition in Children's Argument

Social science researchers investigating children's disputing have proposed various definitions for arguing.[1] Brenneis and Lein (1977:61–62), for example, define an argument sequence as an arrangement of content and/or stylistic categories according to one of three different patterns: (1) repetition, (2) inversion, or (3) escalation. Boggs (1978) uses the term "contradicting routine" in describing the patterning of arguing among part-Hawaiian children. Eisenberg and Garvey (1981:150) analyze what they call "adversative episodes": "the interaction which grows out of an opposition to a request for action, an assertion, or an action,[2] . . . An adversative episode is a sequence which begins with an opposition and ends with a resolution or dissipation of conflict."[3]

Eisenberg and Garvey (1981) provide one of the most coherent definitions of argument in the psychological literature, and their study and others like it have been important in describing a range of basic structures found in argument. However, before proceeding further, it should be noted that recent research has challenged many of the key assumptions in the definition of argument they offered. Thus while Eisenberg and Garvey (1981:150) state that "an adversative episode is a sequence which begins with an opposition," Maynard (1985b) states that it is difficult to predict when arguments start because practically any prior strip of talk may be transformed into something about which there can be dispute.[4] Eisenberg and Garvey also emphasize resolution as a way of terminating disputes. Their research may have been influenced by the fact that children were observed in dyadic rather than multiparty interaction as well as in a laboratory setting.[5] As they report, "The acquainted children were brought by their nursery school teacher to the laboratory playroom in groups of three. The three children were invited to draw straws to see who would go to the playroom first. The dyad was videotaped through one-way observation mirrors" (Eisenberg and Garvey 1981:157). The children in their sample ended arguments with resolutions; Maple Street children, on the other hand, as well as other children observed in multiparty settings (Adger 1984:44–47; Corsaro and Rizzo 1990; Genishi and di Paolo 1982; Maynard 1985a:4–5; Sheldon 1989), display an orientation toward sustaining and promoting rather than dissipating dispute.[6]

Although studies based on role-played data (i.e., Brenneis and Lein 1977) permit us to learn a great deal about the structuring of utterance types, they do not allow us to analyze how dispute arises in interaction in the first place; nor can we learn what functions dispute might serve for social processes among peers (Maynard 1985a, 1985b). Most data on children's arguments have been gathered in a particular situation: the school. It seems quite likely that this setting imposes constraints upon children's interaction that are not found in the neighborhood. Genishi and di Paolo (1982:66), for example, report that because of the availability of a teacher for intervention in disputes, it was "unnecessary for children to formulate their own solutions to conflicts." On Maple Street, by way of contrast, it was customary for children to "fight they own battles" free from adult intervention.

7.1 AGREEMENT, REPAIR, AND OPPOSITION

In order to highlight as clearly as possible the procedures used to build opposition, it is useful to compare the organization of opposition turns with that of talk that displays a preference for agreement. In her work on agreement and disagreement in assessment sequences, Pomerantz (1984:64) distinguishes a *preferred-action turn shape*, which maximizes the salience of actions performed with it, from a *dispreferred-action turn shape*, which minimizes the action performed with it. In the data she examined, disagreement was a dispreferred activity, and its occurrence was minimized through use of phenomena such as (1) delays before the production of a disagreement, and (2) prefaces that mitigated the disagreement. Indeed, these prefaces sometimes took the form of agreements that were then followed by the disagreement.[7] The following provide examples:

(1)   A: She doesn't uh usually come in on
                    Friday, does she.
        B: Well, yes she does, sometimes,

(2) 1   John: *You* could live in thih- in this area.
    2   I belie:ve you c'd *really* live in this
    3   area inna *t*ent.
    4   (0.7)
    5   John: Y'know?
    6   Don: I think you'd if- if- if (you did it
    7   you'd be) ro(h)bbed,

The disagreement in #1 is mitigated by both the hesitant "Well" which precedes it and the qualifier "sometimes" which follows it. In #2 the statement being disagreed with is followed by a long pause (line 4), and the explicit disagreement occurs only when initial speaker in line 5 requests a response. The disagreement that is at last produced is further modulated by being prefaced by a hedge ("I think"). In these examples, although disagreement occurs, it is organized as a dispreferred activity through use of phenomena such as delays in its occurrence and prefaces that mitigate it when it at last emerges.

By way of contrast, when the Maple Street children oppose one another, they organize their talk so as to highlight that opposition. Rather than being preceded by delays, turns containing opposition are produced immediately. Moreover, such turns frequently contain a preface which announces right at the beginning of the turn, characteristically in the first word that is said, that opposition is being produced. Two types of prefaces are used.

1. First, opposition may be signaled immediately through an expression of polarity (Halliday and Hasan 1976:178) that is used to initiate the turn:[8]

(3)   Chopper: Get outa here you wench!
                     You better get outa here.
   → Bea: No! You don't tell *me* to get out!

(4)   *Talking about Martha's hair*

        Billy: Wet it!
   → Martha: No. I don't *w*anna wet it.

(5)   Billy: ((*singing*)) You didn't have to go to
                     school today did you.
   → Kerry: Yes we *did* have to go to school today!

In these data a term displaying opposition to what has just been said is placed at the very beginning of the turn (in #5 "yes" rather than "no" signals polarity in that the preceding utterance was phrased as a negative statement using "didn't"). The shape of these disagreements is such that they do not delay or disguise the alignment a participant is taking up with respect to a prior move but instead emphasize such opposition.

2. A second type of preface used to begin opposition turns consists of repetition of part of the talk that is being opposed:

(6)   *On reaching a city creek*

        Bea: Y'all gonna walk in it?
        Ruby: *W*alk in it, You know where that water come
                     from? The toilet.

(7)   *The girls are trying to trick the boys into*
                                      believing that they have found some frogs.

        Bea: We found a frog.
        Chopper: A *frog*, Y'all did not.

Partial repetition of prior talk selects out a particular part of prior speaker's talk to be focused upon. In addition, it allows present speaker to provide a particular affective reaction to what prior speaker has just said. Partial repetition occurs in a variety of conversational activities, including disagreements with prior speakers' self-deprecations (Pomerantz 1984:83–84) and other-initiated repair (Schegloff, Jefferson, and Sacks 1977). In these activities, as well as in opposition, the partial repeat is used to locate a trouble source in another's talk.

The partial repeats that occur at the beginning of opposition moves differ from the repetitions in other activities in several important respects. In other-initiated repair, the discovery of error is characteristically modulated through use of markers of uncertainty; for example, the partial repeat might be spoken with rising intonation. Moreover, locating the trouble source is frequently the only activity performed in the turn. The following provides an example:

(8)   A: He likes that waiter   A: *Trouble source*
                  over there,
    →   B: Wait-*er*?   B: *Find trouble*
       A: Waitress, sorry.   A: *Provide remedy*

In these data the activities of locating the trouble and providing a remedy are separated into distinct turns performed by different individuals. Although B points to something problematic in A's talk, A is allowed to do the correction her/himself. By restricting the activity in one's turn to locating the error, B proposes that the party who made the error has the competence to remedy it, and provides initial speaker with an opportunity to do so (see Schegloff, Jefferson, and Sacks 1977 for further analysis of this process).

Prefaces of turns performing aggravated opposition differ from other-initiated repair in two basic ways:

1. First, the partial repeat does not characteristically stand alone, but instead is immediately followed by further talk which explicitly opposes what prior speaker said.[9] By providing this correction, the party opposing prior talk portrays prior speaker as lacking the ability or competence to remedy the error on his/her own.[10]

2. A second way in which opposition prefaces differ from other-initiated repair is in terms of the intonation pattern used. Rather than modulating the discovery of a trouble source with a tentative, rising inton-

ation, opposers use distinctive contours that not only focus attention on the trouble *as trouble* but also call into question the competence of the party who produced such an object. Thus the partial repeats in #6 and #7 are spoken with falling-rising contours (Gunter 1974:61), a pattern that Ladd (1980:150) notes may be used to "do something like a holistic 'contradiction' or questioning of speaker A's assumptions."

The use of such an intonation contour has other consequences as well. First, current speaker is able to display a particular affective reaction—e.g., shock, offense, amazement, or incredulity—at what prior speaker has just said. Second, by repeating prior speaker's talk in such a way, current speaker is able to caricature prior speaker by portraying his/her actions as ridiculous or inappropriate. Within the opposition preface, current speaker is thus able to both build a small effigy of the party being opposed, and display his/her own affective alignment to the actions that such a person performs.[11]

The challenge that is intrinsic to an aggravated opposition preface can also be conveyed by preceding a partial repeat with "who" or "what" produced with falling intonation (as in #9 and #10) or the words "what" or "huh" produced with emphatic rising intonation (as in #11 and #12 below).

(9)   Juju: Kerry go and get your pick.
         Kerry: *Wh*at pick. I'm not goin in the house now.

(10)   Martha: When it snows outside where y'all have gym at.
         Billy: In the basement.
         Vincent: *Wh*at basement. *No* we ain't.

(11)   *Discussing bottles for making rings*

         Ossie: Can't use this kind.
         Kerry: *What*? We already- sh-
                     Candy show him them things.

(12)   *Discussing a foster child*

         Billy: Her mother didn't want her.
         Bea: *Huh?* She said cuz her sister ran away
                     and she ain't have nobody to take care of her
                     while she go to work so,

Rather than simply disagreeing with something in prior talk, the aggravated character of the intonation used in such opposition prefaces actively challenges what was just said.

Despite such differences, in other ways aggravated opposition and modulated disagreement have much in common with each other. For example, both use many of the same underlying resources to accomplish what they are doing (e.g., prefaces that characterize the action being performed in the turn, distinctive intonation patterns, careful placement of action, attention to how the other is portrayed, etc.). This suggests that these activities might indeed have real structural ties to each other, i.e., that they might be constructed from alternative choices from the possibilities provided by a basic set of common resources.

7.2 PERSON DESCRIPTORS AND INSULT TERMS

Looking at opposition sequences from a slightly different perspective, one can see that what is being called into question in such sequences is not simply the trouble source in the prior talk but the competence or status of the party who produced that talk. In essence, what is being opposed is not only a position but also an actor responsible for stating such a position. In view of this, it is not surprising that another phenomenon found quite frequently in opposition turns is an explicit characterization of the person who produced the talk being opposed. For example:

(13)   *Discussing slings*

    Chopper: I don't want these big thick ones.
→ Malcolm: You is crazy boy. I swear to God.
                  You need that- thick like that.
                  Cuz that hurts people.

(14)   *Boys are discussing slings they*
                          are making for a slingshot fight.

    Tokay: All right we *g*ot enough *al*ready.
→ Malcolm: No- man! *Y*ou must be *cra*zy. (0.8)
                  *M*ust be. (0.6)
                  Talkin' about I got *enough*!=Boy.
                  You must- I *know* you have never played *now*.
                  Thinkin' I got *enough*. (0.8)
                  Ma:n you need three *thous*and to have *enough*.
                  (1.8) I *al*ways like to have-
                  I *al*ways like to have more than my enemy has.
                  Cuz if *I* don't have more than my *e*nemy ma:n
                  I is *doom*ed.

In both of these examples, the party who produced the talk being opposed is characterized as "crazy" for having said what he said. In #13 such portrayal of prior speaker is further intensified with the idiom "I swear to God" and the account that follows, contradicting prior speaker's statement. In #14 the characterization of prior speaker is heightened by repetition of the talk that is being held up to ridicule: "Talkin' about I got *enough!*" (note also how prior speaker's "we" is changed to "I" in the repeat—the entity who would say such an absurd thing no longer includes the current speaker). What happens here is structurally similar to what occurs in opposition prefaces when a subsequent speaker repeats part of prior speaker's talk. By recycling another's talk and creating a new framework for interpreting it, current speaker can both display his own alignment toward what was just said and comment on the action produced by prior speaker. Malcolm's commentary on Tokay's remark is further elaborated to include the judgment that a party who would produce such talk must be unfamiliar with the activity being talked about.

Opposition can thus call into question not only what has been said but also the general competence of someone who would produce such talk. Moreover, such an action provides the opportunity for a reciprocal display of opposer's expertise; as Kochman (1981:24) has argued, "winning the contest requires that one outperform one's opponents: outthink, outtalk, and outstyle them." Thus the talk does not simply portray its recipient as defective but rather invokes a particular relationship between speaker and addressee that categorizes each of these participants in an alternative way. Data such as these emphasize the fact that in analyzing opposition it is not sufficient to focus exclusively on the talk through which opposition is produced; one must also take into account how actors are portrayed and constituted through that talk.

Looking at opposition from such a perspective sheds light on another frequent component of opposition turns: pejorative person descriptors and insult terms. Such objects provide resources that are used to build a turn that not only opposes prior talk but also explicitly characterizes the person who produced it.

(15)   Malcolm: Me and Tony saw- we saw um:
                    The Witch and the Hangman.
    →   Tony: The *Hangman* and the *Witch* knucklehead.

(16)   Tony: *Gi*mme the *things*.
    →   Chopper: You sh:ut up you big lips.

(17)   *Tony is arguing why he is justified*
                    in taking the pliers for making slings.

        Tony: Oh shut up. You didn't do nothin' with yours.
    →   Chopper: Why don't you *make* me faggot.

(18)   *Rhonda walks quickly toward Kerry.*

   Kerry: ***What*** you want!
→ Rhonda: Watch that's your ***club*** sister punk.

(19)   *Discussing whose bus is faster*

   Freddie: We was first this afternoon.
→ Vincent: We was first this ***morn***in' baby.

(20)   *During a confrontation interrogation*

   Bea: I'm just askin' you how you know.
→ Ruby: And I'm just *t*ellin' you honey.

Contest terms such as the above constitute optional elements of a turn which serve to portray current speaker's alignment toward prior speaker. When a contest term is preceded by "you" (as in #16), the term may be used to display that speaker is specifically tying recipient to the categorization provided by the term. Contest terms and pejorative person descriptors are characteristically placed at the end of argumentative turns, with the talk preceding them being occupied with the work of displaying opposition.[12] When they are positioned at the close of a turn, an affinity of shape with a prior move is achieved and the work of opposition is highlighted.

Data such as these demonstrate how a single opposition turn can contain a variety of components that attend to and operate on differential phenomena (e.g., one component of the turn might deal with something said in prior talk, while another addresses the character of the person who produced that talk). The multiplicity of action within individual turns raises questions about the common practice of analyzing argument by glossing a turn as an instance of a particular kind of speech act.

7.3 SUBSTITUTIONS

As the data just examined demonstrate, opposition can be signaled at many places within a turn. I now examine a way of displaying opposition in places other than the turn preface through use of what Halliday and Hasan (1976:146) call "substitution," or "the replacement of one item in a sentence with another having a similar structural function." For example:

(21)   *During a slingshot-planning session*

   Chopper: Get your four guys,
   Malcolm: You get ***three*** guys.

(22)   *Discussing when something was said about Kerry*

Deniece: An' that happened *last year*.
Kerry: That happened *this* year.

(23)   *Discussing dead blocks*

Malcolm: How'd you lost those two games.
Chopper: *One* game.

(24)   Tommy: You got on a blouse too. I can see the sleeves.
Kerry: I got a *sweat*er on dear heart.

Although substitution occurs in mid-turn, it has some of the same structural consequences that opposition prefaces do. Thus, like an opposition preface, a substitution does not provide the party being opposed a place to remedy the trouble source on his/her own. For example, in #24 Kerry does not give Tommy an opportunity to change "blouse" to "sweater" before providing it herself. However, if Kerry had wanted to make her correction as other-initiated repair rather than as opposition, a turn consisting only of "Blouse?" could have been produced.

When the substitution format is used to create opposition, a number of phenomena are used to heighten the salience of the term being offered as a correction. First, the utterance containing the correction characteristically repeats some of the prior talk while changing the item being challenged. Such repetition of another's talk frames the item being repaired and helps to emphasize that what is being effected is a correction of something the other said. Second, the replacement term is typically spoken with heightened emphasis, giving it "contrastive stress" (Ladd 1980:78).[13] Finally, at the close of the turn, a pejorative person descriptor (i.e., "dear heart" as in #24) may be used. Such a way of signaling a correction differs from that found by Yaeger (1974, Yaeger-Dror 1985) for talk among adults, in which a preference for agreement is operative. In her data, nonsalient intonation was used over expressions of disagreement.[14]

7.4 ALTERNATIVE TYPES OF OPPOSITION: RETURNS AND DISCLAIMERS

We will now briefly investigate how the components of opposition turns can engender subsequent argumentative turns. To examine this process, it is useful to distinguish two contrasting types of opposition moves:

1. Disagreement (#25) or refusal to perform some requested action (#26):

(25)	William:	Boy you broke my skateboard.
	Carl:	No I *di*dn't.
	William:	Did *too*.
	Carl:	Did *not*.
	William:	Did *too*.

(26)		*Discussing Martha's hair*
	Billy:	Wet it.
	Martha:	No. I don't *wa*nna wet it.

2. Return and exchange moves (Pomerantz 1975:26) in which a move equivalent to the one being opposed is returned:

| (27) | Sheridan: | You cheat. |
| | Chopper: | *You* cheat. |

Note that even though the words in both turns may be the same (as in #27), second speaker's action is a *reciprocal* one, not an identical one, since features of it, such as who is referred to by the pronouns in it, change as the participation framework changes. What is preserved is the relationship of action, current speaker, and current recipient.[15]

A single return move can include both of these types of action. Thus in the following, Ossie first disagrees with Lee and then accuses Lee of having performed the action that Lee just accused Ossie of:

(28)	Lee:	Y'all just changed the whole *ga*me around!
	Ossie:	We didn't change *no*thin' around.
		Y'*all* changed it around.

Although both types of action can occur in a single opposition sequence, these procedures are alternative to each other in that they provide for quite distinctive types of sequencing:

  • Disagreement and correction sequences involve the assertion (and reassertion) of positions. Such assertions can be buttressed by justifications, which have sequential consequences of their own.
  • Exchange and return sequences, by way of contrast, are not concerned with the validity or invalidity of a position. In that the truth value of a statement is not at issue, a prior move is responded to with a reciprocal action, rather than with an action which tries to prove or disprove a point of view.

    These distinctions also have consequences in detail for how subsequent moves are spoken. Responses in return and exchange sequences emphasize through intonational stress the agent of the action or subject associated with the pejorative attribute, rather than contrasting features of the truth or falsehood of the action on the floor.

- A third way of responding to a prior argumentative action is by producing talk that comments on the prior move, providing what Halliday and Hasan (1976:206–217) have termed an "indirect response":
    1. a "disclaimer" (an action that denies the *relevance* of a prior action rather than disagreeing[16] with it), or
    2. a "commentary" (an action that comments upon what was said in a prior turn).

Frequently turns containing disclaimers have distinctive prefaces. Thus terms such as "so," "I don't care," and "I know" can be used to begin turns containing reasons why current speaker considers prior speaker's talk to be of no consequence.

There are some subtle differences in the ways in which these prefaces are used. "So" and "I don't care" generally follow utterances interpreted as moves that are attempting to put their recipient in a disadvantageous position.

(29) Billy: *((singsong voice))*
       *Rhon*da an' 'em hadda go to schoo::l,
 → Rhonda: So, *I ain't* have to go to school
       *y*esterday.

(30) Benita: I'm eight and a half. I'm almost nine.
 → Larry: So, my *bro*ther older than *you*.

(31) Kerry: Why you wanna bother with him.
       He smaller than you.
 → Earl: So:, He keep mouthing off with me.

(32)   *Billy compares going to school at the*
       Franklin Institute with attending Bea's school.

    Billy: Better than Shaw,
 → Bea: So, I don't care about my school anyway.

(33) Tommy: I'm a tell Mommy.
 → Kerry: I don't care what you *do*.

(34)   *Jolyn complains about a command her*
       sister has given her.

    Jolyn: I'm a tell Mommy.
 → Kerry: I don't care. You always actin' up
       you old fresh thing. You better hold my hand
       or I'll get mad at you.

(35)   Kerry: Jimmy gonna be in *our* club.
                        Jimmy *and* um Freddie.
      → Stacey: I don't care. Never mind.
                        I don't like Freddie cuz Freddie say
                        he gonna kiss me.

By way of contrast, moves prefaced with "I know" argue that what prior speaker is presenting is not newsworthy:

(36)   Carl: Some people is spot-uh: light freckles.
      → Harold: Yeah I *know*. *I* know that.
                        I know it.

(37)   *In the midst of a confrontation*

          Stacey: Fight yourself.
          Ruby: Well you *make* me fight myself.
          Stacey: I can't *make* you. Cuz it's a free world.
      → Ruby: I *know* it's a free world.

Disclaimers such as "I don't care" or "so," arguing for the irrelevance of prior speaker's talk, constitute especially apt moves following statements such as warnings (#33 and #34), criticisms (#31), and attempts to show oneself at an advantage vis-à-vis others (#29, #30, #32, and #35), when the statements made by the other cannot be disputed. "I know" can be used to challenge the appropriateness of what the other just said, i.e., to argue that s/he offered something as news when current speaker in fact already knew it.[17]

A second form of indirect response involves categorizing what prior speaker just said as a culturally defined offense. Categorizations which Maple Street children use include phrases such as "basing" or talking loudly about someone in a pejorative manner (#38 and #39), talking "trash" (talking in what the recipient considers an inappropriate manner, as in #40),[18] "showing off" (#41), "acting smart" (#41), and "telling stories" (#42) or lying. Other expressions include "laming" (insulting with respect to personal attributes),[19] "acting hard" (putting on a front of being tough), "having smart answers," "bragging," etc. Such characterizations may occur in association with other argumentative actions such as partial repeats (#38), disagreement (#40), or warnings (#41):

(38)   *Pete has said Carl's mother has*
                        four eyes.

          Carl: You must need some glasses.
      → Pete: I need some glasses, Well you-
                        you *base* too much.

(39)   Kerry: What you *want.*
     → Rhonda: Now don't come basin' at *me*!

(40)   *Playing with yoyos*

          Ossie: I don't know how to do it with this yoyo.
          Malcolm: You can't do it *p*eriod.
     → Ossie: I could *so* do it.
                        You talkin' that trash.

(41)   *Jolyn puts the hood of her jacket*
                        down on a cool day.

          Kerry: Don't put that down. Put that back up.
                        It's sup*posed* to be that way.
          Jolyn: *No* it's not Kerry.
     → Kerry: *You* always showin' off. You always
                        actin' smart. I'm a spank you.
                        Always gotta show off.
                        That's what you get for bein' so fresh.
                        ((spanks Jolyn))

(42)   *Stacey has provided numerous excuses to Ruby*
                        for not coming down the street to fight.

          Ruby: Why is you so afraid to come down Maple.
          Stacey   First I gotta look for some money.
     → Ruby: Tellin' all them different stories ain't you.
                        Just got finished sayin'
                        cuz you had to wait for your mother.
                        Now you gotta look for the money.
                        It ain't gonna take you that long
                        to go down Maple.

Such moves have a deep affinity with actions that use pejorative person descriptors. In both cases the person being opposed is explicitly categorized in a negative fashion. However, instead of nouns being used to describe targeted individuals, verb phrases are used to depict the other in an offensive way by categorizing the action s/he has performed. In view of such underlying structural similarity it is not surprising to find insult terms and pejorative characterizations cooccurring in a single turn:

(43)   Kerry: Now you always gotta show off
                        just cuz Jimmy did somethin'.
          Tommy: *I* ain't showin' off.
     → Kerry: STOP! Act so funny. Hey Ignorant.
                        You better stop actin' like a fool.

Responses such as these can initiate a new exchange and return trajectory. Insofar as talk built in this way portrays the other in a negative fashion, it can itself be seen as calling for a reciprocal argumentative action from its addressee. Thus, while these actions constitute subsequent moves, they are also capable of sustaining a dispute sequence by simultaneously constituting new first actions to further argumentative responses from their addressees.

7.5 SUSTAINING DISPUTE: THE SEQUENCING OF ARGUMENTATIVE TURNS

In many anthropological descriptions of legal dealings, two concepts— mediation and settlement—are taken for granted as parts of the dispute process (Cohn 1967:148; Collier 1973:19; Gulliver 1969a:19, 1969b:67–68; Nader 1969:85). For example, Nader (ibid.:85) reports that in Oaxaca, Zapotec ideology "requires the *officials* to 'make the balance,' to restore relations between litigants to a former condition of equilibrium." Recently Gulliver (1979:3) and Nader and Todd (1978:10) have argued that mediation is not a necessary feature of all dispute. However, most anthropologists (with the exception of Yngvesson 1976) have left unchallenged the idea that disputes terminate in settlement.

The disputes of the children of Maple Street differ from disputes reported in the anthropological literature in two important ways: (1) they are conducted without mediators, and (2) they rarely end in compromise or settlement. At play on the street without adults present, Maple Street children argue that individuals should "take up they own battles" without others "jumping in."[20] Indeed, requiring the assistance of an adult is treated as a form of cowardice and can result in extensive ridicule. Children state that the intervention of adults in their disputes is unnecessary:[21]

(44) Vincent: That stupid Mr. Dan gonna come up there
and say (0.4)
"Y'all better come on and shake hands."
Don't mean nothin' cuz we be playin' together
next day anyway,

7.6 DISPUTE ENDINGS

A central feature of disputes is the phenomenon of different parties' taking alternative positions on the same issue. Structurally, one of the clearest ways that this process can be terminated occurs when one of the disputing parties abandons his own stance, while acknowledging the correctness of the perspective advanced by his opponent. For example:

(45)   *In the midst of slingshot planning*

       Chopper: Get your four guys,
       Malcolm: You get *three* guys.
 → Chopper: I mean three guys.

(46)   *Playing dead blocks or coolie*

       Malcolm: You go to fourteens dummy.
       Vincent: I go to my *six*teens.
       Malcolm: You do not cuz you hit him.
 →   Oh: that's right. You missed him.

In that both parties now hold the same position (e.g., in #45 both Malcolm and Chopper agree that the number being disputed is not *four* but *three*), opposition on this issue has been brought to an end.

The party who reverses a previously stated stance is faced with the task of displaying a change in perspective, and accounting for that change. Very frequently this is done through use of what Heritage (1984b) has analyzed as a "change-of-state token," i.e., a particle such as "Oh" which signals a change in speaker's current knowledge or apprehension of the phenomena being discussed. Thus in #46 Malcolm accounts for his change from "you hit him" to "you missed him" by placing "Oh: that's right" between the two statements, the "Oh:" signaling a change in his perception of the facts at issue. Other ways of marking such a change include prefaces such as "I mean" (#45) which signal a repair of a prior statement.

Another structural possibility is for a participant to revise her/his own position and/or partially acknowledge another's stance through phrasings such as "well," "I know, but," etc. Closing trajectories such as the above examples resemble "repair" (Schegloff, Jefferson, and Sacks 1977) or "re-medial sequences" (Goffman 1971:138–148). As Goffman (1971:140) argues, the closing moves of remedial exchanges accomplish "ritual work" which "allows the participants to go on their way, if not with satisfaction that matters are closed, then at least with the right to act as if they feel that matters are closed and that ritual equilibrium has been restored."

Movement to a common perspective constitutes one of the classic ways that disputes are perceived to end, and this form of termination seems to lie at the heart of assumptions about the importance of "conflict resolution" in the disputing process. However, in point of fact, this is a rather rare outcome in the data currently being examined. Maynard (1985a:220) has argued that disputes need not reach resolution because the process of building the dispute itself provides children with the opportunity "to produce fundamental forms of social and political organization." On Maple Street the end of an argument generally occurs without any sharp indication that either position has "won" or "lost." A conflict tends to terminate when one of the two disputing parties does not tie talk to the topic of the prior dispute, but instead produces an action that breaks the ongoing argument frame.

Insofar as participants frequently have the option of moving past argument, instead of focusing analysis on the issue of how conflict can be resolved, one can instead pose the question of how argument can be sustained. We will now investigate a range of procedures available to participants for keeping a dispute open without moving toward termination.

7.7 ALTERNATIVE TRAJECTORIES: EXTENDING DISPUTE AND ATTEMPTING CLOSURE

Within children's disputes, participants work to sustain a state of disagreement both through the forms of opposition displayed within a single turn, and through the sequencing of dispute moves. Two basic ways of sequencing turns may be used to promote extended debate: (1) recycling positions and (2) providing justifications for stances and countering those justifications.

In many of the sequences that we will examine, more than two speakers participate, although the dispute itself is focused on two opposing positions. It is therefore necessary to distinguish opposing *participants* from opposing *positions*. In his analysis of collaboration in argument, Maynard (1986b) distinguishes a range of alignment patterns that are possible within multiparty disputes. Thus he notes that outside parties can differentially align either with a position or with a counterposition, with the effect that "parties can dispute a particular position for different reasons and by different means" (ibid.:264). Parties outside an original conflict can offer to collaborate with one of its protagonists by taking "a stance that is parallel or consistent with that of a principal party" (ibid.:267). Principal parties within the dispute can reject as well as accept such offers of collaboration. In many of the sequences that will now be examined, a position is sustained through the collaboration of several participants.

7.7.1 RECYCLING POSITIONS

One clear way of continuing argumentation is through sustained contradiction or "recycling." Each of *two opposing parties repeats* a prior position with the effect that an extended series of disagreements is produced. In the following, two opposing points of view are presented. By adopting a stance similar to that of Malcolm, Ossie (line 4) in effect aligns himself (Maynard 1985a) with Malcolm and opposes William. Such displays of support can be quite influential in effecting a dispute outcome:

(47)   *During a slingshot-making session*

    1   William: I'm on Malcolm side.
    2   Malcolm: *No* you not.

3	William:	Yes I is.
4	Ossie:	No you *ain't*.
5	Malcolm:	Yeah? You gonna get shot too you come here.

Turns 2, 3, and 4 are remarkably similar in structure. Opposition is displayed immediately with turn prefaces that contain terms of polarity ("yes" and "no") which signal disagreement with the prior utterance. Opposition is further heightened through contrasting verb forms ("is" vs. "ain't" and "not"). These turns are occupied principally with displaying a position of opposition; no accounts or explanations accompany the assertions. Such extended recycling of positions constitutes what Piaget (1926:66) has called "primitive argument."[22] In Piaget's terms, the sequence shifts from a "primitive argument" to a "quarrel" in the fifth turn, a quarrel being a type of dispute in which divergence in position and actions is "accompanied by actions or promises of actions" (ibid.:66).

Recycling of positions can also occur when opposition is produced through use of replacement terms. Opposing sides can argue their points of view through the use of a single term indexing a stance. In the following Martha and Bea playfully object to Jimmy's version of his age, fourteen, and recycle their version of his age, thirteen, throughout several turns.

(48)		*Jimmy, age 12 going on 13, is*
		discussing his upcoming birthday.
	Jimmy:	Till I be fourteen,
	Martha:	How old are you? Thirteen?
	Jimmy:	Fourteen.
	Martha:	*Thir*//teen.
	Jimmy:	*Four*//teen.
	Bea:	*Thir*teen.
	Jimmy:	*Four*teen.
	Bea:	*Thir*//teen.
	Martha:	*Thir*teen.
	Jimmy:	*Four*//teen.
	Martha:	*Thir*teen.
	Bea:	Thirte(hh)n. heh.
	Jimmy:	I'll be thirteen next week.

Although #47 and #48 seem quite similar, the different ways in which opposition turns are built in each have alternative consequences for the detailed organization of each sequence. In #47 subsequent speakers wait until the completion of a prior turn before initiating a countermove. This appears to be responsive to the details of how turns are being constructed in this sequence. Opposition is shown both in the preface of the turn and in the verb form that completes the turn. Subsequent speakers wait until both displays of opposition have been completed before countering that action.

By way of contrast, most of the turns in #48 are overlapped by a counter before they have been completed. Moreover, the turns here are shorter than those in #47. Indeed, they consist of only a single word that provides a substantive alternative to what prior speaker just said. However, these words have a distinctive format: the second syllable of the word is always the same—"teen"—while the first syllable contains the information that is being disagreed with (e.g., "Thir" vs. "Four"). In this situation subsequent speakers frequently do not wait for prior speaker to complete his or her turn (i.e., actually produce the expected "teen") but instead oppose prior speaker as soon as the position being disagreed with has been stated unambiguously, an event that occurs one syllable into the turn. Such systematic placement of overlap is quite compatible with Jefferson's (1973) analysis of how participants can organize their action in conversation so that they produce talk at the precise moment (i.e., neither sooner nor later than) a particular event unambiguously occurs.

Sequences such as the preceding two examples are composed of an *extended series* (Jefferson and Schenkein 1978) of recycled positions. A clear example of how Maple Street children work to sustain a dispute across numerous turns, despite the attempt of a disinterested third partly to close it down, is provided in the following. The color of Jimmy's bike, which is an orangey gold, is being disputed. Although four people are present, the argument is limited to two sides, Martha and Bea against Kerry.

(49)		*Jimmy's bike is leaning against a tree where the children are seated. Alfie is a neighborhood dog.*
1	Vincent:	Donchu got a bike **Ma**rtha.
2		(0.3)
3	Martha:	Yes.
4		(0.4)
5	Vincent:	What color you got.
6	Martha:	It's something like Jimmy bike.
7		It's hot hot ⌜( )
8	Kerry:	⌞Jimmy's bike is
9		*orange* you egg.
10	Bea:	Is- this is **gold**.
11	Kerry:	Jimmy's *bike* is *ora*nge.
12	Bea:	=⌜Gol:d.=
13	Martha:	⌞Gol:d.
14	Kerry:	=It's orange.=
15	Bea:	=⌜Gol:d.
16	Martha:	⌞Gol:d.
17	Kerry:	Jimmy's *bike* is *ora*nge.

18	Bea:	Gold.
19	Kerry:	It's *ora*nge.
20	Bea:	*No* Kerry.
21	Kerry:	Is Jimmy's bike *ora*nge,
22		(0.4)
23	Bea:	Gol:d.
24		(0.4)
25	Kerry:	*Ora*nge.
26	Bea:	It's gold.
27	Vincent:	It's mix⌈ed.
28	Kerry:	⌊OR::ANGE::,
29	Bea:	Gol:d 'hh
30	Kerry:	*Or:*ange,
31	Martha:	⌈Gol::d.
32	Bea:	⌊GOL::D.
33	Vincent:	It's more ⌈orange.
34	Bea:	⌊Gol::d.
35	Kerry:	Eh- now!
36	Martha:	⌈Gold.
37	Bea:	⌊Gold.
38	Kerry:	It's *ora*nge.
39	Martha:	Two ⌈against two.
40	Bea:	⌊Gold.
41		(1.0)
42	Bea:	Two against two ⌈we won.
43	Kerry:	⌊It's *ora*nge.
44	Martha:	It's *gol*d.
45	Bea:	Two against two ⌈we won.
46	Kerry:	⌊Who beat *who.*
47	Vincent:	( ) girl got on top
48	Bea:	((*chanting*)) Two against-
49		⌈Two against two we *won,*
50	Vincent:	⌊I betcha I c'd ( ) I'll bring-
51		I betcha I'm the only one three a them
52		gonna ask ta bring *Al*fie out
53		she bring it out to me.
54	Martha:	You like Ralphie don't you.
55	Kerry:	*Ral*phie,
56	Vincent:	*Ral*phie,
57	Martha:	*Al*fie. *Al*fie.

The moves which oppose prior moves in this sequence are constructed through one-word replacements or substitutions. Frequently substitutions follow descriptions within prior turns which are unequivocal, as in examples #22–#24 (e.g., "that happened *last* year" vs. "That happened *this* year"). The disagreed-with description in #49, however, is marked as somewhat ambiguous. Martha in line 6 states that her bike is "something like" the color of Jimmy's. Argument begins in lines 8–9 when Kerry disagrees with Martha about the color of the bike the group is looking at:

(49)   Martha: It's something like Jimmy bike.
          Kerry: *Jimmy's bike is **orange** you egg.*

Kerry's move is strongly contrastive with Martha's; although Martha's move is designed to permit differences without promoting disagreement, Kerry actively works to display disagreement. Her utterance is constructed out of both an alternative to a prior description and an insult person descriptor, "you egg," in which the pronoun "you" explicitly marks that prior speaker is to be targeted with the insult.

Forms of aggravated disagreement occur repetitively throughout this dispute, and indeed one can see the participants actively working to shape their turns so as to heighten their salience as argumentative actions. Consider, for example, line 10:

(49)   Kerry: *Jimmy's bike is **orange** you egg.*
 →   Bea: Is- this is **gold**.

Placing the verb "is" in turn-initial position is one of the characteristic techniques used to build a question in English (as, for example, in a question such as "Is it orange?"). Moreover, such a format constitutes one of the standard techniques for modulating other-correction and disagreement. However, Bea quickly abandons this format in favor of the nonquestion form that openly highlights her disagreement with what has just been said. The salience of her disagreement is intensified at the end of her turn with heightened stress placed on *"gold,"* which is thus formulated as a term to be heard in opposition to previous speaker's *"orange."* An opportunity for less aggravated disagreement is thus explicitly rejected in this turn. The pattern of opposition that Bea initiates here is sustained as the subsequent sequence unfolds. Numerous other one-word replacements follow. They occur as the only elements in turns, they are accented, and indeed some are produced as screams (as indicated by capital letters in the transcript).

One further demonstration of the participants' orientation toward heightened disagreement is provided by examination of a rejected move toward reconciliation. Vincent in line 27 states, "It's mixed." Such a description could possibly lead to a resolution, in that this description admits the validity of both positions in the dispute. Instead, however, it is overlapped by Kerry's screamed "OR::ANGE::" in line 28, a one-word replacement marked by increased volume and lengthening of sounds. Further rounds of one-word replacements follow, and when Vincent enters a second time, in line 33, with "It's more orange," he sides with one of the parties against another.

In this sequence a statement allowing considerable room for variation in its interpretation is selectively heard as erroneous and answered with an argumentative next action. Throughout, participants make use of highly aggravated rather than modulated forms of opposition. Once disagreement has begun, an attempt by a third party to move toward reconciliation is explicitly rejected. The party who might himself have effected a compromise instead promotes further argumentation. Finally upon the termination of one argumentative sequence (lines 48–49), another is initiated (lines 55–57), as Kerry, with falling-rising intonation in her voice, challenges Vincent's naming of the dog as Ralphie rather than Alfie. Rather than working to minimize disagreement and preserve each other's face, the participants in this sequence work actively both to heighten the salience and aggravated character of their disagreement with each other, and to extend that sequence in the face of possibilities for closing it.[23] From a slightly different perspective, it can be noted that since disputes may be highly charged with affect, the attitude of moral indignation itself justifies and motivates the repetition of one's position over several turns.

7.7.2 JUSTIFICATIONS AS STRATEGIES FOR WORKING TOWARDS CLOSURE

Rather than repetitively recycling their positions, participants might attempt to effect closure to a dispute by offering accounts or explanations for the positions they have assumed.[24] Eisenberg and Garvey (1981:166) have postulated that a justification "is significantly more likely to lead to a termination of the episode." The Maple Street data demonstrate quite the opposite. Though the children do attempt closure by providing justifications for their positions, this action can in fact lead to further argumentation as the focus of the dispute shifts to debate about the new justification. This is particularly evident in the following example in which Martha and Kerry attempt to undercut the grounds for a position taken by William. Justifications are indicated in the left-hand column by a "#."[25]

(50)		*While children skate William bumps into Kerry.*
1	Kerry:	Get off William. Get off!
2	Martha:	Now Kerry just aim at William butt
3		and let's see if we could knock him down.
4	Kerry:	Oh yeah you- you be // you better
5	William:	Y'all better *not* knock me *down*!=
6	Kerry:	Yeah?
7 #	Martha:	If we do that's what we // playin'.
8 #	Kerry:	Play and you gonna get knock down.
9	William:	Nuh *uh*:!
10	Kerry:	Mm *hm*!
11 #	William:	Nuh *uh* y'all. I ain't playin'.

12	Kerry:	Yes you *are* playin'.
13	William:	I can't af//ford
14 #	Kerry:	If you- if you put a skate on you playin'.
15	William:	*No* it ain't.
16	Kerry:	*Yes* it is.
17	William:	I ain't playin' // nuttin!
18	Kerry:	Is you playin' Martha,
19	William:	Nope!
20	Kerry:	Huh // aren't we playin' Martha,
21 #	Martha:	If you-
22		if you put that skate on // you are.
23 #	Kerry:	Yep. If you put the skate on˙you playin'.
24		(2.2)
25	Kerry:	Bea! If they
26		p//ut a skate on // aren't they playin',
27	William:	This her skate.
28	Martha:	You want this?
29	Kerry:	If they put a skate on?
30		(1.4)
31	Kerry:	All except Carl.

This argument is composed of two sequences in which recycling of positions (similar to #48 above) and arguments about justifications occur. In this interaction Martha and Kerry treat William's bumping into them while skating as an offense. Kerry commands him to "get off" (line 1) and Martha proposes knocking him down (lines 2–3), which William objects to in line 5: "Y'all better *not* knock me *down*!" In lines 7 and 8 Martha and Kerry legitimate their proposed course of action, knocking down William, by stating that such actions are appropriate within the context of the activity: "If we do that's what we playin'." "Play and you gonna get knock down."

The first recycling of positions occurs following a justification:

(50)

7#	Martha:	If we do that's what we//playin'.
8#	Kerry:	Play and you gonna get knock down.
9	William:	Nuh *uh*:!
10	Kerry:	Mm *hm*
11#	William:	Nuh *uh* y'all. I ain't playin'.

William's justification for his position of disagreement, "I ain't playin'," becomes the lead-in to a new series of recyclings of positions. Kerry and Martha now attempt to establish the invalidity of William's perspective by arguing that the act of wearing a skate provides evidence for their position that he *is* playing. The very justification which William uses to support his perspective ("I ain't playin' ") thus generates a new arena for dispute:

(50)

11#	William:	Nuh *uh* y'all. I ain't playin'.
12	Kerry:	Yes you *are* playin'.
13	William:	I can't af//ford
14#	Kerry:	If you- if you put a skate on you playin'.
15	William:	*No* it ain't.
16	Kerry:	*Yes* it is.
17	William:	I ain't playin'//nuttin!
18	Kerry:	Is you playin' Martha,
19	William:	Nope!
20	Kerry:	Huh//aren't we playin' Martha,
21#	Martha:	If you-
22		if you put that skate on//you are.

The dispute is eventually dissipated when Martha in lines 21–22 explicitly agrees with Kerry's position in lines 14 and 20. Displaying that a position is shared by two (or more) people is a move that children frequently make in their attempts to assert a particular position. Indeed, Maynard (1985a) has argued that the ability to form such alliances demonstrates that even very young children are in fact engaged in political processes. The present sequence moves past argument in line 27 when William begins a nonargumentative move (see also line 45 in #49). In sum, this example demonstrates how successive justifications may themselves be countered, leading to argument structured through a series of positions presented in couplets.

7.7.3 NONSPECIFIC PROOF STRATEGIES

The justifications so far examined have all been tied to the details of the immediately prior talk. However, participants also have access to strategies that can be used across a range of disputes. Thus people engaged in a dispute might (1) display heightened commitment to a position by invoking supernatural sanctions (swearing) or offering to place a "bet" on a particular stance; (2) claim that others share the argued perspective; (3) establish that there are inconsistencies in prior speaker's talk.

In the following, children dispute whether or not Freddie's mother will let his brother go with Kerry to the library. Freddie argues for the seriousness of his position by stating that he is willing to bet on it:

(51)	Kerry:	She said that when she was over at my house!
→	Freddie:	She ain't- Bet you a dime he'll-
		Bet you a dime Kerry he ain't goin'!
	Kerry:	((starts humming))

In the next example Jimmy attempts to convince Malcolm that he had sex with Ruby by "swearing on [his] mom":

(52)   Jimmy: She gave it to *me* Malcolm.
                               (0.4)
          Ruby: Wha:?
                               (0.5)
          Jimmy: Me and her was out in the school yard.
                               (1.4)
   → Jimmy: I swear on my//mo:m.
          Ruby: You *keep* on lyin' now- come here.

A second strategy through which a disputant may attempt to persuade
an opponent that his or her own position is more valid is by arguing that
that point of view is shared by at least one other person, in some cases
even summoning another party as a witness. If two parties agree on a
common version of the event being disputed, this is felt to "prove" the
correctness of that version:

(53)   → Derrick: Okay. I can *prove* that we went.
                          Randy! Come here. (0.8)
                          Um, didn't we go to the Moore College of Art?
                          Don't we go every Wednesday?

(54)   *Annette is accusing Benita; Arthur*
                          is riding by on his bike.

          Annette: HEY Arthur, *STOP*!
                          *Did*n't you *t*ell me that um,
                          Ni:ta, was talkin' 'bout me.=Um,
                          said that I think I was cute
                          cuz I had that blouse on,

(55)   Deniece: Hey Gwen come here. Remember that time
                          we was at that party at Sissy house?
                          Wasn't Gloria talkin' about Ruby and um, Bea?

When positions are continuously recycled over several turns, witnesses
or third parties may be summoned in attempts to assert the validity of
one's perspective:

(56)   *Making sling boards*

   1   William: You usin' my *nails*.
   2   Carl: I ain't use *none* a your nails.
   3   William: Did *so*.
   4   Carl: Did *not*.
   5   William: Where are they//now.
   6   Carl: This is *none* a your nails.
   7   William: Where are they//then.

8	Carl:	They *Vin*cent nails.
9	William:	They *my* nails//egghead.
10	Carl:	((*falsetto*)) Eh!
11 →	William:	Ain't they Vincent.
12 →	Vincent:	°Yeah, they are William's nails.
13	William:	*N*ow:.

(57)   *Returning from a frog hunt in a city creek*

	Bea:	We caught a frog.
	Freddie:	A frog, Y'all did not.
	Bea:	We did so.
	Freddie:	Where it at then.
	Bea:	In that bag.
	Freddie:	Ain't nothin' in there.
	Ruby:	((*about frog*)) Dog he got
		⌈somp'm in his throat.
→	Freddie:	Did they Candy,
	Ruby:	I'm lettin' him on my step.
→	MHG:	I went *with* them,
		What are you *t*alkin' about.

A third tactic that may be utilized to assert a speaker's position consists of attempting to invalidate another's perspective by undercutting the grounds upon which argument rests:

(58)   *Bea has borrowed a jump rope belonging*
                        to a Colombian family on the street.

1	Martha:	Bea those Spanish people gonna *t*ell on
2		y(h)*ou*(h)!
3	Bea:	*They* ain't *Sp*anish. They *P*ortariccan.
4	Martha:	*H*ow ya know they Portariccan.
5		(0.7)
6	Bea:	They TALK POR*t*ariccan.
7	Martha:	AH YOU DON'T EVEN KNOW HOW PORTARICCAN
8		people *t*alk. So shut up.
9	Bea:	⌈Yes they um- yes they *are* Portariccan.
10	Drucilla:	Stop.
11	Bea:	I don't know what they-
12	Pris:	⌈Okay. You got your other jump.
13	Martha:	I don't know what they are but I know
14		they not Portariccan.

((*Girls begin turning rope for Bea*
to "One Two Three Footsies"))

| 15 | Bea: | Ten twenty thirty forty |

Martha in line 4 requests that Bea provide an account for her statement
that the family who owns the rope is Puerto Rican. Subsequently in lines
7–8 Martha states that Bea's competence to have produced her prior statement is undermined: "AH YOU DON'T EVEN KNOW HOW PORTA-
RICCAN people *t*alk. So shut up." Martha's "how you know" question
sets up for her recipient to provide a justification; she then challenges Bea's
grounds for having made her initial statement. Bea, in line 11, backs down
from her position, and the girls resume jumping rope.[26]

Invalidating prior speaker's position by switching the frame of argument
occurs in the next example:

(59)

1	Vincent:	Let me hold your yoyo.
2	Carl:	I just *got* it.
3	Vincent:	You let Freddie hold it.
4	Carl:	I know. But I was eatin'.
5	Vincent:	You *still* eatin'.
6	Carl:	You don't see nothin'//in my hand.
7	Vincent:	You eating in*vi*sible.
8	Carl:	Know what? You crazy. You fat tack.
9	Vincent:	That girl got beat up.

Vincent's request for a yoyo is countered twice by Carl (lines 2 and 4).
Vincent (line 3) argues that Carl earlier allowed Freddie to borrow his yoyo;
Carl (line 4) states that he let Freddie borrow it because at that time he had
nothing better to do: he was eating. Vincent (line 5), with "You *still* eatin',"
argues that current circumstances still hold and therefore he should get
the yoyo. Carl counters this by saying, "You don't see nothin' in my hand."

In line 7 Vincent reframes the domain of the dispute by moving from
a depiction of actual events to a description of hypothetical ones. By providing a justification which is fanciful rather than serious, Vincent not only
attempts to undercut the grounds for Carl's argument, but also tries to
provide a move which will transform the argumentative talk into something
far more playful.

Moving between real and imaginary events is a routine feature of children's experience. One common ploy by Maple Street children is to try to
trick others into believing something they say or do and then transform
that activity; children use the term "psych" to mark that talk immediately
preceding it should be taken as having been a put-on, not talk to have been
taken seriously:

(60)   Ruby: I'll be back. I'm goin' in the house. (1.0)
                     Eat my giddy up rice. (1.4) Psych.
                     I'm goin' in the house and make up my bed.
                     I might make a little sandwich.

(61)   Vincent: Popped a corn! (1.0) Psych.
                  I ain't hardly got no corn.

(62)   MHG: *((begins to jump rope))* Now don't laugh.
       Bea: We ain't gonna laugh. It's your jump.
                       (4.0) *((ethnographer jumps poorly))*
       Bea: *((laughing at ethnographer))* AH: HA. HA.
                  Psych. You know how to jump.

Such a strategy is extensively used by the children to get someone to buy into a pretend reality that is then subsequently overturned.

Reframing of a more elaborate sort occurs in the next example as a disputant points to a paradox in two expressed positions. In what follows, Jimmy applies a statement his codisputant Ruby introduces early in their argument, "Everything he say, Candy, *h if he said I (0.2) everything he sai:d is no:t true," as the frame within which to interpret a point he and Ruby are debating—whether or not Jimmy "got" (had sex with) Ruby:

(63)

1	Ruby:	Everything he say, Candy, *h if he said
2		I (0.2) everything he sai:d is no:t true.=
3		Hear?
4		(0.2)
5	Jimmy:	All right.
6	Ruby:	Cuz that was Ma:rlene.
7		And I hope he know that.
8		And he need // to get it through his brai:n see,
9	Jimmy:	This ain't true neither.
10	Ruby:	[*h and I can go and // get Marlene *too*!
11	Jimmy:	I didn't I didn't get her. I didn't get her!
12		[That's the truth!
13	Ruby:	And I can go and get Mar:*lene*!
14	Jimmy:	That's the truth.= Right Candy?
15		I didn't get her.
16	Ruby:	I- I don't need *you*!
17		[I can go and *get* Marlene.
18	Jimmy:	I didn't get you!
19	Ruby:	I *know* you didn't.
20	Jimmy:	But you said everything I say ain't true. // I
21		didn't get you.
22		That mean it ain't tr(h)ue! Ha ha!
23	Ruby:	I'm not talkin' 'bout what you // just said.
24	Jimmy:	Na::!
25	Ruby:	I ask you another one.
26	Jimmy:	What I said.
27	Ruby:	What happened to you and Gwendolyn.

Jimmy's turn in lines 20–22—"But you said everything I say ain't true. I didn't get you. That mean it ain't tr(h)ue"—performs the jobs of both referencing other talk and framing it such that his position wins the argument. The conjunction "but" at the beginning of Jimmy's utterance in line 20 ties his talk as a counter to prior talk: Ruby's statement in line 19 that she agrees with Jimmy that he didn't "get" her. Two prior utterances are referenced in Jimmy's talk in lines 20–22: (1) the framing for interpreting his talk which Ruby set up in lines 1–3 (that everything Malcolm says is not true), and (2) his statement in line 18 that he didn't "get" Ruby. The third utterance in Jimmy's turn shows the implication of using Ruby's prior talk in lines 1–3 as a frame within which to interpret his statement "I didn't get you!", talk ratified by Ruby in line 19. By pointing to a logical paradox, Jimmy's utterance "That mean it ain't tr(h)ue. Ha ha!" argues his perspective that he indeed "got" Ruby. Ruby does not accept his position but instead continues the dispute by entering a new round of questioning with her "I ask you another one" in line 25.

We've seen some of the ways in which participants sequence talk in argumentative exchanges. Although arguments may close when one party's position is accepted as more valid, they generally end in stalemates, with neither position being established as the clear winner. A participant can use a range of justifications, commitments, entrapments, and alignment displays to attempt to convince others of the truth of his or her own position, or the incorrectness of the opponent's. However, another, rather different, strategy is also available. A disputant may produce talk which is tied to the subject of the argument but which shifts frame, for example, by introducing humorous or metaphorical speech. Whether or not this frame shift will be accepted as the termination of the dispute depends on how it is treated by one's coparticipants (i.e., in #63 the dispute continues as a new round of debate is opened up).

7.7.4 Playful and Metaphorical Frame Switches as Techniques for Attempting Closure

When children switch to a humorous rendering of what prior speaker said, they invoke a domain for which argumentative talk is no longer appropriate; making a serious counter to a move intended in jest would violate certain implicit understandings about framing, i.e., subsequent speaker would put himself in the position of acting as someone who insists on treating seriously what others are obviously being playful about.[27] A number of basic strategies are used to switch frame: providing a humorous reading of prior talk; changing from the realm of "everyday talk" to speech from another domain, such as a stereotyped expression or song; or attending to the sound properties of talk rather than its substance.

The following provides an example of an outcome of changing frame by recasting talk about a past event into a hypothetical domain. In the midst of a discussion about go-carts, Ossie attempts to get someone to pay attention to his depiction of himself as a wild go-cart driver. Malcolm declines to talk into Ossie's talk, constructing his own monologue about racing (lines 3–5) and commenting that he wants to get some wooden wheels for the cart (line 7). By not responding to Ossie, Malcolm in effect displays his disinterest or disagreement with Ossie's line of talk. In a desperate attempt to get someone to ratify his perspective, Ossie in line 6 summons Tony into the dispute; however, this proves fruitless as Tony effects a humorous frame switch:

(64)   *Discussing riding go-carts*

1	Ossie:	ONE TIME I FLEW OUT AND
2		I//FLEW OUT THE CAR!
3	Malcolm:	When you make a real hard//turn say sshhh!
4	Ossie:	I DID! Y' ASK *TONY*.//I WAS THERE.
5	Malcolm:	Like that and turn.
6	Ossie:	*I* FLEW OUT OF IT. *D*IDN'T I Tony.
7	Malcolm:	Da//g I wanna get some wooden wheels.
8 →	Tony:	In his *dre*ams.
9	Ossie:	It not no dreams nuttin' eh heh heh!
10	Malcolm:	Where can we get some wooden wheels from.
11		*((Talk switches to debate between*
12		*Malcolm and Tony.))*

In response to Ossie's request that Tony ratify his claims about himself as a menacing go-cart driver, Tony replies (line 8) "In his *dre*ams." This talk transforms the claims being made by Ossie into a hypothetical domain. Although Ossie counters this ("It not no dreams nuttin' "), with his laughter at the end of line 9 he acquiesces to the implications of the frame change, and drops the line he has been trying to pursue.

A related type of frame switch involves employing speech from another domain of discourse, such as a stereotypic saying or song, in one's justification. In the following, Ossie and Malcolm argue about the sharpness of various pairs of pliers used to cut coat hangers. Malcolm in line 8 asks Ossie how he knows that he can't use a particular pair of pliers to cut wire: "How you know. Did you ever try it?" Closure is reached when Ossie in line 9 answers Malcolm with a stereotypic saying:

(65)   *Boys are cutting coat hangers with pliers*
                                     to make slingshots.

1	Ossie:	I could step on 'em and they'd cut.
2	Malcolm:	This ain't they- these aren't that-
3		aren't that- aren't that sharp.
4	Ossie:	Just these is like them only you can
5		step on *them* and you can't step on these.

6	Malcolm:	How you know. Did you ever try it?
7	Ossie:	No.
8	Malcolm:	Then how do you say you can't step on 'em.
9 →	Ossie:	I just *know* it. I can feel it in my *bones*.
10	Malcolm:	((*turning to making slings*)) They gonna
11		be cut,

In line 9 Ossie answers Malcolm's leading question with "I just *know* it" and follows this with "I can feel it in my *bones*." With Ossie's response, Malcolm drops the argument and switches to a new activity. By entering into a nonserious state of talk, a disputant may propose that argumentative talk is no longer on the floor. In this case Malcolm ratifies this claim.

In the next example, a speaker combines both of the strategies that have just been examined. In lines 10–26 Malcolm moves talk to a future hypothetical time frame, and within it uses song (lines 27–30) to ridicule his opponent. By switching frame in this fashion, Malcolm is able to effectively close down the dispute. The argument begins when Jack asserts that in a previous encounter Malcolm and Chopper were not able to shoot him with a slingshot.

(66)   *In the midst of making slingshots,*
              boys discuss past instances of hitting
              one another with metal coat hanger slings.

1	Jack:	I got you one time. I know I got somebody.
2	Malcolm:	That faggot.
3	Chopper:	⌈Somebody say "ow." Somebody say "ow."
4	Jack:	You ain't touched me jack.
5		You ain't touched me.
6	Malcolm:	I got you. I got you.
7	Jack:	I must didn't *feel* it.
8		Cuz you hit me on my coat.
9		I had my heavy coat on.
10	Malcolm:	Well you ain't *play*in' with no co-
11		no heavy coat this time
12		cuz I want you to *feel* it.
13		Like if you don't *feel* it
14		I'm a pop you in your hea:d.
15		*hh *The*n you'll *feel* it.
16	Jack:	You couldn't get me in my hea:d.
17		⌈heh heh.
18	Malcolm:	Ye:s. *I*'ll get through that
19		*b*ush on your head. (1.5)
20		*Big* bush. (1.6)
21		That big thing on your head is cama*f*lage.
22		Aheh! Looks *just* like dirt.
23		*All* you gotta do is lay in the dirt

24		and I'll think it's *d*irt.
25		And all I gotta do is step on it
26		and then I know it's *you*.
27		((*singing Jackson 5 song*)) Everybody loves a star
28		When he's on the top.
29		But no one ever comes around
30		When he starts to drop.
31		((*spoken*)) And you started to drop
32		so nobody ever comin' around no more.
33		Eh heh!
34	Jack:	Whose this. ((*pointing to hanger wire*))
35	Malcolm:	That's mine.

In this example Jack (line 1) argues that during a past slingshot fight he hit one of the boys. In lines 1–6 Chopper and Malcolm argue with Jack about who hit whom. Jack answers that with his heavy coat on he didn't feel getting hit (lines 7–9). In response to Jack's statement about a *past event*, Malcolm (lines 10–15) provides a scenario of *hypothetical happenings* in which his version of events could be heard as possible:

(66)

10	Malcolm:	Well you ain't *play*in' with no co-
11		no heavy coat this time
12		cuz I want you to *feel* it.
13		Like if you don't *feel* it
14		I'm a pop you in your hea:d.
15		*hh *Th*en you'll *f*eel it.

When Jack objects again in lines 16–17, stating, "You couldn't get me in my hea:d," Malcolm in lines 18–26 begins to playfully insult Jack's hair, calling it a "big thing" that looks like "camouflage." He then presents another hypothetical version of what he could do to Jack's head:

(66)

18	Malcolm:	Ye:s. *I*'ll get through that
19		*b*ush on your head. (1.5)
20		*Big* bush. (1.6)
21		That big thing on your head is cama*fl*age.
22		Aheh! Looks *j*ust like dirt.
23		*All* you gotta do is lay in the dirt
24		and I'll think it's *d*irt.
25		And all I gotta do is step on it
26		and then I know it's *you*.

Note how the fanciful trajectory of hypothetical events that emerges here is structurally similar to what happens in the sequencing of argument with justifications, i.e., as a new phenomenon enters the talk, it shifts the focus of discussion into new directions.

Malcolm's next move is to launch into a new mode, song, with lyrics that metaphorically depict Jack as someone losing whatever status he might have had. By using the words to the Jackson Five song "Everybody Loves a Star," Malcolm compares the way in which Jack's reputation is floundering with the way in which "no one ever comes around when [a star] starts to drop." Malcolm's shift into a domain of discourse anchored in song leads to the termination of the dispute; the talk that Jack then produces deals with nonargumentative matters.

Another phenomenon that can be subject to reframing is the structure of the talk itself. In the following, argument is terminated when one participant deals with prior talk in terms of its sound properties instead of its intended meaning:

(67)

1	Tokay:	Can you beat *Thom*as,
2	Malcolm:	H//eck no.
3	Dave:	*We* don't know.
4		(2.0)
5	Malcolm:	*Thom*as could- *Thom*as can't beat: *h*im.
6	Dave:	Beat *who*.
7	Malcolm:	Y:ou.
8	Chopper:	*He* can s:o.
9	Malcolm:	No he *can*'t.
10	Chopper:	*Thom*as-
11	Pete:	*Thom*as can't beat *Da*ve.
12	Pete:	⌈*Thom*as *bigg*er than
13	Malcolm:	*Could* you.
14	Dave:	*We*- s:o *we* don't know.
15	Dave:	⌈S:o everytime-
16	Malcolm:	*Get* him sport.
17	Dave:	Everytime we get in a fight always
18	Malcolm:	Oh: *That*'s right.=*He* was gettin' ready
19		to beat *y*our butt that *night*.
20		*I* remember.
21	Dave:	Who. Nope.=He didn't *do* nothin'.
22	Tommy:	⌈Well *who*-
23	Malcolm:	(Was you with him?)
24	Tommy:	Well *who* ran all the way around the *co*rner.
25	Malcolm:	*Who* ran down there to *save* your butt.
26	Dave:	Wh:o.
27	Malcolm:	Ha ha
28	Dave:	Who ran down to save *my* butt,
29	Malcolm:	That's *r*ight.
30	Dave:	=*No*body saved m//e.
31	Chopper:	Dan,

32	Malcolm:	*hh An if they *did*n't they-
33		[You was gettin' ready to get your ***butt*** *k*icked.
34	Dave:	*Me*:,
35	Malcolm:	Eh heh.
36	Dave:	By *who*.
37	Malcolm:	By *h*im. // eh heh
38	Dave:	I wasn't- I wasn't *s*cared,
39	Tommy:	I wasn't gonna hit him.
40	Malcolm:	You- y'all was just got get-
41		*You* was gonna get *your* butt kicked.
42	Dave:	*Wh*o.
43	Malcolm:	So Dan ran around-
44		down there and saved *your* butt.
45	Dave:	°I wasn't-
46		I wasn't doin nothin' but *stan*din' there,
47	Malcolm:	I *know*. // That's *r*ight.
48	Dave:	Before he *h*it me,
49	Malcolm:	You was *s*tandin' there.
50		That's *all* you was // *do*in' there,
51	Chopper:	Woo:,
52	Malcolm:	Cuz if you would of *do*ne it
53		you would of got your *b*utt kicked.
54	Dave:	*Wh*o.
55	Malcolm:	Y:OU:.
56	Dave:	I wasn't // standin' there.
57	Malcolm:	Who you think I'm *ta*lkin' to,
58		There no *ow*:ls in here,
59	Ossie:	((*hooting*)) °Who: who: who: who:
60	Dave:	You goin' out past nine o'clock again to play?

In this dispute Malcolm, Chopper, and Ossie make claims about the way Dave handles himself in fights; they characterize him as incapable of carrying off a successful fight, acting like a scaredy-cat, and needing an adult to come to his rescue. In lines 18–20 Malcolm proposes that Tommy was getting ready to beat Dave one night (note again the importance of hypothetical domains in the building of argumentative moves). Siding with Malcolm, Tommy asks Dave, "Well *who* ran all the way around the corner." Later Malcolm, alluding to Dave's uncle Dan, rhetorically asks, "*Who* ran down there to save your butt," and then in lines 43–44 provides an answer: "So Dan ran around- down there and saved *your* butt." In line 46 Dave attempts to get himself off the hook by claiming, "*I* wasn't doin' nothin' but *stan*din' there." This argument, however, only gets him into more hot water since Malcolm uses Dave's move to hang him. Malcolm answers (lines 49–50, 52–53) that Dave's problem is that he never takes a definitive stand in fights: "You was *s*tandin' there. That's all you was *do*in' there, Cuz if you would of *do*ne it you would of got your *b*utt kicked."

In attempting to defend himself, Dave makes repetitive use of denials
prefaced by "Who":

(67)
18	Malcolm:	Oh: *That*'s right.=*He* was gettin' ready
19		to beat *y*our butt that *night*.
20		*I* remember.
21 →	Dave:	Who. Nope.=He didn't *d*o nothin'.

(67)
24	Tommy:	Well *who* ran all the way around the corner.
25	Malcolm:	*Who* ran down there to *s*ave your butt.
26 →	Dave:	Wh:o.
27	Malcolm:	Ha ha
28 →	Dave:	Who ran down to save *my* butt,

(67)
32	Malcolm:	*hh An if they *did*n't they-
33		⌈You was gettin' ready to get your *butt* *k*icked.
34	Dave:	⌊*Me*:,
35	Malcolm:	Eh heh.
36 →	Dave:	By *who*.

(67)
52	Malcolm:	Cuz if you would of *d*one it
53		you would of got your *b*utt kicked.
54 →	Dave:	*Who.*
55	Malcolm:	Y:OU:.
56	Dave:	*I* wasn't // standin' there.

Dave's attempts to close down dispute lead to further argument from
others attempting to press their point of view. Malcolm explicitly answers
Dave's defense with a definitive "Y:OU:" in line 55 and then adds, "Who
you think I'm *talk*in' to." Malcolm and Dave now transform the meaning
of Dave's talk by playfully reinterpreting his "Who" counters as owl calls:

(67)
57	Malcolm:	Who you think I'm *talk*in' to,
58		There no *ow*:ls in here,
59	Ossie:	((*hooting*)) °Who: who: who: who:

Shifting frame from the *substance* of Dave's talk to a playful rendering of
its *sound properties* ends the dispute.

Children in the midst of argument can thus make creative use of the
language provided by their opponents in prior turns, shaping it to their
own ends. By dealing with prior talk in a manner that treats a disputant's

talk as nonserious, participants may reframe the operative dispute domain. This may occur in a number of ways: through switching from an actual past to a hypothetical future domain (#64), providing a justification which includes a cliché or stereotypic expression (#65), using the words of a song as a metaphor for one's position (#66), or interpreting prior talk with reference to its sound properties rather than its substance (#67). In the examples which have so far been presented, providing a humorous or metaphorical rendering of talk leads to closure of the dispute; however, another structural possibility is the transformation from a playful to a serious mode of discourse, as occurs in #5, examined above.

7.8 FORMAT TYING

Much research in discourse and pragmatics has made a distinction between the surface structure of the utterance (that is, the actual words spoken) and the actions embodied by the utterance (that is, its illocutionary force), and has argued that sequencing between utterances occurs on the level of action. For example, Labov and Fanshel (1977:25)[28] state: "Sequencing rules do not appear to be related to words, sentences, and other linguistic forms, but rather form the connections between abstract actions such as requests, compliments, challenges, and defenses." One effect of such a position is that sequential and discourse phenomena, such as speech acts, are treated as distinct and separable from the phonological, syntactic, and semantic phenomena traditionally analyzed by linguists. There is evidence, however, that approaching sequencing entirely from the perspective of larger speech acts misses much of the work being done by participants in conversation. Thus the work of Sacks (1967) on tying techniques has demonstrated that much of the connectedness between separate turns is achieved through systematic syntactic operations, procedures that are quite relevant to the analysis of the organization of parallelism in language (Jakobson 1966, 1968).[29] This type of perspective sheds important light on a range of phenomena central to the use of language in argument sequences.

In producing a subsequent argumentative move, participants frequently tie not only to the type of action produced by last speaker but also to the particulars of its wording.[30] Consider the following:

(68)   *Billy, who has been teasing Martha*
                       about her hair, has just laughed.

Martha: I don't know what you *l*aughin' at.
Billy: I know what I'm laughin' at.
           Your *h*ead.

If all that was at issue in this sequence were an exchange of information, the second line of Billy's turn by itself could constitute a complete reply to

Martha: "Your *head*" tells Martha what is being laughed at. However, Billy precedes this component of his turn with another, longer sentence that semantically seems to state the obvious, i.e., that he knows what he is laughing at. If this sentence is not providing relevant information, what is it doing? When one looks at it in relationship to Martha's talk, one finds not only that it is closely tied to the particulars of what she just said, repeating many of the exact words that she used,[31] but that it in fact constitutes a systematic transformation of her sentence. The skeleton of her structure is retained, but Martha's "you *laughin'*," is changed to "I'm laughin'," and the negation in her sentence is deleted.[32] These are precisely the minimum and adequate changes necessary to transform her talk into a reply to that very talk. In an almost literal sense, Martha's own words are used against her. To focus analysis of this sentence on its information content, the presuppositions it entails, or the speech act it embodies would be quite misleading. This sentence constitutes an adequate reply to what has just been said by virtue of the way in which it reuses the materials provided by that talk to shape a counter to it.

7.8.1 FORMAT TYING IN ARGUMENTATIVE SEQUENCES

Some demonstration of how important such format tying is to the organization of the talk that is occurring here is provided by what happens next:

(69)   *Billy has been teasing Martha about*
                                  her hair.

1	Billy:	Heh heh!
2	Martha:	I don't know what you *laughin'* at.
3	Billy:	I know what I'm laughin' at.
4		Your *head*.
5	Martha:	I know I'm laughin' at *y*our head too.
6	Billy:	I know you ain't laughin'
7		cuz you ain't laughin'.
8	Martha:	((*mirthless laughter*)) Ha ha.
9	Billy:	Ha ha. I got more hair than *you*.
10	Martha:	You do not. Why you gotta laugh.
11		You *know* you ain't got more hair than me.
12	Billy:	((*taking out shoestrings*))
13		Fifty-four inches.

The talk examined earlier in #68 is found in lines 2–4 of the above example. In line 3, the "I know what I'm laughin' at" framework provides a point of departure for yet another return, this time from Martha to Billy: "I know I'm laughin at *y*our head too." In line 6 it is used again, and indeed the same type of transformations that were applied to line 2 to produce line

3, changing pronoun structure to keep action constant over shift of participants and adding or deleting negation, are used in line 5 to build line 6. Although speakership changes, the underlying pattern used to construct the utterance of the moment is preserved.

Conceptualizing what happens here as a sequence of abstract actions obscures the way in which the participants, in an almost musical way, are exploring one after another the possible variations provided by the detailed structure of the utterances they are producing. The surface structure of the talk in these data is anything but superficial in terms of its power to provide organization for the sequencing of the exchange.

In line 8 the particular pattern that we have been examining is abandoned when Martha shifts from talking about laughter to laughter itself. However, in line 9 the practice of building a return action from the materials just provided by the other party continues as Billy uses laughter to begin his reply to her laughter. In line 10 Martha challenges what Billy has just said, and in line 12, rather than disputing her, Billy shifts to a different topic.

Format tying can occur in many different ways. The following provides an example of one of the simplest—exact repetition of what the other has said:

(70) *Douglas is sitting on Kerry's top step as Joey approaches him from the street. The initial talk refers to an incident in which Douglas was reported to have cried because he lost a key.*

1	Joey:	He- he was gettin' ready to cry.
2	Douglas:	But that wasn't mine.
3		(1.0)
4	Douglas:	Mole!
5		(1.0)
6	Joey:	Mole.
7		(0.3)
8	Douglas:	Ah shut up.
9		(0.4)
10	Joey:	Ah shut up.
11	Douglas:	Make me.
12		(0.3)
13	Joey:	Make me!
14		(0.4)
15	Douglas:	Why donchu make *me*.

In lines 6, 10, and 13, Joey constructs a counter to Douglas by using the exact words Douglas himself has just used.[33] However, although the surface structure of the original and the repeat is identical, their meaning is not; the change in discourse structure produced by the change in speakers requires a new interpretation of each utterance. Thus "me" refers in line 11 to Douglas but in line 13 to Joey, and in all cases agent and recipient of action are changed. By holding the linguistic form constant, Douglas is able to highlight changes in interactive organization by reversing the participation framework created by Joey's prior utterance.

The dispute is escalated in lines 11–13 when each party dares the other to make good on a prior command. In line 15 this leads to a more complex type of format tying. Rather than simply repeating what Joey has said, Douglas, by prefacing Joey's "Make me" with "Why donchu" (and stressing "*me*"), creates a new sentence that includes Joey's prior talk as an embedded component within it[34] and reverses the agent of the proposed action.

Embedding such as this is in fact one of the prototypical ways of taking the words of the other and returning them in a reciprocal action. Consider the following, in which Chopper transforms Tony's command into a challenge. This is achieved by reusing the structure of the prior utterance and adding the words "make me" (while dropping the possessive reference to the yard that the children are in). Tony's sentence is now embedded within a new sentence of Chopper's:

(71)   Tony: Why don't you get out my yard.
          Chopper: Why don't you *m*ake me get out the yard.

Tony's request that Chopper leave is thus transformed into a challenge to Tony to enforce such an action.

As #68 demonstrated, prior speaker's talk can be transformed by the deletion of elements of a prior utterance as well as by the embedding of such talk within a new action. Consider the following:

(72)   Chopper: Don't gimme that.
                       I'm not *t*alkin' ta you.
          Tony: I'm talkin' ta *y*:ou!

Here, rather than embedding prior talk in a new sentence, Tony constructs a return to Chopper by deleting the negation in Chopper's sentence.

The format tying and embedding that occur in #71 and #72, rather than operating on a "linguistic" level that is distinct from the "discourse" level of speech acts, are intrinsic components of the way in which the actions produced in these examples are constructed to be the things that they are. While it is possible to escalate an argument with a subsequent action whose structure is unrelated to that of the action being dealt with, the utterances of #70 and #71 display their status as escalations[35] of prior actions—and challenges to the producers of those actions—by making use of the talk of prior speaker and transforming it to their advantage; in essence, they turn the prior action on its head. Indeed, there is a very nice fit between the social activity of escalating a sequence and challenging a prior move, and the syntactic structure of these utterances, in which the prior move becomes an embedded subcomponent of the sentence used to answer it.

Looking at these data from a slightly different perspective, it can be seen that by performing such embedding the children are openly making use of, and creatively playing with, the syntactic resources provided by their language as they transform prior sentences into new sentences appropriate to their current projects. Tony's talk in #72 consists of almost the same words as Chopper's (with the exception of the negation). However, it is not a repetition of what Chopper just said. First, as was noted above, both pronoun reference and participation framework change when the party producing the talk changes. Second, in reusing the words provided by prior speaker, subsequent speaker can substantially modify what is being done with those words by the way in which he or she speaks them.[36] For example, in these data the emphasis in Chopper's sentence falls on the action that is the topic of the sentence, "*t*alkin'," while in Tony's version the emphasis is shifted to the recipient of that action "*y*:ou!" The focus and import of the sentence are thus modified by the way in which it is spoken.

The following provides a more vivid example of how the way in which something is spoken can substantially change what is being done with those words:

(73) Billy: ((*singing*)) You didn't have to go to school today
                 did you.
      Kerry: Yes we *did* have to go to school today!

Kerry's utterance maintains a structure parallel to that of Billy's with two major exceptions: (1) the word "Yes" at the beginning of her talk which, through its display of polarity, constitutes an opposition preface, and (2) the replacement of Billy's "didn't" with "*did*," which is spoken with contrastive stress (Ladd 1980:77).[37] Both the contrast replacement and the opposition preface enable Kerry to substantially modify the import and focus of the talk she is reusing, i.e., to turn it into a challenge of what that talk originally proposed. However, the changes she is able to accomplish through her pronunciation of the talk go beyond this. Billy's statement, with its singsong intonation, could have been interpreted as a bid for an alliance with its recipient against the school establishment. Instead of participating in the proposed alliance, Kerry focuses on Billy's error for having said what he said. Through the way in which she speaks, Kerry is able to display indignation, something that contrasts quite strongly with the playfulness that was found when Billy spoke these words. In essence, Kerry changes not only the semantic meaning of the prior utterance but also the affect it had conveyed.

Looking at the change from "didn't" to "*did*" from a slightly different perspective, we can see that such replacement in fact constitutes an instance of contrast class replacement or substitution. Since the use of substitution in the construction of counters has already been examined, it will not be looked at in detail here, except to note that it is very common in format tying. Indeed, the repetition of structure provided by format tying frames the substitution so that it becomes highlighted as a noticeable event. Format tying and substitution thus work hand in hand, with the similarity of structure between two utterances provided by format tying making the relevant difference in the second utterance, the substituted term, stand out with particular salience.[38]

In addition to operating on the semantic, syntactic, and propositional structure of a prior utterance, the children may also play with its phonological structure. Consider lines 14–15 of the following:

(74)   *Ruby is sitting on top of Bea.*

1	Bea:	Get off!
2	Ruby:	No. Ain't there's another way?
3	Bea:	Come on, Ruby.
4	Ruby:	Come on, Where we *goin'.*
5		Don't say that either.
6	Bea:	Come on. // Get off. All y'gotta do-
7	Ruby:	Cuz I gotta answer.
8	Bea:	⌈Get off.
9	Ruby:	All ya gotta say *is* (0.2) I mean get-
10		I mean um- um- *Move* please
11		and I can't get no rhymes on that one.
12	Bea:	°Move please.
13	Ruby:	Where the *move* at.
14	Bea:	I'm tryin' to get off rather,
15	Ruby:	*Wa*ther, wh- oh: the weather you want?
16		The day is sunny and tomorrow's gonna
17		be ra-

In line 15, by systematically varying its phonological structure, Ruby transforms "rather" into "weather." This is accomplished by first changing the "r" in "rather" to "w" and then changing the "æ" in "rather" to "ε":

rather
wather
↓ weather

Through this stepwise transformation, Ruby is able to humorously change Bea's request for her to move into a request for information about the weather.

This sequence contains a number of additional playful mishearings that demonstrate yet other ways that children might transform a prior utterance in a subsequent move. For example, within the sequence occurring here, the words "Come on" in line 3 are quite clearly a recycle of the request made in line 1, that Ruby get off Bea. However, when abstracted from a particular context, the words could have a range of different meanings. In line 4 Ruby plays with this fact, first repeating what Bea has said and then treating it as a request to go somewhere, rather than a request to get off. In line 12 Bea makes a request—"Move please"—that has the following format:

[Verb (action requested)] + [Please]

However a very similar format is used with nouns when asking for objects (for example "Salt, please" to request salt at the dinner table):

[Noun (object requested)] + [Please]

In line 13 Ruby treats the verb in line 12 as a noun by asking, "Where the *move* at."

While sitting on top of Bea, Ruby is in fact playing in rather abstract ways with a range of basic structures utilized by her group to not only construct their talk but also interpret its meaningfulness. In line 11 she refers to the process through which she is able to avoid providing next moves to Bea's requests as "having rhymes" on Bea's utterances. Such an expression describes as aptly as any outside analyst could the process of playful but systematic transformation in which she is engaged.

We are now in a position to better investigate how a range of different strategies for format tying might be combined within a single dispute. In the following, a group of girls are practicing steps for a future dance contest against the boys:

(75)   *Girls sing as they practice original*
        dance steps.

1	Tony:	You sound terrible.
2	Martha:	We sound just like you *look*.
3	Malcolm:	What's the matter.
4	Kerry:	What's the matter with *you*.
5	Malcolm:	Same thing that's the matter with *y*ou.

6	Kerry:	Well *n*othing's the matter with me.
7	Malcolm:	Well nothing the matter//with *m*e then.
8	Kerry:	Well then *go* somewhere.
9	Malcolm:	Well I wanna stay *h*ere.
10	Kerry:	Ah: I hate you.
11	Martha:	Go ahead, go ahead. Go ahead y'all.
12		Act like he just ain't even here.

In these data a variety of argumentative actions are organized through format tying into a series of rounds. While attending to the details of the structure of prior talk, the participants also play with the operations used by that talk to reference phenomena.

In line 1 Tony delivers an insult to the girls: "You sound terrible." In her return action, Martha reuses the *[girls] sound* structure but replaces "terrible" with talk that equates how the girls sound to an attribute of the boys: "We sound just like you *look*." Instead of producing an explicit insult term of her own, Martha uses the power of talk to refer to other talk to create a boomerang so that the boys now become the target of their own insult.

For clarity, format tying has so far been discussed in terms of the operations on explicit phonological, syntactic, and semantic elements of prior talk. It can, however, be more abstract than this, as is demonstrated by lines 3–5 of this exchange. Malcolm's talk in line 3 is disjunctive with the talk that just preceded it, but it quickly becomes the template for a new sequence of format-tying operations in lines 4 and 5. Since the way in which actions such as these reuse the materials provided by prior talk has already been examined, this process will not again be looked at in detail here. Rather, I wish to focus attention on the way in which Malcolm in line 5 makes the pejorative attribute of his being asked about by Kerry (i.e., the answer to the question "What's the matter with *you*") an attribute of Kerry as well ("Same thing that's the matter with *y*ou"). In effect, he constructs another boomerang. Thus, although the surface structure of the talk in lines 3–5 is completely different from that found in lines 1–2, Malcolm nonetheless makes use of material from that earlier sequence. However, what is being reused is not specific words or phrases but rather a particular structural solution found by Martha to the problem of building an appropriate return.

The talk in lines 3–5 refers to phenomena, the answer to the "What's the matter" question, that have not yet been specified. In lines 6 and 7 this issue is resolved in a way that takes into account the fact that it has now become an attribute of both contesting parties, i.e., it is defined as "nothing." Parenthetically, it can be noted that if one were to approach argument from the perspective of resolving conflict, this would appear to constitute a prototypical example of conflict resolution, i.e., both contesting parties come to agreement, and moreover agree in a way that is not disparaging to either of them. Clearly, such an approach to what is happening here would be seriously in error.

In lines 8 and 9 the pattern of providing reciprocal actions through format tying is broken. In line 9 Malcolm provides an account rather than a reciprocal move to Kerry. Despite the fact that similarity in action is not achieved, similarity in structure is maintained. Malcolm's utterance ("Well I wanna stay *here*") repeats the "well" of the talk just before it and produces contrast class substitutions for both verbs ("stay" is substituted for "go") and adverbs ("here" replaces "somewhere"). In addition, both tied utterances share the same stress and rhythmic pattern.

7.8.2 FORMAT TYING AND RITUAL INSULT

The way in which format tying poses the task of using the immediately prior talk to build an appropriate return casts light on how this process might be related to a range of other phenomena. For example, it would appear to have close structural ties to "sounding" or "ritual insult" (Abrahams 1970:157–161; Hannerz 1969:129–130; Kochman 1970:157–161, 1972:241–264; Labov 1972a, 1974; Mitchell-Kernan 1971). The recipient of an initial ritual insult (an insult about an attribute of the target known not to be literally true)[39] must utilize the scene described in prior speaker's talk to produce a second description which turns the initial insult on its head and is even more outrageous. As noted by Goffman (1971:179), "the structure of these devices establishes a move that is designed to serve as a comparison base for another's effort, his object being to exceed the prior effort in elegance or wit."[40] A successful return insult leaves the other party with nothing more to say and is responded to with laughter (Labov 1972a:325). For example, in the following ritual dispute over whose school—a junior high attended by Martha or Billy's school, the Franklin Institute (which sponsored a special program for fifth- and sixth-graders)— is better, Billy can produce no successful retort to Martha's characterization of Billy and his school in lines 4–5:

(76)

1	Billy:	((*singsong*)) You don't have no *roo*:ms,
2	Martha:	We do *so* have a room.
3	Billy:	((*singsong*)) Not one block *lon*::g.
4	Martha:	You do not. Y'all just go to a museum
5		cuz y'all on dis*play*.
6	Billy:	((*singsong*)) That's *righ*::t.
7	Martha:	Y'all on dis*play*.
8	Billy:	((*singsong*)) That's *righ*::t.
9		That's *righ*::t.

Labov (1974:115) has argued that excellence may be achieved in ritual insult through "striking semantic shifts with minimal changes of form." For example:

(77)   Malcolm: She a dropout.
           Ruby: I *know* you a dropout.
     → Malcolm: She says she know she a dropout.

Here the referent of the description becomes the prior speaker and the action is redirected, although the description itself remains unchanged.[41]

The following are excerpts from a lengthy playful ritual insult battle:[42]

(78)
39	Ruby:	One day- (0.2)
40		*My br*other was spendin' the night with *you,*
41		*h And//the next mornin' he got up,
42	Malcolm:	I don't wanna hear about it.
43		Your brother//ain't *never* been in *my* house.
44	Ruby:	THE NEXT TIME HE GOT UP,
45		*heh He was gonna brush his teeth
46		so the roach tri(h)ed ta(h) bru(h)sh hi(h)s!
47	Malcolm:	Don't//swag.
48	Ruby:	*h *Ha ha ha ha ha *hh!//*h
49		Eh heh heh//*heh* he he he he
50	Malcolm:	An' if he was up there
51		If the roach was tryin' ta *brush* it
52		he musta brought it up- it up there *with* him.
53	Ruby:	*heh!
54		*h *Eh*//he heh heh heh he he he he
55	Malcolm:	*h eh heh!
56	Tommy:	((*falsetto*)) Ha//he! he
57	Ruby:	He he he he ha//ha ha//ha
58	Jimmy:	*heh!

In this fragment Ruby (lines 45–46) describes her brother finding roaches brushing their teeth in Malcolm's house. Malcolm's response builds upon this description in lines 50–52, stating that if that is so, her brother must have brought the roaches with him. The point is not to negate or contradict prior talk but to show that second speaker can take a feature of first speaker's talk (here, the statement about roaches) and transform it.

In the following, a three-part insult sequence occurs. Ruby's initial description of talking roaches at Malcolm's door is answered by a return insult from Malcolm in lines 97–98, which is subsequently overturned by a response in lines 99–100:

(79)

72	Ruby:	Ah ha:. (0.2) And one *more* thing!
73		One day (0.2) *I* went in your hou-
74		*I* was gonna walk in the door
75		for *two* sets//a roaches.
76	Malcolm:	For what.
77		For what.
78	Ruby:	One roach here (0.2) and one roach here.
79		THE ONE RIGHT HERE,
80	Malcolm:	Oh you tryin' ta *sell*//'em for him.
81	Ruby:	THE ONE RIGHT HERE W-
82	Malcolm:	You tryin' to se(hh)ll 'e(hh)m.
83	Ruby:	THE ONE RIGHT HERE//WAS UP HERE SAYIN'-
84	Malcolm:	*Some*body gonna buy your//damn roach.
85	Ruby:	THE ONE RIGHT here was up here sayin'-
86		(0.2) "People movin' *ou:t*?" (0.2)
87		And the one right here was sayin' (0.2)
88		"*Peo*ple movin' in-"//Why?
89		Because of the odor of their//ski(hh)n.
90	Malcolm:	You understand their language.
91		You must be one of 'em.
92	Jimmy:	((*falsetto*)) Eh *heh!* Heh he heh!
93	Ruby:	What'd he s(hhhh)ay? Wha(h)d he(h) say(h)y?
94		*H What he(h) sa(hh)y?
95		What he sa(heh heh)y? What you say?
96		Whad's he//say Candy?
97	Malcolm:	You understand their language
98		cuz you *one* of 'em.
99	Ruby:	I(h) *know(h)* you(h) ar(hh)re!
100		You was *born* from the roach fam//ily.

In each of the insult sequences, subsequent speaker does not refute a prior statement but instead uses the scene it sets to build a logical counter to it. In essence, second speaker argues that if the initial statement is true, then the consequence is that an even more pejorative description can be made of prior speaker. In lines 85–89 Ruby sketches a scene of roaches on either side of Malcolm's doorway quoting the words of the Jackson Five song "Ball of Confusion": "People movin' ou:t" and "People movin' in." Malcolm then, in lines 90–91, states that Ruby is able to understand talking roaches because she herself is "one of 'em." In response Ruby (lines 99–100), using the preface "I know," transforms Malcolm's insult about her into a statement authored by him about himself and tops his insult; she argues that Malcolm "was *born* from the roach family." In brief, ritual insults do not constitute an activity or genre that is totally distinct from other, less stylized talk. Rather, through the way in which participants use the material provided by prior talk to construct return actions, ritual insults build from resources that are already present in opposition sequences.[43] From a slightly different perspective, although almost all of the previous literature on ritual insults has talked about it as a male activity, here we find that girls not only participate but are able to build returns that top those of the boys.

7.9 COOPERATION IN COMPETITION

There are a number of different procedures for carrying out disputes. We have examined both how opposition is accomplished and how more extensive argument sequences are constructed from basic oppositional moves and procedures for format tying. As these examples show, both boys and girls have access to similar ways of disputing. These data are thus important with regard to the relationship of language and gender. Researchers investigating black language and culture have repeatedly argued (e.g., Abrahams 1970, 1975a, 1976; Abrahams and Bauman 1971; Hannerz 1969:129–130; Kochman 1970, 1981; Reisman 1970, 1974b) that such character contests are particular to Afro-American males. However, as studies of everyday arguments among black and white families (Vuchinich 1984) and in white middle-class Anglo-American children's groups (Brenneis and Lein 1977; Cook-Gumperz 1981; Corsaro 1985; Eisenberg and Garvey 1981; Genishi and di Paolo 1982; Hughes 1983; Maynard 1985a, 1985b) as well as among working- and lower-class white adolescent girls' groups (Eder 1990), Italian children (Corsaro and Rizzo 1990), part-Hawaiian children (Boggs 1978), and children in a culturally diverse suburban American school setting (Adger 1984, 1986, 1987),[44] have shown, contest frameworks for interaction occur among other groups as well.[45] Moreover, as will be discussed in greater depth in Chapter 8 with respect to a gossip dispute event called "he-said-she-said," females make wide use of interactive frameworks for carrying on dispute.

Although compromise is seldom reached (or oriented toward as a goal of the interaction), by shifting to noncompetitive talk, parties cooperate in bringing about closure to the dispute. Despite the absence of a clear outcome, disputing allows participants the opportunity to construct and display character, a process important in their social organization as well as social development. Argument among peers permits the elaboration of what Piaget (1965) sees as "mutual understanding," considered an important aspect of the mature self; comparison, contrast, and confrontation "obliges individuals to 'place' themselves in reciprocal relationship with each other without letting the laws of perspective . . . destroy their individual points of view" (ibid.:397). In the neighborhood peer group, in contrast to the school situation, children cannot call upon an external system for resolving their differences. The situation of interaction between coequals thus provides for what Youniss (1980:7–8) has described as children's understanding of "the cooperative production of meaning."

CHAPTER EIGHT

He-Said-She-Said

This chapter will examine a particular type of gossip dispute that occurred almost exclusively in the girls' peer group.[1] In this activity, which the children call "he-said-she-said," one girl accuses another of a particular breach: having talked about her behind her back. The offended party confronts an alleged offending party because she wants to "get something straight." While some he-said-she-said disputes can be brief and even playful, on other occasions accusations can lead to an extended dispute which the girls treat as quite consequential for the social organization of their group (one he-said-she-said confrontation culminated in the ostracism of a girl for several months), as well as an event of high drama within which character and reputation can be gained or lost. Indeed, an upcoming confrontation can become the focus of the entire group's attention.

The statements used to initiate these confrontations are intricate, highly structured objects. Within the scope of a single utterance, a girl making a he-said-she-said accusation is able to invoke a coherent domain of action, indeed a small culture, that includes identities, actions, and biographies for the participants within it, as well as a relevant past that justifies the current accusation.

The past depicted in a he-said-she-said accusation includes events at three separate moments in time:

1. An initial gossip stage in which the current defendant is alleged to have talked about her accuser in her absence.
2. An intermediate stage in which the girl who was talked about learns about the offense committed against her from a third party.
3. The confrontation itself.

The series of stages enacted parallels Turner's (1980:150–151) formulation of "social drama":

> A social drama first manifests itself as the breach of a norm, the infraction of a rule of morality, law, custom, or etiquette, in some public arena. . . . The incident of breach may be deliberately, even calculatedly, contrived by a person or party disposed to demonstrate or challenge entrenched authority. . . . Once visible, it can hardly be revoked . . . a mounting crisis follows, a momentous juncture or turning point in the relations between components of a social field.

Since he-said-she-said accusations encapsulate the entire process, I will begin my analysis with them. However, before we look at these accusations in detail, it is useful to provide an overview of the range of phenomena relevant to them that will be examined in this and subsequent chapters.

The offense located by a he-said-she-said accusation is talking about someone behind her back, and indeed the girls recognize the dangers inherent in this activity. In Chapter 11, which deals with the stage preparatory to the confrontation, we will look at some of the ways in which girls talk about other girls, paying special attention to how they work to avoid implicating themselves in gossip until they can determine others' positions regarding the person being talked about.

The high drama in this process occurs during the confrontation stage, when accuser and defendant face each other. However, that situation is precipitated by events at the second stage, in which a third party tells the accuser about the offenses committed against her. While this third party might initially appear a rather peripheral figure in events that focus on accuser and defendant, she can, in fact, be the one who engineers the confrontation, and indeed the girls call the activities she engages in "instigating." One of the ways in which a potential accuser can learn about what has been done to her is through an elaborate storytelling procedure in which the instigator not only talks about the offensive actions of the party who will be the defendant, but also portrays herself and others in the group as allied with her current recipient (i.e., the potential accuser) against the party who has offended her. Crucial to this storytelling process are the responses of recipient to it, and indeed the instigator seems to be attempting to elicit a promise to initiate a he-said-she-said confrontation. Instigating stories will be the subject of Chapter 11.

The present analysis differs from most previous studies of gossip with respect to (1) the type of data which are analyzed, and (2) its focus on how language provides social organization for participants. Generally, informants' reports *about* gossip, rather than actual sequences of talk, are used as the primary data for research (Colson 1953; Gluckman 1963; Harris 1974).[2] Most investigators of gossip have been primarily interested in explaining its social functions (Almirol 1981; Colson 1953; Epstein 1969; Frankenberg 1957; Gilmore 1978; Gluckman 1963, 1968; Harris 1974), its information-management functions (Campbell 1964; Cox 1970; Hannerz 1967; Paine 1967), its "performance standards" (Abrahams 1970), and its individual, network, or interest group motivations (Campbell 1964; Cox 1970; Gilmore 1978; Hannerz 1967; Hotchkiss 1967; Paine 1967; Szwed 1966). Haviland (1977:5), in his study of gossip in Zinacantan, is concerned with "how native actors examine, use and manipulate cultural rules in natural contexts." This study, however, is concerned with how a particular phase of gossip, the confrontation, is constructed through conversation.

8.1 A HE-SAID-SHE-SAID
CONFRONTATION

The he-said-she-said event makes use of a form of public dispute process termed "negotiation" by Nader and Todd (1978:10).[3] It can be distinguished from other possible types of legal procedure such as "lumping it," avoidance, adjudication, arbitration, and mediation (ibid.:8–11). In this procedural mode, two principal parties dispute the case without the aid of a third mediating party.

The outcome of the he-said-she-said confrontation differs from that of most disputes in that neither compromise nor a clear form of settlement occurs. This in part is a result of the unique shape of utterances which open the dispute and provide an operative realm of action for participants.

The following provides an example of a he-said-she-said confrontation:

(1)   *Julia, Barbara, and Kerry meet Bea,*
                        Martha, and Drucilla on Poplar Street.

1	Julia:	*WE* AIN'T *SAY* THAT *BEA:.*
2	Barb:	You said that // I said-
3	Bea:	°Where. Where.
4	Julia:	[°Sh'said-
5	Bea:	(°Lemme see.)
6	Julia:	Um-
7	Barb:	They // say y'all say I wrote *everything*
8		o//ver there. I ain't // wrote
9		everythi:ng.
10	Julia:	*They* say-
11	Julia:	Y'*all* said that she
12	Julia:	wrote that um,
13	Julia:	They wrote // that bi:g
14	Kerry:	You // said-
15	Barb:	Only thing // is the car.
16	Kerry:	*Bea* tol: // *me-*
17	Bea:	*UH*UH.=*THAT* WAS *VIN*CENT SAID.
18	Kerry:	But y//ou told *me* that
19	Barb:	I know it was Vincent cuz Vincent was
20		the one that wrote that // on that *car.*
21	Martha:	((*falsetto*)) *Uh*uh.=We started to tear
22		that- *h uh that out. We tol- we said
23		that we- *all* said- *h I said // all-
24	Julia:	((*falsetto*)) I said, "Who wrote it on
25		the car." Martha say "Either Vincent,
26		(0.2) or, *Vin*cent or um- [*Barbara."*
27	Bea:	[*Bar*bara.
28	Martha:	*Bar*bara.

29	Martha:	I put th//is
30	Barb:	*Vin*cent *di:*d it. *Vin*cent had that
31		crayon more than *any*body.
32		(0.7)
33	Martha:	*h An' plus- an'=
34	Barb:	Oo this's *cold* out *here* // t'day.
35	Kerry:	WELL WHY YOU TELL HER *I* said it.
36	Bea:	YEAH BUT *JU*LIA- YEAH BUT *JU*LIA WAS SAYIN *WE*
37		*WRO*:TE ALL OVER THE STREET AND WE
38		*DIDN'*T.=
39	Barb:	[*We* ain't write over no street *noth*in'.
40	Kerry:	I'm~not~talkin'~'bout- B'//t why did-
41	Julia:	Vincent say he wrote in the street. *((sigh))*=
42	Martha:	=Well I ain't write // in the street.
43	Barb:	Oh *you* fin' s'n in the st//r:eet then.
44	Bea:	I ain't *wrote nutt*in' in no str:ee://t,
45	Kerry:	Well how come *you told Bar*bara that I
46		said that *she* wrote it.
47		(0.6)
48	Martha:	I said that *who* wrote it.=
49	Kerry:	=*Not* you.=Bea.
50	Pris:	°Well // who did.
51	Bea:	That *she* wrote it,
52	Bea:	[°That- that you was-
53	Pris:	All they hadda do is // look in the street.
54	Martha:	Well come on out here. Let's see it.
55		(1.2)
56		*((Girls move to the site where*
57		*pejorative things were written about*
58		*Kerry on a car and garage door.))*
59	Barb:	I only said- // so that when I- when we
60		were goin' to the car.
61	Bea:	That *she* that *she* wrote it, I TOLD YOU
62		THAT // Barbara WROTE,
63	Martha:	( )
64	Julia:	I'm gonna stay *out* from *now* on.
65	Kerry:	Well cuz you- you said that she wrote it.
66	Barb:	*UH*UH. *UH*UH CUZ I ONLY WROTE *ONE* THING
67		IN *RED.*
68		(0.4)
69	Bea:	S:o did I. *I* only- *h // Besides- I
70		only di:d that where *Yolan*da did cuz
71		Landa wrote on that *thing.*
72	Barb:	Vincent did *that.* Yolanda wrote where.
73	Bea:	Yolanda wrote on that thing.=And // I
74		only traced what- Yolanda wrote on it,
75		*h cuz Yolanda wro//te it *sm*:all.
76	Martha:	On the side?

77	Kerry:	I know.=I'm not *talk*in' 'bout *that*. But
78		how come you told her that I that I was
79		*talk*in' 'bout her.
80	Bea:	=YOU WA:S.
81	Kerry:	*WH*en.

The division of the conversation at
this point into two groups is indicated
by separate columns.
Simultaneous talk occurs on the same
horizontal line.

82	Bea:	Remember when um- um- that's when um:		
83		(0.8) Uh: uh: remember when you sai:d,		
84			Barb:	(°Well he
85				started it) cuz
86	Bea:	that um,		he got some of
87				it off.
88	Martha:	Yep.		
89	Bea:	nuh-		
90		remember when you	Barb:	( )
91		jus- When you		*Vin*cent did
92		sai:d, When you		that.
93		sai:d,	Julia:	['N' who did this.
94		"Bar-uh	Dru:	Bar:,
95		Barbara don't	Barb:	All this the
96		got nuttin to do		same handwritin'
97		with it."		an' it ain't
98				*mi*:ne.
99	Kerry:	*Uh*uh.	( ):	How 'bout right
100		*Ju*lia said that.		up there.
101	Bea:	Oh *Ju*lia said that.		
102	Julia:	*((from distance))* SAID WHAT.=		
103	Barb:	=Julia // said what.		
104	Bea:	said-//that you ain't		
105	Kerry:	That Barbara don't have nothin' to *do* with		
106		it.= 'Member? // We was arguin'?		
107	Julia:	Y:OU DON'T- She's not- (1.0) Cuz- She		
108		ain't mean nuttin'- t'do nuttin' to you.		
109		(1.4)		
110	Barb:	I was just writin' for *fun* cuz I ain't		
111		do it till nuttin' was happenin'.		

8.2 THE STRUCTURING OF ACCUSATIONS IN THE HE-SAID-SHE-SAID

He-said-she-said confrontations,[4] such as that in #1, begin with accusations in which one girl is charged with having talked about another behind her back. These accusations have a number of interesting properties, and their structure will be investigated in detail. Sequentially, these accusations are unusual in that they can occur as the first utterance of an encounter[5] and need not be tied to prior talk in the local interaction; such utterances in effect create their own context.[6] In essence, he-said-she-said accusations set the stage for the dispute which subsequently unfolds by building a particular cultural scene that includes (1) a set of relevant participants, (2) occasion-specific social identities for those participants,[7] (3) a set of relevant actions that these participants are expected to perform, and (4) a relevant past that culminates in the present. This past is highly structured and the events within it both account for the current accusation and provide a past history of participants and actions in the event, in essence a set of occasion-specific biographies for relevant participants. The structure of these opening accusations will now be examined in more detail.

8.2.1 BASIC STRUCTURE OF THE ACCUSATION

The confrontation presented above (#1) begins with utterances from Julia and Barbara directed to Bea:

(2) 1   Julia: *WE* AIN'T *SAY* THAT *BEA:*.
    2   Barb: You said that//I said-

Then Barbara states:

(3) 6   Julia: Um-
    7   Barb: They say y'all say I wrote *every*thing
    8   over there.

The structure of this utterance closely parallels the structure of other utterances used to initiate activities of this type:

(4)   *In the midst of play, Annette*
                    confronts Benita.

    Annette: And *Ar*thur said that *you* said
                    that *I* was showin' off just because
                    I had that *bl:ou*se on.

(5)   *Annette has just walked down the*
                    street from her house to a shade tree
                    in front of Vettie's house.

    Bea: Kerry said *y*ou said that (0.6)
                    I wasn't gonna go around *Pop*lar no more.

Each of these utterances provides an ordering of participants and events in a past leading to the present. The ordering is achieved through use of the format "she/he-said-you-said-I-said." This pattern might be most easily seen through use of a simple diagram. A horizontal arrow will mark an utterance from speaker to hearer. A vertical line will indicate some third party located by the utterance.

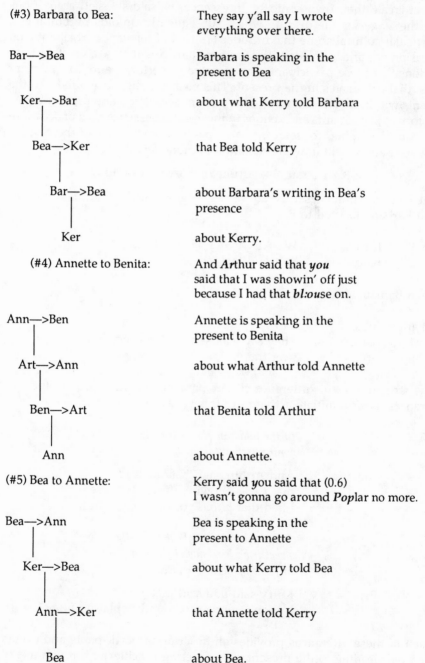

(#3) Barbara to Bea:

They say y'all say I wrote *e*verything over there.

Bar—>Bea

Barbara is speaking in the present to Bea

Ker—>Bar

about what Kerry told Barbara

Bea—>Ker

that Bea told Kerry

Bar—>Bea

about Barbara's writing in Bea's presence

Ker

about Kerry.

(#4) Annette to Benita:

And *Ar*thur said that *you* said that I was showin' off just because I had that *bl:ou*se on.

Ann—>Ben

Annette is speaking in the present to Benita

Art—>Ann

about what Arthur told Annette

Ben—>Art

that Benita told Arthur

Ann

about Annette.

(#5) Bea to Annette:

Kerry said *y*ou said that (0.6) I wasn't gonna go around *Pop*lar no more.

Bea—>Ann

Bea is speaking in the present to Annette

Ker—>Bea

about what Kerry told Bea

Ann—>Ker

that Annette told Kerry

Bea

about Bea.

Disregarding particular participants, we can let A stand for the speaker in the present, B stand for the hearer in the present, and C stand for the party talked about:

A—>B	A is speaking in the present to B
|	
C—>A	about what C told A
|	
B—>C	that B told C
|	
A	about A.

The pattern contains three basic stages. At each stage two parties in the immediate presence of each other are situated as speaker and hearer. A third party, neither speaker nor hearer, is talked about. Participants change positions within this basic triad at each stage in a regular fashion:

↓	**Time 1**	Speaker	Hearer	Spoken About
↓	**Time 2**	Spoken About	Speaker	Hearer

The ordering of events at each stage and the rules for sequencing stages through a regular rotation of participants provide a past with a particular structure that makes relevant specific types of next moves in the present. In essence the current hearer is charged with the offense of having talked about the current speaker behind her back, with the report of the third party establishing the grounds for that charge.[8]

The social and interactive possibilities of this structure will be investigated in more detail in a moment. First, however, the triadic pattern found here deserves further comment. Generally, the arguments of children analyzed by previous researchers (e.g., Eisenberg and Garvey 1981) have been dyadic in structure. This may be in large part because characteristically such researchers investigate children in a controlled environment. From another perspective, the structure of argumentation itself seems to bias the interaction so that it becomes focused upon two opposing positions, as occurs in previous argument fragments we have examined. However, even in such cases, participants other than the principals may align themselves with one of the positions on the floor, so that while the arguments are bipolar in terms of position, they are not intrinsically dyadic with respect to numbers of participants (see Maynard 1986b for a similar argument, as well as analysis of further complexities about the ways in which participants align themselves to positions). Moreover, as data in this chapter will demonstrate, within the he-said-she-said, children may occupy several positions concurrently. In brief, while most analysis of children's disputes has used a dyadic model, such a framework does not adequately conceptualize the richness of organization that children themselves bring to their spontaneous arguments.

8.2.2 Participants' Information States

The organization of events displayed within a he-said-she-said utterance (i.e., the patterning of events in the past leading to the present that was analyzed above) proposes that speaker and her addressee have differential access to the events that are the subject of the dispute:

1. The defendant has personal knowledge of what she said about her accuser.
   - The accuser however, does not have personal knowledge of this event, because it was spoken when she was absent. Her only access to it is via the report of the intermediate party.
2. The accuser has personal knowledge of what the intermediate party told her in the stage just prior to the present confrontation (for example, what Arthur said in #4).
   - Her addressee, however, was not present at this event, and indeed is being informed of it with the present utterance.
3. Accuser, as the party who purportedly performed the action that defendant told others about, is defined as someone who has direct knowledge of this action (including whether or not it did in fact occur).[9]
   - Defendant is also claiming to be knowledgeable about this event, but this is precisely the claim that is being challenged with the present accusation.

These differential information states can be diagrammed as follows. A plus sign indicates personal knowledge of the relevant event:

	Accuser's Original Action	Statement about Accuser by Defendant	Intermediate Party's Report to Accuser of What Defendant Said
Accuser	+	—	+
Defendant		+	—

The differential information states (Chafe 1976:30–33; Goffman 1974:133–134; Sacks 1973:139–141, 1974:343; Terasaki 1976:123) of accuser and defendant have a number of consequences for the organization of the activity in which the participants are engaged. First, the structure of the utterance locates the statement made by the defendant about the speaker as having been made in the speaker's absence. The act of the hearer thus constitutes what the children describe as "talking behind my back"; this act is considered an offense.[10]

Second, the accuser's action can be formulated in at least two different ways. In the data so far examined, the accusation has been formatted as a declarative statement (e.g., "Kerry said *y*ou said that I wasn't gonna go around *Pop*lar no more"), and this is indeed the characteristic form that such actions take when they are used to initiate a confrontation. However, insofar as the defendant is proposed to possess relevant knowledge that the accuser lacks—what she actually said about the accuser—these actions could also be formulated as explicit "requests for information" (Labov 1972a:57) to the defendant, asking her if she did in fact say what the intermediate party said that she said. This occurs when accusations are recycled as the confrontation develops:

(6)   Ruby: Did you say it Stacey?

(7)   Kerry: W- were *you* the girl at the *par*ty?
                  That was talkin' 'bout Ruby?

(8)   Ruby: I just wanna know did you say somp'm about
                  me.

In these actions no explicit reference is made to the intermediate party. The request for information references only the act of talking about the speaker, an activity known about by the hearer and unknown directly to the speaker.

By way of contrast, the declarative statement *informs* the defendant of something she does not know: that at a prior stage an intermediate party told the accuser about an act committed against her. Such differences account in part for the differential placement of these alternative forms of the accusation in a he-said-she-said confrontation. The more elaborated declarative form establishes the accuser's grounds for the accusation (for example, how she learned about the offense) and thus constitutes an appropriate move to begin a confrontation. Indeed, one of the striking features of such accusations is that, unlike most utterances, which rely upon the immediately prior talk for their interpretation, the declarative accusation is able to create a new context that ignores what has just been said in the current encounter, and uses as its frame of relevance events in other encounters. By way of contrast, the more elliptical request for information assumes knowledge of some of the information in the elaborated declarative form (for example, what constitutes "it" in #6), while simultaneously intensifying focus on the actions of the defendant by eliminating reference to the intermediate party.

8.2.3 Responses to He-Said-She-Said Accusations

Despite differences in the way that they are formatted, both forms of the accusation constitute first-pair parts of adjacency pairs (Schegloff and Sacks 1973:295–296). Recipients regularly respond to them with denials:

(1)	7	Barb:	They say y'all say I wrote *everything*
	8		over there.
			…
	17 →	Bea:	*UH*UH.=*THAT* WAS *VIN*CENT SAID.

(9)		Ruby:	I just wanna know did you say somp'm about
			me.
	→	Stacey:	*Uh* uh. I ain't *say* anything.

(10)		Ruby:	Did you say it Stacey?
		Stacey:	What you mean.
		Ruby:	What Kerry just got finished sayin'
			she said about me.
	→	Stacey:	I ain't say nothin' to-
			I ain't say nothin' *to* her.

(11)		Kerry:	W- were *you* the girl at the *par*ty?
		Gloria:	Huh::?
		Kerry:	That was talkin' 'bout Ruby?
			(0.8)
	→	Gloria:	*I* ain't say nothing 'bout *her*.

The children themselves label the act of responding to an utterance of the form he/she-said-you-said-I-said *denying*. The first-pair part is viewed as "asking about something" for the larger purpose of *getting something straight*. This activity of formally bringing a grievance before someone, presenting one's case, and talking things out is viewed as an alternative to physical fighting. The children do not use a particular term for the action of accusing. However, the way in which formal he-said-she-said statements systematically elicit denials is consistent with the argument that they are in fact interpreted as accusations, and I will continue to refer to them as such.

8.2.4 Framing the Accusation through an Intermediate Party

In bringing an action against an offending party, the offended constructs an accusation in a form which differs from those typical of male speakers, made baldly and directly, as in the following:

(12)   Malcolm: You took the hangers that I took off your bed.

(13)   William: Boy you broke my skateboard!

(14)   Lee: Y'all just changed the whole game around!

(15)   Vincent: You messin' up my *pap*er.

In he-said-she-said accusations, instead of being stated directly, thus making the hearer the sole actor implicated in the wrongdoing, the offense is instead phrased in terms of a report by some intermediate party (cf. #1–#5). Bringing the offense via an intermediary party has major implications. First, because "reported speech" may be regarded as a "message belonging to someone else" (Vološinov 1973:149), the speaker is not the sole party responsible for the report.[11] This feature of the accusation has sequential import in that it constrains the choice of next moves for the defendant. Following many types of accusations in children's arguments, a defendant may counteraccuse his accuser:[12]

(16)   Lee: Y'all just changed the whole game around!
          Ossie: We didn't change *no*thing around.
    →   Y'*all* changed it around.

(17)   Vincent: You messin' up my *pap*er.
          Ossie: Shut up.
    →   *Y*ou the one messin it up.

(18)   Ossie: Don't know what he *ta*lkin' about.
          Carl: Don't know what *you* talking about.

With reference to the pattern accusation/counteraccusation, Emerson (1969:167) has stated that "in making a denunciation a person automatically opens up his own motives and moral character to examination and evaluation, with the distinct possibility that they will be found wanting." Since this is the case, the denouncer must "establish a right to undertake such action" (Emerson 1969:166). By including in her accusation the statement of another party, the accuser argues that her charge is warranted and supported by at least one other person.[13] She not only establishes a form of license to bring the charge but also argues that an alignment of "two against one"[14] exists against the defendant. By way of illustration, consider the following speech Ruby makes to her adversary during a confrontation:

(19)   Ruby: Well I'm a get it straight with the people.
                        What *Ke*rry, (1.4)

It's between Kerry, and you, (1.0)
See *two* (0.5) two against one. (0.7)
Who wins? The one is two.=Right? (0.5)
And that's Joycie and Kerry. (0.5)
They both say that you said it.
And you say that you didn't say it.
Who you got the *proof* that say
that you *did*n't say it.

From a slightly different perspective, the utterance form selected by accuser can be seen to be holding conflict within certain bounds. In that the intermediate party, rather than current speaker, is credited with authorship of the report of the offense, the defendant cannot bring a counteraccusation against her accuser, claiming *she* is making up the offense, lying, or unjustly accusing her. The appropriate target of a counteraccusation is not the accuser but rather the absent intermediate party; therefore, the argument trajectory accusation/counteraccusation, which permits both parties the opportunity to accuse one another, does not develop.

The statement opening the he-said-she-said might thus be viewed as an action of a particular type arguing for the relevance of a third party. In that information concerning the offense at issue was obtained and mediated through a third party, a situation in which characters possess differing information states is constructed. This leads to the possibility of an extended drama; a puzzle without any clear resolution is provided for participants.

8.3 THE SEQUENCING OF ACCUSATION/RESPONSE PAIRS IN AN EXTENDED CONFRONTATION

The long he-said-she-said confrontation introduced in #1 will now be examined in more detail to investigate how accusations and their responses provide a structured field for the ordering of participants relative to one another and for the organization of their actions. A variety of different phenomena are implicated in the organization of this fragment. Analysis, however, will be confined to the more salient features used to construct it: in particular, the adjacency pair accusation/response and the identities provided for participants. It should be noted that although the accusations in this activity are unique to the he-said-she-said, the responses to them to be considered are common "counters" in children's arguments.

8.3.1 Four-Stage Accusations

The confrontation begins as Bea, Martha, Drucilla, and I meet Barbara, who has been talking with Julia and Kerry. Barbara directs a he-said-she-said accusation statement to Bea: "*You* said that *I* said-." This is elaborated in Barbara's next utterance (#1, lines 7–8): "They say y'all say I wrote everything over there." By again diagramming the accusation we can examine the configuration of occasion-specific identities which it constructs:

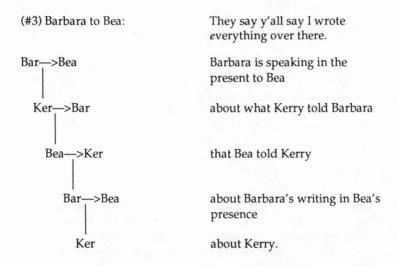

(#3) Barbara to Bea:

Bar—>Bea

Ker—>Bar

Bea—>Ker

Bar—>Bea

Ker

They say y'all say I wrote everything over there.

Barbara is speaking in the present to Bea

about what Kerry told Barbara

that Bea told Kerry

about Barbara's writing in Bea's presence

about Kerry.

Unlike those examined earlier in #4 and #5, this accusation contains four rather than three stages. Further, while the spoken-about party is generally absent, in this case she (Kerry) is present.

Four-stage accusations emerge systematically from three-stage accusations. First, the same procedures used to project a third stage from a second stage can be used to construct a fourth from a third. Second, there are systematic reasons why a three-stage he-said-she-said would be expanded to four stages. We saw earlier that accusations are framed in indirect speech in terms of the report of an intermediate party. This provides some immunity for the accuser against a counteraccusation by the defendant. However, by expanding the he-said-she-said to a fourth stage, a defendant can bring an action not against the accuser but against the party who informed on her to the accuser. The repeated application of the procedures used to construct these events thus generates subsequent stages.

Note that in a four-stage accusation, the act at issue is no longer the bottom layer of the charge. Irrespective of the number of stages, the accusation refers to the third stage down from the present. For convenience I will label the three relative stages as follows: the stage occurring in the present is the *confrontation*, the stage occurring immediately prior is the *reporting*, and the third stage from the present is the *offense* stage. When the he-said-she-said reaches the fourth stage, participants become located in several fields of orientation simultaneously:

(1) Barbara to Bea: They say y'all say I wrote
                            everything over there.

Bar—>Bea   Barbara speaks to Bea   4   Confrontation
  |
  |
    Ker—>Bar   about what Kerry told Barb   3   Reporting
      |
      |
      Bea—>Ker   that Bea told Kerry   2   Offense
        |
        |
          Bar—>Bea   about Barbara's writing in   1
            | Bea's presence
            |
          Ker   about Kerry.

In the present example, Barbara is both accuser to Bea (stage 4) and defendant to Kerry (stage 3). Bea is defendant to Barbara (stage 4) and the
intermediate party who told Kerry about what Barbara did (stage 2). Kerry
is intermediate party between Barbara and Bea (stage 4) and accuser of
Barbara (stage 3).

To examine what happens as the structure is transformed beyond three
stages, the structure of occasion-specific identities created by this procedure
will be briefly described. At each moment in time, the participants are
located in a particular configuration relative to each other. However, participants change their positions in this configuration in an orderly fashion
through time. That is, not only does the application of the procedure provide a history of relevant events; it also provides a biography for each
participant, a career of positions occupied in the unfolding course of located
events. Further, the biography of each participant is unique. Specifically,
the fact that the participants are located in separate positions at the first
stage of the activity and, in addition, that there exist definite rules for the
rotation of the participants from stage to stage provides that at any moment
in time no two participants will have the same biography.

These biographies and the types of occasion-specific identities they construct have a dynamic character as the process unfolds through time. A
party who was the offended party at one stage becomes the accuser two
stages later, but she gains the latter position only by virtue of having previously occupied the former. Because the biographies of the participants
accumulate in this fashion, the complexity of both the structure of actions
and the occasion-specific identities created for the participants is progres-
sively increased as the structure is applied repeatedly through time.

As transformations are extended beyond the third stage, the structure of occasion-specific identities ordering the immediate exchange remains the same. Consider again the diagram of #1. Speaker and hearer in the top stage stand to each other as accuser and defendant. However, the participants as well as the act at issue have changed. The defendant at the immediately previous stage, stage 3, has become the accuser. Furthermore, in that the act at issue is the act committed by the party located as defendant, that act is located in the third stage back irrespective of how far the stages extend below that point. Insofar as this is a next stage in the action, the new fourth-stage accusation also counts as part of the speaker's defense to the action of the previous speaker against her in the third stage. If the speaker in the fourth stage can obtain a denial or retraction from the defendant, the case brought against her by the previous speaker in the third stage collapses. Of course, if the present defendant issues a denial she may then bring an accusation against the previous speaker, and yet another stage will be entered.

A party may thus be simultaneously situated in several fields of orientation, e.g., as defendant to one party and accuser to another. Furthermore, within this process the criteria for the various occasion-specific identities are being both achieved and negotiated such that a subset of these types of persons may be retrospectively restructured. A subsequent interaction may reveal that although at one point in time a party was heard as, for example, an offender, she did not in fact possess the necessary criteria to be heard as that occasion-specific identity; when that point in time is viewed from this later stage, she may be found to have held the position of a party wrongly accused, and in fact to have been the offended party. The intersection of two features—a comparatively simple procedure for ordering events and the accumulation of separate biographies for participants in the form of a history of the positions they are heard to have occupied in the cited events—makes it possible through repeated application of the procedure for situations of increasing complexity to be generated.

The different fields of orientation are linked such that they are interdependent. A single move can have consequences for the various identities of all participants. For example, in #1, if Barbara can get Bea to deny that she made the statement at issue to Kerry, then (1) the grounds for Kerry's accusation in the immediately prior (reporting) stage are lost so that Barbara is no longer a defendant to an accusation from Kerry, and (2) in stage 4 Kerry can by inference be located as an intermediary who did not tell the truth.

8.3.2 CONSTRUCTING A DENIAL

An accused can build a denial to a he-said-she-said accusation in several different ways, by responding to different parts of the allegation. Thus she can deny that she committed the offense cited in the offense stage, or alternatively couple such a denial with a statement that the intermediate party lied about her in the reporting stage:

	Action	Defense
A—>B:	Accuser tells Defendant	
C—>A	that C said	← "C is lying."
B—>C	that Defendant said something	←"I ain't say it."
A	about A.	

The first type of construction is illustrated by #20 and #21. In #20 Stacey denies that she said what she was accused of saying and in #21 Benita states that someone else said it:

(20)   Stacey: I ain't say that.

(21)   Benita: *Wan*da said *that*. That's all I know.

In that they challenge the charge being made, such denials also imply that what was said by the intermediate party was in error (i.e., defendant denies that she said what she was reported to have said). This alternative type of construction is illustrated by #22–#25:

(22)   Deniece: Well *I* know that *they* tellin' a *lie*
                    cuz *I* know I ain't *say* nothin' about you.

(23)   Deniece: Well he *lie*. I ain't *say* that.

(24)   Stacey: I don't know who said it but- now- I-
                    now if *I* ain't say it,
                    whoever told you musta said it.

(25)   Stacey: I know *I* ain't say it. (2.4)
                    Cuz I ain't- I ain't even say nothin'.
                    I just said just what I just now told you.
                    And I should know what I did.
                    She must- they must-
                    She put those two words in there herself.

Denials thus may focus on either the offense or the reporting stage of the accusation. In some cases, the denial may contain a new accusation. Either some other party is charged with the offense (e.g., #21), or the intermediate party is charged with having lied #22–#25. Although some denials reference only the offense stage, they can nonetheless be seen to also contain an implicit accusation that the intermediate party misquoted the defendant.

On some occasions defendants do admit that they said something about the accuser. However, in such cases, as noted by Goffman (1963:2), a party charged with an offense can attempt to restore the expressive order by reframing the event being challenged: "An attempt can be made to show that what admittedly appeared to be a threatening expression is really a meaningless event, or an unintentional act, or a joke not meant to be taken seriously, or an unavoidable, understandable product of extenuating circumstances." Thus a defendant who acknowledges saying something argues that what was said either was not an offense or at worst was not intended as one.[15] For example, in the following Gloria argues that although she did say something, what was said was in fact a compliment:

(26) Gloria: The only *thing I* said,
                   only thing I said about them,
                   *h that they can *dance* nice. (1.0)
                   And I said- "Every time I see that-
                   that girl that came around here? (1.3)
    →   She go to Franklin Institute."=I s-
                   "*She* wear some *nice clothes.*"

One of the most powerful techniques available for reframing quoted talk is embedding the quote being disputed within another event that recontextualizes it. Most frequently this encompassing event is the talk of another. Thus defendants may portray what was said as a justified response to the offensive actions of another:

(27) Gloria: But I ain't even *say* nothin'.
    →   *h I- I knew I said s-
                   She said somp'm 'bout *me.*
                   Then I said somp'm about her.

(28) Stacey: I ain't *say* nothin' 'bout you.
                   I was only talkin' 'bout um, Sister. (2.4)
                   And when I told Sister about y'all sayin' that,
    →   first they said "I think Ruby and Sister
                   a little mad at you." And I said
                   "I don't *care* if they mad at *me!*"

(29)   Deniece: That time me and *Tom*my was arguin'
          →   he w'talkin' 'bout "I'm gonna get *my*
                         *si*ster to kick *your* butt."
                         I said "Go ahead." That's all I said.

In this way, defendants are even able to explicitly admit saying what they
have been charged with, while arguing that insofar as their talk constituted
a warranted response to the talk that elicited it, it should not be considered
an offense:

(30)   Deniece: Bu:t *you* was *talk*in' about them though.
          → Gloria: But *she* was talkin' about *me*!

The ability to recontextualize disputed talk by embedding reported speech
within other quoted speech provides participants with a powerful resource
for negotiating the meaning and interpretation of the events in which they
are engaged.

The fact that he-said-she-said accusations systematically evoke denials[16]
has a number of consequences. If the hearer were to agree to the description, the speaker would have grounds to seek redress. Although physical
fights do not occur, they are discussed as possible trajectories following
an admission of guilt:

(31)   Annette: You gonna beat her up today?
          Ruby: If I find out that she said it.
          Annette: You are?
          Ruby: If she said- if she admit that she said it.

By denying the accusation, the hearer avoids any possible reading that she
participated in acts of wrongdoing against the accuser. In addition, she
prevents the accuser from being viewed as someone who delivers empty
threats. By way of example, consider the following, in which by answering
rather than denying the charge, Malcolm frames Tony's action as nonthreat-
ening:

(32)   Tony: Who was- who was throwin' the *r*ocks.
          Malcolm: *Me* and- and Tokay, and everybody else.

Making use of actions which deny the accusation, attribute guilt to
another, or disclaim intentional insult to the offended party not only helps
keep within limits the potential for conflict inherent in a dispute such as
the he-said-she-said, but also preserves the face and status of both parties
even as they are engaged in vigorous dispute with each other. Should the
defendant *not* respond, keeping her head bowed and remaining silent, she
tacitly admits to having committed the offense in question (as occurred in

only one very serious he-said-she-said dispute). In such a case the confrontation event is constructed out of talk *about* the defendant's offenses rather than volleys of accusation/denial sequences.

8.3.3 THE TRAJECTORY OF A SPECIFIC HE-SAID-SHE-SAID DISPUTE

Returning to the specific accusation in #1, Bea's denial charges a nonpresent party, Vincent, with having committed the offense:

(1)	7	Barb:	They say y'all say I wrote *everything*
	8		over there.
			...
	17 →	Bea:	*UH*UH.=*THAT* WAS *VIN*CENT SAID.

Through this denial Bea introduces a new party into the dispute. Because Vincent is not present, certain next moves cannot be performed. For example, Vincent cannot counter the charge against him and Barbara cannot question him. After Bea's denial, Barbara's accusation is terminated. In fact, Barbara agrees with Bea in her next utterance:

(1)	7	Barb:	They say y'all say I wrote *everything*
	8		over there.
			...
	17	Bea:	*UH*UH.=*THAT* WAS *VIN*CENT SAID.
	18	Kerry:	But y//ou told *me* that
	19 →	Barb:	I know it was Vincent cuz Vincent was
	20		the one that wrote that on that *car*.

Bea's denial not only closes down Barbara's accusation to her, but it also reshapes the field of activity. Bea's assertion that the statement being disputed was made by Vincent implicitly accuses Kerry of having lied. In response, Kerry starts to provide a defense, a counteraccusation or objection to Bea ("But you told *me* that" in line 18). Kerry's action is overlapped by Barbara's agreement with Bea's assertion that Vincent said it. However, before Barbara has finished speaking, one of Bea's allies, Martha, starts to provide an answer to Kerry's defense (lines 21–23). As she hesitates in providing the answer, Julia continues (lines 24–26), saying that it was either Vincent or Barbara. The two separate lines of talk that have briefly emerged here (Barbara tying across Kerry's defense to Bea's talk and Martha tying across Barbara's talk to Kerry's) are now joined with a statement that, instead of letting Barbara off the hook, implicates her with Vincent. Indeed, as Barbara's name emerges in Julia's talk, Bea and Martha join her (lines 26–28), with the effect that three separate parties simultaneously announce her name.

(1)

17	Bea:	*UH*UH.=*THAT* WAS *VIN*CENT SAID.
18	Kerry:	But y//ou told *me* that
19	Barb:	I know it was Vincent cuz Vincent was
20		the one that wrote that // on that *ca*r.
21	Martha:	*((falsetto)) Uh*uh.=We started to tear
22		that- *h uh that out. We tol- we said
23		that we- *all* said- *h I said // all-
24	Julia:	*((falsetto))* I said, "Who wrote it on
25		the car." Martha say "Either Vincent,
26		(0.2) or, *Vin*cent or um- ⌜*Bar*bara."
27	Bea:	⌜*Bar*bara.
28	Martha:	⌞*Bar*bara.
29	Martha:	I put th//is
30	Barb:	*Vin*cent *di*:d it. *Vin*cent had that
31		crayon more than *any*body.
32		(0.7)
33	Martha:	*h An' plus- an'=
34	Barb:	Oo this's *cold* out *here* // t'day.
35	Kerry:	WELL WHY YOU TELL HER *I* said it.

Barbara answers the chorus of voices accusing her by first saying that Vincent did it "more than *any*body" (line 31), and then in line 34 by attempting to shift frame to a topic other than the he-said-she-said dispute. Her talk here is the only utterance in the confrontation that does not deal with the dispute.

This sequence effectively closes the accusation sequence with Barbara. However, a new accusation from Kerry immediately follows: "WELL WHY YOU TELL HER *I* said it" (line 35). This accusation appears two more times (lines 45–46, "Well how come *you* told *Bar*bara that I said that *she* wrote it," and lines 78–79, "But how come you told her that I that I was *talk*in' 'bout her"), and it may be diagrammed as follows:

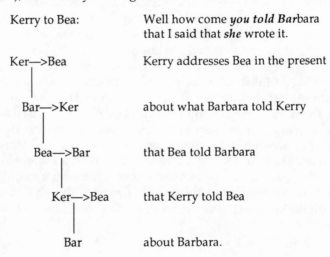

Kerry to Bea:	Well how come *you told Bar*bara that I said that *she* wrote it.
Ker—>Bea	Kerry addresses Bea in the present
Bar—>Ker	about what Barbara told Kerry
Bea—>Bar	that Bea told Barbara
Ker—>Bea	that Kerry told Bea
Bar	about Barbara.

Unlike many he-said-she-said accusations, these do not ask whether or not the act in question was committed; rather they take for granted that it was and ask "why" and "how come."

The accusation is recycled two times because Bea repetitively avoids answering it. Before we consider the answer that the accusation finally evokes, the procedures Bea uses to avoid providing a second pair part to the accusation will be considered. Bea's first response is a countercharge, which is also an explanation for the offense:

(1)
35	Kerry:	WELL WHY YOU TELL HER *I* said it.
36	Bea:	YEAH BUT *JULIA*- YEAH BUT *JULIA* WAS SAYIN' *WE*
37 →		*WRO*:TE ALL OVER THE STREET AND WE
38		*DIDN'T*.=

Instead of accusing Kerry, Bea accuses one of Kerry's allies, Julia, of having said something about her first. This action also constitutes a defense. Although it admits that the act at issue did in fact occur, the action argues that it was justified in that an offensive act of another preceded it.

Bea's utterance in lines 36–38 reorganizes the relevant domain of talk. Conversation is tied no longer to Kerry's accusation to Bea (line 35) but rather to Bea's action to Julia. A series of denials and a challenge to the reported accusation follow:

(1)
35	Kerry:	WELL WHY YOU TELL HER *I* said it.
36	Bea:	YEAH BUT *JULIA*- YEAH BUT *JULIA* WAS SAYIN' *WE*
37 →		*WRO*:TE ALL OVER THE STREET AND WE
38		*DIDN'T*.=
39 →	Barb:	[*We* ain't write over no street *noth*in'.
40	Kerry:	I'm~not~talkin'~'bout- B'//t why did-
41	Julia:	Vincent say he wrote in the street. *((sigh))*=
42 →	Martha:	=Well I ain't write // in the street.
43 →	Barb:	Oh *you* fin' s'n in the st//r:eet then.
44 →	Bea:	I ain't *wrote nutt*in in no str:ee://t,
45	Kerry:	Well how come *you told Bar*bara that I
46		said that *she* wrote it.

Bea does not attempt to deny the accusation made against her by Kerry (note how her turn in line 36 begins with "Yeah but"). However, by quoting the talk of another, she is able to immediately place herself in the position of one who has been wrongly charged (only now by Julia rather than Bea) and moreover to display the affect appropriate to someone in such a position (for example, righteous indignation at the injustice done her). This is done in the very turn that admits the validity of the current charge against her. What happens here provides a vivid demonstration of the power of reported speech to recontextualize not only the talk being quoted but also the activity of the moment that encompasses that talk.

At the end of the flurry of activity generated by Bea's move, Kerry (lines 45–46) reintroduces her accusation to Bea:

(1)
```
45      Kerry:         Well how come you told Barbara that I
46                     said that she wrote it.
47                            (0.6)
48      Martha:        I said that who wrote it.=
49      Kerry:         =Not you.=Bea.
```

For a second time, the answer to her question is impeded. Although the "points of orientation" (Brecht 1974:491) of the pronouns "you" and "she" in Kerry's utterance are clear, Martha argues that they are ambiguous. Martha rather than Bea answers the accusation and argues that the referent of "she" is uncertain. The misapprehension (Jefferson 1972:304–308) concerning who is recipient of Kerry's accusation is resolved immediately (line 49). Several features of the interaction demonstrate that the referents of the pronouns are not unclear, and that this is, in fact, recognized by the participants. First, as we just saw, a similar accusation was answered by Bea in line 36. Second, Barbara, through her repetitive denials of the offensive act of having written something, has previously identified herself as a party implicated in the act of writing (e.g., "I ain't wrote everything over there," lines 8–9; see also lines 19–20 and 30–31).

A series of side sequences (Jefferson 1972) and repairs (Schegloff, Jefferson, and Sacks 1977) which do not address Kerry's accusations to Bea (lines 45–46) follow in lines 51 through 76. The next time Kerry recycles her accusation to Bea she prefaces her action by signaling a "satisfactory termination of preceding talk" (Jefferson 1972:317) and categorizing the prior talk as having been off topic:

(1)
```
77      Kerry:         I know.=I'm not talkin' 'bout that. But
78                     how come you told her that I that I was
79                     talkin' 'bout her.
80      Bea:           =YOU WA:S.
81      Kerry:         WHen.
```

This time no counteraccusation or side sequence develops. Bea answers in line 80 "YOU WA:S," arguing that the statement Kerry is calling her on was a true report of Kerry's actions. After some debate, following Kerry's challenge in line 81 ("When") and Bea's replaying of the scene when Kerry reportedly said something about Barbara (lines 89–97), Kerry states that it was Julia rather than she who was talking about Barbara:

(1)

89	Bea:	nuh-		
90		remember when you	Barb:	( )
91		jus- When you		*Vin*cent did
92		sai:d, When you		that.
93		sai:d,	Julia:	['N' who did this.
94		"Bar-uh	Dru:	Bar:,
95		Barbara don't	Barb:	All this the
96		got nuttin to do		same handwritin'
97		with it."		an' it ain't
98				*mi*:ne.
99	Kerry:	*Uh*uh.	( ):	How 'bout right
100		*Ju*lia said that.		up there.
101	Bea:	Oh *Ju*lia said that.		
102	Julia:	*((from distance))* SAID WHAT.=		
103	Barb:	=Julia // said what.		
104	Bea:	said-//that you ain't		
105	Kerry:	That Barbara don't have nothin' to *do* with		
106		it.= 'Member? // We was arguin'?		
107	Julia:	Y:OU DON'T- She's not- (1.0) Cuz- She		
108		ain't mean nuttin'- t'do nuttin' to you.		
109		(1.4)		
110	Barb:	I was just writin' for *fun* cuz I ain't		
111		do it till nuttin' was happenin'.		

As soon as Kerry says this, Bea (line 101) changes her position, signaling this change with "Oh," a prototypical change-of-state token (Heritage 1984b). In that the party being accused of having given an inaccurate report now agrees that it is inaccurate, debate on this issue is closed, and focus shifts to the new charge against Julia (lines 102–108).

Unlike many forms of argument in which the subject of discussion may shift radically from moment to moment as new moves are put forward (C. Goodwin and M. H. Goodwin 1990 and Chapter 7 of this volume), the he-said-she-said is highly topicalized. Throughout this sequence, with the sole exception of Barbara's "Oo this's *cold* out *here* t'day" (line 34), attention is focused on accusation/response sequences, and a clear division is maintained between those two who are principals and those who are spectators. The integrity of confrontation events is maintained, as accusers actively monitor them—ignoring or sanctioning those who make statements irrelevant to the business at hand.

The procedures we have been examining not only provide for utterances with a particular structure but also create a coherent domain of action, an entire drama for the participants implicated in these utterances. As the current accusation on the floor switches, so the relevant configuration of identity relationships of participants in the event is rearranged.

8.4 CLOSING HE-SAID-SHE-SAID DISPUTES

Confrontations can end in a variety of ways. The way in which they terminate is influenced by a number of issues, including the availability of a party other than accuser or defendant to debate the charge, and the seriousness with which participants treat the offense at issue.

The presence of an intermediate party in the sequence just examined helps close debate about whether Kerry actually said something about Barbara. Since the sequencing of events and stages is complex here, it is useful to look again at the diagram of Kerry's accusation:

Kerry to Bea: Well how come *you told Bar*bara
                                 that I said that *she* wrote it.

		Stage
Ker—>Bea	Kerry asks Bea	4
Bar—>Ker	about what Barbara told Kerry	3
Bea—>Bar	that Bea told Barbara	2
Ker—>Bea	that Kerry told Bea	1
Bar	about Barbara.	

In stage 3 Barbara accuses Kerry of having said that Barbara wrote things about Kerry. Bea is the party who (at stage 2) told Barbara what Kerry had said. The defendant at stage 3, Kerry, then initiates a new confrontation at stage 4. Here Kerry confronts Bea about her actions as an instigator who told on her to Barbara at stage 2. Initially Bea argues that what she said was true, i.e., that Kerry did talk about Barbara (line 80). However when Kerry disputes this by saying "*Uh*uh. *Ju*lia said that," Bea acknowledges that Kerry is in fact correct and she is wrong (line 101, "Oh *Ju*lia said that"). Thus Bea, the party who through her storytelling had engineered a situation in which particular girls were led to confront each other, admits that she was in error about who was at fault.

The confrontation closes with a repair-like utterance from Bea (line 101), a move from Julia (the new guilty party) implicating Barbara (lines 107–108), and a defense from Barbara (lines 110–111):

(1)
101	Bea:	Oh *Jul*ia said that.
		…
105	Kerry:	That Barbara don't have nothin' to *do* with
106		it. 'Member?//We was arguin'?
107	Julia:	Y:OU DON'T- She's not- (1.0) Cuz- She
108		ain't mean nuttin'- t'do nuttin' to you.
109		(1.4)
110	Barb:	I was just writin' for *fun* cuz I ain't
111		do it till nuttin' was happenin'.

Reaching agreement on who in fact said what is one way that he-said-she-said disputes can not only end but have the issues being debated within them actually be resolved. For example, in another confrontation Annette accused Benita of having talked about her behind her back. The dispute ended when both parties agreed that it was not Benita, the current defendant, but someone else, Wanda, who had committed the offense:

(33)	Annette:	Wanda said she said it.
	Benita:	Yep. Wanda said it.
		(4.0)
		((*Girls resume play.*))

In both of these arguments the contesting parties were able to reach agreement about the events being debated. Moreover, both disputes ended without serious repercussions. In #33 the girls started playing together immediately after the dispute. In #1, Kerry played with the other girls an hour later. Coming to agreement thus seems to help prevent the confrontation from disrupting ongoing social relationships. However, it also seems to be the case that it is precisely those arguments that are less serious to begin with that are able to be resolved.

More frequently, confrontations end in a stalemate. Consider the following, which ends with Annette simply walking away:

(34)
1	Bea:	Kerry said *y*ou said that (0.6)
2		I wasn't gonna go around *Pop*lar no more.
3	Annette:	You *s*aid you weren't.
4	Ruby:	She- Kerry say-
5	Bea:	And Kerry said that um that *y*ou said
6		that *B*ea wasn't gonna go around *P*oplar
7		no more.

8	Annette:	That's what Kerry said.
9	Bea:	Well I *know* what Kerry said that you said.
10		She said- She sat there and looked at you.
11		And Kerry- And she said-
12		And if you have anything to say about *me*
13		you come and say it in front of my *face*.
14		And *here* and *right* here
15		You say whatever you got to say.
16		Cuz *every* time you go around Poplar
17		you always got something to say.
18	Ruby:	Kerry said it *too*.
19	Bea:	And I'm tellin' Kerry *too*
20		that she said it.
21		(6.5)
22 →	Annette:	I gotta go somewhere.
23		(1.5)
24 →	Annette:	I'll be back. Okay Candy?
25		((*Annette walks up the street to her house.*))
26 →	Ruby:	She doesn't really have to go somewhere.

Following Annette's first defense (line 3), Bea, the plaintiff, recycles the initial accusation (lines 5–7). When Annette provides a second defense (line 8) addressing actions in the reporting stage ("That's what Kerry said"), Bea refutes Annette's account ("Well I *know* what Kerry said that you said") and provides a descriptive detail of her previous encounter with Kerry to justify her position (line 10).[17] Bea closes up the he-said-she-said with an admonition to Annette, as well as with a framing of this particular offense as representative of Annette's more general way of behaving: "every time you go around Poplar you always got something to say." Ruby, an onlooker, both aligns herself with Bea's position in this dispute (line 18) and in line 26 explicitly comments on how lame Annette's excuse for breaking off the confrontation is: "She doesn't really have to go somewhere."

This sequence also contains an example of another very typical move toward closure, an aphorism: "And if you have anything to say about *me* you come and say it in front of my *face*" (lines 12–13). Schegloff and Sacks (1973:306) have noted the power of aphorisms to bound topics by stating the "moral" or "lesson" of the topic underway. By virtue of their ability to withdraw from the details of the topic toward its more general import, such techniques constitute apt moves for attempting closure (although of course such moves can be rejected, and in the he-said-she-said frequently are). The aphorism used here, a general admonition to say things directly to the accuser rather than behind her back, occurs frequently in he-said-she-said confrontations, and indeed encapsulates in general terms the offense at issue in such confrontations.

Stalemate also occurs when parties accept that their opponents are simply going to continue recycling their positions. The following confrontation between accuser Kerry and defendant Deniece has gone on for several minutes. After Deniece has produced one of many denials, Kerry tells the girls they might as well go home:

(35)   Deniece: Well *I* know *I* ain't say that.
                     I know for my*self* I ain't *say* that.
  → Kerry: Come on y'all. *She* s-
                     she say she ain't say it.
       Deniece: *R*ight. I ain't say nothin' about *her*
                     and I ain't say nothin' 'bout *her*.
                     ((*Girls walk home.*))

Although such a sequence of moves might appear to close off confrontation (indeed Jimmy, a spectator to this argument, states, "Y'all got it straight. Now y'all can go: home") the conflict may be opened up at a later time during the day. For example, a short time after the above interaction, Kerry returns to Deniece's house and confronts her (#36, lines 1–21). However, Deniece skillfully redirects the dispute (lines 22–28) so that Kerry has to confront Gloria (lines 46, 49):

(36)
  1   Kerry: Deniethia? (1.4) *Jim*my and them
  2   was goin' around there tellin' everybody
  3   that *I* swag. Cuz *right*?
  4   Cuz didn't I say I was gonna fight you?
  5   You said you ain't say nothin'?
  6   But I want you to get it straight.=Okay?
  7   Cuz I don't- cuz I- Listen. Y-
  8   If I *fight* you I *fight* you.=
  9   And if I *don't* I *don't*.=But-
 10   but see the only reason that I-
 11   Cuz *they* told me, *they* were tellin' me
 12   "Why don't you go around there
 13   and kick Deniece *butt*=
 14   Because *she* tellin' everybody
 15   *h *she* can kick *your* butt."
 16   And that ain't *true*. (0.4)
 17   That's the only reason why I came around
 18   here.=Wasn't *no* other *rea*son.
 19   That I wanted to or that I *di*dn't want to.
 20   Just that *they told* me
 21   what you was gonna *do*.
 22   Deniece: Well *I* know *they* tellin' you a *lie*
 23   cuz *I* know *I* ain't *say* nothin' about you.
 24   (0.6)
 25   And so, when I went over Gloria house
 26   t'tell her what Ruby said

27		she said Ruby ain't have no business
28		talkin' about her.
29		(0.5)
30	Kerry:	She home now?
31	Deniece:	Uh huh.
32	Kerry:	Can I go visit her?
33	Deniece:	((nods))
34	Kerry:	Where she live at.
35	Deniece:	Straight over there.
36		((We walk to Gloria's house during
37		23 seconds of silence.))
38	Deniece:	Gloria!
39		(3.5)
40	Deniece:	Gloria come here. (2.8)
41		Somebody wants you at the door.
42		(11.0)
43	Kerry:	That's Gloria?
44	Deniece:	Uh huh,
45		(1.5)
46	Kerry:	Were *you* the girl at the *party*?
47		(0.8)
48	Gloria:	Huh::?
49	Kerry:	That was talkin' 'bout Ruby?

The rather abrupt closing up of the argument between Kerry and Deniece (lines 22–23) indicates the readiness with which Kerry is prepared to terminate their dispute and continue argumentation with another party. When Deniece mentions (lines 25–28) that Gloria had said something about a friend of Kerry's (Ruby), Kerry does not hesitate in taking steps to confront Gloria on Ruby's behalf (lines 30, 32, 34). A certain lack of seriousness is keyed in other ways as well. This dispute, taking place between two playmates who only rarely play together (and therefore do not compare themselves with one another in the same intense way that Maple Street playmates do), opens with a soliloquy rather than a first-pair part accusation. In fact, Kerry states at the beginning of her talk (lines 1–3) that the reason she is confronting Deniece is not to accuse her but to go on record with Jimmy and her peers as having not been afraid to confront Deniece (lines 1–21), i.e., so she herself is not accused of "swagging."

Different outcomes seem to be related to the seriousness of the dispute. After nonserious confrontations, participants can interact together in a playful, nonconfrontational mode. However, more serious confrontations end with one of the parties physically removing herself from the other's presence, as in #34, line 22, in which Annette leaves to "go somewhere." Such withdrawal can in fact become far more extensive. In an effort to prevent future conflict from taking place at school, a girl may intentionally be absent for several days; "turning in sick" is one strategy for terminating disputes quite similar to the practice of avoidance in other societies.

8.5 THE HE-SAID-SHE-SAID AS
A DISPUTE PROCESS

Most analysis of the disputing process in the social science literature has focused on situations in which males are the principal protagonists. Indeed, it has sometimes been suggested that one of the attributes of female speech is its relative lack of concern for the elaboration of legalistic debate (Gilligan 1982, 1987; Lever 1976; Piaget 1965:83). According to Gilligan's (1982) argument, girls are more concerned with the ethics of care and responsibility than with moral principles of justice and rights.[18] However, within the he-said-she-said, preadolescent girls formulate charges that their individual rights have been violated with respect to how they are to be treated in the talk of others. They do so by constructing opening accusation utterances of considerable sophistication that not only state the charge formally but also provide the grounds for it—invoking what is in fact a vernacular legal process.[19] Through this dispute, the alignment of principals to the argument shifts as various stages of the initial accusation statement are dealt with and related offenses are brought up. This provides for a speaking floor of much greater complexity than that which exists when only two positions to an argument are debated, the general situation in most boys' and cross-sex disputes.

According to Gilligan (1982), females are less likely to dominate and more likely to negotiate than males. However, the accuser within the he-said-she-said can repetitively recycle her position throughout several turns, refusing to back down from her initial accusation. Abrahams (1976:77) has suggested that the "contest element" in speech lasts for a shorter duration among black females than among males. However, because of the topical focus it provides, a he-said-she-said dispute can be significantly more extended than the disputes found in the boys' or cross-sex groups. Indeed, because of the way in which it creates both a relevant past and an anticipated future, the he-said-she-said can provide an arena for action and drama that lasts for several days (and in more extreme cases several weeks), with participants anticipating, reviewing, and evaluating the playing out of the confrontation.

The confrontation event provides a framework for action that is quite relevant to the larger concerns of the girls' group. Generally, the activity of he-said-she-said is carried out among girls who regularly interact and compare themselves with one another.[20] Among a group of individuals for whom it is culturally inappropriate to insult, command, or accuse another person openly, the confrontation provides an event—a political process—through which complaints about others may be aired and character may be generated. What was said about someone behind her back is what gets disputed in a he-said-she-said, while other deep-seated concerns and breaches underlying disputes are left unspoken.

Initiating a dispute may in part be influenced by jealousies among play group members or the perception that someone considers herself above others of the social group.[21] For example, with reference to the extended confrontation in #1, the girls were annoyed with Kerry because although she was the same age as they were she had skipped a grade and got straight A's on her report card. In addition, she would often talk about how her mother made her save money for college (a future event never discussed by the other girls). The fact of her being in a higher grade was accentuated by her constantly anticipating for Bea and Martha what to expect in junior high school. Girls were jealous of Stacey and Deniece because of their popularity with boys. When Stacey was asked to join Ruby, Kerry, and Bea's social club, she refused, saying that she already had a club, and one with more desirable boys as members. Deniece received more attention from boys than any other girl in the neighborhood, and in contrast to Bea, Martha, Kerry, and Ruby, she was both thin and shapely.

Specific friendship alignments causing jealousies may also lead to arguments. For example, in the following Kerry describes as the reason for a confrontation the incident of Sister's cousin Joyce choosing to play with Kerry rather than Sister:

(37)   MHG: Kerry what happened with uh Stacey
                    and Sister and all them.
        Kerry: Oh they was gettin' ready to fight
                    because she came around here and Sister
                    thought I was gonna take Joyce away from her.

She further elaborates to me the reasons for Sister's jealousy of Kerry as follows:

(38)   Kerry: And she come around the corner wolfin' and all
                    so then Bea came around there and stopped her?
                    And said "Sister you think that
                    Kerry gonna take Joyce away from you."
                    And I and I said, "That's right.
                    Joyce gonna be your cousin *all* the time."
                    And then- then a- and Stacey say
                    "I don't even know why you thinkin' that way."
                    She start cryin'. And then she up there sayin'
                    "Everybody jump on me."
                    And Bea don't even know what she talkin'
                    about.

To provide a sense of the events surrounding a confrontation, one particularly serious he-said-she-said case will be briefly reviewed. The girls became jealous of Annette, who the girls felt acted as if she were better than the others; this was in part because her mother provided her a more extensive wardrobe than anyone else could afford. Most of the girls wore clothes handed down to them by other relatives or purchased at a thrift store; their only new outfits were purchased for wear on the first day of school. Once a week Annette's mother would return from shopping with something new for Annette. In addition, one of Annette's aunts was a seamstress, and she was constantly making her new outfits in the latest styles; for example, Annette was the first girl on the street to have a jump-suit. Complaining about Annette's mother, Martha said the following:

(39)   Martha: She don't want us playin' with Annette
                   so why sh- She try to be so different.
                   She want Annette to have everything best.
                   That's why Annette ain't gonna have no friends.
                   She try to be so selfish.

An additional source of friction resulted from complaints lodged by An-nette's mother against the character of both Bea and her mother:

(40)   Bea: And her mother talkin' 'bout
                   "You stay out day and night.
                   Why don't you go in the house somewhere."
                   I said- so- she said- she said
                   "Don't your mother ever be home?"
                   I said "Yeah sometimes she go out Friday,
                   sometimes she go away."

The dispute structure provided by the he-said-she-said was used to initiate proceedings against Annette, who was believed to have stepped out of line with respect to group norms. After the confrontation, Annette was ostracized from her peers for a month and a half. As part of an extended degradation ceremony (Garfinkel 1967:205), whenever Annette was seen on the street she was made fun of in taunts (line 2) and insults modeled after ritual insults which poked fun at her large lips (lines 9–12) as well as in reformulated cereal jingles such as the "We love you Alphabits" com-mercial (lines 25–42):

(41)
1	Martha:	Hey Annette.
2	Bea:	Hey hey with the BIG LIPS.
3	Kerry:	Eh heh // heh
4	Martha:	Eh heh!
5	Bea:	Walk down the street with it hangin.
6	Kerry:	Eh heh // heh
7	Martha:	Ha ha ha
8	Kerry:	We're the beauty generation.

9	Martha:	Yeah, // she can use her lips
10		to cover her at nighttime.
11	Kerry:	((singing)) We got somp'm to say-ay
12	Martha:	⌈For a, for a blanket.
13	Kerry:	Yep. When it's cold- When she go to
14		school // she don't have to wear no
15		clothes.
16	Kerry:	*h Ulp. Uhl // from her nose down, *h
17	Martha:	Ha ha
18	Kerry:	Hah ha ha
19	Bea:	Heh heh heh heh
20	Kerry:	And tie 'em around her. ((chanting))
21		Dn ne ne neh.
22	Martha:	((singing)) Walkin' down the street
23	Kerry:	When when she went she // when she comes
24		we gonna go w- we gonna go,
25	Bea:	Alphabits.
26	Kerry:	((singing)) We love you Alphabits,
27		⌈Wherever you go
28	Martha:	((singing)) Wherever I go,
29		You're A B C delicious, Oh we love Big Lips.
30	Bea:	You so
31	Kerry:	Heh heh
32	Bea:	Big Lips! We don't love Big Lips. // I'm
33		a say
34	Kerry:	I hate Big Lips.
35	Bea:	((scream))
36	Kerry:	((singing)) We hate you Alphabits,
37		⌈Wherever you go
38	Martha:	Wherever I go,
39	Kerry:	⌈You're A B
40	Bea:	You're A B C D
41	Kerry:	Hateful, now let me see. A B C D nasty.
42		Oh we hate Big Lips.

Annette's brother and mother were also the targets of ridicule. During the ostracism, Annette spent much of her time inside watching television and doing homework. She came outside only for the purpose of watching boys' activities at a time when Bea, the initiator of the proceedings against her, was not around. Even her best friend during that period avoided her as Bea had directed. The ridicule and exclusion from the neighborhood group caused Annette a deep sense of pain, and she told me that it frequently made her cry. Her mother considered moving to another neighborhood, despite the fact that she had a mortgage on their home on Maple Street. The period of ostracism finally ended on one of the most important of children's holidays, Halloween night. Bea met Annette as the two were in costume and invited her to go to several houses together trick or treating. Annette's reincorporation into the group thus occurred on an occasion of heightened ritual impact fitting to the intensity of emotion experienced during the prior degradation ceremony.[22]

While jealousies about girls' relationships with others or displeasure with someone's self-perceptions may lie at the root of ill feelings, such concerns do not become the official issues in arguments between girls. The act of talking about someone behind her back does, however, provide a culturally recognizable offense which entities a girl to make displays of righteous indignation and thus may trigger formal confrontation proceedings. This forum allows for the accuser to discuss complaints which she has against the defendant. That which gets debated in a formal legal case, therefore, might not be what generated the dispute but rather what anyone knowledgeable of the culture could see as an offense warranting verbal retributive action.

Although dispute is an essential component of the he-said-she-said process, this does not mean that all confrontations have the same character or level of seriousness. Instead, the possibilities for organization provided by the basic structure of the he-said-she-said can be keyed (Goffman 1974) in a variety of different ways, to produce events that range from playful short disputes, which resemble games more than fights, to confrontations so serious that girls are driven from the play group. Upon completion of a nonserious confrontation, children may continue the play that occurred prior to the event. Indeed, the entire he-said-she-said can be seen as an elaborate procedure, at times almost a game, in which participants create and reform alliances of two against one, a type of social structure typical of the nonhierarchical girls' group.[23] In fact, the long he-said-she-said dispute involving Kerry, Julia, and Bea analyzed in this chapter is played out in this manner; Kerry, the target of the offenses, rejoined the play group after a brief separation during which she ate lunch and took her younger sister to school.

Although talk about talk can lead to serious consequences—depriving someone of her basic right to interact with others in her play group for a period of time—confrontations did not lead to permanent ruptures in social relationships (the ostracism noted above was the strongest action taken) or to more violent behavior, as in some societies. Indeed, as argued by Katriel (1985:487) with respect to a form of Israeli children's argument called *brogez*, ritualized ways of handling disagreement provide a way of expressing aggression without disrupting the group's social order.

In most societies, public disputes involve third parties as mediators and compromises are possible outcomes. According to Nader and Todd (1978), "conflict" phases are characteristically dyadic, while "disputes" (events in which conflict becomes public) involve "a third party who intervenes either at the behest of one or both of the principals or their supporters" (ibid.:15). The he-said-she-said presents an exception to this generalization. Third parties in the he-said-she-said are important not in the confrontation but rather in the reporting stage; they act as instigators setting up a confrontation at a future stage.[24] Disputes in the confrontation stage are handled directly by those who are either defendant or plaintiff, or parties acting in one of these roles. Although spectators can align themselves with one of the protagonists, if they attempt to get the dispute off track they may be sanctioned by the principals. By participating in a public dispute, accusers attempt to generate moral character through displays of righteous indignation and try to demonstrate that they are capable of "fighting they own battles." Compromises do not occur in the he-said-she-said confrontation.

Despite the fact that the social organization of the confrontation is dyadic, the structure of the utterances defining the field of action is triadic. Although "third parties" are not present as mediators, their relevance is invoked in the opening accusation statements. In framing the offense as a report from an intermediary party, the accuser provides an "out" for the defendant in her next move. In that the defendant has available a number of procedures for denying the charge, she need not admit the offense, thereby leaving the accuser exposed as someone who delivers empty accusations. Thus both accuser and defendant cooperate in maintaining each other's sense of face in the confrontation. The type of legal proceeding being described occurs neither in a specifiable place nor at a specific time. Yet although it occurs within what appears to be an unstructured setting, the event itself has a highly formalized structure.

Although the analysis of gossip has been an important concern in anthropology, as yet few studies have described cultural practices for *generating* actual sequences of conversation which *construct* social organization. Here I have described quite precisely how the he-said-she-said activity is built through an underlying set of cultural procedures that provide a particular ordered field of events, including such things as relevant actions and identities for participants in both the past and the present. The procedures employed to construct opening he-said-she-said accusations do not simply produce sentences with a particular syntactic structure but in addition create a social order through the use of complex linguistic structures of embedding. A next speaker will have to analyze the structure of a preceding utterance and display her understanding of it in order to tie appropriately to the previous speaker; the production of a next utterance requires the integrated use of both cultural and social competence (Moerman and Sacks 1988). Phenomena within the he-said-she-said do not obtain their meaning in isolation, but rather from their position within the entire structure. Thus, categories of person, the structure and interpretation of events, forms of action, and the sequencing of these phenomena through time are interdependent aspects of a single whole. The he-said-she-said event thus provides a resource for realigning the social organization of the moment and reconstituting occasion-specific identities. In that the he-said-she-said itself is a dispute performed in a public arena, such a situation may also be used to rearrange social relationships of the girls' group, through airing grievances and initiating periods of ostracism. This event—with its sequencing of phases (breach, crisis, redress, and reintegration)—resembles what Turner (1980) has discussed as a "social drama."

Section 4

Stories within Dispute Processes

CHAPTER NINE

Perspectives on Stories

Among the children on Maple Street, the word "story" is used in a rather restricted way, primarily in the expression "telling stories"; this sense of the term refers to a false account made in response to an accusation, as in "And she gonna tell you another story anyway." However, I will use the term in a much broader way to refer to narratives and other tellings in conversation. The story in this more general sense has received extensive study within many different disciplines.[1] Thus,

- Stories are the primary speech genre analyzed by folklore.
- Narratives constitute a key locus for Labov's attempts to move sociolinguistics to the analysis of units larger than the sentence.
- For conversation analysts, stories provide crucial data for the study of the interactive organization of multiunit turns.
- Goffman used narrative to demonstrate how speakers in everyday life are able to create through the resources of talk a whole theater, animating both characters and the reactions of others to them.
- The process of scripting stories has received extensive study within cognitive science.
- Literary criticism has always taken the story as its primary object of study, and in recent research, largely through the influence of Bakhtin, an expanded view of the dialogic organization present in written stories has provided fresh insights into how stories are organized within talk itself.

Substantively stories are one of the principal places where members of a society use language to encode and shape complex events that are central to the organization of their culture. It is therefore not surprising that anthropologists have paid particular attention to them in a wide variety of forms, from gossip and legal dispute to myths, and that they have provided key data for some of the more important paradigms for the study of culture, including Lévi-Strauss and the ethnography of speaking.[2] Stories have thus been especially important in many different attempts to analyze the distinctively human capacity to use language to think about the world in systematic ways, create art, and build culture.

One question that emerges immediately is, what constitutes a story?

For reasons that will become clear in a moment, I will not attempt to provide a precise answer to this question. Instead, in this chapter I will use the problems posed in attempting to define a story to compare some of the approaches to the study of narrative that are most relevant to my own analysis. In Chapters 10 and 11, some of this research will be applied to analysis of how the Maple Street children use stories both to strategically restructure the social organization of the talk of the moment and to initiate larger social events.

9.1 THE COMPLEXITY OF STORIES

Despite the ease with which both analysts and participants identify a strip of talk as a "story," stories are in fact extraordinarily complex speech events. One very simple indication of this is their length. While many of the speech acts that occur within conversation can be performed within an utterance or two (consider, for example, greetings, accusations, insults, promises, questions, requests, etc.), stories typically contain many utterances. Moreover, they may contain within their boundaries a range of different kinds of talk and action. Thus, while some of the utterances within a story might report a sequence of events, others will provide the current speaker's evaluation of those events. Yet other parts will contain talk that is to be attributed not to the current narrator but rather to the characters being animated within the story. Stories thus provide a prime example of heteroglossia.

The diverse voices and events that constitute a story are woven together into a coherent whole through use of syntactic devices of considerable complexity. Such linguistic structure is complemented by an equally vivid use of intonation, gesture, and other paralinguistic phenomena. As Goffman (1974) has noted, by telling a story a speaker is able to bring alive in the midst of ordinary conversation what is in essence a vernacular theatrical performance; the teller enacts the characters whose exploits are being recounted and, with talk of a different type, sets the scene for those events, provides necessary background information, and comments on their meaning. By incorporating such dramatic and aesthetic elements, stories become a central locus for artistic performance within talk; and folklorists and others interested in verbal art have devoted considerable attention to them. From a slightly different perspective, stories are one of the prototypical places where events from beyond the immediate interaction are reported on and incorporated into that interaction.

Finally, stories are told to an *audience*, and although this feature of their organization has frequently been overlooked, what work has been done,[3] as well as the analysis to be developed in Chapters 10 and 11, demonstrates that both *who* stories are addressed to and *interaction between speakers and recipients during their telling* are quite central to their organization.

9.2 COMPLEMENTARY APPROACHES TO THE ANALYSIS OF NARRATIVE

In view of the complexity of events found within stories, it is not surprising that different research approaches to them have focused on different types of phenomena, data, and issues. Several of the approaches that are most relevant to the analysis to be developed in Chapters 10 and 11, including the *narrative analysis* of Labov and his associates (Labov and Waletzky 1968, Labov 1972a), Goffman's (1974) *frame analysis*, and work on stories within *conversation analysis*, will now be briefly described.

9.2.1 LABOV'S NARRATIVE ANALYSIS

One of the more influential recent approaches to the study of stories has been the analysis of narrative developed by Labov. Labov and Waletzky (1968:287) define narrative as "one method of recapitulating past experience by matching a verbal sequence of clauses to the sequence of events which (it is inferred) actually occurred."[4] Such a definition includes elements of both *content* (restricting narrative to reports about past events) and *structure* (a particular ordering of clauses). Work to be developed in Chapter 11 will reveal that limiting narrative to reports about *past* events is far too restrictive. For example, the girls on Maple Street can use the procedures available for constructing he-said-she-said events to build *future stories*, hypothetical descriptions of confrontations that have not yet occurred. Despite this, Labov's definition constitutes an important point of departure.

One of Labov's goals in analyzing narrative was the development of method and theory within linguistics that could move beyond the sentence. As part of this project, he paid particular attention to tying the temporal organization of narrative to linguistic structure. For example, Labov and Fanshel (1977:107) state that "the structure of narrative is established by the presence of *temporal junctures* between these narrative clauses." The stories that Labov collected were not composed only of narrative clauses, but instead contained many *free clauses* (Labov 1972a:361) that did not form part of the temporal sequence of events being reported within the narrative; for example, a narrator might comment on the events being reported. To account for such phenomena, Labov (1972a) developed a rather elaborate, and very influential, model of the internal structure of a narrative. Among the features identified (ibid.:370) are the following:

A: *The Abstract*	What is this story about?
B: *Orientation*	Who, When, What, Where?
C: *Complicating Action*	Then what happened?
D: *Evaluation*	So what?
E: *Resolution*	What finally happened?
F: *The Coda*	Signals that the narrative is complete.

Such a structure has a clear affinity to the classic plot typologies developed within folklore (for example, Propp 1968).[5] However, a key question for Labov was the issue of what constituted an *effective* narrative, and he analyzed the structure he found in terms of how it contributed to forestalling a recipient's "so what." Thus he notes (Labov 1972a:370) that only C, the complicating action, is necessary to recognize what he calls a narrative (i.e., an ordered report of past events). The other components of this structure function to ensure the effectiveness of the narrative by providing information necessary for the proper understanding of the events being reported.

Crucial to the appropriate understanding of a story is "evaluation," described by Labov and Waletzky (1968:200) as a means used by the narrator to indicate the point of the narrative, its raison d'être—why it was told and what the narrator is getting at. Within such a perspective, *evaluation* of the import of a narrative takes on special importance. Labov identifies a particular place in the narrative structure (i.e., just before the resolution) where this process of assessing the events in the story is focused. However, he also examines how processes of evaluation[6] function throughout the narrative (Labov 1972a:369). Moreover, evaluation can be done in a range of different ways. For example, the narrator can explicitly tell the listener what the point of the story is (ibid.:371); however, a storyteller can also *embed* the evaluation by having characters themselves comment on the significance of the events they are engaged in, or by having reported actions demonstrate the import of what is being reported. Such processes of evaluation, and in particular the way in which the actions of a character can be used to display teller's alignment to an event, are quite central to some of the analysis that will be developed in Chapters 10 and 11.

9.2.2 Goffman's Frame Analysis

A different perspective toward examining the internal structure of stories is taken by Goffman (1974:496–559) in his essay on "the frame analysis of talk." Goffman (ibid.:516–544) argues that while telling a story, a speaker not only portrays events but also animates characters who produce talk of their own, and provides indications of her own alignment toward the events being recounted.[7] Building on Vološinov's (1973) analysis of *reported speech*, Goffman notes that quoted talk in stories poses problems in "framing" for both analyst and listener; at one and the same time, quotations are the words of a present speaker, replaying past experience, as well as those of a character in the story who is being animated by the teller. He argues that such phenomena provide a way of moving beyond the limitations of traditional sociological analysis which "breaks up the individual into multiple roles but does not suggest that further decimation is required" (Goffman 1974:516).[8] Goffman finds it necessary to subdivide the speaking individual, "I," for example, into a number of different entities; instead of occupying alternative roles in separate domains of action, these entities coexist as different levels of an intricately laminated participation structure. Consider the following brief excerpt from a story told by Barbara about a policeman who chased people away after a fight during a school strike:

```
(1) 1    Barbara:    An' boy I ran across~the~street
    2                Say "Ikay.=I LIVE RIGHT HERE."
    3                     (1.2)
    4    Barbara:    He said ((thuggishly in bass voice))
    5 →              "You better- you better live right here."
    6                That cop. Ool::: (5.4) That was ba:d today.
```

In order to answer the question "Who is talking" in line 5, it is necessary to distinguish at least the following entities:

1. The *principal* or *originator* of a statement, the party "held responsible for having willfully taken up the position to which the meaning of the utterance attests" (Goffman 1974:517), i.e., the policeman whose talk is being quoted. Note, however, that there are many situations, such as a candidate's statement delivered through a spokesman, in which the *speaker* of the statement and the *principal* will not be the same individual. On Maple Street, older children would sometimes tease younger ones by enacting the talk of an adult threatening a younger child. Here the enacted adult, not the actual speaker, is the party credited with the force behind the threatening statements.

2. The *emitter* of the statement in the current interaction, "the current, actual sounding box from which the transmission of articulated sound comes," in the present data Barbara.

3. However, Barbara does not simply speak these words but rather enacts the character who performs them. It therefore is necessary to see Barbara operating in another capacity as well, as an *animator*, who both enacts the talk and the speaker being quoted, and simultaneously comments on them.

4. The character who is being enacted, or *figure*, i.e., the enacted policeman. In these data the figure is the same as the principal, but that need not always be the case.

5. In some circumstances it is possible to also have a *strategist* (ibid.:523), an entity who diagnoses situations and decides what positions a principal should take. For example, in Chapter 11 we will see how girls on Maple Street can project an upcoming he-said-she-said confrontation, and debate the effectiveness of various statements that the principals involved in the dispute might make.

6. Finally, it is possible to have something like a presidential speech writer, a party who is the *author* of statements used by a principal but not herself the party who becomes socially responsible for making those statements (ibid.).

In order to see the complexity that structures make possible for even a brief strip of talk, and the way in which these structural possibilities provided the children on Maple Street with rich resources for strategically manipulating talk and interaction, consider what happened after I answered an apparently innocuous question from Bea:

(2)   *Boy skates down the street.*

     Bea: That boy have ugly sneaks don't he.
     MHG: Mm yeah.
     Bea: HEY BOY
  →   THAT GIRL SAY *YOU* HAVE UGLY SNEAKS!

Here I become the *principal* responsible for a statement whose content was *authored* by Bea (perhaps as part of a larger *strategy*), and which is indeed also *emitted* by Bea. In addressing the boy, Bea *animates* both talk that is attributed to me[9] and me as a *figure*. Finally, such structures can be used strategically to pursue larger projects, for example, to attempt to initiate a he-said-she-said confrontation.

9.2.3 Conversation Analysis

Labov's description of evaluation and Goffman's analysis of the laminated entities involved in the framing of talk are two approaches to the study of narrative that are quite relevant to the analysis to be developed in Chapters 10 and 11. A third, very important, perspective is provided by Sacks's (1970, 1974, 1978) work on stories. Sacks's point of departure is not the isolated story, or specific events within it, but rather the way in which stories are embedded within conversation and interaction. In this respect his work differs from that of Labov and Goffman, as well as from most other approaches to the study of narrative.

Since the approach taken by Sacks not only provides a particular framework for the analysis of stories but also has strong theoretical and methodological consequences for what will be included within the scope of analysis, it is relevant to briefly note the consequences his perspective has for the collection and analysis of data. It is quite common for anthropologists, linguists, and folklorists to extract stories from the processes of interaction within which they emerge in a particular culture before even starting to perform analysis on them (Lévi-Strauss 1963 provides a particularly vivid and important example), and indeed to ignore indigenous interaction by eliciting stories themselves. Thus all too frequently, research investigating the internal structure of stories is based on those that are "collected" by the researcher. The interviewer generally solicits the story from an informant by making an initial request for one. For example, Watson (1973:260) reports, "A child who wished to tell a story responded to the eliciting frame, *Tell us a story.*" While such an approach is valuable for the collection of linguistic data and for understanding the structure of a story produced in response to a question, it does not aid us in understanding how the story might have been initiated in conversation without having been initially warranted by the interviewer's question, how it might have been told to another member of the culture instead of an outsider, or how it might have functioned as a component of larger social practices within the culture. Even in circumstances in which stories are recorded in indigenous speech settings, there is frequently a tendency to extract the story from its interactive context for purposes of analysis. For example, despite the great, and productive, effort of folklorists to gather data in indigenous settings, there is as yet little analysis of how recipients of stories shape their emergent development. Unfortunately, elicitation practices seem typical of much anthropological fieldwork.[10] Levinson (1983:369) has raised the possibility that "humans as a species are as much characterized by conversational activity as they are by differing cultures, complex social systems and tool-making." If interaction does in fact provide the ground upon which stories (and other forms of talk) are shaped (Goffman 1964), it is tragic if anthropologists working in societies that could provide important comparative information return with only the products of this process (for example, *texts* of myths and stories) while ignoring Margaret Mead's (1973) call to bring back records of the interaction itself.[11]

Among the issues to which Sacks devotes special attention in his analysis is the question of how stories emerge within conversation in the first place. His investigation of this process permits us to see some of the structural features of stories identified by Labov and Waletzky (1968) from a complementary, interactive perspective.

Most analysis of stories takes as its point of departure the fact that stories are long stretches of talk, in the sense that they contain not just one but multiple sentences or clauses. It is precisely this internal differentiation within a single speech form that makes it possible to identify structurally distinct components within the story, and to analyze both their patterning and the alternative functions that different components might perform. When stories within conversation are examined, it is found that the multiunit turn containing the body of the story is characteristically preceded by a particular two-part sequence: (1) in a single-unit turn, the party who wishes to act as teller *announces* the availability of a story; (2) recipients then ask to hear the story, or provide grounds for rejecting it. For example:

(3)   Barbara: My aunt died.
        Martha: Died, what happened.
        Barbara: ((*tells story*))

The body of the story thus occurs only after speaker and recipient(s) have systematically provided for its occurrence:

Teller   *Story Preface*
Recipient   *Request to Hear Story*
Teller   *Multiunit Story*

By virtue of the interactive work that they are doing, story prefaces systematically contain particular components. For example, in order to tell recipients that the story will be news to them (and thus intercept one of the most common grounds for rejecting a story), the preface frequently contains a statement about *when* the incident to be recounted occurred (e.g., "The funniest thing happened to me *last night*"). Agreeing to hear a story poses systematic tasks for recipients; for example, at its climax or conclusion they will be expected to respond to it in an appropriate way. Prefaces thus contain a *characterization* of the story about to be told. Recipients can use this characterization first to analyze the talk being heard for what might constitute a possible conclusion, and second, as a guide to the type of response that is expected from them (e.g., if speaker characterizes the story as being about "a terrible thing," recipient is *not* being asked to laugh at its conclusion). In other work, Sacks (1978) provides extensive analysis of the internal structure of stories, including how particular aspects of their structure shape their possibilities for transmission, the different interactive and cognitive consequences of a story built from personal experience as opposed to the telling of a preformulated joke or tale, how different audiences might glean very different types of information from the same story, and what the organization of stories can tell us about how human beings organize their experience of the events they encounter in the world.

The way in which a story articulates with the conversation that it both emerges from and returns to has been analyzed in detail by Jefferson (1978). According to Jefferson (ibid.:220), "stories emerge from turn-by-turn talk, that is, are *locally occasioned* by it, and, upon their completion, stories reengage turn-by-turn talk, that is, are *sequentially implicative* for it." Jefferson (ibid.:245) notes in addition that "There is . . . evidence that a story not only articulates with turn-by-turn talk at its edges, but throughout. Roughly, a story is not, in principle, a block of talk, but is constructed of 'segments' via which teller's talk can alternate with recipient's."

In analysis of the *participation structures* provided by a story, C. Goodwin (1984) finds first, that the telling of a story can partition its audience by providing telling-specific identities for different kinds of recipients, and second, that participants attend in detail to differences between alternative types of story components, and indeed use such structure as a resource for the organization of their interaction while the story is in progress. A storytelling is thus constituted by the collaborative but differentiated work of multiple participants.

In brief, work in conversation analysis has demonstrated that the basic shape that stories take in conversation, the way in which they articulate with the talk that surrounds them, and events that occur in the midst of the telling itself are all interactively organized. In addition, they have provided detailed analysis of a range of types of organization found in the midst of stories, such as laughter (Jefferson 1979, 1984) and assessments (C. Goodwin and M. H. Goodwin 1987; M. H. Goodwin 1980b). Such analysis demonstrates the importance of collecting stories in their indigenous interactive contexts, and the contributions that conversation analysis has made by analyzing stories as interactive phenomena.

9.2.4 OTHER RELEVANT RESEARCH

The work of researchers in diverse fields has converged upon the problem of how the telling of a story is accomplished as a *joint production*.[12] Linguists such as Tannen (1981) and Polanyi analyze interactive work in storytelling. For example, Polanyi demonstrates that "the point of a story should not be taken as a fixed formal aspect of the story as originally told" (Polanyi 1979:207). She discusses how speaker and audience jointly "negotiate for what the story will be agreed upon to have been about" (ibid). Conarration in storytelling has also been analyzed by linguists (Ochs, Taylor, Rudolph, and Smith 1989; Ochs, Smith, and Taylor 1989), anthropologists (Watson-Gegeo and Boggs 1977; Scollon and Scollon 1980:17), sociologists (Eder 1988), and medical researchers (Mishler 1986). Feminist social scientists such as Jenkins (1984), Fishman (1978), and Edelsky (1982) have investigated coparticipation in the telling of a story by women; they argue that the type of floor (Edelsky 1982) or "support work" (Fishman 1978; Jenkins 1984) which females provide differs from the competitive nature of male conversational style.[13]

Recent work in folklore and the ethnography of speaking has analyzed the relationship of storytelling to larger social scenes (Abrahams 1982; Bauman 1972, 1986; Ben-Amos 1975; Briggs 1985; Duranti 1988; Georges 1969; Kirshenblatt-Gimblett 1974; McCarl 1976, 1980).[14] Such "performance-centered" (Abrahams 1968, 1970, 1972; Bauman 1977; Hymes 1962, 1972) studies argue for the need to investigate the relationship between folkloristic materials, such as "storytelling events" (Georges 1969), "and other aspects of social life *in situ* . . . where that relation actually obtains, the communicative events in which folklore is used" (Hymes 1972:46).[15] In moving toward a performance-centered approach, folklorists have begun to seriously explore the long-neglected study of folklore's social functions.[16] Analysis of features of the internal structure of stories has been the primary focus of research by sociolinguists, anthropologists, and folklorists influenced by Labov and Waletzky's (1968, Labov 1972a) studies of narrative (Brady 1980; Kernan 1977; Polanyi 1979, 1985; Pratt 1977; Stahl 1977; Watson 1973; Wolfson 1978) and Goffman's (1974) notion of "frame" (Babcock 1977; Bauman 1986; Schiffrin 1980; Sherzer 1980; Tannen 1979). As yet, however, few researchers have investigated specific texts in detail to examine how social organization is achieved and negotiated within them. Neither have researchers examined how the fact that stories can be part of larger speech

events embedded in social processes extending beyond the immediate social encounter[17] is consequential for the construction of a story by speaker
and its interpretation by hearer.

Chapters 10 and 11 will examine the ways that boys and girls make use
of stories in a particular context—disputes. I examine how stories are jointly
constructed by hearers and speakers, as well as how stories emerge within
interaction and function to accomplish specific social tasks. The contrasting
ways in which stories are built and used within dispute processes reflect
differing concerns of boys' and girls' cultures.

CHAPTER TEN

Stories as Participation Structures

In order to investigate how stories constitute tools for accomplishing particular social tasks, we must look at how they can be used to structure events and situations within argumentative sequences. As noted by Turner (1986:39–43), a world of theater is often created while redressing grievances, as conflict provides the quintessential arena in which "the structures of group experience (*Erlebnis*) are replicated, dismembered, remembered, refashioned, and mutely or vocally made meaningful" (ibid.:43). When stories are used in dispute processes, they permit the playing out of an event in full dramatic regalia; through a multiplicity of voices (Bakhtin 1981), the teller of the story, as well as her hearers, animates principal figures in the story and offers her commentary upon the unfolding action and characters.

In the present chapter I will examine how the distinctive structural properties of a *story* can be used to restructure the social organization of an emerging argument. To do this I analyze in some detail a single dispute between some of the Maple Street boys. Initially the argument is shaped as a sequence of paired exchanges between its two principal protagonists. One of the disputing parties then introduces a story. This switch involves more than simply movement from one genre of talk to another. More important, the story *expands the participation framework* of the dispute. This makes it possible for parties not initially involved in the argument to align themselves with particular positions within it, and introduces into it events from beyond the immediate interaction. These phenomena are quite consequential for the subsequent development of the dispute. As recipients are recruited into the story, they may transform talk they hear into next moves appropriate to their positions vis-à-vis the characters and events in the story.

The complete dispute can be found in Appendix C, and the reader might want to look at it now. Because of the length and complexity of this material, I will focus on extracts from the complete exchange, and introduce the unfolding dispute bit by bit as the analysis develops.

10.1 DISPUTES BUILT THROUGH RECIPROCAL COUNTERS

One very common way in which the boys on Maple Street built disputes was by producing a series of *paired counters*. Before we turn to the sequence that will be the principal focus of analysis in this chapter, another exchange that illustrates some of the properties of paired counters will be briefly examined. Nine boys, aged nine through fourteen, are making slingshots in the back yard of Malcolm and Tony Johnson. The boys have informally divided themselves into two teams, one under the direction of Malcolm (aged 13), and the other led by Tony (aged 14). Tony is not only the oldest but also the strongest boy present, and indeed he usually spends his time with an older group of boys.

The fact that play is occurring in their yard provides Malcolm and Tony with a strategic resource that they can invoke in a variety of ways. For example, if other boys challenge them, Malcolm or Tony can demand that the offender leave their property, although this demand will not automatically be obeyed. Note how Chopper challenges Tony's demand in lines 3, 5–6, and 8 of the following:

(1)

1	Chopper		The heck with you.
2	Tony:	⌈	Why don't you get out my yard.
3	Chopper:	⌊	Why don' you *make* me get out the yard.
		⌈	
4	Tony:		I *know* you don't want that.
5	Chopper:		You're not gonna make me get out the yard
6		⌊	cuz you can't.
		⌈	
7	Tony:		Don't force me.
8	Chopper:		You can't. Don't force *me* to *hu*rt you.
9			((snickering)) Khh Khhh!
		⌊	
10	Tony:		((to his team)) Now you gotta make
11		⌈	your noodles.
12	Chopper:		You hear what I said boy?

Argument in this exchange proceeds through a sequence of paired counters. The three left brackets in the data display mark two-turn sequences in which a first challenge or threat is answered by a counter to it.

The first utterance of the bracketed pair is in addition an answer to the prior action.

Using such couplets to build an argument shapes the interaction of the moment in distinctive ways. First, it both focuses talk and restricts participation in the debate. Although nine people are present, only two parties speak in the sequence. Focusing participation in this fashion is a systematic consequence of the type of talk that is occurring here. Within each couplet,

- B challenges what A has said.
- This makes it relevant for A to answer that challenge.
- A's answer in turn provides for the relevance of a new response from B, etc.

Using reciprocal counters to build opposition thus has the effect of restricting participation in the sequence to a small set of *focal participants*,[1] most frequently just two speakers (although there is the possibility of more than one participant siding with a particular stance). Other forms of dispute, such as arguments about the truth or falseness of events, are not as restricted to interchange between parties representing two competing positions (Maynard 1986b); however, return and exchange moves characteristically return the floor to prior speaker, as each subsequent challenge selects prior speaker as next speaker.

Second, the protagonists in this sequence talk in relatively short turns which typically are not interrupted. Within the context of the event that has been in progress, this is striking. The boys have divided themselves spatially into two separate teams, each making its own ammunition in preparation for the slingshot fight, and during most of this work parties within each group have been carrying on separate conversations. The effect has been considerable simultaneous talk. The emergence of the dispute sequence creates a point of focus for all present. It thus provides organization not only for those who talk within it, but also for the others present who become *ratified overhearers* to it.

Third, within such couplets subsequent speakers display the aptness of a return, as well as its immediate local relevance, by systematically reusing, but changing, elements of the talk being responded to. An opponent's own words are used against him.

These same structures are found again in another exchange that occurred a short time later:

(2) 1   Tony: Gimme the *things*.

2   Chop: You sh:ut up you *big* lips. (Y'all been
3   hangin' around with thieves.)
4   Tony: (*Shut* up.)

```
 5   Chop:  ⌈  Don't gimme that.=I'm not talkin' to
 6          |  you.
 7          |       (1.4)
 8   Tony:  ⌊  I'm talkin' to y:ou!


 9   Chop:  ⌈  Ah you better sh:ut up with your
10          |  little- di:ngy sneaks.
11          |       (1.4)
12   Tony:  |  I'm a dingy your hea:d.=How would you
13          ⌊  like that.
```

Once again talk becomes restricted to two focal participants, who challenge each other in comparatively short turns which are not interrupted. Moreover, in line 3 of #1 Chopper constructs a return by making use of Tony's own sentence—"Why don't you get out my yard"—as an embedded component of the counter to that very sentence:

(1) 2   Tony: Why don't you get out my yard.
    3   Chopper: Why don't you *make* me get out the
                   yard.

Similarly, in line 8 Chopper uses what Tony said in line 7 as the point of departure for his counter:

(1) 7   Tony: Don't force me.
    8   Chopper: You can't. Don't force *me* to *hu*rt you.

In brief, argumentative sequences built from paired counters shape both the interaction of the moment and the talk occurring within it in distinctive ways.

Insofar as each next action establishes the relevance of prior speaker's producing a subsequent return, one issue that can arise is how such sequences are ended. Looking at line 10 of #1, we find that at a certain point Tony simply turns his attention from Chopper to other activities. Thus, despite the fact that Chopper wants to pursue the sequence—note his "You hear what I said boy?" in line 12—he is unable to do so without Tony's continuing coparticipation. Moreover, although an extended dispute occurs here, there is no clear demonstration that one of the protagonists has gotten the upper hand over the other.

One might ask how a speaker in the midst of a sequence such as this could design talk that would prevent a move such as the one made by Tony.

For example, would it be possible to build a participation framework in which such a unilateral exit would no longer be a strong possibility?

10.2 RESTRUCTURING
A DISPUTE

Further examination of the second dispute between Chopper and Tony provides one indication of how a speaker might design a new form of participation framework which would preclude the liabilities incurred in the strategy of switching topic, which Tony utilized in #1 above. In line 15 Chopper initiates what becomes the first in a series of stories about Tony (lines 19–25) that portray him as having acted in a cowardly fashion in the past.

```
(2)
  12    Tony:       I'm a dingy your hea:d.=How would you
  13                like that.
  14                     (0.4)
  15    Chopper:    No you won't you little- ⌈*h Guess what.
  16    Jack:                              ⌊(°foul) foul
  17                thing.
  18                     (0.4)
  19    Chopper:    Lemme~tell~ya.=Guess what. (0.8) We
  20                was comin' home from practice, (0.4)
  21                and, three boys came up there (.) and
  22                asked~us~for~money~and~Tony~did~like~
  23                this. (0.6)
  24                *hh ((raising hands up))
  25                "I AIN'T GOT n(h)(hh)⌈o (°m(h)oney)"
  26    Pete:                           ⌊Ah~hih~ha,
  27                *hh Hah~hah!
```

Let us look in more detail at how this story is introduced. In line 15 Chopper starts a counter to what Tony has just said but breaks it off before it reaches completion. He then produces a prototypical story preface, "Guess what," and subsequently in lines 18–24 tells a story about Tony. With his preface he signals that he has a multiutterance unit to complete which will extend over several turns. Although generally following such a preface a recipient provides a warrant for the telling by responding at that point, here storyteller launches quickly into a story.

```
(2)
  12    Tony:       I'm a dingy your hea:d.=How would you
  13                like that.
  14                     (0.4)
```

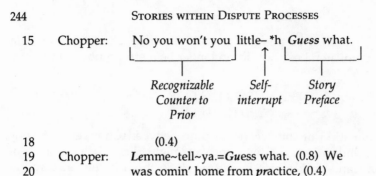

18		(0.4)
19	Chopper:	Lemme~tell~ya.=Guess what. (0.8) We
20		was comin' home from practice, (0.4)

Such a move has a range of consequences. First, since the utterance containing Chopper's counter is not brought to completion, Tony is not given the opportunity to respond to it. The return and exchange sequence has in effect ended.

Second, the story invokes a participation framework that is quite different from that provided by the aborted counter. The *counter* locates Tony as its specific addressee—for example, with the second-person pronoun in line 15—and makes relevant particular types of next actions, such as return counters, from him and not others. Dialogue is restricted to two persons. By way of contrast, *the story is addressed to all present*, and indeed Tony, who is now referred to in third person, is no longer the exclusive or even the principal addressee of Chopper's talk. Rather than being situated as onlookers to a dispute that does not concern them, others present now become the *audience* to the story.

Third, the actions that become relevant as responses to a story are quite different from those appropriate to the counters. Recipients have the opportunity to *evaluate* the events heard in the story, and publicly display that evaluation. Insofar as members of the audience are active coparticipants in the production of a story (C. Goodwin 1984, 1986), they gain rights to participate in the telling in distinctive ways. Moreover, through the way in which it is organized, Chopper's story proposes that the evaluation of events within it will be of a distinctive type: one that will challenge the stance that Tony is trying to assert in the current encounter. To examine this process in more detail, we will look first at how Tony is depicted within the story, and second at the *alignment displays* and commentary on Tony's actions provided by Chopper as he describes them.

10.3 ENACTING THE TALK
OF ANOTHER

Within the story, Tony is portrayed as having acted in a cowardly fashion. When approached by three boys who asked him for money, Tony is described as having displayed fear through his actions—holding up his hands in the face of the threat—and words—"*I AIN'T* GOT n(h)(hh)o °m(h)oney":

(2)
```
19    Chopper:    Lemme~tell~ya.=Guess what. (0.8) We
20                was comin' home from practice, (0.4)
21                and, three boys came up there (.) and
22                asked~us~for~money~and~Tony~did~like~
23                this. (0.6)
24 →              *hh ((raising hands up))
25 →              "I AIN'T GOT n(h)(hh)[o °m(h)oney"
26    Pete:                           Ah-hih-ha,
```

To portray Tony as a coward, Chopper *quotes* something that he said. In terms of Goffman's (1974) frame analysis, Chopper uses the quoted talk to *animate* Tony as a *figure* who displays a particular type of character through the actions he takes in a moment of stress. The quoting of another's past words is common in storytelling. Indeed, Bakhtin (1981:337) has argued that "The transmission and assessment of the speech of others, the discourse of another, is one of the most widespread and fundamental topics of human speech. In all areas of life and ideological activity, our speech is filled to overflowing with other people's words." Moreover, Vološinov (1973) has argued that a speaker never simply reports the talk of another but instead, in the very process of animating that talk, comments on it and shows his or her own alignment to it (see also the discussion of *footing* in Goffman 1981). The present data provide a particularly clear example of this process. As Chopper speaks the words "no(h)(hh)o m(h)oney," he starts to embed laugh tokens in the talk being quoted. This laughter is heard not as something that Tony said within the past event being recounted, but rather as comments by the current speaker, Chopper, on those words. While quoting Tony's talk, Chopper is simultaneously laughing at what Tony said. Events such as this demonstrate the importance of distinguishing, within a single strip of talk, between a *principal* responsible for a statement and the *animator* who quotes that talk while commenting on it in the present (Goffman 1974). Such phenomena are crucial to the way in which *evaluation* is accomplished within stories.

In the present data, such a process is heightened by the way in which, instead of simply reporting what Tony said, Chopper *enacts* his behavior at the moment of climax. First with the phrase "Tony did like this," Chopper announces that he will perform an enactment. He then nonvocally mimics the way in which Tony lifted his hands up. Vocally the talk that follows this action is marked as an enactment by animation cues such as increased volume (indicated by capital letters) and emphasis (italicized words, the italicization marking high pitch) which focuses attention on the initial part of the reported denial: "*I AIN'T* GOT."

10.4 THE AUDIENCE TO
THE STORY

What Chopper does not only demonstrates the complexity of talk that can occur in the midst of conversational narratives—their intrinsic intertextuality (as text from one scene is embedded within the talk of another) and the way in which speakers in the midst of ordinary conversation can author, enact, animate, and comment on indigenous dramatic performances (Goffman 1974)—but also reshapes the field of action within which interaction is occurring. Thus, instead of treating people other than Tony as overhearers to a dispute with two ratified protagonists, Chopper is now inviting an *audience* to participate in the talk of the moment. Indeed, other work (M. H. Goodwin 1980b) has demonstrated that heightened dramatizations in the midst of speech, such as the enactment performed by Chopper, can function to obtain *enhanced* responses from recipients. Moreover, Chopper proposes that the talk being heard should be evaluated and responded to in a particular way. For example, the laugh tokens he embeds within this talk can function not simply as an individual commentary on what is being reported, but as *invitations* to recipients to coparticipate in the laugh (Jefferson 1979). Indeed, that is precisely what happens here. Before Chopper's animation has reached its conclusion, Pete (lines 26–27) is laughing with him:

(2)

25	Chopper:	*"I AIN'T* GOT n(h)(hh)$_\lceil$o °m(h)oney."
26 →	Pete:	Ah~hih~ha,
27 →		*hh Hah~hah!
28	Chopper:	((snicker)) khh
29	( ):	(° look $_\lceil$good.)
30	Pete:	*hh
31 →	Tokay:	You *di:*$_\lceil$d, ((smile intonation))
32	Pete:	Aw:,
33	Chopper:	*hhh~ ((snicker)) Khh $_\lceil$°Hey O(h)ssie.
34 →	Malcolm:	Ah~*ha*~aa~aa Ah~*ha*//ha

Just after the conclusion of the animation, Tokay and Malcolm join Chopper and Pete in the laughter. Thus, very shortly after Chopper abandons his return counter and switches to a story, Tony finds four people laughing at him.

Members of the audience can also provide requests that lead to expansion of the story or replaying of its key scenes. Indeed, asking for such elaboration is one of the prototypical methods available to recipients to demonstrate that the story has engrossed them and to display their interest in the events that it is reporting. In the present data, Tokay responds to the story with a number of requests to parties implicated in it:

(2)

25	Chopper	*"I AIN'T* GOT n(h)(hh)ᵣo °m(h)oney."
26	Pete:	Ah-hih-ha,
27		*hh Hah-hah!
28	Chopper:	((*snicker*)) khh
29	( ):	(° look ᵣgood.)
30	Pete:	*hh
31 →	Tokay:	You *di:*ᵣd, ((*smile intonation*))
32	Pete:	Aw:,
33	Chopper:	*hhh~((*snicker*)) Khh ᵣ°Hey O(h)ssie.
34	Malcolm:	Ah~*ha*~aa~aa Ah~*ha*//ha
35 →	Tokay:	You there *Mal*colm,
36	Chopper:	((*snicker*)) *hhKh He was the(hh)re.
37 →	Tokay:	What'd he say *Ch*opper, ((*smile*
38		*intonation*))
39	Chopper:	*hKh Yeah.=
40	Tony:	=You was there ᵣTo*kay!*
41	Chopper:	*hih *hih
42	Chopper:	Lemme~tell ya, An h(h)e sai(hh)d,

Tokay not only requests elaboration of the event being described. Through his questions he also displays intense interest in the report, and with the smile intonation in his voice (lines 31, 37) he aligns himself with Chopper's characterization of Tony.

Actions such as Tokay's are appropriate responses for one who did not participate in the event being described, in that they suggest that recipient does not have direct access to or knowledge of the reported event. There is, however, a systematic possibility for ambiguity with such moves. While an utterance such as "What'd he say *Ch*opper" can be interpreted as a request for unknown information, such a statement can also be used to request a *replay* of a known event. Issues of information management and appreciative response become intertwined here.

Tokay's moves are answered by parties representing two different positions. First, they are answered by the teller, Chopper, who intercepts a request directed to Malcolm ("You there *Mal*colm," line 35) and answers Tokay's request for elaboration of the story ("What'd he say *Ch*opper," line 37). Second, they are answered by the protagonist in the story, Tony, who argues that Tokay's introducing questions into the story is inappropriate— "You was there To*kay!*" (line 40). Since the smile intonation Tokay uses to make his request displays the type of elaboration he is soliciting, an attempt by Tony to intercept a response to it is quite understandable.

The different types of responses that recipients produce here demonstrate that Chopper's talk is not simply addressed to an audience as an amorphous, homogeneous entity, but rather that there is internal differentiation within the audience that is quite consequential for how the story is being analyzed and dealt with. Most analysis of stories has focused almost exclusively on the actions of the teller. Both the active role of the audience and the way in which members of it differ significantly from each other in ways relevant to the organization of the talk in progress emphasize the importance of treating the audience as an active coparticipant, and actually studying what members of it do.

Although the introduction of the story constitutes a marked transformation of the dispute, it remains very relevant to it. Of crucial importance is the way in which the story allows Chopper to create *a visible multiparty consensus* against Tony. Chopper moves to a structure that provides parties not initially designated as ratified participants the opportunity to participate in it. Maintaining and shaping their participation in particular ways, Chopper is able to demonstrate publicly that his characterization of Tony is one that others share. Through their laughter, Pete and Malcolm affiliate themselves with Chopper's position.

What happens here demonstrates the crucial importance of *participation structures* in the organization of argument (and other interaction). By aborting his counter and beginning a story, Chopper has effected a marked change in the participation framework of the moment. By shifting the conversational activity from a contest of challenges to *stories about contests of challenges*, Chopper can provide an elaborated instancing of his version of Tony's character, as he depicts his opponent's cowardly actions in the past through a series of related stories. Moreover, within the new framework for interaction provided by the structure of a story, recipients are able to participate visibly in the actions being performed by Chopper, with the effect that Chopper is able to create a perceptible alliance against Tony.

10.5 COUNTERS TO THE STORY BY ITS PRINCIPAL CHARACTER

One of the ways in which stories told in conversation differ from those studied by literary critics, as well as many folktales, is that parties being portrayed as characters within a story are frequently present at its telling. Such a situation creates a range of interesting interactive possibilities. In the present data Tony attempts to counter the portrayal of him being drawn by Chopper in a number of different ways. All of Tony's attempts boomerang and paradoxically have the effect of giving Chopper even greater opportunities to depict Tony in a negative light. This process will now be examined in more detail.

10.5.1 Disputing Events within the Story

In lines 45–51 Tony disputes what Chopper is saying about him, and explicitly denies raising his hands up in cowardice when confronted by the boys:

(2)

42	Chopper:	Lemme~tell ya, An h(h)e sai(hh)d,
43	Tokay:	WH:en!=
44	Chopper:	="I ain't got no(h) mo₁(h)ney."
45 →	Tony:	Member=
46	Pete:	₁Whew::,
47 →	Tony:	that night when we was goin ₁there,
48	Chopper:	((snicker)) Khh
49	Tony:	and ₁them boys came down the street,
50	Chopper:	((snicker)) Khhh!
51 →	Tony:	I ain't rai:sed my hands ₁up.
52	Chopper:	Go
53	Chopper:	ahead.=You're gonna say it- I know:.
54		*hh Didn't he g'like this? (0.4)
55		"I ain't go(hh)t
56		no(hh)n₁(h)e."
57	Malcolm:	Ah~ha~ha~ha~ha~ha~ha
58	Chopper:	((snicker)) *hkh
59	Malcolm:	Aw::::
60	Chopper:	*H ((snicker)) KHH
61	Malcolm:	((baby voice)) "I ain't got no money."
62		Ah~₁ha~ha.
63	Chopper:	((snicker)) Khhhhheh!

Despite the way in which Tony's denial is designed to refute what Chopper is saying, it in fact provides Chopper with an opportunity to replay his enactment of Tony while soliciting yet further recipient laughter. In lines 52–53 Chopper counters Tony's defense by proposing that such a response is expected: "Go ahead.=You're gonna say it- I know:." He then switches explicit addressees from Tony to the audience[2] and in line 54 invites them to agree with his characterization of what happened: "Didn't he g'like this?" The format of this request provides distinctive dramatic and interactive resources. Chopper uses the task of identifying what the audience is being asked to agree to (i.e., the referent of "this") to *replay* his earlier enactment (lines 55–56): "I ain't go(hh)t no(hh)n(h)e." What Tony is purported to have said is now embedded within yet another lamination. While the talk that Chopper produces here again animates Tony as a figure, and reports something he (purportedly) said in the past, it also quotes an incident from Chopper's own earlier talk that is now being disputed.

Although the words spoken in lines 55–56 are substantially the same as those spoken in line 25,[3] they now index an additional context: the earlier report, as well as the incidents being described within the report. Within the initial story these words not only provided information (what Tony said) but also commented on that talk while inviting others to participate in it, which they indeed did. By replaying the enactment, Chopper is able not only to invoke the earlier story but also to reactivate the participation possibilities it provided. Thus, as Chopper's animation of Tony comes to completion in line 56, it is received with laughter from Malcolm. The talk being quoted now has the character of a *refrain* that can invoke both the story that constitutes its home environment, and the interactive framework for participation and alignment that it first offered in that environment.

A moment later, in line 61, the refrain is picked up by someone other than Chopper when Malcolm uses a baby voice to animate "*I ain't* got no money." Note once again how in talk such as this, recipients do not simply repeat what they have heard, but also provide a commentary on that talk (in this case through the baby voice used in the animation) that is relevant to the organization of the events in progress. Through the way in which he speaks, Malcolm mocks Tony and displays his affiliation with Chopper's version of the events being disputed.

What happens here demonstrates another structural consequence of shifting the participation framework of the initial dispute from paired counters to a story. By constructing a story, Chopper can invoke an activity that *anchors* the talk of the moment; although Tony may dispute how he is being portrayed, the story frame creates a point of focus to which story-teller, as well as other participants, may return.

Attempts by Tony to refute what he is saying thus benefit Chopper and provide him with an opportunity to further elaborate the story he wants to tell. In the counters exchange that began the dispute, control over the emerging sequence was far more evenly balanced. There Tony could answer an action with an equivalent action. Within the story framework, he is put in the defensive position of trying to dispute a pejorative description of his actions that not only his opponent but others present as well have already agreed to. Instead of disputing whether Tony will throw Chopper out of his yard, an expanded set of participants is now arguing about whether Tony is a coward. As Tony attempts to defend himself within such a situation, he gets into greater and greater trouble. Indeed, his counters make possible both further descriptions by Chopper of his cowardice, and ratifications of that description by others, through laughter and recycling of the quoted refrain.

10.5.2 Building a Return Story

Perhaps in response to the structural constraints imposed by Chopper's story, Tony attempts to turn the tables on Chopper. Instead of disputing descriptions of his own actions, he builds a hypothetical story in which *Chopper* becomes the principal character, and moreover a character who is beaten by his opponents:

(2)
61	Malcolm:	((*baby voice*)) "*I ain't* got no money."
62		Ah-⌐ha-ha.
63	Chopper:	((*snicker*)) Khhhhheh!

```
64 →  Tony:       If he had money. If ⌈he had money
65    Chopper:                       ⌊*hihh
66 →  Tony:       ⌈and he said he didn't=
67    Chopper:    ⌊*hih
68 →  Tony:       =them boys kicked his b'hi(hh)nd. °eh heh
69    Chopper:    I ain't had no mon- I only had a penny
70                they didn't even find it.
71                     (0.4)
72    Jack:       °mmYeah.
73                     (0.8)
74    Chopper:    At least I didn't go up there and say,
75                     (1.2)
76    Chopper:    "I ain't got none."
```

Tony's story constitutes a systematic transformation of Chopper's. Thus it presents an equivalent situation—a group of boys demanding money from the main protagonist in the story—but changes the identity of the principal character. Sacks (1970) has investigated in detail the organization of such *second stories*, including the way in which their parasitic organization displays a relevant analysis of the prior story. In the present data, the structural transformations that tie Tony's story to Chopper's are most relevant to the organization of the dispute between them. By placing both protagonists in equivalent situations, Tony is able to compare them with each other. Thus he is able to depict Chopper as someone who would lose in a physical encounter (and this was indeed one of the underlying themes of the original dispute, in which Chopper challenged Tony to "make him" get out of the yard). On a more general level, sets of stories in which different protagonists (including characters who represent particular social categories in a society such as "husband," "father," or the "reasonable man") are compared in equivalent, socially relevant situations are a widespread feature of arguments within dispute processes in many different societies (see, for example, Gluckman's [1955] discussion of legal dispute among the Barotse).

Tony attempts to replicate not only the structure of Chopper's story but also its participation framework. Thus he embeds laugh tokens in his talk as he says "b'hi(hh)nd" (line 68). However, no one responds to these invitations to laugh. Chopper was able to use his story to align recipients against his opponent. Tony now tries to do the same thing but fails. One reason may be the fact that Chopper's prior story has already created a multiparty alliance against Tony, and a consensus about how the issues being disputed are to be interpreted. However, such a consensus could always be called into question by subsequent events in the argument.

In lines 69–70 Chopper answers Tony's description of him with a counter that argues for its irrelevance (i.e., he did not, in fact, have any money). The parasitic structure of Tony's story now provides a way for Chopper to return to his own stories about Tony. By using the preface "At least," in line 76 he is able to compare what Tony said he did with what Tony did in an equivalent situation, and once more recycle his enactment of Tony's cowardice:

(2)

64	Tony:	If *he* had money. If ⌜he had *money*
65	Chopper:	*hihh
66	Tony:	⌜and he said he didn't=
67	Chopper:	*hih
68	Tony:	=them boys kicked his b'hi(hh)nd. °eh heh
69	Chopper:	*I* ain't *had* no mon- *I* only had a penny
70		they didn't even *find* it.
71		(0.4)
72	Jack:	°mm*Yea*h.
73		(0.8)
74	Chopper:	At least I didn't go up there and say,
75		(1.2)
76	Chopper:	⌜"I *ain*'t got none."
77 →	Tony:	*Well* there'd be some problems if *he*
78		came found it *did*n't it.
79 →	Chopper:	Nope. And ⌜guess what Mal⌜*colm.*
80	Malcolm:	°He said said
81		((*baby voice*)) "I ain't got no money."=
82	Chopper:	=Guess what Malcolm.=Them boys out
83		there said, *hh "Your football player
84		ca:n't, play," And guess where *To:*ny
85		was. (0.6) All the way ar(h)ound the
86		cor(hh)n(h)er.

Tony overlaps Chopper's enactment with further elaboration of the points in his story. However, Chopper quickly dismisses this with a simple "Nope" and in line 82 launches yet another story preface followed in lines 82–86 by another story about Tony's cowardice. In brief, despite numerous attempts by Tony to counter the way that Chopper has depicted him, the anchoring of the story frame works once more to Chopper's benefit, providing him with a point of focus to which he, as storyteller, may return.

As Chopper elaborates his new story, Tony once again challenges what is being said within it:

(2)

79	Chopper:	Nope. And ⌜guess what Mal⌜*colm.*
80	Malcolm:	°He said said
81		((*baby voice*)) "I ain't got no money."=
82	Chopper:	=Guess what Malcolm.=Them boys out
83		there said, *hh "Your football player

```
84                      ca:n't, play," And guess where To.ny
85                      was.  (0.6) All the way ar(h)ound the
86                      cor(hh)n(h)er. (0.5) *hih ⌈Remember=
87      (    ):                                ⌊°What?
88      Chopper:        =that night? Them little boys said
89                      "That little p:unk can't fight?" And
90                      Tony started runnin' across the s:treet.
91      Jack:           Hey:⌈:,
92      Chopper:            ⌊Not e⌈ven waitin' for 'em.=
93      Ray:                       ⌊eh~heh~heh.
94 →    Tony:           =WHAT?!
95      Chopper:        'Member that time, (0.5) Lemme see we
96                      got about- where we was playin'
97                      basketball at? (1.2) And // you had
98 →    Tony:           Where who w'playin' basketball at.
99      Chopper:        You know, where we were playin'
100                     basketball? And you wasn't even waitin'
101                     for us, you was up there r:unnin',
102                     Until you got way around the
103                     corner.=Them boys said, those boys kep,
104                     those boys kept on (I said,) "Hey Tony
105                     what you runnin for." He said "I ain't
106                     runnin." Them boys woulda come next to
107                     me I(h) woul(hh)da, ((snicker)) *hKkh I woulda
108                     k:icked their ass. And // Tony was
109                     all the way ar(h)ound the corner.
```

Although Tony's questions are designed to undercut the story that Chopper is trying to tell by challenging its credibility, in each case they have the reverse effect of providing Chopper with an opportunity to elaborate his story. Thus Chopper explicitly answers Tony's "Where *who* w'playin' basketball at," but instead of treating it as a challenge he uses the request for information it contains as a warrant to produce material that is relevant to the further development of the story.

In lines 106–108, Chopper turns the tactic used a moment ago by Tony, telling a hypothetical second story, against him. Chopper depicts himself in a situation comparable to that described for Tony; however, in contrast to Tony's running "all the way around the corner," Chopper portrays himself as having stood up to the boys confronting him.

By this time members of the audience have become quite active in both mocking Tony and countering some of his counters to Chopper. Note, for example, the actions of Jack and Malcolm in the following:

```
(2)
109                     And ⌈Tony was all the way ar(h)ound the corner.
110     Tony:              ⌊I don't know what you talkin' 'bout.
```

```
111 →  Jack:       °Talkin' // 'bout bein' kicked. That's
112                what it // is.
113    Pete:       'Member that time,
114    Tony:       I don't remember // what you talkin'
115                about.
116    Pete:       that we was goin' around the corner on
117                Poplar?
118    Chopper:    "I ain't got no(hh) mo(hh)ney."
119    Pete:       That boy down there
120 →  Malcolm:    ((baby voice)) "I ain't got no money."
121                "I ain't got no money."
122    Tokay:      Remember when that boy down in the
123                park, °that time, when he was talkin'
124                to ⌈Tony for
125    Tony:          ⌊What he- When is he talkin' ⌈about.
126    Chopper:                                  ⌊OH YEAH!
127                    (0.5)
128    Chopper:    "I know you ain't talkin' to
129                me!" Down in the park! ((snicker)) Khh~heh!
130    Pete:       eh~heh~heh.
131    Chopper:    *hh We was down the park, (0.7) and we
```

As Pete and Tokay begin to reminisce with Chopper, they introduce another type of move which enables him to continue the story. Pete (" 'Member that time, that we was goin' around the corner on Poplar?" lines 113, 116–117) and Tokay ("Remember when that boy down in the park," lines 122–123) request that Chopper tell another story about a past related experience. Chopper chooses to ignore Tony's counters in lines 114–115 and 125 and recognizes Tokay's request by providing what Labov (1972a:363–364) has analyzed as an "abstract" to his story: "I know you ain't talkin to me!" (line 128). This abstract is Chopper's animation of a line in the story to come (in line 146); it is the action delivered by a "big boy" that Tony backed down from during a confrontation:

```
(2)
122    Tokay:      Remember when that boy down in the
123                park, °that time, when he was talkin'
124                to ⌈Tony for
125    Tony:          ⌊What he- When is he talkin' ⌈about.
126    Chopper:                                  ⌊OH YEAH!
127                    (0.5)
128 →  Chopper:    "I know you ain't talkin' to
129 →              me!" Down in the park! ((snicker)) Khh~heh!
130    Pete:       eh~heh~heh.
131    Chopper:    *hh We was down the park, (0.7) and we
132                was- (0.6) and wh- wh- what was he
133                doin',=
```

134	Tony:	=You can ask *Ralph* what happened down
135		the *park* Malcolm Johnson cuz *this*
136		sucker *lie* too much.
137	Chopper:	*Uh* UH. We was playin'- (0.3) we was
138		makin' a *d*arn *r*aft, (0.5) and them
139		boys (.) was throwin' things at Tony,
140		(0.7) And *he* said, (0.6) "Boy!" And-
141		lemme tell.=(*They*) were talkin' to that
142		*li*ttle boy. Th'he said, "Boy you
143		better watch them *things!*" That big
144		boy said,
145	Tony:	°What ones.=
146 →	Chopper:	="I *know* he ain't talkin' to *me*!" I
147		said (0.4) and he said-
148		"NO: not ⌜you: du(hh)mmy-"
149	Tony:	What things.
150	Pete:	Ah:~*heh*~heh~⌜heh.
151	Chopper:	"The *li*ttle bo:(hh)y."
152		Eh~heh~heh. ((*snicker*)) *hKh
153	Malcolm:	That-
154	Chopper:	That big boy woulda kicked his butt!
155	Malcolm:	That *li*⌞ttle boy.
156	Tony:	That's a lie *too* Chopper.
157	Chopper:	Why you talk to that *li*ttle boy.
158		(1.0)
159	Tony:	*I* said *what?*
160	Chopper:	Got you got you *got* you!
161		(1.2)
162	Chopper:	Say Hey heh *heh*
163		heh, Hey hey HEY! HEY HEY *HEY*! "I
164		ain't go(h)t no(h)" (0.8) Da:g!

Despite differences in the incidents being described, this new story is
built around the same structural framework as Chopper's earlier stories.
In all of them Tony encounters a group of bigger boys who threaten him
and in response produces a statement that demonstrates his cowardice and
makes him look ridiculous. The structure of Chopper's original telling has
now become a template that generates not simply a second story but a
whole set of subsequent narratives that have structural parallels to the
original recounting.[4] From this perspective, the precise form of Chopper's
abstract becomes interesting. Instead of providing an overview of what the
story will be about, he animates talk attributed to Tony. By this point in
the sequence, such animation has become such a recognizable part of the
narratives being told that it can serve to preview a story not yet heard.[5]
Participants are thus attending to not only the content of what is being
said but also visible patterns for the organization of that content, and using

such *bricolage* as a resource for the production and recognition of their subsequent action.

Chopper's new story engenders further counters from Tony. However, Chopper is able to continue the depiction of Tony's character by elaborating a further example of Tony's cowardice. In response, Tony states that Chopper is lying (lines 134–136) and pleads that Malcolm consult a disinterested third party. Chopper's answer is to deny the charge of lying and to continue the story (line 137). Throughout the telling of this third story, Tony counters Chopper's telling of it (lines 145 and 149).

Chopper eventually puts an end to Tony's objections by trapping him in an inconsistency:

(2)
```
154      Chopper:   That big boy woulda kicked his butt!
155      Malcolm:   That liₜttle boy.
156      Tony:             That's a lie too Chopper.
157 →    Chopper:   Why you talk to that little boy.
158                       (1.0)
159 →    Tony:      I said what?
160 →    Chopper:   Got you got you got you!
161                       (1.2)
162      Chopper:   Say Hey heh heh
163                 heh, Hey hey HEY! HEY HEY HEY! "I
164                 ain't go(h)t no(h)" (0.8) Da:g!
```

In line 157 Chopper asks, "Why you talk to that *li*ttle boy?" Tony responds with "*I* said *what*?" Chopper interprets this as an admission that he *did* talk to the little boy, and says in triumph, "Got you got you *got* you!" and gloats on his one-upmanship in lines 162–164.

Shifting the conversational activity from a contest of challenges to stories about contests of challenges in which counters can occur has several advantages for Chopper. The confrontation takes place on Tony's property and thus puts him in a better position to enforce his threats. By constructing a story, Chopper shifts the activity of argumentation away from the immediate situation, a domain in which Tony has a clear advantage, to the past, a domain where Tony's position relative to others can be called into question. The story format, which invites others to participate, allows Chopper to provide an extended, ratified account, an instancing of his version of Tony's relative status, by discussing Tony's cowardly actions in the past.

More important, the rearrangement of the argument mode also calls into play a different configuration for social organization. The event shifts from one designating only two parties to dispute to one inviting the participation of all those present. In that others may join in the activity, even without being officially summoned as witnesses, they may align themselves with a particular side of the dispute, and their participation may display whose version has more support. Chopper's story elicits agreement with his position from others present. The structure of the recounting itself allows for displays of appreciation, both laughter and repetition of his lines, as well as requests for elaboration of the story, which grant Chopper a warrant to develop his line. Even though Chopper's description may be countered, topic shifts or exits from the dispute by his opponent are precluded in that the narrative format provides a point of focus to which Chopper as storyteller may return.

Examining detailed structuring of stories and responses to them permits us to analyze how children achieve their social organization of the moment, and provides materials for comparative study. For example, given the same story and dispute resources, girls construct quite different types of events.

CHAPTER ELEVEN

Instigating

Unlike the boys, girls do not generally utilize direct methods in evaluating one another. They seldom give each other bald commands or insults, and making explicit statements about one's achievements or possessions is avoided. Such actions are felt to indicate someone who "thinks she cute" or above another, thus violating the comparatively egalitarian ethos of the girls. These different cultural perceptions lead to different ways in which stories which are part of dispute processes are built by the teller, and involve others in the process of storytelling. Rather than directly confronting one another with complaints about the actions of a girl in the play group, girls characteristically discuss their grievances about other girls in their absence. Through an elaborated storytelling procedure called "instigating," girls learn that absent parties have been talking about them behind their backs, and commit themselves to future confrontations with such individuals.

The activity of reporting to a recipient what was said about her in her absence constitutes an important stage preliminary to the confrontation event. It is the point at which such an event becomes socially recognizable as an actionable offense. The party talked about may then confront the party who was reportedly talking about her "behind her back." Such informing typically is accomplished through use of stories by a girl who will stand as neither accuser nor defendant. This type of storytelling is called "instigating" by the children. Girls talk about the activity of deliberately presenting the facts in such a way as to create conflict between people in the following way:[1]

(1)   Martha: Everytime she- we do somp'm she don't like
                  she go and tell somebody a lie.
                  She make up somp'm and then she always
                  go away.

The instigator may initiate a sequence of events which leads to conflict as part of a process of sanctioning the behavior of a girl who steps outside the bounds of appropriate behavior or as a way of demonstrating her ability to orchestrate such events.

Instigating possesses features of the black speech event analyzed as "signifying" by Kochman (1970) and Mitchell-Kernan (1971, 1972). According to Mitchell-Kernan (1972:165, 166), signifying refers to "a way of encoding messages or meanings in natural conversations which involves, in most cases, an element of indirection" either with reference to "(1) the meaning or message the speaker is adjudged as intending to convey; (2) the addressee—the person or persons to whom the message is directed; (3) the goal orientation or intent of the speaker." In discussing signifying, Kochman (1970:157) has stated that "the signifier reports or repeats what someone else has said about the listener; the 'report' is couched in plausible language designed to compel belief and arouse feelings of anger and hostility."

The sequence of events which occurs as a result of stories' being told about what was said in a story recipient's absence is parallel to the sequencing of events resulting from the "signifying" which occurs in one of the most popular of black folklore forms, "The Signifying Monkey" (Abrahams 1964:147–157; Dorson 1967:98–99). In that tale's "toast" form, the monkey provokes a dispute between the lion and the elephant by telling the lion that the elephant was insulting him behind his back. The lion then confronts the elephant:

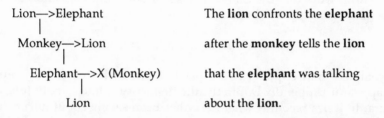

Lion—>Elephant   The **lion** confronts the **elephant**

Monkey—>Lion   after the **monkey** tells the **lion**

Elephant—>X (Monkey)   that the **elephant** was talking

Lion   about the **lion**.

In the girls' he-said-she-said event, a parallel series of events occurs when an intermediary party (like the monkey) reports to someone what was said about her in her absence.

In both the he-said-she-said and "The Signifying Monkey," past events are reported in such a way as to lead to confrontation; however, the offenses at issue in the folktale are not the more general activity of having talked about someone in her absence but rather personal insults. The folklore form of "The Signifying Monkey" crystalizes what in everyday life is a recognizable event configuration in black culture; however, the positions in the he-said-she-said drama are transformed into animal figures,[2] and thus involvement in the story is not contingent on personal involvement with its characters.

The larger framework of the he-said-she-said dispute provides organization for the storytelling process in several ways:

1. It provides structure for the cited characters and their activities within the story.
2. It influences the types of analysis recipients must engage in to appropriately understand the story.

3. It makes relevant specific types of next moves by recipients: for example, evaluations of the offending party's actions during the story, pledges to future courses of action near the story's ending, and rehearsals of future events at story completion and upon subsequent retellings.

11.1 STRUCTURE IN TELLING AND LISTENING TO "INSTIGATING" STORIES

Bringing about a future confrontation has direct bearing upon the way speaker structures her instigating story and recipients respond to it. Through dramatic character development, speaker skillfully guides her recipients to interpret the events she is relating in the way she wants them to, and attempts to coimplicate hearers in forms of future activity. Recipients' responses to instigating stories are differentiated, depending upon the identity relationship of listeners to figures in the story. Much of Goffman's (1974) work on "the frame analysis of talk" and animation of characters (ibid.:516–544) will be relevant here.

11.1.1 COIMPLICATING LISTENERS

The complete transcripts of two separate stories which will be analyzed here appear in Appendix D. Briefly, the first story is told to both Julia and Barbara. In it Bea recounts what Kerry has been saying about Julia behind her back. Julia then leaves, and Bea starts a new set of stories in which she tells Barbara what Kerry said about *her* (Barbara).

The description of the past is organized so as to demonstrate that the events being recounted constitute *offenses*. Moreover, the presentation of past events is carefully managed so as to elicit from its recipient, now positioned by the story as an *offended party*, pejorative comments about the party who offended her, without this appearing as the direct intent of the speaker's story.

We will start by examining the initiation of Bea's first story, recounting what Kerry said about Julia:

(2)

11	Bea:	*How- how-* h- um, uh h- h- how about me
12		and *Ju*lia, *h and all them um, and
13		*Kerry*, *h ⌈and all them-
14	Julia:	⌊Isn't *Kerry mad* at
15		*me* or s*:omp*'m,
16		(0.4)
17	Bea:	*I'on'* kn//ow.

18	Barbara:	Kerry~*al*ways~mad~at somebody.
19		°*I* ['on' care.
20	Julia:	[Cuz- cuz cuz I wouldn't, cu:z she
21		ain't put my *n*ame on that *p*aper.
22	Bea:	*I* know cuz OH yeah. *Oh* yeah.

This story beginning has the form of a reminiscence. Bea requests that others remember with her a particular event: "*How- how-* h- um, uh h- h- how about me and *Jul*ia, *h and all of them um, and *Ke*rry." The numerous hesitations in her speech contribute to the highly charged framing of this talk. The proposed story concerns negative attributes of Kerry. The telling of derogatory stories, especially in the context of the he-said-she-said, poses particular problems for participants. That is, such stories constitute instances of talking behind someone's back, the very action at issue in a he-said-she-said.

Among Maple Street girls, responding to another's pejorative statement about an absent party is viewed in a particular way: it is seen as "getting involved." Participants themselves display an orientation toward the structured possibility of there being a "slot" (Sacks 1972:341–342) for an evaluative comment following a pejorative statement of a prior speaker. Consider the following:

(3)	Kerry:	You know I was gonna have Jimmy-
		I was have a Hallow-
		I'm havin' a Halloween party?=So I said um,
		so I said uh: Martha-
		All Julia wanna do is *dance* at the party.
		Tch! She don't wanna play no *g*ames or nothin'.
→	Bea:	I ain't gonna say *no*thin'
		cuz I don't wanna be involved.
→	Martha:	Me neither. I don't wanna say nothin'
		about nobody else business.

A party who tells about another runs a particular risk: current recipient might tell the absent party that current speaker is talking about her behind her back.[3] The activity of righteously informing someone of an offense against her can itself be taken and cast as an offense. Are there ways in which a party telling such a story can protect herself against such risk? One way might be to implicate her recipient in a similar telling so that both are equally guilty and equally vulnerable. However, this still poses problems; specifically, it would be most advantageous for each party if the other would implicate herself first. This can lead to a delicate negotiation at the beginning of the story: in #2, lines 11–13, when Bea brings up Kerry's offenses toward Julia, she requests the opinion of others, while refusing to state her own position. In response, Julia asks a question that describes her relationship to Kerry in a particular way: "*Isn't Kerry mad at me* or *s:omp'm*" (lines 14–15). If Bea in fact provides a story at this point demonstrating how Kerry is mad at Julia, Bea will have talked negatively about Kerry before Julia has coimplicated herself in a similar position. Bea subsequently passes up the opportunity to tell such a story by saying "*I 'on' know*" (line 17). Then Julia provides an answer to her own question: "*Cuz- cuz cuz I wouldn't, cu:z she ain't put my name on that paper*" (lines 20–21). Only after Julia implicates herself does Bea begin to join in the telling (line 22).

11.1.2 CITED CHARACTERS AND CURRENT PARTICIPANTS

Instigating stories concern others within one's play group who are judged to have behaved in an inappropriate fashion. Such stories share certain features in common:

1. The principal character in the story is a party who is not present.
2. The nonpresent party performs actions directed toward some other party.
3. These actions can be seen as offenses.

   Although much of girls' gossip concerns negative evaluations of female agemates' activities, such conversation need not necessarily lead to a confrontation if the activities of the absent party were not in the past directed toward the present recipient of the teller's talk. Thus the feature of instigating stories which distinguishes them from other types of stories used in dispute processes (such as those of the boys discussed earlier) is that:

4. The target of the offense is the present hearer.

The placement of present recipient within the story as a principal figure provides for her involvement in it and, consequently, for the story's rather enduring lifespan by comparison with other recountings.

Some evidence is available that the teller takes into account the four features listed above in the construction of her instigating stories. In the data being examined, Bea's initial stories (#2) involve offenses Kerry committed toward Julia. These include having said that Julia was acting "stupid" and inappropriately when girls were telling jokes, and having intentionally excluded Julia's name from a hall bathroom pass. During these stories, both Julia and Barbara are present. However, Julia then departs, leaving only Barbara as audience to Bea. Bea now starts a new series of stories (#4) in which Barbara is the target of a different set of offenses by Kerry. These involve Kerry's having said something about Barbara in her absence (that she had nothing to do with writing on the sidewalk and street about her) and having reported to Bea that "Barbara need to go somewhere." Thus when one hearer (Julia) leaves (prior to the beginning of #4), the speaker modifies her stories. In both sets of stories, the absent party who commits the offenses, Kerry, remains constant. However, the recipient of her actions is changed so that the target of the offense remains the present hearer. Through such changes, the speaker maintains the relevance of her story for its immediate recipient. What happens here demonstrates the importance of not restricting analysis of stories to isolated texts or performances by speakers, but rather including the story's recipients within the scope of analysis, since they can indeed be quite consequential for its organization.

Stories may also be locally organized with respect to the figure selected as the offender. The fact that Kerry is reportedly the agent of offensive talk in the story to Julia may well be why she is selected as a similar agent in the stories to Barbara several minutes later. When the confrontation is played out, it is discovered that it was actually Julia, rather than Kerry, who said something about Barbara in the past (see #1 in Chapter 8, line 100). Bea is found to have misrepresented the person who performed the offensive actions in order to create conflict between Barbara and Kerry.

Larger political processes within the girls' group might also be relevant to the selection of Kerry as offender in these stories. Gluckman (1963:308) has noted that gossip can be used "to control aspiring individuals." In the present data, Kerry is the same age as the other girls but has skipped a year in school, and they are annoyed at her for previewing everything that will happen to them in junior high. The structure of the immediate reporting situation, as well as larger social processes within the girls' group, is thus relevant to how past events are organized within these stories, and the way in which particular members of the girls' group become cited figures (Goffman 1974:529–532) within the stories.

In replaying past events, the teller animates (Goffman 1974) the cited figures within her stories in ways that are relevant to the larger social projects within which the stories are embedded.[4] In a variety of ways, the absent party's actions toward the current hearer are portrayed as offensive. Thus, in describing what Kerry said about Julia, Bea (lines 26–31) reports that Kerry had characterized Julia as having acted stupid:

Teller
Animates
↓
Absent Party
Animating
↓
Current Hearer

(2)

26	Bea:	*She* said, *She* said that um, (0.6)
27		that (0.8) if that *girl* wasn't
28		there=*You* know that girl that always
29		makes those funny jokes, *h Sh'aid if
30		that *girl* wasn't there *you* wouldn't be
31		*ac*tin', (0.4) a:ll *stu*pid like that.

Continuing on, Bea (lines 34–35) animates Kerry's voice as she reports that Kerry had said that Julia had been cursing:

(2)
| 35 | Bea: | And she said that *you* sai:d, that, |
| 36 | | "*Ah*: go tuh-" (0.5) somp'm like tha:t. |

As Bea further elaborates her story about Kerry, she relates how Kerry had attempted to exclude Julia's name from a permission slip to go to the bathroom, or "hall pass." At the same time that she describes Kerry's actions as offensive, she portrays Julia as someone whose actions were appropriate and exemplary (lines 64–66) and herself as someone who took up for Julia (lines 68–69):

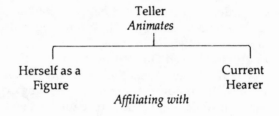

(2)
64	Bea	An' j- And Julia w'just sittin'
65		up there actin'- actin':, ac- ac- actin'
66		sensible. An' she up- and she up there
67		talking 'bout, and she- *I* said, I s'd I
68		s'd I s'd "This is how I'm- I'm gonna
69		put Julia *na*:me down here." Cu- m- m-
70		Cuz she had made a pa:ss you know. *h
71		She had made a *pa*:ss.

Bea's stuttering adds to the dramatic quality of her talk as she expresses excitement about what she is relating. As Bea animates Kerry's voice, she colors her talk with a whiny, high-pitched, defensive tone, enacting Kerry's distaste for having to include Julia's name. Immediately following, however, Bea again portrays herself as someone who *defended* the position of her present hearer against the offender:

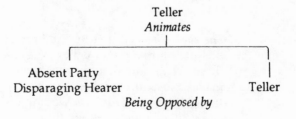

(2)

77	Bea:	I s'd- I s'd "*How*: *co*:me you
78		ain't put Julia name down here." *h So
79		she said, she said ((*whiny, defensive tone*))
80		"That other girl called 'er so,
81		she no:t *wi*:th *u*:s, so,"
82		That's what she said too. (0.2) So *I*
83		said, s- so I snatched the paper
84		wi'her. I said wh- when we were playin'
85		wi'that paper?

(2)

93	Bea:	But she ain't even put your *na*me down
94		there. *I* just put it *down* there. Me
95		and Martha put it down.=An' I said, and
96		she said "*Gi*mme-that-paper.=I don't
97		wanna have her *n*ame *d*own here." I s- I
98		s- I s- I said "She woulda allowed *you*
99		name."

Quite different forms of affect and alignment toward Julia's perspective are conveyed by Bea's animation of Kerry and of herself. While Bea portrays Kerry as having willfully excluded Julia from the group going to the bathroom, Bea describes herself as having actively defended Julia against Kerry. She talked back to Kerry, arguing that Julia would certainly not have conducted herself as Kerry had, and even snatched the bathroom pass from Kerry to write down Julia's name so that she would be included. Bea structures her stories so that her characters take up contrasting stances with reference to the issues at stake, and they thus stand in sharp relief.

Speaker not only carefully crafts her own description of events; she also acts upon any indication by recipient of her alignment toward the absent party. For example, when Julia makes an evaluative comment—"OO: r'mind me a-you old b:aldheaded Kerry" (lines 108–109)—at the close of the story about Kerry's actions toward Julia, Bea states, "*I* should say it in fronta her *f*ace. (0.8) Bal': head" (lines 110–111). Bea presents a model of how she herself would confront the offending party and invites recipient to see the action in question as she herself does: as an action deserving in return an aggravated response, such as a personal insult.

Suggestions for how to act toward the absent party may also take the form of stories in which *speaker* rather than recipient appears as principal character reacting to actions of the offending party. Briefly, the speaker makes her suggestions by telling her present recipient the kinds of actions that *she herself* takes against the offender, these actions being appropriate next moves to the offenses described in the informing stories:

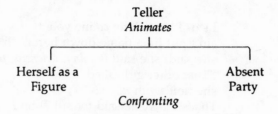

Teller
Animates

Herself as a   Absent
Figure   Party
Confronting

(4)

58	Bea:	Oh yeah, oh yeah.=*She* was, *she*- w's
59		*she* was in Rochele: house you know, and
60		she said that um, that- I heard her
61		say um, (0.4) um um uh uh "*Jul*ia said
62		y'all been talking behind my back."=I
63 →		said I'm a- I'm a say "H:oney, I'm gl*a*:d.
64		that *you* know I'm *t*alkin' be*hind your*
65		*back.* Because *I*- because *I meant*
66		for you to know *any*way." An' she said,
67		I- said "I don't have to talk behind
68		your back.=I can talk in front of your
69		*face too.*"

(4)

142	Bea	*h And she was leanin'
143		against- I- I said, I s'd I s'd I s'd I
144		said, "*Hey* girl don't lean against that
145		thing cuz it's *w*eak *e*nough." *h And
146		she said and she said *h she- she did
147		like that.=She say, "Tch!" ((*rolling*
148		*eyes*)) // like that. I s'd- I said "You
149		c'd *roll* your eyes all you *want* to.
150	Barbara:	Yeah if somebody do that to her-
151		And if ⌜you know what?
152	Bea:	⌞Cuz I'm *t*ellin' you. (0.5)
153		*T*ellin'- I'm not *ask*in' you." (0.4) An' I
154		ain't say no *plea*:se *ei*ther.

In these stories Bea tells how she confronted Kerry with aggravated insults. Specifically, she describes how she told Kerry to her face that she had talked about her behind her back (lines 63–66). In addition, Bea describes having performed insulting actions directly to Kerry's face, issuing a direct command to her: "Cuz I'm *t*ellin' you. (0.5) *T*ellin'- I'm not *ask*in' you" (lines 152–153). The bald on-record nature of the command is highlighted by placing it in contrast to a more mitigated form which was not said: "An' I ain't say no *plea*:se *ei*ther" (lines 153–154).

Providing evaluation through descriptions of past activities is quite consequential for the process of eliciting from recipient a promise to confront the offender in the future. On the one hand, objectionable actions performed by the absent party can be interpreted as explicit offenses against current recipient. On the other hand, speaker's description of her own actions in response to such offenses, i.e., confronting the offender, can provide recipient with a guide for how she should act toward that party. Thus Julia's statement that she will confront Kerry occurs right after Bea has described how she confronted Kerry about having excluded Julia's name from the bathroom pass.

(2)

| 86 | Julia: | I'm a I'm a *t*ell her about herself. |

Reports of actions in the past can thus lead to commitments to perform relevant answers to them in the future.

Thus through a variety of activities—passing up the opportunity to align herself with a definitive position before hearer does at story beginning, presenting herself as having defended the offended party in the past, and portraying how she boldly confronted the offending party—speaker carefully works to coimplicate her present recipient in a next course of action. Features of indirection are evident in the reporting in several ways. In accordance with Kochman's (1970:157) definition of indirection, the teller presents a believable picture of past events involving what was said about the recipient which arouses feelings of anger and hostility. In keeping with Mitchell-Kernan's (1972:166) analysis of indirection, the goal orientation of speaker in presenting her stories is obscured. Although the report is supposedly a narrative account of past events involving teller and offending party, and speaker's alignment of righteous indignation toward these acts, it may also function to suggest future courses of action for present recipient.

11.1.3 DIFFERENTIATED RECIPIENTS' RESPONSES

As we have seen, the stories used in instigating contain extensive reported speech (Vološinov 1973) as speakers animate the characters in their talk. The recipients of the present reports, in accord with Goffman's (1974:503) idealization of listener response, display that they "have been stirred" by the events the narrator describes. A current participant who was absent when the things said about her were reported to have been said can now answer those charges. In addition, in that these recountings are embedded within a larger realm of action, one which provides for the dynamic involvement of coparticipants and is not restricted to the present encounter, recipients are invited by the narrator to be moved to action. The report of offenses in the he-said-she-said event is specifically constructed to inform someone that she has (from the teller's perspective) been offended and thereby to invite her to take action against the offender. This prospect of future involvement may provide for recipients' participation and engross-

ment in the present in more active roles than generally occur in response
to stories.

In responding to talk, participants pay close attention to the differential
access they have to the events being talked about. Listeners as well as
speakers occupy multiple identities vis-à-vis both the teller in the present
and the cited figures in the reported story. They thus differ with respect
to their involvement or engrossment in the events being recounted. Parties
who were present when the action described occurred and are figures in
the story not only may respond to the story but also may participate in its
telling, as Julia does in response to Bea's first instigating story:

(2)

47	Julia:	So: *she* wouldn' be *a*ctin' *l*ike *that*
48		wi' that *other* girl.=*She* the one picked
49		*me* to *sit* wi'them.=*h She said ₍"Julia you
50	Bea:	Y:ahp.
51	Julia:	sit with her, *h and I'll sit with her,
52		*h an Bea an'- an' Bea an'-
53		an' an' Martha sit together."

(2)

101	Julia:	I said Kerry "°How come you ain't put my
102		name."
103	Barbara:	Here go B//ea, "uh uh uh well-"
104	Julia:	"You put that *other* girl (name down)
105		didn't you. I thought *you* was gonna
106		have- owl: a hall pass with that *other*
107		girl." That's °what Kerry said. I said
108		(What's~her~problem.)

Such a collaborative telling is dependent upon knowledge of the event and
generally utilizes past tense.

Implicated recipients are not restricted to making comments about
events that they directly experienced. A listener who has had attacks made
upon her may respond to these attacks in the present, despite the fact that
her attacker is not present but exists only as a cited figure in another's story.
One form of counter is a challenge to the truth of statements concerning
her. For example, when Bea reports that Kerry had accused Julia of swearing, she quickly denies the charge:

(2)

35		Bea:	She- and she said that *you* sai:d, that,
36			"*Ah*: go tuh-" (0.5) somp'm like ₍tha:t.
37	→	Julia:	°No I
38			didn't.

A dialogue between events and participants who are separated from each other by both space and time thus occurs, as a present participant addresses actions performed against her in the past by someone who is now absent. Moreover, as will be seen shortly, such events can have consequences for the future as well.

Bea's report that Kerry characterized Julia's actions in the past as "acting stupid" (lines 28–30) is likewise countered by Julia, who says in an aggravated tone:

(2)

| 33 | Julia: | But *was* I actin' stupid with them? |

Such a response not only answers charges in the past but also solicits an alliance with the current teller against the offender. A second form of counter to a reported statement which denigrates the current recipient may be a return pejorative statement about the cited figure:

(2)

45	Bea:	She said, hh that *you* wouldn't be *a*ctin'
46		*like that* aroun'- around *peo*ple.
47 →	Julia:	So: *she* wouldn' be *a*ctin' *like that*
48		wi'that *oth*er girl.

When Barbara is told that Kerry has said that she didn't have anything to do with the writing that is the subject of another dispute, she answers that past action with a current challenge. Even though the events at issue would seem to be positive ones from Barbara's perspective—not being found guilty for having written pejorative things about Kerry—the fact that Kerry *said* something about Barbara in her absence makes relevant a response from her. The identity of the offended party is thus a position which is collaboratively brought into existence through both teller's description of a third party's past activities and recipient's orientation toward absent party's past actions as offenses:[5]

(4)

32	Barbara:	If I *wro*:te somp'm then I *wrote*
33		it.=Then I got somp'm to do with
34		it.=W'then I *wrote* it.

(4)

| 48 | Barbara: | WELL IF I WROTE SOME'EN *I* HAD SOMP'M |
| 49 | | T'*DO* with it. |

The present encounter encompasses a dialogue not only between participants and events in the present, but also between participants and events from previous encounters. As seen above, a present participant may answer charges made by someone absent from the present interaction who currently exists only as a cited figure in the talk of another speaker. Parties denied the opportunity to counter offensive statements about them in the past when the offenses were committed may deal with them in their re-telling. In this way the offended party may also discover the present speaker's alignment toward the cited speaker's statements by observing her next utterances to the counter.

All of the responses examined so far were made by current recipients who were figures in the cited story. The offense committed against them in the past warranted their indignant responses to the charges made against them. However, responses of this type, denials for example, are not avail-able to a current listener who is not mentioned in the story and has not been maligned. How can a party in such a position respond to the telling? During the first set of narratives about how Kerry acted toward Julia, Bar-bara is in precisely this position. She is not a character in the recounting and has not been offended. When her actions are examined, it is found she provides general comments on the offender's character, referring to ongoing attributes of her in the present progressive tense. For example:

(2)

| 18 | Barbara: | Kerry~*al*ways~mad~at somebody. |
| 19 | | °*I* 'on' care. |

(2)

40	Barbara:	Kerry *al*ways say somp'm.=When you
42		*jump* in her *face* she gonna de*ny*
43		it.

In the first story (#2), Barbara's evaluations provide a structural alter-native to the way in which Julia, a figure in the event recounted, participates in it. While Julia has access to the events being talked about, Barbara does not. Julia can therefore answer Kerry's charges with her own version of the incidents at issue. The events recounted thus have a differential rele-vance to the current situation of each participant; while Julia's character has been called into question, Barbara's has not. Julia, unlike Barbara, has both motivation and standing to answer the charges raised by Kerry.

The structures used by Barbara provide a creative solution to the prob-lem of talking about the event that is currently on the floor. Despite the fact that this event does not involve her in the way that it does the others present, Barbara helps to constitute it. In brief, the talk of the moment creates a field of relevance that implicates those present to it in a variety of different ways, and this has consequences for the detailed organization of the action that each party produces.

11.2 PREPLAYINGS: FUTURE STORIES IN RESPONSE TO INSTIGATING STORIES

By telling stories, instigators portray how they treated an absent party in the past, as a way of suggesting how their current addressee should treat that party in the future. Through their descriptions, instigators report events which can be seen as offensive and provide recipients the opportunity to assume the identity of offended party. However, the mere reporting of offenses is not itself sufficient to bring about a future confrontation; rather, a recipient must publicly analyze the event in question as an offense against her and state that she will seek redress by confronting her offender:

(2)
```
86    Julia:       I'm a I'm a tell her about herself
87                 today.
```

Actions such as these constitute far stronger evaluations than mere complaints about the prior actions of offending party. In essence, current recipient commits herself to taking action in the future against the party who offended her.

In comparing the kinds of evaluative responses Julia and Barbara give to the stories Bea tells, Barbara in #4 takes a much stronger stance vis-à-vis Kerry's reported actions than Julia. In response to instigating stories, offended party (Barbara) produces a series of future stories in which she projects what she will do when she confronts her offender (Kerry):

```
(4) 6    Barbara:    Well you tell her to come say it in
    7                front of my fa:ce. (0.6) And I'll put
    8                her somewhere.

(4)
    22   Barbara:    So, she got anything t'say she
    23               come say it in front of my face. (1.0)
    24               I better not see Kerry today. (2.5) I
    25               ain't gonna say- I'm~a~say "Kerry what
    26               you say about me."

(4)
    101  Barbara:    I better not see Kerry today. I'm a
    102              say "Kerry I heard you was talkin' 'bout
    103              me."

(4)
    157  Barbara:    W'll I'm tellin' ya
    158              I better not catch Kerry today. Cuz if
```

159   I catch her I'm gonna give *her* a wor:d
160   from my *mou*th.

Bea's stories about past events in which Barbara was offended permit Barbara to describe future scenes that are the contingent outcome of events
emerging in the present. To provide strong demonstrations of her understanding of Bea's stories, Barbara makes herself a character who confronts
Kerry, just as Bea had in the past. These stories not only give Barbara the
opportunity to seriously answer Bea's suggestions, they also permit her to
construct a future scene in which she carries out a confrontation with Kerry.
In these scenes Barbara is the accuser and Kerry is the defendant. These
enacted sequences have certain regular features: (1) an evaluation of the
offending party's actions, (2) an accusation, and (3) a response to the accusation.

Barbara evaluates Bea's stories by making statements about how the
offender should have acted:

(4)
22   Barbara: So, she got anything t'say she
23   come say it in front of my face.

Her evaluations also include warnings for Kerry:

(4)
118   Barbara: I better not catch you t'day.=I'm a
119   *tell her butt o*:ff.

(4)
157   Barbara: W'll I'm tellin' ya
158   *I* better not catch Kerry to*day*. Cuz if
159   I catch her I'm gonna give *her* a wor:d
160   from my *mou*th.

Combined with the warning may be a statement of how she will confront
Kerry with a formal complaint:

(4)
101   Barbara: I better not see Kerry to*day*. I'm a
102   say "Kerry *I* heard *y*ou was talkin' 'bout
103   me."

(4)
24   Barbara: I better not *see Kerry* today. (2.5) I
25   *ain*'t gonna say- I'm~a~say "Kerry *what*
26   *you say* about me."

Following the offended's enactment of her own future action as an accuser, she projects how the defending party will respond with denials, actions that are expected following opening accusations:

(4)
```
26    Barbara:    She gonna say
28                "I ain't say nuttin'."
```

(2)
```
105   Barbara:    Then she gonna say "I ain't-
106               What I say about you."
```

At the close of the future stories, Barbara enacts additional parts of the drama, which are contingent on Kerry's response to Barbara:

(4)
```
121   Barbara:    An if she get bad at me:e: I'm a,
122               punch her in the eye.
```

(4)
```
160   Barbara:    An' if she jump in
161               my face I'm a punch her in her fa:ce.
```

Note that these projected accusations differ from actual he-said-she-said accusations in that Barbara does not include reference to Bea, the party who told her about the offenses. The lack of specificity concerning the reporter is adaptive to the immediate interaction. The party who informed the accuser of an offense is someone within the present interaction. Were the accusation to contain a reference to a specific person who informed on the offending party, this would call attention to the fact that at the next stage of the event the party in the present interaction who had reported the offense could be identified as someone who talked about the defendant in her absence.

Offended parties' responses which constitute plans to confront the offending party are made in the presence of witnesses; they thus provide displays of someone's intentions to seek redress for the offenses perpetrated against her. Failure to follow through with a commitment statement such as "I'm a tell her about herself to*day*" can be remarked on as demonstrating inconsistencies in a person's talk and actions, thus reflecting negatively on her character. Indeed, when Julia later fails to confront Kerry, others use her actions in the present exchange to talk about the way in which she had promised to tell Kerry off but then did nothing:

(5)   Bea: Yeah and Julia all the time talking
                 'bout she was gonna tell whats-her-name
                 off. And she ain't do it.

Alignments taken up in the midst of an exchange such as this can thus be interpreted as commitments to undertake future action for which parties may be held responsible by others. People who refuse to confront once they have reported their intentions are said to "swag," "mole," or "back down" from a future confrontation and may be ridiculed in statements such as "You molin' out." The fact that a statement about future intentions can be treated as a relevantly absent event at a future time provides some demonstration of how responses to instigating stories are geared into larger social projects.

These enactments of possible worlds (Lakoff 1968) in which Barbara is confronting Kerry not only provide strong displays of her commitment to carry out a confrontation with Kerry but also enable her to rehearse future lines in that encounter.[6] Such enactments might be viewed as idealized versions (Werner and Fenton 1973:538–539) of the sequence of activity in the actual confronting. That is, a minimal he-said-she-said sequence would, given this model, contain an accusation, a defense, and a warning or evaluation of offender's actions.

Typically anthropologists, and ethnoscientists in particular, employ *elicited informants' accounts* to substantiate their statements about the "ideational order." Quite frequently such accounts occur as the product of interaction between informants and researchers (Briggs 1986; Jordan and Suchman 1987; Mishler 1986) fitted to the expectations participants have for such encounters. Alternatively, anthropologists might make use of talk between members of the group being studied. As these stories show, participants in their talk to one another provide rather precise images of confrontation encounters, specifying minimal sequences of appropriate utterance types.

11.3 STORIES RETOLD BY INSTIGATOR TO PERIPHERAL PARTIES

He-said-she-said confrontations are dramatic events that the whole street looks forward to with eager anticipation. Between the instigating and the confrontation stages, selective reporting of prior talk occurs when the instigator meets someone who is not a principal to the dispute but will act as audience to it. After the storyteller secures recipient's commitment to confront the offending party, an instigator may tell a friend not involved in the conflict about what happened. This occurs as Bea (instigator) meets Martha (peripheral party) and relates what had just occurred with Barbara (offended party). As argued earlier, narrative generally is told from the perspective of teller about her own past actions. However, in the stories related to peripheral figures, instigator emphasizes offended party's past statements which are important to the future confrontation but eliminates her own work in soliciting such statements. In her retelling, Bea omits entirely the stories she told to Julia. She downplays her own role in the past stories, summarizing her participation with a single statement—"I had told Barbara what um, what Kerry said about her?" (lines 1–3)—and then launches into her story about the offended party's promise to confront the offending party. Informing Barbara of these events had in fact involved the major portion of the informing process. However, this is reported succinctly and in indirect speech. By way of contrast, Bea reports in direct speech Barbara's response to her informings (lines 4–11):

```
(6)  1    Bea:        Hey you- you n- you know- you know I-
     2                I- I had told Barbara, what um,
     3                what Kerry said about her? And I-
     4                and she said "I better not see um,
     5                um Kerry, b'cause" she said she said
     6                "Well I'm comin' around Maple
     7                and I just better not see her
     8                b'cause I'm- b'cause I'm gonna tell her
     9                behind her- in front of her face
    10                and not behind her-
    11                I mean in front of//her face."
    12   Martha:      She call her baldheaded and all that?
    13   Bea:         Yep. And she said- she said- she said
    14                I'm gonna-
```

In the initial storytelling session, the crucial events at issue were the actions of the offending party (Kerry). Such events were important in that they constructed a portrait of the absent party as an offender. When a story is retold to someone who may be a future witness to the confrontation, a detailed chronology of past events is not key to the activity of involving a listener in some future stage of the he-said-she-said events. The crucial aspect of the past story is, rather, responses of the offended party to the report: in particular, whether or not she will seek a confrontation. Indeed, it is this latter action that brings into existence the drama that will engross the spectator. As Martha, after hearing Bea's report (and anticipating the future confrontation), states:

```
(7)    Martha:     Can't wait t'see this
                   A::Ctio:n. Mmfh. Mmfh.
```

In that offended party's responses projected a future confrontation, they are relevant to the peripheral figure's future participation. Bea marks the importance of these responses not only by placing them very early in the story, but also through their elaboration.

11.4 FUTURE HYPOTHETICAL STORIES TOLD BY INSTIGATOR AND PERIPHERAL PARTY

In response to Bea's replaying of her informing to Barbara, both Bea and Martha collaborate in constructing a future story. They elaborate hypothetical events occurring when offended meets offending party; however, their projections, which include admissions of guilt and personal insults, do not, in fact, occur in confrontation sequences.

(8) 1	Martha:	Can't wait t'see this
2		A::Ctio:*n*. Mm*fh*. Mm*fh*.
3	Bea:	But if *Bar*bara say // she
4	Martha:	I laugh- I laugh I laugh if Kerry say-
5		Bea s- I laugh if Barbara say,
6		"*I wrote* it
7		so what you gonna *do* about it."
8	Bea:	*She* say, she- and- and- and she
9		and she probably gonna back out.
10	Martha:	I know.
11	Bea:	*Boouh boouh* // *boouh*
12	Martha:	And then she gonna say "You didn't
13		*have* to *write* that about me Barbara."
14		She might call her Barbara *fat* somp'm.
15		=Barbara say "Least I don't have no long:
16		bumpy legs and bumpy neck. *Sp*ot legs,
17		*h Least I don't gonna fluff my hair up
18		to make me look like // I hadda bush."
19	Bea:	Y'know *she's*- she-
20		least she *fat*ter than her.
21	Martha:	Yeah an' "Least I got bones.=
22		At least I got *shape*."
23		That's what she could say. (0.6)
24		Barbara *is* cuter than her though.
25	Bea:	Yah:p. And Barbara got *shape* too.

In this sequence the party who was a nonparticipant in the informing stories but is present at the replaying of such stories, Martha, projects herself as a spectator to an upcoming confrontation (lines 5–7): "I laugh if Barbara say, '*I wrote* it so what you gonna *do* about it.' " The enactment of the future event, however, is made up of forms of utterances which contrast with those which are actually enacted in a confrontation. Martha notes that it would be an event which would evoke an unusual response, laughter, were Barbara actually to admit the offense. In dramatizing what Kerry and Barbara would say to each other, Martha and Bea use personal insults (lines 15–22), actions which among girls rarely occur in someone's presence.

The informing about a past meeting with an offended party serves to recruit potential spectators to the event. It provides for forms of enactments about possible future events for those not occupying the identity of offended or offending party in the confrontation, in much the same way that informing about offenses to an offended party provides for enactments by that party.[7] License in building dialogue in future stories occurs in part because girls are talking about absent parties rather than involving themselves in providing an accurate depiction of an event. In addition, the reporting is a way of recruiting potential spectators to the event, in that it provides for their involvement at a future time.

The way in which Bea presents her description of past events to Martha differs from her informings to Julia and Barbara. Although in the stories Bea told to Julia and Barbara (#2 and #4) she took precautions to elicit responses from them with regard to their alignment toward the offending party, building in opportunities for them to do so before indicating her own orientation toward Kerry, with Martha (#6 and #8) she launches into her story in an unguarded fashion. While Julia and Barbara appear as cited characters in the stories Bea tells, Martha does not. Moreover, in that Martha and Bea are best friends who complain to one another about both Kerry and Barbara, Bea can expect Martha to side with her on most issues. In fact, as seen earlier when this he-said-she-said is played out, after Kerry confronts Bea for having talked about her, both Martha and Bea provide denials (see Chapter 8, #1). The friendship alignments between girls are thus important in the structuring of gossip stories.

Stories tied to the he-said-she-said event thus take a variety of forms; they include (1) initial instigating stories between instigator and offended party, (2) future stories of offended party in response to instigating stories, (3) retold stories about the instigating session between instigator and offended, and (4) hypothetical stories between instigator and peripheral parties. In delivering her stories, instigator carefully shapes them to elicit from her listeners responses which will promote involvement in a future confrontation. She embellishes past dialogue which will evoke recipient response and downplays talk of her own which could be viewed in an objectionable way. Offended party for her part, too, carefully omits the role of instigating party in evoking a future stage. Finally, hypothetical future stories provide a way for instigator and peripheral party to talk about absent parties and play with speech actions which are generally taboo in female interaction.

The form of listener analysis and participation examined here demonstrates the competence of listeners to interpret events in culturally appropriate terms. Questions and enactments of future scenes display to the teller that the listener is performing at each point in the story an ongoing analysis of events. In order to demonstrate understanding in a relevant way and to have this understanding ratified, listeners make use of procedures for projecting future stages in the he-said-she-said.

11.5 A COMPARISON OF BOYS' AND GIRLS' DISPUTE STORIES

We may now compare the forms of participation which are made available in boys' and girls' dispute stories. Within dispute processes, girls' and boys' stories share several features in common: (1) the principal topic is offenses of another, and (2) one of the characters in the story is a *present participant*. In the case of boys' stories, cited offenses deal with wrongdoings of a present participant. Among girls, however, offenses concern *reported deeds of absent parties*. Although both girls and boys oppose the reported descriptions, such structural differences lead them to make alternative types of responses. While boys who are offended parties direct counters to *principal storyteller*, girls direct their counters to *cited figures* who offended them in the past. In that the offending party is absent from the instigating event, girls, in contrast to boys, cannot resolve their disagreements in the present interaction.

A second point of contrast in boys' and girls' dispute stories is that *principal hearer* is portrayed in different ways. While in Chopper's story Tony has performed objectionable actions in the past as a coward, in girls' instigating stories the present hearers (Julia and Barbara) have performed exemplary actions in the past, which sharply contrast with the objectionable actions of an absent party (Kerry). The portrayal of characters and events within dispute stories has consequences for the form and timing of interaction which ensues. Thus, while boys' dispute stories engender disagreements which permit negotiation in the *immediate setting*, girls' stories engender alignments of "two against one" against an absent third party who will be confronted *at some future time*. Offended party reacts to the story by stating not only that she disapproves of the offending party's actions toward her in the past but that she is prepared to confront her offender. Although boys' stories have little motive power beyond the present situation, girls' instigating stories are embedded within a larger social process. They constitute a preliminary stage in a larger procedure of sanctioning inappropriate behavior which may extend over several weeks and provide for the involvement of participants in multiple phases of activity.

In both girls' and boys' stories, recipient response from parties other than those who are principal figures in the story aids in the teller's depiction of the offending party; nonfocal participants provide comments on the offender's character. In the boys' stories, this is accomplished largely through laughter, requests for elaboration, and repetition of quoted refrains of the principal character's speech in a past event. Girls' comments or evaluations likewise blatantly display that the story instances inappropriate behavior of an offending party. Among the girls, nonfocal participants make their commentary principally by referring to ongoing objectionable attributes of the offender.

The girls' and boys' stories investigated here tell of future and imaginary events as well as past occurrences. In boys' stories, the party cast as the offender may initiate hypothetical stories; in an attempt to counter pejorative descriptions made about him, offended party may portray storyteller in imaginary events in which he appears cowardly. With respect to girls' instigating stories, the primary organization of the descriptions in them as well as responses to them is to be found not in properties of the past events being described but rather in the structure of the present interaction, which includes an anticipated future. That anticipation is possible because of the embeddedness of this entire process, including the constructing and understanding of the stories, within a larger cultural event, the he-said-she-said. Such stories therefore differ from the forms of those most frequently dealt with by students of stories. Although Goffman (1974:505) has noted the possibility of "preplays," most researchers have a narrower vision of what constitutes a narrative; generally narrative is considered "a method of recapitulating past experience by matching a verbal sequence of clauses to the sequence of clauses which (it is inferred) actually occurred" (Labov 1972a:359–360).[8] Given this orientation toward the structuring of stories, it is not surprising that researchers of narratives make use of role-played data or elicited texts, assuming that narratives can be analyzed in isolation from the course of events in which they are embedded. While accounts informants give anthropologists can perhaps best be depicted as social constructions (Bruner 1986:141), they are most frequently portrayed as context-free renderings of experience.

Anthropologists frequently rely on reports as primary data sources, and one of their central concerns has been how accurately the report corresponds to the initial events which it describes (Bilmes 1975).[9] By way of contrast, Sacks (1963, 1972:331–332) argues that the central issue is not the correspondence between the report and the event it describes but rather the organization of the description as a situated cultural object in its own right. In the present investigation I have been concerned not with how accurately a story reflects the initial event it describes, but rather with the problem of how the description of the past is constructed in the first place[10] such that it is a recognizable cultural object appropriate to the ongoing social project of the moment. Indeed, I wish to argue, as does Vološinov (1971), that the context of reporting itself provides the description with its primary organization. Such an argument concerning the nature of reports is important for the enterprise of ethnography. Anthropologists, rather than accepting reports as instances of the events they describe, must seriously investigate the process of reporting itself.

Section 5

Conclusion

CHAPTER TWELVE

Conclusion

The preceding ethnographic study of children's talk has integrated the analysis of conversation within anthropological fieldwork.[1] In several ways, this approach differs from most other studies of children. First, it locates the *peer group*, rather than caretaker-child or adult-child units, as the locus for study. As Piaget (1965:396) argues, the peer setting provides the most appropriate of all settings for observing the fullest elaboration of children's speech activities.[2] Research emphasis on adult-child rather than peer group interaction may occur because it has become common to treat socialization as a fundamentally *psychological* process; children, who are believed to gradually internalize adult values, are seen as in need of "integration into the social world" (Richards 1974):[3]

> The child . . . remains for social theory *negatively defined*, because s/he is de-
> fined only by what the child is *not* but is subsequently going to be, and not
> by what the child presently *is*. The child is depicted as pre-social, potentially
> social, in the process of becoming social—essentially undergoing socialization.
> (Alanen 1988:924)

Such a perspective is also characteristic of anthropology, which views children as "raw material, unfinished specimens of the social beings whose ideas and behavior are the proper subject matter for a social science" (LaFontaine 1986:10). This book, in its concentration on the dynamics of *peer interaction*, has argued against such traditional views of socialization. I have instead treated children as *actors actively engaged* in the construction of their social worlds rather than as *passive objects* who are the recipients of culture.

A further way in which my fieldwork differs from other studies of children by social scientists, and in particular psychologists, is that I made no attempt to manipulate the situation observed; I neither elicited[4] speech acts nor created artificial social units such as dyadic pairs to be studied. Rather, I observed spontaneous encounters within the most ordinary of children's social constellations: multiparty interaction. Moreover, in contrast to studies of peer interaction that focus on events within the school setting (a situation in which adults dominate), this study was situated within the children's neighborhood. Such a vernacular setting constitutes

a key locus for the analysis of children's competencies. In the neighborhood, children of different ages interact with members of the opposite sex
as well as their own. Moreover, events are controlled and organized by the
children themselves, rather than by adult caretakers. Within such a rich
social environment, speech activities become more elaborated. Indeed,
some of the speech events that showed the greatest syntactic complexity
and conceptual strategy—arguing, for example—are actively sanctioned in
settings controlled by adults.[5] By observing the neighborhood setting over
an extended period of time (one and a half years), I was afforded a rich
natural experiment and could investigate how the organization of talk
changes as children move from one activity to another.

Such a strategy is particularly important given some of the typifications
of female speech which argue that females speak "in a different voice"
(Gilligan 1982),[6] and unwittingly may support the view of females as pow-
erless speakers. Many task activities among Maple Street girls are conducted in a way which emphasizes relative equality and solidarity among
participants and avoids disagreement. However, activities such as pretend
play, jump rope (M. H. Goodwin 1985b), and argument can be actively
constructed so as to display difference or asymmetry. While in both task
activity and pretend play, the accounts girls provide in their directives deal
with relationships and their connections to others, the moral concerns
within the he-said-she-said confrontation involve issues of "justice and
rights" rather than an ethic of "care and responsibility" (Gilligan 1982).
Thus the type of social structure as well as the moral themes expressed in
speech actions varies from activity to activity and argues for a situated
rather than unidimensional view of girls' concerns.[7] Cooperation and competition are not mutually exclusive agendas and often coexist within the
same speech activities. In both pretend play and he-said-she-said confrontations, participants work together to sustain a coherent activity with a
well-defined structure. However, the specific type of joint action which is
exhibited does not resemble "supportive" forms of collaboration described
elsewhere as characteristic of female speech (see Maltz and Borker
1983:211). For example, there is no "underlying aesthetic or organizing
principle" of "harmony," as Kalčik (1975) found in the adult female storytelling group she studied. Moreover, the talk of the argumentative sequences examined in this book displays anything but "a tone of relaxed
sweetness, sometimes bordering on the saccharin," which Hannerz
(1969:96) finds typical of black female adult speech, in contrast to black
males' argumentative style. In Abrahams's view, female values of respect-
ability and the home are contrasted with male values of reputation and the
public world (Abrahams 1976:64); however, displaying one's character in a
public arena is precisely what is at issue in a he-said-she-said, and girls
can hold their own in arguments with boys.

Dichotomies such as domestic and public (Rosaldo 1974) or nature and culture (Ortner 1974) are of relatively little use in explicating how boys and girls on Maple Street come to process experience in different ways. Indeed, gender asymmetry, considered the social-structural principle leading to polar contrasts such as public and private, does not constitute a relevant feature of social organization among Maple Street children.[8] In this sense the neighborhood appears to differ from the school, where teachers sort children on the basis of gender (Maccoby and Jacklin 1987; Thorne 1986). The diversity of activities children on Maple Street engage in across age/ gender groups is remarkable. More studies of neighborhood groups are needed to see how extensively other groups of children have access to the range of activities or possibilities for cross-sex or cross-age interaction which occur on Maple Street. Such studies could be important in promoting more diversity within the school environment as well as in guiding child-development workers in their planning of after-school programs.[9]

Girls and boys on Maple Street have in common not only a similar social space but also procedures for carrying out numerous conversational events. I therefore focused on the construction of conversational activities in organizing my data rather than on sex differences in building such speech activities. While studies of girls' peer groups fill a large void in our understanding of female social organization, most studies (among white, predominantly middle-class girls)[10] tend to focus on distinctions between age/ sex groups and boundary maintaining mechanisms, ignoring the features of social interaction girls and boys share in common. Indeed as Overing (1986:142) has argued, "stress in anthropology has probably been too much on *difference*, while not sufficient attention has been paid to how conceptually the sexes can be viewed as *sharing* a common humanity."

Much the same argument can be made about ethnicity. In the literature on black speech events, there has been a strong bias toward concentrating on what *differences* can be discerned between groups. A rich body of research by linguists, sociolinguists, and students of folklore exists on the grammar of the language of black children (Baratz and Shuy 1969; Dillard 1972) and adolescents (Baugh 1983; Labov, Cohen, Robins, and Lewis 1968), as well as on a variety of speech acts in black culture (Abrahams 1963, 1976; Folb 1980; Kochman 1972, 1981; Labov 1972a:297–353; Mitchell-Kernan 1971). However, such studies of black speech events tend to focus on the uniqueness of patterns of black communication (Abrahams 1974, 1975b, 1976; Kochman 1970, 1981; Reisman 1970, 1974a, 1974b)[11] rather than investigating the underlying structure for accomplishing those activities. If, as Goodenough has argued, the ethnographer should try to provide a "how to do it" book that makes explicit the structures and procedures used to build, interpret, and participate in the ordinary scenes in a society, then focusing study only on what distinguishes a group from those around it inevitably distorts the analysis and leads to study of only a small subset of the cultural resources available to that group. The present work provides analysis of a range of complex speech events not described previously by students of black culture, without, however, making the claim that access to these events is restricted to a single ethnic group.[12]

The salience of speech in structuring social relationships is given a great deal of attention in my analysis. It is common when describing the relationship between language, culture, and society to state that language *reflects* some aspect of the social order. For example, Sherzer (1987:296) argues that language is social in that it "reflects and expresses group memberships and relationships." This analysis has examined ways in which aspects of gender are manifested in speech activities, but more important, I have investigated how speech events can themselves *provide for* social organization, shaping alignment and social identities of participants to the present interaction. Through investigation of how language is used in daily interaction, I have attempted an examination of how language constitutes a powerful tool for organizing social groups.

The particular way in which talk is structured creates *participation frameworks*: an entire field of action including both interrelated occasion-specific identities and forms of talk; a speaker may transform the social order of the moment by invoking a different speech activity. For example, as we saw in Chapter 10, by switching from a contest of verbal contention to a story, a participant may dramatically reshape a dyadic form of interaction into a multiparty one; this may permit an opponent to recruit others to visibly confirm his/her position. Similarly, within the he-said-she-said confrontation, a field of negotiated action, complete with its own relevant history, is invoked through the structure of an opening accusation statement; a single utterance creates a complex past history of events, providing operative identity relationships for participants. Through careful framings of experience and "tactical uses of passion" (Bailey 1983) in instigating stories, girls can call forth feelings of righteous indignation that are relevant to the shaping of a dispute which can last for over a month. The interactive frame created by the he-said-she-said event thus links together several speech events—stories, gossip, and argument—within a single process, the management of breaches. Such analysis of vernacular conflict expands the scope of dispute mechanisms encompassed by legal anthropology.

Treating language as "a mode of social action rather than a mere reflection of thought" (Malinowski 1959:312–313) necessitates investigation of how competent members of a society use language to deal with each other. This requires first, methods of data collection that maintain the sequential structure of indigenous interactive events (i.e., ones which exclude the ethnographer's intervention through elicitation) and make visible the process that these events are both embedded within and constitute; and second, a mode of analysis that, rather than treating talk as either a means for obtaining information *about* other phenomena or a special type of verbal performance, focuses on how competent members use talk socially to act out the ordinary scenes of their everyday life.[13]

The study of ordinary conversation not only focuses attention upon what cross-culturally constitutes one of the most pervasive of all human activities. It also requires that we examine critically the very process of reporting, which constitutes the anthropologist's primary means for learning about culture. If "describing a culture in a way that allows one to have some confidence in a claim to have revealed a bit of reality rather than to have created a bit of fantasy" (Frake 1980:333) is recognized as a critical problem for ethnographic description, then *providing texts for the scrutiny of others* should be of primary rather than incidental concern. Conversation analysis, through its emphasis on documentation of interaction among members of a society, furthers the methodology of anthropology and facilitates comparative research. In addition, a focus on ongoing interaction in everyday encounters enables anthropologists to describe institutions (such as social control mechanisms) within a society as dynamic rather than static cultural processes. Indeed, talk constitutes one of the most basic forms of social order in which human beings take part. It should be at the core of a general theory of human social organization, one that embodies linguistic and cultural competence.

It has frequently been assumed that the speech of working-class children, and black children in particular,[14] is deficient, and that talk produced in actual situations of use is too degenerate for systematic analysis (Chomsky 1965:3–4). The present analysis demonstrates that, to the contrary, the speech of children at play, in particular talk taken to be "aimless activity" (Malinowski 1959:315), constitutes a powerful manifestation not only of linguistic competence, but of social and cultural competence as well.

Finally, I would like to make a plea for the primacy of conversational materials in anthropological understandings of how people structure their lives. Radcliffe-Brown (1973:310) was of the opinion that while there may be "certain indirect interactions between social structure and language . . . these would seem to be of minor importance." My investigation of the ways in which language can construct social order indicates, to the contrary, that it is possible to analyze language as a functionally integrated component of a group's social organization and culture. Analyzing language, culture, and social organization from such a perspective would seem to be quite consistent with the traditional, holistic goals of anthropology. By making use of the techniques of conversation analysis and the documentation of the sequential organization of indigenous events, we can avoid the pitfalls of "interpretive anthropology," which tends to focus its attention on ethnographer/informant dialogue rather than interaction *between participants*. This will enable us to move away from reports to ethnographers of how people play out their lives toward an "anthropology of experience" concentrating on how people themselves actually perform activities—an endeavor at the very heart of anthropological study.

Appendix A
The Children

Although boys usually played in groups of no more than eight, the following list identifies all of the boys who provided a pool of potential participants in the older boys' group and their ages in 1970:

Boys	Age	Grade	Street
Tommy	9	5th	Maple
Derrick	10	5th	Maple
William	10	5th	Maple
Vincent	10	5th	Maple
Alan	11	6th	Maple
Carl	11	6th	Maple
Freddie	11	6th	Maple
Lee	11	6th	another neighborhood
Tickey	11	6th	Poplar
Earl	11	6th	Poplar
Harold	11	6th	Maple
Charles	11	6th	Maple
Chopper	12	7th	Maple
Billy	12	6th	Poplar
Dave	12	7th	Maple
Sheridan	12	7th	another neighborhood
Tokay	12	7th	another neighborhood
Jimmy	13	8th	Maple
Juju	13	8th	Maple
Malcolm	13	8th	Maple
Pete	13	8th	Maple
Ossie	13	8th	Maple
Tony	14	8th	Maple

Girls generally played in groups no larger than four or five; however, the larger pool of girls from which groups were formed included the following:

Girls	Age	Grade	Street
Annette	10	5th	Maple
Yolanda	10	5th	Poplar
Patrice	10	5th	Poplar
Sister	10	5th	Maple
Ruby	11	5th	Maple
Bea	12	7th	Maple
Martha	12	7th	Poplar
Julia	12	7th	Maple
Kerry	12	8th	Maple

Older girls who socialized with other girls or who had boyfriends included:

Barbara	13	8th	Poplar
Joanie	13	8th	Maple
Rhonda	14	9th	Poplar

Girls from beyond the one-block radius of Maple and Poplar streets who sometimes played with the Maple Street group included:

Stacey	10	5th	
Deniece	10	5th	
Sheila	10	5th	

Members of the younger girls' group included:

Girls	Age	Grade	Street
Jolyn	4	nursery school	Maple
Prestina	5	kindergarten	Poplar
Wanda	7	2nd	Maple
Drucilla	7	2nd	Poplar
Benita	8	3rd	Maple
Rochele	9	4th	Maple
Annette	10	5th	Maple
Vanessa	10	5th	Maple

The younger boys' group included:

Boys	Age	Grade	Street
Larry	6	1st	Maple
Douglas	6	1st	Maple
Arthur	7	2nd	Maple

Appendix B
Ritual Insult Sequence

1	Malcolm:	Shoes all messed up.
2		(1.0)
3	Ruby:	You say somp'm? I- come on let me have it.
4	Malcolm:	You been che(hh)win' o(hh)n e(hh)//m.
5	Ruby:	Eh heh heh heh heh!
6		*h I *know* you been.
7		*You* all me://ssed up.
8	Malcolm:	*h You bee(h)n chewin' o(h)n e//(h)m.
9	Ruby:	Eh heh!
10		No I *hav*en't.
11	Malcolm:	Yes you ha://ve.
12	Ruby:	You took a(h)n' got your dog
13		your dog 'd chew 'em up
14		cuz he ain't have nothin' ta // eat.
15	Malcolm:	If he pick up a piece of wood
16		and I say no ( ) then it's in the-
17		in the // ( )
18	Ruby:	Ah you shu:t up.
19		⌈You can't even kees // a
20	Malcolm:	⌊You slap
21		You just slappin' on wood!
22	Ruby:	You can't even *keep* a (0.2)
23		a decent (0.2) pair a shoe://s.
24	Malcolm:	Don't swag.
25		(0.3)
26	Ruby:	I'm not *swa*:ggin'.
27	Malcolm:	You // are too cuz you go to the (0.2)
28		you go to the John
29	Ruby:	Mole mole cheek cheek. Psychedelic.
30		(0.2) that'//s all.
31	Malcolm:	You go to the John Baldwin's store
32		and get them five-dollar shoes.
33		(0.8)
34	Malcolm:	Eh // heh!
35	Ruby:	What?
36	Malcolm:	Cuz the closest thing
37		is the Thrifty Sto(heh-heh//heh)re!
38	Ruby:	You go and get them *one* dollar. Okay?
39		One day- (0.2)
40		H{my} *bro*ther was spendin'the night with *you*,
41		*h And // the next mornin' he got up,

42	Malcolm:	I don't wanna hear about it.
43		Your brother // ain't *never* been in *my* house.
44	Ruby:	THE NEXT TIME HE GOT UP,
45		*heh He was gonna brush his teeth
46		so the roach tri(h)ed ta(h) bru(h)sh hi(h)s!
47	Malcolm:	Don't // swag.
48	Ruby:	*h *Ha ha ha ha ha *hh*!// *h
49		Eh heh heh // *heh* he he he he
50	Malcolm:	An if he was up there
51		If the roach was tryin' ta *brush* it
52		he musta brought it up- it up there *with* him.
53	Ruby:	*heh!
54		*h *Eh*//he heh heh heh he he he he
55	Malcolm:	*h eh heh!
56	Tommy:	((*falsetto*)) Ha// he! he
57	Ruby:	He he he he ha // ha ha // ha
58	Jimmy:	*heh!
59	Jimmy:	*H!
60	Ruby:	*h and I // saw-
61		I sawed you on (0.2)Ni:nth Street *knit* on
62		tryin' ta catch a *sale* for a dollar!
63	Jimmy:	*H heh.
64	Malcolm:	Don't swag.
65	Ruby:	Ah: shut up. ((*singsong*)) Poor little Malcolm,
66	Malcolm:	What? Do you have a knit?
67	Ruby:	⌜Sittin' onna fence,
68	Malcolm:	Do you have a knit?
69	Ruby:	Troyina make a dollar
70		outa ninety-noine cents. He heh!
71		(0.3)
72		Ah ha:. (0.2) And one *more* thing!
73		One day (0.2) *I* went in your hou-
74		*I* was gonna walk in the door
75		for *two* sets // a roaches.
76	Malcolm:	For what.
77		For what.
78	Ruby:	One roach here (0.2) and one roach here.
79		THE ONE RIGHT HERE,
80	Malcolm:	Oh you tryin' ta *sell* // 'em for him.
81	Ruby:	THE ONE RIGHT HERE W-
82	Malcolm:	You tryin' to se(hh)ll 'e(hh)m.
83	Ruby:	THE ONE RIGHT HERE // WAS UP HERE SAYIN'-
84	Malcolm:	*Some*body gonna buy your // damn roach.
85	Ruby:	THE ONE RIGHT here was up here sayin'-
86		(0.2) "People movin' *ou:t*?" (0.2)
87		And the one right here was sayin' (0.2)
88		"*Peo*ple movin' in-"

89		[Why? Because of the odor of their //ski(hh)n.
90	Malcolm:	You understand their language.
91		You must be one of 'em.
92	Jimmy:	((*falsettto*)) Eh **heh!** Heh he heh!
93	Ruby:	What'd he s(hhhh)ay? Wha(h)d he(h) say(h)y?
94		*H What he(h) sa(hh)y?
95		What he sa(heh heh)y? What you say?
96		Whad's he // say Candy?
97	Malcolm:	You understand their language
98		cuz you *one* of 'em.
99	Ruby:	I(h) ***know(h)*** you(h) ar(hh)re!
100		You was ***born*** from the roach fam//ily.
101	Malcolm:	Don't swag.
102		(1.2)
103	Ruby:	Don't ***you*** swa::g.
104		(1.2)
105		You know one thing ((tch!))
106		uh when you was *li*ttle,
107		All you did every roach
108		you see crawl on the floor
109		you get it and save it for a souvenir.=
110	Malcolm:	Don't swag. You used to go out there
111		and put the roaches in the- in the-
112		in the jar at night. (0.2) And put 'em
113		and let 'em out in the mornin'.

Appendix C
Boys' Dispute Stories

(1)

1	Tony:	Gimme the *things*.
2	Chopper:	You sh:ut up you *b*ig lips. (Y'all been
3		hangin' around with thieves.)
4	Tony:	(*Sh*ut up.)
5	Chopper:	Don't gimme that.=I'm not *t*alkin' to
6		you.
7		(1.4)
8	Tony:	I'm talkin' to *y*:ou!
9	Chopper:	Ah you better sh:ut *up* with your
10		little- *di*:ngy sneaks.
11		(1.4)
12	Tony:	I'm a *d*ingy your hea:d.=How would you
13		like *that*.
14		(0.4)
15	Chopper:	No you won't you little- ⌜*h *Guess* what.
16	Jack:	(°foul) foul
17		thing.
18		(0.4)
19	Chopper:	Lemme~tell~ya.=*Gu*ess what. (0.8) We
20		was comin' home from *pr*actice, (0.4)
21		and, three boys came up there (.) and
22		asked~us~for~money~and~Tony~did~like~
23		this. (0.6)
24		*hh ((*raising hands up*))
25		"*I AIN'T* GOT n(h)(hh)⌜o °m(h)oney."
26	Pete:	Ah-hih-ha,
27		*hh Hah-hah!
28	Chopper:	((*snicker*)) khh
29	( ):	(° look ⌜good.)
30	Pete:	*hh
31	Tokay:	You *di*:⌜d, ((*smile intonation*))
32	Pete:	Aw:,
33	Chopper:	*hhh~((*snicker*)) Khh ⌜°Hey O(h)ssie.
34	Malcolm:	Ah~*ha*~aa~aa Ah~*ha*//ha
35	Tokay:	You there *Ma*lcolm,
36	Chopper:	((*snicker*)) *hhKh He was the(hh)re.
37	Tokay:	What'd· he say *Ch*opper, ((*smile*
38		*intonation*))
39	Chopper:	((*snicker*)) *hKh Yeah.=
40	Tony:	=You was there ⌜To*kay*!
41	Chopper:	*hih *hih

```
42 Chopper:    Lemme~tell ya, An' h(h)e sai(hh)d,
43 Tokay:      WH:en!=
44 Chopper:    ="I ain't got no(h) mo⌈(h)ney."
45 Tony:                             'Member=
46 Pete:     =⌈Whew::,
47 Tony:        that night when we was goin' ⌈there,
48 Chopper:                                ((snicker)) Khh
49 Tony:       and ⌈them boys came down the street,
50 Chopper:        ((snicker)) Khhh!
51 Tony:       I ain't rai:sed my hands ⌈up.
52 Chopper:                             ⌈Go
53             ahead.=You're gonna say it- I know:.
54             *hh Didn't he g'like this? (0.4)
55             "I ain't go(hh)t
56             no(hh)n⌈(h)e."
57 Malcolm:          Ah~ha~ha~ha~ha~ha~ha
58 Chopper:    ((snicker)) *hkh
59 Malcolm:    Aw:::
60 Chopper:    *H ((snicker)) KHH
61 Malcolm:    ((baby voice)) "I ain't got no money."
62             Ah-⌈ha-ha.
63 Chopper:       ((snicker)) Khhhhheh!
64 Tony:       If he had money. If ⌈he had money
65 Chopper:                        ⌈*hihh
66 Tony:     ⌈and he said he didn't=
67 Chopper:  ⌈*hih
68 Tony:       =them boys kicked his b'hi(hh)nd. °eh heh
69 Chopper:    I ain't had no mon- I only had a penny
70             they didn't even find it.
71                (0.4)
72 Jack:      °mmYeah.
73                (0.8)
74 Chopper:    At least I didn't go up there and say,
75                (1.2)
76 Chopper:  ⌈"I ain't got none."
77 Tony:       Well there'd be some problems if he
78             came found it didn't it.
79 Chopper:    Nope. And ⌈guess what Mi⌈chael.
80 Malcolm:              ⌈°He said        said
81             ((baby voice)) "I ain't got no money."=
82 Chopper:    =Guess what Malcolm.=Them boys out
83             there said, *hh "Your football player
84             ca:n't, play," And guess where Tony
85             was. (0.6) All the way ar(h)ound the
86             cor(hh)n(h)er. (0.5) *hih ⌈Remember=
87 (    ):                            ⌈°What?
```

88 Chopper: =that night? Them little boys said
89 "That little p:*unk* can't fight?" And
90 Tony started *r*unnin' across the s:treet.
91 Jack: Hey:ₗ:,
92 Chopper: Not eₗven waitin' for 'em.=
93 Ray: eh~*heh*~heh.
94 Tony: =WHAT?!
95 Chopper: 'Member that time, (0.5) Lemme see we
96 got about- where we was playin'
97 basketball at? (1.2) And // you had
98 Tony: Where *who* w'playin' basketball at.
99 Chopper: You know, where we were playin'
100 basketball? And you wasn't even waitin'
101 for us, you was up there r:unnin',
102 Until you got way around the
103 corner.=Them boys said, those boys kep,
104 those boys kept on (*I* said,) "Hey Tony
105 what you runnin' for." He said "*I* ain't
106 runnin'." Them boys woulda come next to
107 *me* I(h) woul(hh)da, *((snicker))* *hKkh I woulda
108 k:icked their *a*ss. And // Tony was
109 all the way ar(h)ound the corner.
110 Tony: I don't know what *you talk*in' 'bout.
111 Jack: °Talkin' // bout bein' *kick*ed. That's
112 what it // is.
113 Pete: 'Member that time,
114 Tony: I don't remember // what *you talk*in'
115 about.
116 Pete: that we was goin' around the corner on
117 Poplar?
118 Chopper: "*I ain*'t got no(hh) mo(hh)ney."
119 Pete: That boy down there
120 Malcolm: *((baby voice))* "*I ain*'t got no money."
121 "I ain't got no money."
122 Tokay: Remember when that boy down in the
123 park, °that time, when he was talkin'
124 to ₗTony for
125 Tony: What he- When is he talkin' ₗabout.
126 Chopper: OH YEAH!
127   (0.5)
128 Chopper: "I *know* you ain't talkin' to
129 *me!*" Down in the park! *((snicker))* Khh~heh!
130 Pete: eh~heh~heh.
131 Chopper: *hh We was down the park, (0.7) and we
132 was- (0.6) and wh- wh- what was he
133 *do*in',=
134 Tony: =You can ask *Ralph* what happened down

135		the *park* Malcolm Johnson cuz *this*
136		sucker *lie* too much.
137	Chopper:	*Uh* UH. We was playin'- (0.3) we was
138		makin' a *darn raft*, (0.5) and them
139		boys (.) was throwin' things at Tony,
140		(0.7) And *he* said, (0.6) "Boy!" And-
141		lemme tell.=(*They*) were talkin' to that
142		*little* boy. Th'he said, "Boy you
143		better watch them *things!*" That big
144		boy said,
145	Tony:	°What ones.=
146	Chopper:	="I *know* (he ain't talkin' to *me!*")
147		I said (0.4) and he said-
148		"NO: not ⌐you: du(hh)mmy-"
149	Tony:	└What things.
150	Pete:	Ah:~*heh*~heh~⌐heh.
151	Chopper:	└"The *little* bo:(hh)y."
152		Eh~heh~heh. ((*snicker*)) *hKh
153	Malcolm:	That-
154	Chopper:	That big boy woulda kicked his butt!
155	Malcolm:	That *li*⌐ttle boy.
156	Tony:	└That's a lie *too* Chopper.
157	Chopper:	Why you talk to that *little* boy.
158		(1.0)
159	Tony:	*I* said *what*?
160	Chopper:	Got you got you *got* you!
161		(1.2)
162	Chopper:	Say Hey heh *heh*
163		heh, Hey hey HEY! HEY HEY *HEY*! "I
164		ain't go(h)t no(h)" (0.8) Da:g!

Appendix D
Girls' Instigating Stories

(2)

Bea, Barbara, and Julia are sitting on Julia's steps discussing substitute teachers during a teachers' strike.

1	Barb:	Teach us some little *six*th-grade work.
2		(0.4) *That*'s how these volun*teers* doin'
3		now. A little um, *h *Ad*din' 'n' all
4		that.
5	Bea:	Yahp. Yahp. // Yahp. An' when
6		we was in the-
7	Barb:	Twenny and twenny is // forty an' all
8		that.
9	Bea:	How 'bout when we was in-
10	Barb:	Oo I *hate* that junk.
11	Bea:	*How- how-* h- um, uh h- h- how about me
12		and *Ju*lia, *h and all them um, and
13		Kerry, *h ⌜and all them-
14	Julia:	⌞Isn't Kerry *mad* at
15		*me* or s:*omp*'m,
16		(0.4)
17	Bea:	*I'on'* kn//ow.
18	Barb:	Kerry~*al*ways~mad~at somebody.
19		°*I* ⌜'on' care.
20	Julia:	⌞Cuz- cuz cuz I wouldn't, cu:z she
21		ain't put my *na*me on that *pa*per.
22	Bea:	*I* know cuz ⌜OH yeah. *Oh* yeah.
23	Barb:	⌞An' next she,
24		(0.3)
25	Barb:	⌜talk~'bout~*peo*ple.
26	Bea:	*She* said, *She* said that um, (0.6)
27		that (0.8) if that *girl* wasn't
28		there=*You* know that girl that always
29		makes those funny jokes, *h Sh'aid if
30		that *girl* wasn't there *you* wouldn't be
31		*ac*tin', (0.4) a:ll *stu*pid like that.
32		⌜°Sh-
33	Julia:	⌞But *was* I actin' stupid w⌜ith them
34	Bea:	⌞Nope, no,=And
35		she- and she said that *you* sai:d, that,
36		"*Ah*: go tuh-" (0.5) somp'm like ⌜tha:t.
37	Julia:	⌞°No I
38		didn't.

39	Bea:	She's- an' uh- somp'm like *that*. She's-
40	Barb:	Ke⌜rry *al*ways say somp'm.=When you=
41	Bea:	⌞She-
42	Barb:	=*jump* in her *face* she gonna de*ny*
43		it.
44	Bea:	Yah:p Y⌜ahp.=An' she said, *h An'- and
45	Julia:	⌞°Right on.
46	Bea:	she said, hh that *you* wouldn't be *a*ctin'
47		*li*ke *that* aroun'- around *pe*ople.
48	Julia:	So: *she* wouldn' be *a*ctin' like *that*
49		wi'that *oth*er girl.=*She* the one picked
50		*me* to *sit* wi'them.=*h She said ⌜"Julia you
51	Bea:	⌞Y:ahp.
52	Julia:	sit with her, *h and I'll sit with her,
53		*h an' Bea an'- an' Bea an'-
54		an' an' ⌜Martha sit together."
55	Barb:	⌞SHE TELLIN' Y'ALL WHERE TA SIT
56		AT?
57		(0.2)
58	Bea:	An' so *we* sat together, An' s- and s- and
59		so Julia was ju:st s:ittin' right
60		there.=An' the girl, an'- an'- the girl:
61		next to her? *h and the girl kept on
62		getting back up. *h Ask the teacher
63		can she go t'the bathroom. An' Julia
64		say she don' *wa*nna go t'the bathroom
65		w'her. An j- And Julia w'just sittin'
66		up there actin'- actin':, ac- ac- actin'
67		sensible. An she up- and she up there
68		talking 'bout, and she- *I* said, I s'd I
69		s'd I s'd "This is how I'm- I'm gonna
70		put Julia *na*:me down here." Cu- m- m-
71		Cuz she had made a pa:ss you know. *h
72		She had made a *pa*:ss.
73		(0.2)
74	Bea:	⌜For all us to go down to the bathroom.
75	Barb:	⌞Y'all go down t'the bathroom?
76	Bea:	For ALLA- yeah. Yeah. For u:m, (0.4)
77		for- for alla us- t'go to the
78		bathroom.= I s'd- I s'd "*How*: *co*:me you
79		ain't put Julia name down here." *h So
80		she said, she said ((whiny, *defensive tone*))
81		"That other girl called 'er so,
82		she no:t *wi*:th *u*:s, so,"
83		That's what she said too. (0.2) So *I*
84		said, s- so I snatched the paper
85		wi'her. I said wh- when we were playin'
86		wi'that paper?

87	Julia:	I'm a I'm a *t*ell her about herself
88		to*da*₍y. Well,
89	Bea:	Huh? huh remember when we're
90		snatchin' that ₍paper.
91	Barb:	An' she gonna tell you
92		another story any*way*. // (Are you gonna
93		talk to her today?)
94	Bea:	But she ain't even put your *na*me down
95		there. *I* just put it *down* there. Me
96		and Martha put it down.=An I said, and
97		she said "*Gi*mme-that-paper.=I don't
98		wanna have her *na*me *d*own here." I s- I
99		s- I s- I said "She woulda allowed *you*
100		name (if you star:ted)."
101		(1.0)
102	Julia:	I said Kerry "°How come you ain't put my
103		name."
104	Barb:	Here go B//ea, "uh uh uh well-"
105	Julia:	"You put that *o*ther girl (name down)
106		didn't you. I thought *you* was gonna
107		have- owl: a hall pass with that *o*ther
108		girl." That's °what Kerry said. I said
109		(What's~her~problem.) OO: r'mind me a-
110		you old b:aldheaded Kerry.
111	Bea:	*I* should say it in fronta her *f*ace.
112		(0.8) Bal': head.
113	Barb:	Hey 'member when what we did th(h)e
114		o(h)ther ti(h)me.

| (3) | | *The following occurs 45 seconds later* |
| | | *after Julia has gone inside.* |

1	Bea:	She shouldn't be *w*ritin' things, about
2		me. (0.5) An' so- An' so- so she said
3		*Ba*rbara, Barbara need ta *go*
4		somewhere.
5		(1.0)
6	Barb:	Well you *t*ell her to *c*ome say it in
7		front of my fa:ce. (0.6) And *I*'ll *p*ut
8		*her* somewhere. (3.8) An' Barbara
9		ain't got nuttin' t'do with *what*.
10	Bea:	*Write*- um doin' um, ₍that- that thing.
11	Barb:	What do y'*all*
12		got ta do with it.
13	Bea:	Because because um, *I* don't know what
14		we got to do with it. Bu₍t she said-
15	Barb:	W'll *she*
16		don't know what *she ta*kin' 'bout.

17	Bea:	But- but she- but we *di:d* have somp'm
18		to do because we was *ma:d* at *her.*
19		Because we didn't *like* her no more.
20		(0.6) And *that's* why, (0.6) Somebody
21		the one ⌈that use-
22	Barb:	⌊So, she got anything t'say she
23		come say it in front of my face. (1.0)
24		I better not *see* Kerry today. (2.5) I
25		*ain't* gonna say- I'm~a~say "Kerry *what*
26		*you say* about m⌈e." She gonna say
27	Bea:	⌊((whiny)) (Nyang)
28	Barb:	"I ain't *say* nuttin'."
29	Bea:	(behind her face) she meant- sh'ent You
30		know you- you know what. She- she
31		chan⌈gin it.
32	Barb:	⌊If I *wro*:te somp'm then I *wrote*
33		it.=Then I got somp'm to do with
34		it.=W'then I *wrote* it.
35		(0.5)
36	Bea:	And *she* said, an'- an'- she u:m ah
37		whah. (I'm sorry oh.) I'm a walk you
38		home. *She* said that um,
39	Barb:	She get on my *n*erves.
40	Bea:	She said that um,=
41	Barb:	=*Nown* I got somp'm ta write about her
42		*now*::.
43		(0.5)
44	Bea:	Oh yeah.=She sai:d tha:t, (0.4) that
45		um, you wouldn't have nuttin' ta do with
46		it, and every*thing*, and *plus*, (0.5)
47	Bea:	⌈um,
48	Barb:	⌊WELL IF I WROTE SOME 'EN *I* HAD SOMP'M
49		T'*DO* with it.
50	Bea:	An she said, *I* wanna see what I was
51		gettin' ready ta say, (2.0) °And um,
52	Barb:	She gonna de*ny* every *word.*=Now *watch.*
53		I c'n put more up there for her the:n.
54		(2.0)
55	Bea:	⌈*What,*
56	Barb:	⌊An' in magic marker °so there.
57		(0.6)
58	Bea:	Oh yeah, oh yeah.=*She* was, she- w's
59		*she* was in Rochele: house you know, and
60		she said that um, that- I heard her
61		say um, (0.4) um um uh uh "*Ju*lia said
62		y'all been talking behind my back."=I
63		said I'm a- I'm a say "H:oney, I'm gla:d.

64		that *you* know I'm talkin' be*hind your*
65		*back.* Because *I-* because *I meant*
66		for you to know *any*way." An' she said,
67		I- said "I don't have to talk behind
68		your back.=I can talk in front of your
69		*face too.*" // And she said-
70	Barb:	That's all I write. I didn't
71		write that. *I* wrote *that.*
72		(1.2)
73	Bea:	Over here. *I* write *this-* I cleared it
74		*off.* Because *La*nda *wrote*
75		and I- *h ⌐and *I* made it *bigger.*
76	Barb:	Mmm,
77		(0.2)
78	Bea:	So she said, ⌐That first-
79	Barb:	And the other I did with
80		my finger on the cars ⌐and all that.
81	Bea:	An'- so- *I* said,
82		an'- an' so we were playin *sch*ool you
83		know at Rochele's house? And *boy we*
84		*t*ore her *all-* we said, I got
85		uh y'know ⌐I was doin' some signs?
86	Barb:	I better *not* go around an
87		catch Kerry.
88	Bea:	And Ro*chele* called her *bald*headed
89		right~in~fronta~her face. She said "You
90		*bald*headed *thing.*" Because she was
91		messin' with Rochele.=I said, and so she
92		said, you know we were playin' around
93		with her? And she said "You *bald*headed
94		thing."=She said, "Rochele YOU DON'T
95		LIKE IT?" I said I said ⌐that's why-
96	Barb:	Yeah she gonna
97		base in some little kid's ⌐face.
98	Bea:	Yeah. And
99		she said, //I said AND I SAID= I said I
100		said "What~are~ya doin' to her."
101	Barb:	I better not see Kerry to*day*. I'm a
102		say "Kerry *I* heard *you* was talkin'
103		'bout me."
104	Bea:	I a s⌐ay-
105	Barb:	Then she gonna say "I ain't- *What*
106		*I* say about you." I say "Ain't none
107		yer *bus*iness what you said.=You come
108		say it in front a my *f*ace since what=
109		you been tell everybody *else*." (0.4)
110		((falsetto)) OO:, And I can put more

111		and I'm a put some- some °bad words in
112		to*day*.
113		(0.5)
114	Bea:	*She* said, and *she* was saying,
115		⌐she said-
116		*Now* I got somp'm to write ⌐a*bout*.
117	Bea:	└*I* said,
118	Barb:	I better not catch you t'day.=I'm a
119		*tell her butt o*:ff.
120		(0.4)
121	Barb:	An' if she //get *bad* at me:*e*: I'm a,
122		punch her in the eye.
123	Bea:	*I* said, *I* s- *I* said, I said, Hey
124		Barbara I said, "Why don't you" um, I
125		s- I- I- I- and "*Why* don' you stop
126		messing with her." And she said she
127		said "She called me baldheaded."
128		=I said,
129	Barb:	That's right.
130	Bea:	=⌐An' so-
131	Barb:	└That's her name so call her name back.
132	Bea:	*Guess* what. *Guess* what. Uh- we- w-
133		an' we was up finger waving?=And I said,
134		I said, I said I said ((*does motion*))
135		like that.=I did.
136		hh An' ⌐just like that.=*h and I said=
137	Barb:	└OO::,
138	Bea:	an' I an' I was doin' all those *sig*:ns in
139		her face and everything? (0.5) *h And
140		she said that um, (1.0) And then she-
141		an you- and she s- °She- roll her eye
142		like that. *h And she was leanin'
143		against- I- I said, I s'd I s'd Is'd I
144		said, "*Hey* girl don't lean against that
145		thing cuz it's *weak enough*." *h And
146		she said and she said *h she- she did
147		like that.=She say, "Tch!" ((*rolling*
148		*eyes*)) // like that. I s'd- I said "You
149		c'd *roll* your eyes all you *want* to.
150	Barb:	Yeah if somebody do that to her-
151		And if ⌐you know what?
152	Bea:	└Cuz I'm *t*ellin' you. (0.5)
153		Tellin'- I'm not *ask*in' you." (0.4) An' I
154		ain't say no *plea*:se *ei*ther.
155	Barb:	mm hmm.
156	Bea:	((*chews fingers*))
157	Barb:	*Don*'t do that. (1.5) W'll I'm tellin' ya
158		*I* better not catch *Kerry* to*day*. Cuz if

159		I catch her I'm gonna give *her* a wor:d
160		from my *mou*th. (0.6) An' if she *j*ump in
161		my *f*ace I'm a punch her in her *fa*:ce.
162		(1.5) And she can talk behind my ba:ck
163		she better say somp'm in front of my
164		face.
165		(1.5)
166		*((Boy walks down the street.))*
167	Barb:	OO: there go the *Tack*. *h *hh *hh Eh
168		That's your na(h)me.
169		(1.5)
170		*((Barbara starts down the street.))*
171	Barb:	°h See y'all.
172	Bea:	*See* you.

Notes

Chapter 1: Talk as Social Action

1. The term "black" rather than "African-American" is used in this book because "black" was the term used by the children on Maple Street in 1970–71 to refer to their ethnicity.

2. It appears that other types of speech-exchange systems such as debates, interviews, talk in institutional settings, etc., are organized by constraining parameters allowed to vary within conversation itself (cf. Sacks, Schegloff, and Jefferson 1974: 729–731) so that conversation can in a serious sense be considered the most basic of these systems.

3. For more detailed exposition of how an action in conversation creates a framework of expectations that constrains and provides for the interpretation of subsequent action, see Schegloff's (1968) discussion of *conditional relevance* and the reviews of work in conversation analysis provided in Heritage (1984a, 1985) and Levinson (1983).

4. Important collections of research in conversation analysis can be found in Atkinson and Heritage (1984), Button and Lee (1987), Schenkein (1978), the special double issue of *Sociological Inquiry* edited by Zimmerman and West (1980), and a special issue of *Human Studies* (1986) edited by Button, Drew, and Heritage. Turn-taking is most extensively analyzed in Sacks, Schegloff, and Jefferson (1974). The investigation of phenomena within the turn, including the interdigitation of verbal and nonverbal behavior in that process, is dealt with at length in C. Goodwin (1981) and Heath (1986). For an analysis of both basic ideas in ethnomethodology and work in conversation analysis that grows from it, see Heritage (1984a). Levinson (1983) provides a review of conversation analysis that focuses on its contributions to pragmatics. For examples of how conversation analysis can be applied to the analysis of larger institutions, see Atkinson (1984), Atkinson and Drew (1979), and Maynard (1984).

5. See Ben-Amos (1981:113) for a similar critique of research within symbolic anthropology.

6. Haviland (1977) is concerned with "how native actors examine, use and manipulate cultural rules in natural contexts." The talk he examines is elicited data.

7. As Gumperz (1972:17) argues, "speech event analysis focuses on the exchange between speakers, i.e., how a speaker by his choice of topic and his choice of linguistic variables adapts to other participants or to his environment and how others in turn react to him."

8. See, however, Berentzen's (1984) study of gender roles in a Norwegian nursery school peer group (among children aged 5–7).

9. Eckert (1988) analyzes the mechanisms involved in the spread of sound change among middle- and working-class adolescents.

10. As noted by Yawkey and Miller (1984:95), prior to interactive approaches to the study of language, psychologists relied on either the behaviorist perspective, in which "explanations of language use rested on the children's appropriate modeling of adults' language and successive approximations of their responses," or the "nativist perspective," which "emphasized the innateness of language and the basic 'language inventiveness' of the child."

11. Relevant literature on children's interaction in a classroom setting includes Bloome (1987); Bremme and Erickson (1977); Cazden, John, and Hymes (1972); Cook-Gumperz and Corsaro (1977); Corsaro (1985); Corsaro and Tomlinson (1980);

Dore (1977); Erickson and Mohatt (1982); Fillion, Hedley, and deMartino (1987); Florio (1978); Garvey (1974, 1977, 1984); Gilmore and Glatthorn (1982); Green and Wallat (1981); Griffin and Shuy (1978); McDermott (1976); McDermott and Gospodinoff (1979); McDermott, Gospodinoff, and Aron (1978); Mehan (1979, 1985); Michaels (1981); Philips (1972); Spindler (1982); and Wilkinson (1982, 1984). Mehan (1985) reviews "classroom discourse." Studies of children's language use in classroom settings investigate speech activities such as access rituals (Corsaro 1977), directives (Andersen 1978; Cook-Gumperz 1981; Ervin-Tripp 1982b; Ervin-Tripp and Mitchell-Kernan 1977), arguing (Adger 1984; Brenneis and Lein 1977; Corsaro and Rizzo 1990; Eisenberg and Garvey 1981; Lein and Brenneis 1978; Maynard 1985a, 1985b; Mitchell-Kernan and Kernan 1977), and pretend play (Schwartzman 1978).

12. See the work of Garvey (1974, 1975, 1977, 1984), Halliday (1975), and Shatz and Gelman (1973) for close studies of young children's language use in experimental situations. Heath (1983) presents ethnographically based descriptions but is primarily concerned with the use of language between adults and children.

13. Rubin (1980:3) argues that children's peer groups were relatively unstudied from 1940 to 1970 because of "the assumption, fostered by psychoanalytic theory, that the mother-child relationship is paramount in the child's development." He argues further that compared to this "first relationship," children's relationships with one another were seen as being of little real importance. See also Denzin (1977:75, 111), Foot, Chapman, and Smith (1980:1), Lewis and Rosenblum (1975:1), Rubin (1980:3). With regard to caretaker-infant language studies, Shatz (1983:877) argues that despite "an explosion of work that has carefully described early interactive patterns between infants and their caretakers," as yet there is little "real evidence that patterns of interaction developed in the early months or even the first year have any direct bearing on the speed or order of language-acquisition skill."

14. A number of social science researchers have recognized the importance of seeing peer culture not as an incomplete version of the adult world but rather as a coherent entity in its own right. See, for example the pioneering work of psychologists Piaget (1965), Sullivan (1953), and Vygotsky (1978) and sociologist Mead (1934) as well as that of more recent researchers within the traditions of psychology such as Damon (1977, 1978); Duck and Gilmour (1981); Hartup (1978, 1980, 1983); Lewis and Rosenblum (1975); Lubin and Forbes (1984:237); Overton (1983); Rubin (1980); Rubin and Ross (1982); Selman (1981); Shantz (1983); Stone and Selman (1982); Sutton-Smith (1982); Youniss (1978, 1980); Youniss and Volpe (1978); sociology such as Alanen (1988); Ambert (1986:23); Cicourel (1974); Cook-Gumperz (1981:49, 1986a); Corsaro (1985); Corsaro and Streeck (1986); Denzin (1977, 1982); Elkin and Handel (1978); Fine (1979, 1981); Glassner (1976); Goodman (1970); Hallinan (1980:322); Savin-Williams (1980:344); Speier (1976); Thorne (1987a); linguistics with the work of Streeck (1983) and anthropology with Berentzen (1984) and LaFontaine (1986:10). See also edited volumes which contain articles across several disciplines, such as Adler and Adler (1986b); Asher and Gottman (1981); Cook-Gumperz, Corsaro, and Streeck (1986); Foot, Chapman, and Smith (1980); Handel (1988); McGurk (1978); Richards (1974); and Skolnick (1976).

15. Adler and Adler (1986a:5) state that because developmental psychology has dominated the advancement of knowledge about children, "there is a gap and a great need for sociological studies of children, to shed light on their interpersonal experiences, perspectives, roles, culture and transformational processes."

16. See also White and Siegel (1984), who emphasize the way in which studies of cognitive development must take into account the cultural scenes and social practices within which that development occurs. White and Siegel (ibid.:2) argue that "to understand cognitive development across time and space requires seeing it as deeply embedded in a social world of occasions, formalities, etiquettes, and dramaturgy."

17. More recent research in everyday cognition (for example, Lave 1988, Lave, Murtaugh, and de la Rocha 1984, and Scribner 1984) is beginning to use ethnographic methods in natural settings.

18. Cazden (1976:151), commenting on the relevance of the naturalistic study of speech for understanding children's communicative competence, states the following: "From a finite experience of speech acts and their interdependence with socio-cultural features they [children] develop a general theory of the speaking appropriate in their community, which they employ, like other forms of tacit cultural knowledge (competence) in conducting and interpreting social life."

19. See Corsaro and Rizzo (1990) for a critique of the use of role-played data in investigating children's conversational activities.

20. In 1975, Shantz (1975:266) reported that "the most extensive model" of interpersonal inference in cognitive-development theory, which had been formulated by Selman (1973; Selman and Byrne 1974), dealt specifically with the changes in role-taking skills of the child and adolescent, conceptualized as structures or stages. She notes that this stage model of role taking "is based largely on children's verbal responses to short stories, some involving moral dilemmas and others simple social dilemmas" (Shantz 1975:266).

21. As noted earlier, some of those working in the field of everyday cognition (for example, Scribner 1984 and Lave, Murtaugh, and de la Rocha 1984) are beginning to do their research in the actual settings in which the events they are studying typically occur.

Chapter 2: Fieldwork

1. The extensive networks which children themselves build are investigated in Salzinger, Antrobus, and Hammer (1988).

2. See Mead (1973:257) regarding the advantages of such a nonselective approach to data collection.

3. For a more recent formulation of such issues, see Hymes (1986:65).

4. This example has been constructed to contain a variety of relevant transcription devices in a brief example. It is not an accurate record of an actual exchange.

Chapter 3: The Maple Street Children's Group and Their Neighborhood

1. Berentzen (in press) studied a West Philadelphia gang of black adolescents within eight blocks of where I did fieldwork.

2. Two of the children, Rochele and Dave, were white. They had a black stepmother and spoke Black English Vernacular.

3. The Maple Street neighborhood thus contrasts with the Philadelphia neighborhood described by Shuman (1986) in her study of adolescent storytelling, where adults were either working or unemployed and on welfare.

4. In 1986, few of the Maple Street children (then in their late twenties) still lived at home. To have children living "on their own," separately from their families of origin, was of major concern to Maple Street parents.

5. This pattern of residence differed from that of poorer neighborhoods in which I did fieldwork, where men were as likely to live with members of their family of origin as with women with whom they had relationships.

6. The names which are used to identify children are pseudonyms.

7. In contrast to the arrangement of space in poor inner-city New York homes videotaped by Scheflen (personal communication 1969), children had their own private space and were not forced to seek privacy for tasks such as doing homework in hallways.

8. Lever (1974:131, 139–142) reports that the middle-class white girls she studied spent more of their playtime indoors than boys; her interviews showed that 80% of girls who were asked, "Where do you usually play after school, indoors or

outdoors?'' replied that they played indoors most of the time. Berndt (1988), in a summary article on children's friendships, recycles such an argument, stating that girls spend more time in indoor play with dolls or toys.

9. Medrich, Roizen, Rubin, and Buckley (1982:80) report that although ''black children played as frequently as white children in their own homes and yards they were less likely to play in those of their friends.''

10. In poorer neighborhoods, parents were less concerned about damage children might do to their house and allowed children greater access to all downstairs rooms as a consequence. My experience, however, contrasts with access norms prescribed for ethnographer Dan Rose by black South Philadelphians (Rose 1987:147, 154).

11. Medrich, Roizen, Rubin, and Buckley (1982:80), in a comparative study of ethnic/class groups of children, report that ''black children playing together more often played outside and in public spaces.'' It should be noted that in the black neighborhood studied by Medrich, Roizen, Rubin, and Buckley (1982), play outside the home was associated with the fact that children lived in multiunit dwellings (in contrast to the attached yet single-unit row homes on Maple Street) and had little privacy. The use of public space for play occurs also among rural blacks (Heath 1983:98, 99, 166), although the public place is a more centralized community ''plaza'' area.

12. As noted by Dobbert and Cooke (1985:13), ''relatively isolated nuclear family dwellings'' (i.e., those in more affluent communities) ''eliminate a very great deal of peer learning experience.''

13. A listing of the names and ages of the children, their grade in school, and the streets on which they live appears in Appendix A.

14. There is overlap in the age distribution of the girls' group because one ten-year-old played with both the younger and the older girls' group. There were no seven- or eight-year-old boys.

15. Such findings are consistent with those of Barker and Wright (1954), who in studying Midwestern small-town children report that infants (0–2) spend an average of 95% of their time in family settings. However, while Barker and Wright (1954) found that preschoolers (2–6) spend an average of 92% of their time with the family, on Maple Street children above four years generally play outside with other children. Hart (1979) found that five-year-old children in a small New England town were limited in their range of play to locations within sight of the home. Such a situation parallels practices in the Maple Street community, where children four to six were usually within view of a relative or neighbor.

16. The effect of physical proximity on group formation was originally noted by Homans (1950), who observed that persons who are near each other have more opportunities to interact and are more likely to become friends. The importance of proximity for the formation of friendships is not unique to working-class blacks, of course. Fine (1980:311), for example, in his study of lower- and upper-middle-class children's friendship groups found proximity to be important. Hallinan (1980) notes the importance of both propinquity and similarity of attitudes, interests, and values in the formation of cliques. Berndt (1988) notes that friendships form most easily when children have regular and frequent opportunities for interaction with each other. For a review of literature discussing the importance of propinquity in human relationships, see Kurth (1970:139).

17. A similar pattern is reported by Medrich, Roizen, Rubin, and Buckley (1982:81) for urban black children and by Dougherty (1978:68) for rural black children.

18. Whiting and Edwards (1973), in a cross-cultural analysis of sex differences in the behavior of children aged three through eleven, found that girls' obligations to care for infants and perform domestic chores result in their staying in the vicinity

of the house and yard. This is in line with their cross-cultural finding that "women have the major responsibility for the care of infants and for domestic chores" (Whiting and Edwards 1973:183). Abramovitch, Corter, and Lando (1979) found that older girl siblings were more likely to engage in nurturing behaviors than were older boys. Ellis, Rogoff, and Cromer (1981:406) hypothesize that around the ages of eight to ten, children are needed for chores; they report that an increase in household responsibilities might explain the difficulty they had in finding nine- to twelve-year-old children (especially girls) outside the neighborhood.

19. In contrast to the situation for the Maple Street group Lever (1974:122) reports that among the middle-class children she studied, children "of both sexes devoted equal time" to household chores.

20. In this regard the play pattern of the older boys resembles that discussed by Foley (1950), Medrich, Roizen, Rubin, and Buckley (1982:77–78), Opie and Opie (1969:10), and Suttles (1975).

21. My findings are consistent with those of Sutton-Smith, Rosenberg, and Morgan (1963) regarding play preferences for girls.

22. Lever (1974:114), citing McGhee (1900) and Sutton-Smith and Rosenberg (1971), argues that "throughout recent history girls have had a wider range of preferred play activities."

23. Lever (1974:171) noted that for the middle-class children she observed on playgrounds, girls spent more time talking than boys and less time at recess actually playing games than boys. Csikszentmihalyi and Larson (1984) have stated that adolescents spend a substantial portion of their time talking with each other about themselves.

24. Lever (1974:126) reports that among the white middle-class girls she studied, clubs were generally "quite short term in duration," generally lasting about two weeks.

25. The younger girls also dabbled in conducting club meetings and having parties. Rubin (1980:95) found that children in their early school years (especially 8–9) form "official" groups. These are typically sex-segregated, and in them children "invest a tremendous amount of energy into deciding on officers and their official titles, find nothing to do after that, and then disband."

26. This game is called skelly in New York (Knapp and Knapp 1976:141). As reported in the *Christian Science Monitor* (Oct. 19, 1987, p. 23) for New York children:

> Boys use skelly tops—milk bottle caps filled with clay and boys shoot them into chalked-in numbered boxes. The idea is to shoot your top into all thirteen boxes, hitting your opponents' tops whenever you can. Then reverse the order, going from thirteen back to one. Next you try to hit everybody's top three times. If you do you're a "killer," a winner.

27. Hartup (1978:144) states that divisions into sex-segregated groups are based on *shared interests* among children of the same sex rather than *avoidance* of the opposite sex. Oswald, Krappman, Chowdhuri, and von Salisch (1985:7) also report that six-year-olds "interact almost as frequently with children of the other sex as with children of their own sex," although this pattern is discontinued when children reach age ten. Ellis, Rogoff, and Cromer (1981:403–404) report that same-sex companionship was no more common than mixed-sex companionship until ages seven or eight among the middle-income U.S. children they studied. Among rural Kenya children, Harkness and Super (1985) argue that the number of available playmates of similar age affects degree of segregation by sex. Among rural U.S. fourth- and sixth-graders studied by Hallinan (1979), children claimed those of the opposite sex as best friends roughly one-fourth of the time; Berndt (1988) argues that this may be because of a relatively small number of same-sex peers.

28. In England the acting game of "Old Mommy Witch" is called "Old Mother Grey" (Opie and Opie 1969:307–310).

29. Sutton-Smith (1968:188) notes that singing games among white American children are much less popular today than during the nineteenth century.

30. Sutton-Smith, Rosenberg, and Morgan (1963:120) found that elementary school boys, significantly more than girls, chose such play activities as baseball, and games involving unrestrained movement or pretend assault such as cowboys, cops and robbers, soldiers, and throwing snowballs. See also Lever (1974).

31. Eisenstadt (1956) proposes that age-heterogeneous groups are basic to societies in which kinship is the primary unit for the social division of labor. Among middle-income children, Ellis, Rogoff, and Cromer (1981) found that children were more likely than not to be in groups containing at least one related child companion.

32. Berentzen (1984:75–76) discusses Norwegian girls as young as five to seven preferring to interact in small groups. He relates this preference to processes of alliance formation among the girls and argues that in groups larger than four or five, disagreements are likely to arise. Berndt (1988) argues that girls interact in smaller groups because indoor spaces can become crowded and uncomfortable; such an argument does not have relevance to girls on Maple, because children seldom played indoors and enjoyed playing with large groups of playmates.

33. Heath (1983:100) reports that "a major purpose of all types of playsongs in Trackton is the involvement of young children."

34. However one liability in caring for younger children was that should they "get in trouble," the older children would be blamed because their parents argued that they were "supposed to have reason" and "should know better."

35. Lever sees such a finding as consequential for interaction more generally, in particular for processes of handling disputes. She maintains that by having the opportunity to observe the model set by older boys during age-mixed games, boys can "maintain social order and resolve their disputes more effectively than girls" (Lever 1974:153). As I argue here, not only do her underlying assumptions about mixed-age groups differ from mine, but as I will demonstrate in Chapter 6, her statements about how girls handle disputes are incompatible with my data.

36. Hartup (1978:132) states that women in 'third world' cultures who have principal responsibilities in agriculture assign infant and toddler care to five- and eight-year-old "child nurses" who are responsible for entertaining, carrying, feeding, and bedding down the infants and young children in their care. See also Dobbert (1981).

37. See, for example, the classic study by Sherif and Sherif (1953). My findings concerning the absence of a fixed hierarchical social structure among children are similar to those of Corsaro (1985:127).

38. Festinger (1954:228) has stated, "To the extent that objective, non-social means are not available, people evaluate their opinions and abilities by comparison respectively with the opinions and abilities of others." With respect to the function of a fixed social hierarchy in a social group, Strayer (1980:172) argues that "the emergence of a stable dominance hierarchy helps to minimize the dispersive effect of social conflict and thus contributes directly to an increase in social cohesion for the group. Given a stable dominance hierarchy each group member is able to anticipate and avoid the adverse consequences of severe social aggression." Although the Maple Street boys organized their social structure with reference to ranking, the absence of any stable hierarchy within any of the Maple Street children's groups resulted in constant jockeying for positions.

39. Corsaro (1979:55), Fine (1979:743), Genishi and di Paolo (1982:57–58), and Maynard (1985b:18) also discuss age as an important dimension in children's comparisons.

40. Berentzen (1984:101, 107) reports similar findings for Norwegian nursery school boys ages five to seven; they evaluate one another with reference to strength, speed, and courage in the games they play and constantly hold competitions involving comparisons of each other's performances.

41. Abrahams (1976:57), Kochman (1981:63–65), and Reisman (1974a:117–119) discuss boasting behavior, which is distinguished from bragging by its lack of seriousness and exaggeration (Kochman 1981:63).

42. Whiting and Edwards (1973:184), in their cross-cultural study of sex differences in children, report that seeking attention, which includes boasting, occurs much more frequently among boys than among girls. In a study of children of affluent parents, Best (1983:93) found that among boys, self-congratulation about achievement was quite acceptable.

43. Immediately prior to this sequence of talk, Tony discussed some of the criteria which can be taken into account in establishing a rank ordering. In the following, Tony laments the fact that Malcolm exerts total control over the use of the go-cart, despite the fact that Tony designed and helped produce it.

10/23/70/346

Discussing go-carts

Tony:	You would *think* that since I gave him
	the de*signs* to *m*ake that thing,
	I should have a little control with it.
	I should have something to say about it,
Ossie:	But you don't!
Tony:	But I don't got a *thing* to say about it.
	What *he* says *goes.*

44. Lever (1974:344) argues that while boys have "universalistic standards of achievement for evaluating boys' athletic skills," girls do not. See also Eifermann (1968:151–152).

45. See Knapp and Knapp (1976:120) for further discussion relevant to this point.

46. Best (1983:99) found that winning and being first in games did not have the same meaning for girls that it did for boys. She notes that among girls there was "no structured group of peers watching and judging a girl's performance." See also Lever (1974:192), who argues that among middle-class girls in jump rope, "no one keeps track of the jumps made but the jumper herself." The pattern she found, however, clearly contrasts with the way in which Maple Street girls play the game of jump rope.

47. In a study of an integrated middle school among sixth- through eighth-graders Schofield (1981:66) found that girls concerned themselves with their hair, clothes, and other aspects of their physical appearance, as well as with the relationships they could claim with boys.

48. In comparing one another, boys also make claims to special relationships with members of the opposite sex (described as "foxy"), although they do so far less than girls.

49. Mitchell-Kernan and Kernan (1977:312) state that "black children, especially girls, insult others by accusing them of being conceited about their physical beauty."

50. Rose (1987:174) discusses the importance of clothing in the black community.

51. Kochman (1981:66) states that attributions of "being conceited" or "thinking himself better than the next person" are used in the black community when discussing someone's bragging about money, possessions, or social status.

52. Indeed, the way in which exclusion of others is often an intrinsic component of friendship alliances raises questions about whether it is appropriate to analyze even two-party friendship in dyadic terms.

53. Hughes (in press [b]) describes incipient team organization in large groups of girls playing the game of four-square.

54. See also Tuma and Hallinan (1979).

55. In her study of peer interaction in a desegregated school, Grant (1984:108) found that "most black females crossed race or gender lines more readily than other children." In general she found that "black girls had more extensive peer contacts than any other race-gender group." This argument runs counter to what was found by Damico (1975): among relatively affluent Florida children in a mixed racial (27% black) group, there was a significantly larger number of cross-race interactions recorded for males than for females.

56. A similar type of social organization has also been observed by Thorne (1986) and Thorne and Luria (1986) in a study of primary school children in California and Michigan.

57. Oswald, Krappman, Chowdhuri, and von Salisch (1985:29) describe patterns of cross-sex interactions involving giving help among preadolescents.

58. As Rose (1987:172) reports, "If to *see* was to *know* someone then to *talk with* was to *go with* someone."

59. See Sacks (1978) for analysis of ways in which girls of an equivalent age display in their telling of a dirty joke a primary orientation toward the concerns of their same-sex peers.

Section 2: Directive/Response Sequences and Social Organization
1. I am deeply indebted to Michel de Fornel for comments on an earlier version of my analysis of directives that led me to substantially rethink some of the issues involved.

Chapter 4: Research on Directives
1. Although Labov and Fanshel (1977) made extensive use of linguistic and philosophic work on speech acts, they incorporated into their very rich model of requests analysis from a sociological tradition as well, especially the work of Goffman and Sacks on interaction and conversation.

2. For a very comprehensive review of linguistic and philosophic analysis of speech acts, and a comparison of that tradition and conversation analysis, see Levinson (1983).

3. See also Cole and Morgan (1975), Fowler (1985:64), and Searle (1969) regarding the use of directives as social control mechanisms among adults.

4. A particularly vivid locale for exploring this issue is provided by Marine boot camp. On the one hand, the drill instructor ↔ recruit identity relationship has a formal "external" existence that is indeed codified in military regulations. On the other hand, particular directive choices by both DI and recruit are one of the principal ways that their relationship is defined, constituted, and made visible as a matter of situated everyday practice, and indeed forcing recruits to obey and respond to directives in a specific way is one of the main techniques used to transform boys into Marines (in line with Goffman's [1961] analysis of the organization of total institutions). Distinctive modes of giving and taking orders (i.e., directives) lie at the heart of military behavior.

5. The practice of focusing analysis on individual directive utterances is clearly based on the linguistic practice of studying sentences as isolated, self-contained objects. Note, however, that the grounds for making such a simplifying assumption are far weaker for directives than they are for sentences in general. While it might be argued that sentences are the intellectual products of individual speakers, and

thus objects that can be studied without reference to the interaction within which they typically emerge (and conversation analysts have raised serious questions about such assumptions), directives are defined precisely by their ability to coordinate action between separate individuals, and are thus intrinsically social objects.

6. For more thorough discussion of issues involved in the analysis of context see Goodwin and Duranti (in press).

Chapter 5: Directive Use in a Boys' Task Activity
1. This same pattern was found by Berentzen (1984) in his analysis of play at a Norwegian nursery school, among children five through seven. It thus appears that such play patterns emerge at a very early age.

2. The organization of boys' activities into "teams" has been extensively commented upon by researchers (e.g., Lever 1974, 1976, 1978). Among the Maple Street boys, making go-carts evolved into play divided into two highly competitive "pit crews," each with its own professional secrets regarding the manufacture of the carts.

3. Tony demanded that those joining his team hand over to him a specified number of slings. Having previously made a large quantity of the slings he himself might well have been content to have been his own one-man team.

4. For more detailed analysis of how the boys negotiated both the emerging structure of the activity and their positions within it, see C. Goodwin and M. H. Goodwin (1990).

5. Berentzen (1984:132) discusses the interactive nature of resource allocation among nursery school boys.

6. For more detailed analysis of the interactive organization of assessments, see C. Goodwin and M. H. Goodwin (1987) and Pomerantz (1984).

7. Some side talk not relevant to the issues now being examined has been omitted for clarity.

8. For more detailed analysis of the social and interactive organization of place reference, see Hanks (in press [b]) and Schegloff (1972b).

9. Brown and Levinson (1978:113) note how "in-group" terms of address are frequently used to soften an imperative "by indicating that it isn't a power-backed command."

10. Indeed, in a data search of all uses of "man" in this two-hour play session, the only cases I found where the term was not used by a superior were in turns such as "((whining)) That's my brother's man," where speaker is complaining about his hanger being expropriated. Here "man" is utilized by someone depicting himself as an offended party, and its use seems congruent with the complaint being lodged against addressee. From a slightly different perspective, the way in which "man" can be used to show disrespect has been noted by novelists. Thus, in describing a New York City mayor confronting hecklers in a Harlem audience, Wolfe (1987:4) writes:

"We don't want your figures, man!"
Man, he says! The insolence!

11. "My," unlike "our," is exclusive and establishes a contrast between speaker and recipient.

12. Lyons (1977:722–723) has suggested that possessives might be analyzed as structures with underlying locative subjects, an idea that sheds interesting light on the way in which the possessives in these data are formulated by positioning participants in space.

13. The use of "need statements" (Ervin-Tripp 1976:29), "desire statements" (Ervin-Tripp 1982b:30), or "explicit statements" (Ervin-Tripp 1982b:35) has been argued (Ervin-Tripp 1976:29; Garvey 1975:52, 60) to constitute one of the most aggravated

ways of formulating a directive. With reference to categorization schemes developed by researchers in developmental cognitive psychology, the types of actions used by leaders such as Malcolm to organize the activity could be classified as a level one "command" type of "social negotiation strategy" (Stone and Selman 1982:169–172), consisting of "unilateral, one-way understanding" (ibid.:172) in that "children express only the self's needs or wishes in a situation. They do not refer to or inquire about the other's needs or wishes" (ibid.) but deal with "justification on the basis of the self's perspective."

14. Note here that an initial request by Malcolm to remember something (line 1) is treated by Tokay (line 3) as the first-pair part of an "initiation-reply pair." When Tokay guesses the completion of Malcolm's utterance, Malcolm subsequently (line 4) evaluates Tokay's guess. Mehan (1979, 1985) notes that a three-part sequence with this structure is characteristic of educational discourse.

15. McTear (1980) and Wootton (1981, 1984, 1986) stress the importance of going beyond analysis of request/response pairs to consider the whole sequence in which the request is embedded. As McTear (1980:25) argues, "the selection of a particular request or response form is determined not only by factors such as the relative politeness of the form in isolation or the nature of the action requested, (whether high or low cost and benefit) but also by the point in the sequence where it occurs." For a study which treats some aspects of the sequential organization of requests ("contingent queries"), see Garvey (1975).

16. For further discussion of how hierarchy is established among these children through an interactive activity, see C. Goodwin and M. H. Goodwin (1990).

17. For further elaboration of the distribution of roles between Malcolm and Tony see C. Goodwin and M. H. Goodwin (1990).

Chapter 6: Task Activity and Pretend Play among Girls
1. Although generally boys' directives are stated quite baldly, those that project major shifts in the group's location or agenda and therefore require group consensus may be formatted more deferentially using the verb "let's." Invitations to play games of various sorts such as "Let's play some football Ossie. Two against two" or "Malcolm! Let's get a game" also use "let's." Although an extremely uncommon usage (there were only four cases of "let's" within two hours of taping), in the next fragment Malcolm through the use of *let's* proposes rather than demands that the group move from his front steps to his back yard.

(A)
Malcolm: All right. It's too crowded in here.
                   Let's go somewhere. ((*Team moves to*
                   pavement part of the back yard.))
                   Pop 'em over here.

(B)
Malcolm: Let's go around back and make the slings.
Pete: Okay. ((*Group moves from front steps to*
                   back yard.))

Here the directives "let's move" and "let's go" are accompanied by talk which speaks to reasons for the proposed action which are beyond the personal whims of the speaker (i.e., the reasons for moving speak to situations of crowding). However, note that immediately following the move to the back yard, Malcolm issues an imperative: "Pop 'em over here." Although the account mitigates the initial request for action, it should be noted that it asserts Malcolm's rather than the group's definition of the situation of the moment. Nonetheless, these examples point to the fact that in limited types of situations, i.e., when cooperation in shifting to a major new phase of the activity is needed, leaders may deviate from their standard practice of using imperative forms.

2. Brown and Levinson (1978:132) note that by using the inclusive "we" form, a speaker may "call upon the cooperative assumptions and thereby redress FTA's (face threatening acts)." According to Blum-Kulka and Olshtain (1984:203), such a "point of view" provides a more mitigated form of directive.

3. In her study of interaction between physicians and their patients, West (1990) reports that female physicians formulate their instructions as suggestions rather than commands, making frequent use of "let's" and modal verbs.

4. Blum-Kulka and Olshtain (1984:203) discuss modals as forms of mitigators of the request. See also Labov and Fanshel (1977:84–86).

5. Cook-Gumperz (1981:36) notes that a change in pronouns may radically shift the social perspective of the directive, i.e., from requesting to persuading.

6. Some features of this sequence, for example, the organization of Ruby's talk in lines 2–3, will be examined in more detail when argumentative moves are studied in Chapter 7.

7. From the point of view of cognitive psychologists who study "social perspective taking" ("an individual's capacity to coordinate psychological perspectives of self and other," Stone and Selman 1982:164) and "social negotiation strategies" (Stone and Selman 1982), it can be argued that girls' directives display taking into consideration the other's point of view to a far greater extent than boys' do. However, it is not at all clear that boys are in fact less able to deal with the perspective of the other than girls are.

8. In the midst of such activities, however, girls establish alliances among themselves against the boys, while attempting to trick them into believing things that are not true, i.e., making believe that they found turtles after their expedition to a city creek. Although they do not one-up each other, girls do attempt to get the best of the boys. In addition, girls also assume caretaking responsibilities in the midst of play, constantly monitoring the actions of younger children; during such activity they assume a dominant position with respect to younger children.

9. Grant (1984:108), in her study of peer interaction in a desegregated school, found that "black girls were above the mean in care-giving in four classrooms."

10. As noted by Zahn-Waxler, Iannotti, and Chapman (1982:153), peers may use many of the same techniques for control as do parents. According to Bellinger and Gleason (1982:1133), "parental modeling is the strongest candidate for the mechanism by which children learn to use the sex-associated strategies for requesting action." They argue that from an early age children associate the more direct ways of requesting action with males and the more indirect ways with females. In the present case, however, girls and boys use a style consistent with that which their mothers use.

11. See also Gleason and Greif (1983:144).

12. See also Bellinger and Gleason (1982:1124).

13. The one situation in which differences in the imperatives of mother and fathers tend to disappear is when there is a degree of urgency in the request. As argued by Bellinger and Gleason (1982:1134), when the urgency of the situation "overrides politeness as a determinant of directive form the imperative is the form most likely to be used."

14. Developmental psychologists argue that in general the sibling system is less egalitarian than the peer system; this provides the opportunity for older siblings "to be assertive and assume a leadership role in initiating and directing sibling interaction" (Pepler, Corter, and Abramovitch 1982:216).

15. The importance of female sibling ties among black families has been discussed

by Aschenbrenner (1975), Ladner (1971), McAdoo (1983), and Stack (1974) and in novels such as Morrison's *Beloved* and Naylor's *Mama Day*. In an ethnographic study of Norwegian children, Berentzen (1984:102) argues that girls fight over who will be mother because in that role "they can most adequately express their gender identity." As Berentzen (ibid.:101) states, in a girls' group "to 'play with' the girl one most prefers to be with can be seen as an expression of how they evaluate each others' ability to practice intimate dyadic relationships." Playing the role of someone's sister or someone's child can thus represent an alliance between two girls. Among Maple Streeters, boys who join the activity for short periods of time play the role of "company" rather than "father." Researchers who have studied preschool children's play (Berentzen 1984:91–92; McLoyd, Ray, and Etter-Lewis 1985:41; Pitcher and Schultz 1983) report that when playing house, girls seldom develop the father role. Berentzen (1984:111) argues that this may be partially because girls are "not interested in having . . . [their] efforts to build up a satisfactory alliance and game spoiled by the boys."

16. Commenting upon the role of parental child within black families, McLoyd, Ray, and Etter-Lewis (1985:41) state, "Older children often assume caretaking responsibilities for younger children (Aschenbrenner 1975; Lewis 1975; Young 1970) and, as a consequence, may acquire advanced role-taking skills."

17. Corsaro (1985:83) also found that requests for permission were most frequently used by children playing younger children to "mothers" and constituted a way of displaying subordination. McLoyd, Ray, and Etter-Lewis (1985:37) found that "children" used more direct forms with each other than with their "mothers." However, they used 62% more declaratives than questions, while only 9% more questions than imperatives in interaction with their mothers. Gordon and Ervin-Tripp (1984:308) argue that "true permission requests imply that the addressee has control over the speaker and that the speaker's wishes are subject to the hearer's approval."

18. Girls playing "mothers" also exchange equivalent types of actions as they tell stories about their "children."

19. Berentzen (1984:76, 87, 121) found for Norwegian nursery school children that while girls recognized those playing mother as directing aspects of the activity, no one person emerged as dominant. He argues, "as distinct from the boys' play the girls didn't have anyone who was clearly the 'chief' in the game."

20. Berentzen (1984:120–121) describes ways Norwegian girls (4–7) expressed their alliances by creating humiliating situations for girls who wanted to join a group.

21. Supportive evidence for girls' competence in developing elaborated forms of social organization while playing games comes from Hughes's (1983, 1988, in press) studies of white middle-class girls; within a nonteam game such as "four-square," girls evolve quite sophisticated forms of social organization which entail contests between incipient teams.

Section 3: Disputes and Gossip

1. For reviews of literature on gendered features of women's talk, see Borker and Maltz (1989), Brown (1976); Kramarae (1981); McConnell-Ginet (1980, 1983); Philips (1980); Thorne and Henley (1975); Thorne, Kramarae, and Henley (1983); West and Zimmerman (1985). See also Lakoff (1973).

2. However, see Brenneis (1988), Duranti (1990) and Grimshaw (1990).

3. Mitchell-Kernan and Kernan (1977:201), in their analysis of role-playing activity of black American preadolescent children, have made similar analyses regarding the use of directives and their responses, which "were constantly used to

define, reaffirm, challenge, manipulate, and redefine status and rank." See also Ervin-Tripp (1982b:31) and Maynard (1985a).

Chapter 7: Building Opposition in Children's Argument

1. Early psychological research on children's arguments includes the work of Dawe (1934), Green (1933a, 1933b), and Piaget (1926).

2. By way of contrast, Maynard (1985b) argues that practically any prior strip of talk may be transformed into something about which there can be dispute.

3. Genishi and di Paolo (1982) also analyze structural features of argument; their definitions are built on those of Boggs (1978) and Eisenberg and Garvey (1981).

4. Maynard's critique, however, does not take into account that Eisenberg and Garvey (1981:165) do note that "the episode began with an initial act of opposition *to a statement of intent, a directive, an attack, or an action.*" Thus they do note that another form of action precedes the initiation of the adversative sequence.

5. For a penetrating critique of the methodology of most research on children's disputes, see Corsaro and Rizzo (1990).

6. Adger (1984, 1986) uses the term "protest sequence" to highlight the oppositional nature of the interaction among children which she observed; Corsaro and Rizzo (1990) state that for Italian children, "one's style or 'metodo di persuasione' " is "more important than any eventual resolution."

7. See also Sacks (1987) regarding preferences for agreement.

8. Such procedures share the principle of opposition observable in the "contradicting routines" of part-Hawaiian children described by Boggs (1978:328). For a review of child language literature dealing with the development of children's "discourse negation," see Maynard (1986a).

9. This same pattern was found in Pomerantz's (1984:83–84) examples of disagreements with prior speakers' self-deprecations, and indeed in such circumstances the disagreements are opposing what prior speakers said in an environment in which they would not be expected to modify initially-taken positions on their own.

10. Corsaro and Rizzo (1990) note that initial opposition prefaces of this sort occurred rarely in their middle-class American children's data; only the black children in their sample made use of such structures.

11. Vološinov (1973) called attention to the importance of studying the way in which reported speech embodies a comment by current speaker on the talk being reported. The ability of participants to animate (Goffman 1974) versions of both their opponents and themselves in the midst of argument through use of reported speech will be investigated in more detail in Chapters 10–11 when we look at how stories function within argument.

12. Insult terms in directive sequences also tend to occur at the end of utterances. It may be that in some cases the inclusion of a contest term provides an additional beat or beats to the utterance and thus also functions to preserve the rhythm of the prior utterance.

13. Lein and Brenneis (1978) note similar patterns of stress in the arguments of black American migrant children they studied. The Fijian Indian children in their sample also used contrastive stress, though far less frequently than did blacks, while "white children did not use stress for contrast in the way which the other two groups did" (ibid.:305).

14. For more detailed analysis of how correction can be formulated either as a salient or as a nonexplicit event see Jefferson (1987).

15. See Pomerantz (1975:26) for an analysis of how return assessments maintain the relationship between referent and speaker.

16. See Haviland (1989) for analysis of the use in argument in Zinacantan of

evidential particles that make it possible for participants to display agreement with what the other has said while maintaining oppositional positions.

17. On the importance of the feature of newsworthiness in conversation, see Sacks (1973:139, 1974:341).

18. Abrahams and Bauman (1971) discuss "talking trash" as involving talk with sexual connotations.

19. The term "sounding" is used by Maple Street children to describe ritual and personal insult (Labov 1972a:128), as in utterances such as "He said a whole lot. He was sounding, boy."

20. This strategy contrasts with efforts toward mediation by third parties in Israeli children's disputes (Katriel 1985:479–481). In American nursery schools (i.e., Genishi and di Paolo 1982:66; Maynard 1985a), third parties who intervene to stop disputes are frequently teachers.

21. Whereas among adults argumentative interactions are thought to lead to rifts in relationships (Labov and Fanshel 1977:88), among children it is expected that peers who argue will play together amicably shortly afterwards.

22. A number of researchers have proposed that disputes constructed through recycling of positions are less complex in structure than disputes with justifications (Eisenberg and Garvey 1981:167; Genishi and di Paolo 1982:55; Keller-Cohen, Chalmer, and Remler 1979; Piaget 1926:68). For example, Genishi and di Paolo (1982:55) argue that more complex arguments include "an acceptance, appeal to authority, compromise or supporting argument."

23. Recyclings of utterances in the absence of "justifications" have been reported to be a dispreferred procedure for constructing arguments among adults (Coulter 1979). However, cycles of "assertion-counterassertion" exchanges (Garvey 1977:43) or "repetitions" (Brenneis and Lein 1977:56) are quite typical among children. From a slightly different perspective, Pomerantz (1975:24) has noted that "in a disagreement the disagreed-with party has the option in next turn of reasserting or reaffirming his prior position." An argumentative move following a previous action can thus lead prior speaker to recycle his initial action.

24. Boggs (1978:341) found that "arguments (statements that attempt to prove other statements, explanations, and explications) are more frequent in the older boys' disputes than in those of younger boys and girls." Similarly, in my data younger children more frequently constructed their arguments out of exchange and return moves than out of positions buttressed with accounts. Nevertheless, the linguistic skill of embedding displayed in format tying in return and exchange moves (to be explored in the next section of this chapter with reference to "format tying") is highly developed, and I do not consider providing accounts "a move beyond inversion or the assertion/counterassertion format of opposition" as does Maynard (1986a).

25. Here line numbers are used to mark talk, although clearly the argument originates before the talk with William's bumping into Kerry while skating.

26. For more extended analysis of this sequence, see M. H. Goodwin (1985b:325–326).

27. Katriel (1985:480) discusses the use of humor as a strategy for "calming down" disputes among Israeli children. See also Maynard (1985b) for a discussion of the uses of humor in middle-class nursery school children's disputes.

28. For a more recent statement of this position, see Maynard's (1985b:213) distinction between "surface level" characterizations of an utterance and deeper analysis of what that talk presumes and presupposes.

29. Bauman (1986:96–97) discusses "parallelism" as "repetition with systematic variation, the combining of variant and invariant elements in the construction of a poetic work. Parallel structures may be developed at a range of formal levels: phonological, prosodic, syntactic, semantic, thematic."

30. Although the present data are drawn from the arguments of children, format tying is not restricted to either children or argumentative exchanges. Consider, for example, the following, which is taken from an adult male joke-telling session (simplified transcript):

Mike:	She said- You better hurry on up
	'fore I get outta the *m*ood. She says.
	He says. I gotta get outta the *m*ood
	before I can get outta the car.

Here second speaker not only repeats the exact words of prior speaker—"get outta the mood"—but also uses the structure provided by that talk as a framework for his subsequent talk—"before I can get outta the car."

The following (reported in the *New York Times*, August 8, 1985, p. 10) occurred at the White House between presidential spokesman Larry Speakes and reporter Helen Thomas:

Speakes:	Do you want to say that I did not tell
	the truth?
Thomas:	→ Aw, come on, get off of that.
Speakes:	→ No, you come on. You've accused me of
	something.

31. Keenan (1974) and Keenan and Klein (1975) describe conversations of two- and three-year-olds, in which replication of form in terms of phonological shape occurred between paired utterances. Keenan (1974:179) states: "It is often acceptable to reply to a comment, command, question or song with an utterance which attends only to the form of that talk." In the data being examined in this book, although the children attend closely to the form of the prior talk, that in itself is not adequate for the construction of a proper return move; it must also provide an appropriate next action to the action being countered. The work of Ochs (see in particular the collection of articles in Ochs and Schieffelin [1983] on substitution, sound play, focus operations, and repetition), though dealing with children younger than those being studied here, is quite relevant to a range of phenomena that are being discussed as format tying.

32. Such a procedure is also used in part-Hawaiian children's arguments. Boggs (1978:332–333) states: "One way of contradicting is by grammatically incorporating and negating another speaker's clause."

33. Such a type of counter is also characteristic in arguments of part-Hawaiian children (Boggs 1978:329) and among white middle-class children (Lein and Brenneis 1978:305). Note also the strict attention to turn taking observable in these data. Such a patterning is similar to that observed by Lein and Brenneis (ibid.:306) for the black migrant and white middle-class children they studied, while contrasting with that for Fijian Indian (ibid.:306–308) children.

34. The term "embedding" is used here in a slightly different way from how it is usually used in linguistic analysis. However, I know of no other term that captures as aptly the way in which specific material from prior talk is implanted within the current talk.

35. On the principle of escalation, see Lein and Brenneis (1978:301).

36. For more extensive analysis of what happens to the talk of another when it is repeated by someone else, see Vološinov (1973).

37. Ladd is careful to state that "contrastive stress" may be signaling not explicit contrast but rather "narrow focus"; that is, it may be doing nothing more than "focusing on the points of difference in otherwise identical phrases" (Ladd 1980:79).

38. Cook-Gumperz (1981:45) notes the importance of stylistic contrast in children's "persuasive talk" and argues, "prosody carries a very significant part of the signaling load as does rhythm." See also Schiffrin (1984:318) for a discussion of such features in adult arguments.

39. Labov (1972a:153–154) proposes that attributes may include negatively assessed values of age, weight, clothes, appearance, sexual behavior, smell, wealth, or food.

40. Lein and Brenneis (1978:302) note that "among the black migrant children and the Indian children insults are repeated or improved on by each succeeding speaker."

41. Semantic shifts with minimal changes in form are also observable in verbal dueling of the Chamula (Gossen 1974, 1976) and Turkish boys (Glazer 1976). For a review of the literature on verbal dueling, see Brenneis (1980).

42. The entire sequence from which this is taken can be found in Appendix B.

43. Ritual insult of this type was not observed in the younger children's group. However, younger children generally construct their extended arguments in rounds of moves attempting to outmaneuver the other (as contrasted to moves which attempt to validate a particular point). The content of these moves generally refers to comparisons of ascribed rather than achieved attributes; for example, ages of children and their relatives are compared, reflecting the idea "more is better" (Genishi and di Paolo 1982:57–58).

44. Adger (1986, 1987) contrasts styles of Orientals with those of blacks and Western cultures.

45. Whiting and Whiting's (1973) studies of childhood in six cultures indicate that what they term "aggressive behavior" constitutes 24% of all behavior to peers. Shantz (1987a:285) cautions that "most conflict does not involve aggression," and argues that the concepts of aggression and conflict need to be distinguished. Shantz (1987b), as well as psychologists Rubin (1980:74), Green (1933a), and Youniss (1980), views arguing as an important and natural process in children's peer relationships.

Chapter 8: He-Said-She-Said

1. In his book about black American street life in Philadelphia, Rose (1987:172) discusses gossip among adults as an event in which talking with someone of the opposite sex holds the possibility of confrontation with "fictitious (or real?) sexual involvements"; "humorous accusations of a third party could lead to fights between the man and woman on whom the game had been started." See his discussion (ibid.:214–222) of the performance dimensions of a specific public litigation.

2. The liabilities inherent in using this form of data in the analysis of gossip have been discussed by Wilson (1974) in his critique of Colson (1953).

3. According to Nader and Todd (1978:10), "In the next procedural mode, negotiation, the two principal parties are the decision makers, and the settlement of the matter is one to which both parties agree without the aid of a third party." This description appears to only partially characterize the type of dispute being analyzed in this paper. The confrontation stage is dyadic; there is no mediating third party. However, settlement or agreement is not an outcome of this stage. Moreover, although the event is carried out between two principal disputants, it constitutes a public event.

4. The term "confrontation phase" is used to distinguish the stage in a he-said-she-said where argument actually occurs from previous stages in which stories are told for the purpose of aligning participants in a particular way. Children refer to the process of dispute within a he-said-she-said as "argument," "fuss," or "fight."

5. In confrontations which are not treated as serious, that is, ones in which participants play together immediately upon dissipation of the conflict, accusations may occur in the midst of talk between peers playing together.

6. Halliday and Hasan (1976:36) have argued that reference in children's speech is characteristically "exophoric," an exophoric item being one which "does not name anything—it signals that reference must be made to the context of the situation" (ibid.:33). In the case of utterances opening he-said-she-said confrontations, however, referents are quite explicitly described.

7. The term "identity" is used by Goodenough to refer to "an aspect of self that makes a difference in how one's rights and duties distribute to specific others" (Goodenough 1965:3). The term "occasion-specific identity," suggested to me by Gail Jefferson (personal communication, 1973), is used in the present analysis to refer to the sets of rights and duties that are expected of participants in local speech events of the type being examined here.

8. A related triadic pattern has been noted by Pike (1973:141–142), although in his analysis the three parties were identified as speaker, addressee, and listener.

9. Note that some of the things the accuser is reported to have done are in fact quite complex with respect to the issue of what kind of knowledge she has of this event. Thus in #4 Annette is accused of "showing off," an action that exists as much in the eyes of the beholder who interprets her behavior as it does in the actions being interpreted.

10. In its simplest form the offense may be described as "saying something about somebody else":

10/12/71/35

Kerry:	She gonna fight Stacey.
Rhonda:	Why.
Kerry:	Cuz she said somp'm about her.

11. See also Goffman (1974:529). In the course of denials in the he-said-she-said, blame is not attributed to the accuser, who could well have modified the message in order to be able to accuse the addressee; parties who relayed the message to the accuser are instead challenged. Thus, an additional form of deference may be seen to be paid to the accuser in the delivery of the defendant's response to an accusation.

12. Emerson (1969:155–171) describes a form of counteraccusation he calls "counter-denunciation," a strategy used by accused parties to "undermine the discrediting implications of the accusation by attacking the actions, motives and/or character of one's accusers" (ibid.:156).

13. In investigating the role-played arguments of first- through fourth-graders, Lein and Brenneis (1978:302) found the following: "In these role-played arguments, both black and white American children rarely employed statements of proof or documentation of their own preceding statement . . . [while] statements of validation are used occasionally, validity does not seem to be a significant arguing point."
Within naturally occurring arguments such as he-said-she-saids, in the opening confrontation statements speakers do provide a form of validation for their positions by including the report of a nonpresent party. It may well be that the role-playing situation is conducive to the delivery of "arguments of fantasy statements that neither participant expects to be validated" (ibid.:302).

14. Caplow (1968) examines coalitions of "two against one" in social psychological experiments.

15. See Hughes (in press) for a description of accounts by girls playing the game of four-square which likewise attempt to frame the act in progress as nonoffensive, given the actor's lack of volition in initiating it.

16. Kochman (1983:336) argues that defensive denials are interpreted in black culture as evidence that "the effect of the remark has been felt, and that, therefore, it must be true"; he further states (ibid.) that "the strategy for those who might conceivably consider themselves accused is to pretend that they have *not* been touched" and, therefore, not to respond. This simply is not the case with regard to children's he-said-she-said accusations, which explicitly call for denials. Silence in response to an accusation is taken as an indication of a party's guilt.

17. Recreating details of the past event is a strategy used by the girls to lend authenticity to the position which they wish to put forward.

18. Gilligan's (1987:22) concern is that Kohlberg's (1984) theory of moral development tends to equate "justice" reasoning rather than an orientation of "care" (which she found to be more prevalent among females) with moral reasoning.

19. Hughes (1988, in press) and Von Glascoe (1980:229–230) describe legalistic debate within the context of girls' games.

20. Katriel (1985:485) notes that among the Israeli children she studied, preadolescent "girls and boys tended to rule each other out as candidates for *brogez*" (a form of "agonistic state characterized by the suspension of ordinary interactional practices," ibid.:467) as "they live in different social worlds, each with its own 'pecking order.' " Almirol (1981:294) also reports that among Filipinos in central California, "one gossips only with someone whom one knows well."

21. Almirol (1981:296) reports that among Filipinos in central California, gossip occurs among people who are in the process of becoming "more prestigious than anybody else" and argues that "persons who are regarded as constant violators of social values" are most prone to be targets of gossip (ibid.:298).

22. Elaborate ritual entailed in repairing breaches in relationships among adults in a black Philadelphia community is discussed in Rose (1987:218).

23. As reported by Rose (1987:172) in his study of an adult black Philadelphia community, the aim of gossip between males and females was "to try humorously to damage intimate ties in order to see what would happen."

24. Instigators are not unlike Turner's (1980:152) "star groupers" who "manipulate the machinery of redress."

Chapter 9: Perspectives on Stories

1. For a review of studies analyzing stories across disciplines, see Mishler (1986:66–116, 145–161).

2. Turner (1980:167) argues that if one regards narrative as "the supreme instrument for binding the 'values' and 'goals' . . . which motivate human conduct into situational structures of 'meaning,' then we must concede it to be a universal cultural activity embedded in the very center of the social drama."

3. For analysis of how the audience of a story is relevant to its interactive organization, see Jefferson (1978), C. Goodwin (1984, 1986), Haviland (1986), and the articles in the special issue of *Text* (volume 6–3, 1986) on "The Audience as Coauthor" edited by Alessandro Duranti and Donald Brenneis.

4. In a subsequent study, Labov (1982:233) reformulates his notion of narrative cohesion, stating that it "does not depend on the sequence of narrative clauses but on the sequences of speech acts and actions that the narrative presents." Smith (1980:227) argues that "absolute chronological order is as *rare* in folkloric narratives as it is in any literary tradition" and that "nonlinearity is the rule rather than the exception in narrative accounts."

5. See especially his later formulation (Labov 1982) which, analyzing the sequencing of speech actions, attempts to "outline the generating mechanisms that produce the narrative backbone" (ibid.:227).

6. On the multiple meanings which "evaluation" may have in research on sto-

ries, see Bauman (1975:290–234), Labov (1972a:267–393), Polanyi (1979, 1985:13–16), Pratt (1977:45–51, 63–68), Robinson (1981:76–76), Tannen (1982:8–13), and Watson (1973:255).

7. Of relevance here is Prince's (1980:21) discussion of how through "dialogues, metaphors, symbolic situations, allusions to a particular system of thought," etc., the narrator in a novel may manipulate "the reader, guiding his judgments and controlling his reactions."

8. For a somewhat parallel conceptualization of roles of "narratees" vis-à-vis the narrator within the tradition of reader-response criticism, see Prince (1980:17).

9. Note also that the first-person pronouns being used here, "I" and "me," are also referring to complex laminated entities of the type analyzed by Goffman. Although lodged in the same individual, the entity who sat on the street as a participant observer, the entity cited as a speaker in the above exchange, the entity now sitting in front of a computer writing the text containing "I" and "me" that cites the participant observer as a character in her text, and the entity visible to you as the author of the print being read in fact differ from each other in interesting and complex ways. As noted by Goffman (1974:519),

> Although certainly the pronoun, "I," refers to the speaker, and although certainly the speaker is a specific biographical entity, that does not mean that the whole of this entity in all of its facets is to be included on each occasion of its being cited. For he who is a speaker might be considered a whole set of somewhat different things, bound together in part because of our cultural beliefs regarding identity.

10. Note, for example, how Chagnon in *A Man Called Bee* collects myths from the Yanamamo and has them perform a myth for the camera. The viewer (or analyst) is given a good record of the words and gestures used in a particular myth, but no information whatsoever about how and where such events are performed *by members of the society for each other*.

11. Despite all of the research done on the aborigines of Australia, Lieberman (1985) is the only study that focuses on the organization of their interaction.

12. Although folklorists advocate analysis of hearers' roles in storytelling (Abrahams 1968:146; Ben-Amos 1972:4; Brady 1980:166; Dégh 1969:83–84; Dégh and Vazsonyi 1971:287–288, 293; Finnegan 1967:67–68; Georges 1969; Leary 1976:37–39), rarely is serious analysis of the precise form of such participation undertaken. However, see Bauman (1986).

13. As I will argue in Chapter 10, analysis of Maple Street boys' stories demonstrates that in fact a considerable amount of cooperation is displayed in boys' listening to each other's stories.

14. Smith (1980:232–234) argues that narrative must be viewed as part of a "social transaction" including audience as well as narrator.

15. In a similar spirit, Abrahams (1968:157) argues that "if we are going to relate folklore to the dynamics of culture we need to develop a methodology which will focus on the movement of items as constructed and performed, as used by people in a living situation." Such a perspective has been adopted by folklorists and anthropologists who feel, as does Darnell, that "folklore as a discipline has all too often existed in a vacuum from which texts are abstracted for the edification of outsiders about the cultural context of their performance" (Darnell 1974:315).

16. See Bauman (1986:113), who reviews work on narrative which takes the perspective that narratives are "constitutive of social life."

17. For ethnographic analysis of how the telling of stories by urban black boys might function within larger social tasks, see Berentzen (in press).

Chapter 10: Stories as Participation Structures

1. Sacks, Schegloff, and Jefferson (1974:708–709) note that the basic organization of turntaking includes a bias for last speaker to become next speaker, which can lead to precisely the type of restricted participation found in the present data.

2. Although the talk in lines 52–53 locates Tony as its explicit addressee with the pronoun "you," it is clearly spoken as much for the audience of onlookers as to Tony. For interesting analysis of the complexities of implicit address within conversation, see Holmes (1984).

3. The main difference between line 56 and earlier enactments of what Tony said (lines 25 and 44) is the replacement of "no money" by "none." Unlike "no money," the term "none" points backward to earlier talk for its interpretation. The way in which the enactment is now referring to the earlier version of the story as well as the incidents being described is thus displayed in the details of the utterance. For interesting analysis of how elliptical processes in story construction display ways in which speakers are expecting recipients to take earlier talk into account for the proper understanding of current talk, see Sacks (1978).

4. In his lectures on stories, Sacks (1970) notes the relevance of such phenomena for not only the organization of second stories but also the study of how members of a society organize and remember their experience of the events they encounter.

5. For other analysis of how existing structure becomes a resource for the creation of subsequent action, see C. Goodwin and M. H. Goodwin (1990).

Chapter 11: Instigating

1. Katriel (1985:480), discussing Israeli children's conflict, describes the role of "troublemaker" as a party who is said to "exaggerate in the direction of bad things."

2. See Sacks (1978:262) for a consideration of the motive power of preformulated talk.

3. Parsons (1966:386–478) describes how in the Oaxacan town of Mitla there is hesitancy in repeating stories to others acquainted with the target of the story because of the fear of initiating a dispute and hostility.

4. Rose (1987:176) discusses the performance features of gossip about another among black adults, arguing that in such talk "one could literally, for the moment, wear the persona and speech of another."

5. In addition, the alignments offended parties maintain with the offending party may also account for different types of responses. Julia is a close friend of Kerry's, while Barbara rarely plays with her or anyone on the older girls' street. Thus Barbara, in contrast to Julia, has little to lose by confronting Kerry.

6. Labov (1972a:395–396) in describing structural complexity in narratives states that the ability of a narrator to move "back and forth from real to imaginary events" is more generally characteristic of adults than of children. In these sequences, however, girls move with little effort from past to future and possible events.

7. The intent and function of audience participation in public litigations of black adults are discussed in Rose (1987:220–221).

8. A reformulation of this definition appears in Labov (1982).

9. A similar concern is expressed by folklorists studying *memorates*. The investigator must attempt to make clear how authentically a memorate reflects original supernormal experience (Honko 1964:11).

10. See Bateson (1947:650).

Chapter 12: Conclusion

1. See also Moerman (1988).

2. The increasing relevance of the peer group in children's development has been recently noted by Ladd, Hart, Wadsworth, and Golter (1988:61) who argue that it constitutes "a much larger part of the young child's life than even a decade

ago and will undoubtedly become an even greater source of companionship, emotional support, and guidance in the future."

3. See Cook-Gumperz (1986a), Corsaro and Streeck (1986), and Thorne (1987a) for recent analysis arguing that "social situations created by children as well as the interpersonal relations which they entertain are 'culturally different' from the adult world rather than being incomplete versions thereof" (Cook-Gumperz and Corsaro 1986:4).

4. As argued by Becker (1982:168), eliciting actions such as requests in an "impoverished social context" is often preferred by psychologists to naturalistic observation because it involves less time in gathering data.

5. See Piaget (1965:396) and Youniss (1980:7–8).

6. For critiques of Gilligan, see Kerber et al. (1986) and Meyers and Kittay (1987).

7. Arguing against the universality of Gilligan's findings and for a more cross-culturally sensitive view of ethics, Stack (Kerber et al. 1986:322–323) reports that among black migrants returning to the rural South, there is a convergence "between women and men in their construction of themselves in relation to others" and in "women's and men's vocabulary of rights, morality and the social good." According to Stack, caste and economic systems within rural southern communities "create a setting in which Black women and men have a very similar experience of class" (ibid.:322).

8. As argued by Yanagisako and Collier (1987:20), distinctions such as domestic/ public, nature/culture, and reproduction/production "are variations of an analytical dichotomy that takes for granted what we think should be explained." Overing (1986:140) argues that close ethnographic description of many societies does not substantiate the notion that females are tied to the domain of the private and the domestic and that this domain is devalued vis-à-vis more public space.

9. Here I am indebted to Donna Eder's insightful comments.

10. See however the work of Eder (1985, 1988, 1990), and Eder and Sanford (1986) on working class- and lower-class girls in the U.S. and Wulff's (1988) study of black and white teenage girls in South London.

11. Abrahams (1975a) discusses differences between male and female patterns of communication as well as black/white distinctions.

12. Indeed, the structure of gossip and storytelling that Shuman (1986) finds in her study of white, Puerto Rican, and black girls in Philadelphia is similar to that I found for the speech events of Maple Street girls.

13. Sacks discusses how in seeking to create "a natural observational science" (Sacks 1984:21), he wanted to be able to use naturally occurring social activities to formally investigate the fullest range of human competences.

14. For example, Bernstein (1964) has proposed that working-class children utilize a "restricted code." Bereiter and Engleman (1966) have stated that the Black English Vernacular is "nonlogical." Although specifically concerned not with either black or working-class speech, but with how "texts" maintain their sense of cohesion, Halliday and Hasan (1976:36) have stated that in the "neighborhood speech" of children in their peer groups, "the context of the situation is the material environment—the 'things' [which] are there in front of one." The present analysis argues against such findings and supports the position of Labov (1970, 1972a, 1972b, 1974) and Labov, Cohen, Robins, and Lewis (1968) that the Black English Vernacular is capable of being used for highly abstract thought.

References Cited

Abrahams, Roger D.
1963 Some Jump Rope Rhymes from South Philadelphia. *Keystone Folklore Quarterly* 8:3–5.
1964 *Deep Down in the Jungle: Negro Narrative Folklore from the Streets of Philadelphia.* Hatboro: Pennsylvania Folklore Associates.
1968 Introductory Remarks to a Rhetorical Theory of Folklore. *Journal of American Folklore* 81:143–158.
1970 A Performance-Centered Approach to Gossip. *Man* 5:290–301.
1972 Folklore and Literature as Performance. *Journal of the Folklore Institute* 9:75–91.
1974 Black Talking on the Streets. In *Explorations in the Ethnography of Speaking.* Richard Bauman and Joel Sherzer, eds. Pp. 337–353. Cambridge: Cambridge University Press.
1975a Negotiating Respect: Patterns of Presentation among Black Women. *Journal of American Folklore* 88:58–80.
1975b Folklore and Communication in St. Vincent. In *Folklore: Performance and Communication.* Dan Ben-Amos and Kenneth S. Goldstein, eds. Pp. 287–300. The Hague: Mouton.
1976 *Talking Black.* Rowley, Mass.: Newbury House.
1982 Storytelling Events: Wake Amusements and the Structure of Nonsense on St. Vincent. *Journal of American Folklore* 95:389–414.
Abrahams, Roger D. and Richard Bauman
1971 Sense and Nonsense in St. Vincent: Speech Behavior and Decorum in a Caribbean Community. *American Anthropologist* 73:762–772.
Abramovitch, R., C. Corter, and B. Lando
1979 Sibling Interaction in the Home. *Child Development* 50:997–1003.
Adger, Carolyn Temple
1984 Communicative Competence in the Culturally Diverse Classroom: Negotiating Norms for Linguistic Interaction. Unpublished Ph.D. Dissertation, Linguistics Department, Georgetown University.
1986 When Difference Does Not Conflict: Successful Arguments between Black and Vietnamese Classmates. *Text* 6:223–237.
1987 Accommodating Cultural Differences in Conversational Style: A Case Study. In *Research in Second Language Learning: Focus on the Classroom.* James P. Lantoef and Angela Lobarca, eds. Pp. 159–172. Norwood, N.J.: Ablex.
Adler, Patricia A. and Peter Adler
1986a Introduction. In *Sociological Studies of Child Development*, Vol.1. Peter Adler and Patricia A. Adler, eds. Pp. 3–9. Greenwich, Conn.: JAI Press.
Adler, Peter and Patricia A. Adler (Eds.)
1986b *Sociological Studies of Child Development*, Vol.1. Greenwich, Conn.: JAI Press.
Agar, Michael
1975 Cognition and Events. In *Sociocultural Dimensions of Language Use.* Mary Sanches and Ben G. Blount, eds. Pp. 41–56. New York: Academic Press.
Alanen, Leena
1988 Growing Up in the Modern Family: Rethinking Socialization, the Family and Childhood. In *Growing into a Modern World: An International Interdisciplinary Conference on the Life and Development of Children in Modern Society.* Karin Ekberg and Per Egil Mjaavatn, eds. Pp. 919–945. Trondheim, Norway: The Norwegian Centre for Child Research.

Allen, Donald E. and Rebecca F. Guy
    1974 *Conversational Analysis: The Sociology of Talk*. The Hague: Mouton.
Almirol, Edwin B.
    1981 Chasing the Elusive Butterfly: Gossip and the Pursuit of Reputation. *Ethnicity* 8:293–304.
Ambert, Annie-Marie
    1986 Sociology of Sociology: The Place of Children in North American Sociology. In *Sociological Studies of Child Development*, Vol.1. Peter Adler and Patricia A. Adler, eds. Pp. 11–31. Greenwich, Conn.: JAI Press.
Andersen, Elaine Slosberg
    1978 Learning to Speak with Style: A Study of the Sociolinguistic Skills of Children. Unpublished Ph.D. Dissertation, Department of Linguistics, Stanford University.
Aschenbrenner, J.
    1975 *Lifelines: Black Families in Chicago*. New York: Holt, Rinehart and Winston.
Asher, Steven R. and John M. Gottman (Eds.)
    1981 *The Development of Children's Friendships*. Cambridge: Cambridge University Press.
Atkinson, J. Maxwell
    1984 *Our Masters' Voices: The Language and Body Language of Politics*. London: Methuen.
Atkinson, J. Maxwell and Paul Drew
    1979 *Order in Court: The Organisation of Verbal Interaction in Judicial Settings*. London: Macmillan.
Atkinson, J. Maxwell and John Heritage (Eds.)
    1984 *Structures of Social Action*. Cambridge: Cambridge University Press.
Austin, J. L.
    1962 *How to Do Things with Words*. Oxford: Oxford University Press.
Babcock, Barbara A.
    1977 The Story in the Story: Metanarration in Folk Narrative. In *Verbal Art as Performance*. Richard Bauman, ed. Pp. 61–79. Rowley, Mass.: Newbury House.
Bailey, F. G.
    1983 *The Tactical Uses of Passion: An Essay on Power, Reason, and Reality*. Ithaca: Cornell University Press.
Bakhtin, Mikhail M.
    1981 *The Dialogic Imagination*. Translated by Caryl Emerson and Michael Holquist. Austin: University of Texas Press.
Baratz, Joan C. and Roger W. Shuy
    1969 *Teaching Black Children to Read*. Washington D.C.: Center for Applied Linguistics.
Barker, R. G. and H. F. Wright
    1954 *Midwest and Its Children: The Psychological Ecology of an American Town*. New York: Appleton-Century-Crofts.
Barrios de Chungara, Domitila, with Moema Viezzer
    1978 *Let Me Speak: Testimony of Domitila, a Woman of the Bolivian Mines*. New York: Monthly Review Press.
Barth, Fredrik
    1959 *Political Leadership among Swat Pathans*. New York: Athlone Press.
Bartz, K. W. and E. S. Levin
    1978 Childrearing by Black Parents: A Description and Comparison to Anglo and Chicano Parents. *Journal of Marriage and the Family* 40:709–719.
Bateson, Gregory
    1947 Sex and Culture. *Annals New York Academy of Sciences* 47:603–663.

Baugh, John
1983 *Black Street Speech: Its History, Structure, and Survival*. Austin: University of Texas Press.
Bauman, Richard
1972 The La Have Island General Store: Sociability and Verbal Art in a Nova Scotia Community. *Journal of American Folklore* 85:330–343.
1975 The Ethnography of Speaking. In *Annual Reviews 4*. Bernard Siegel, Alan R. Beals, and Stephen A. Tyler, eds. Pp. 95–119. Palo Alto: Annual Reviews Inc.
1977 The Nature of Performance. In *Verbal Art as Performance*. Richard Bauman, ed. Pp. 3–58. Rowley, Mass.: Newbury House.
1986 *Story, Performance, and Event: Contextual Studies of Oral Narrative*. Cambridge: Cambridge University Press.
Baumrind, D.
1972 An Exploratory Study of Socialization Effects on Black Children: Some Black-White Comparisons. *Child Development* 43:261–267.
Bearison, D. J.
1982 New Directions in Studies in Social Interaction and Cognitive Growth. In *Social Cognitive Development in Context*. F. Serafica, ed. Pp. 199–239. New York: Guilford Press.
Becker, Judith
1982 Children's Strategic Use of Requests to Mark and Manipulate Social Status. In *Language Development*, Vol. 2: *Language, Thought and Culture*. Stan Kuczaj II, ed. Pp. 1–35. Hillsdale, N.J.: Lawrence Erlbaum Associates.
1984 Implications of Ethology for the Study of Pragmatic Development. In *Discourse Development: Progress in Cognitive Development Research*. Stan Kuczaj II, ed. Pp. 1–17. New York: Springer-Verlag.
Bellinger, David C. and Jean Berko Gleason
1982 Sex Differences in Parental Directives to Young Children. *Sex Roles* 8:1123–1139.
Ben-Amos, Dan
1972 Toward a Definition of Folklore in Context. In *Toward New Perspectives in Folklore*. Americo Paredes and Richard Bauman, eds. Pp. 3–15. Austin: University of Texas Press.
1975 *Sweet Words: Storytelling Events in Benin*. Philadelphia: ISHI.
1981 *Review of* The Social Use of Metaphor: Essays on the Anthropology of Rhetoric. J. D. Sapir and J. C. Crocker, eds. *Language in Society* 10:111–114.
Bereiter, Carl and Siegfried Engelmann
1966 *Teaching Disadvantaged Children in the Preschool*. Englewood Cliffs, N.J.: Prentice-Hall.
Berentzen, Sigurd
1984 *Children Constructing Their Social World: An Analysis of Gender Contrast in Children's Interaction in a Nursery School*. Bergen: Department of Social Anthropology, University of Bergen.
in press The Contextualization of Behavior and Transformational Processes: A Study of Gang Formation in a Black Ghetto. In *Transaction and Signification*. R. Gronhaugh, ed. Oslo-Bergen: Scandinavian University Books.
Bergmann, Jörg
1987 *Klatsch: Zur Sozialform der diskreten Indiskretion*. Berlin: W. de Gruyter.
Berndt, Thomas J.
1988 The Nature and Significance of Children's Friendships. In *Annals of Child Development*, Vol. 5. R. Vasta, ed. Pp. 155–186. Greenwich, Conn.: JAI Press.
Bernstein, Basil
1964 Elaborated and Restricted Codes: Their Social Origins and Some Conse-

quences. In *The Ethnography of Communication*. John J. Gumperz and Dell Hymes, eds.. *American Anthropologist* 66, 6, pt. II:55–69.

Besnier, Niko

1989 Information Withholding as a Manipulative and Collusive Strategy in Nukulaelae Gossip. *Language in Society* 18:315–341.

in press Conflict Management, Gossip and Affective Meaning on Nukulaelae. In *Disentangling: Conflict Discourse in the Pacific*. Karen Watson-Gegeo and Geoff White, eds. Stanford: Stanford University Press.

Best, Raphaela

1983 *We've All Got Scars*. Bloomington: Indiana University Press.

Bilmes, Jack

1975 Misinformation in Verbal Accounts: Some Fundamental Considerations. *Man* 10:60–71.

Binzen, Peter

1971 *Whitetown, U.S.A.* New York: Random House.

Bloome, David

1987 *Literacy and Schooling*. Norwood, N.J.: Ablex.

Blum-Kulka, Shoshana, Brenda Danet, and Rimona Gerson

1985 The Language of Requesting in Israeli Society. In *Language in Social Situations*. Joseph Forgas, ed. Pp. 113–139. Berlin: Springer.

Blum-Kulka, Shoshana and Elite Olshtain

1984 Requests and Apologies: A Cross-Cultural Study of Speech Act Realization Patterns (CCSARP). *Applied Linguistics* 5:196–213.

Boggs, Stephen T.

1978 The Development of Verbal Disputing in Part-Hawaiian Children. *Language in Society* 7:325–344.

Bogoch, Bryna and Brenda Danet

1980 Fixed Fight or Free-for-All? An Empirical Study of Combativeness in the Adversary System of Justice. *British Journal of Law and Society* 7:36–60.

1984 Challenge and Control in Lawyer-Client Interaction: A Case Study in an Israeli Legal Aid Office. *Text* 4 (1–3):249–275.

Borker, Ruth A. and Daniel N. Maltz

1989 Anthropological Perspectives on Gender and Language. In *Gender and Anthropology: Critical Reviews for Research and Teaching*. Sandra Morgen, ed. Pp. 411–437. Washington D.C.: American Anthropological Association.

Brady, Margaret K.

1980 Narrative Competence: A Navajo Example of Peer Group Evaluation. *Journal of American Folklore* 93:158–181.

Brady, Margaret K. and Rosalind Eckhardt

1975 "This Little Lady's Gonna Boogaloo": Elements of Socialization in the Play of Black Girls. In *Black Girls at Play: Folkloristic Perspectives on Child Development*. Margaret K. Brady and Rosalind Eckhardt, eds. Pp. 1–56. Austin: Early Elementary Program Southwest Educational Development Laboratory.

Brecht, Richard D.

1974 Deixis in Embedded Structures. *Foundations in Language* 11:489–518.

Bremme, Donald W. and Frederick Erickson

1977 Relationships among Verbal and Nonverbal Classroom Behaviors. *Theory into Practice* 16:153–161.

Brenneis, Donald

1980 Fighting Words. In *Not Work Alone: A Cross-Cultural View of Activities Superfluous to Survival*. Jeremy Cherfas and Roger Lewin, eds. Pp. 166–180. London: Temple Smith.

1984 Grog and Gossip in Bhatgaon: Style and Substance in Fiji Indian Conversation. *American Ethnologist* 11:487–506.

1988 Language and Disputing. In *Annual Review of Anthropology*, Vol. 17. Alan R. Beals and Stephen A. Tyler, eds. Palo Alto: Annual Reviews, Inc.

Brenneis, Donald and Laura Lein
  1977 "You Fruithead": A Sociolinguistic Approach to Children's Disputes. In *Child Discourse*. Susan Ervin-Tripp and Claudia Mitchell-Kernan, eds. Pp. 49–66. New York: Academic Press.
Briggs, Charles
  1985 Treasure Tales and Pedagogical Discourse in Mexicano New Mexico. *Journal of American Folklore* 98:287–314.
  1986 *Learning How to Ask: A Sociolinguistic Appraisal of the Role of the Interview in Social Science Research*. Cambridge: Cambridge University Press.
Brown, Penelope
  1976 Women and Politeness: A New Perspective on Language and Society. *Reviews in Anthropology* 3:240–249.
  1980 How and Why Are Women More Polite: Some Evidence from a Mayan Community. In *Women and Language in Literature and Society*. Sally McConnell-Ginet, Ruth Borker, and Nelly Furman, eds. Pp. 111–149. New York: Praeger.
Brown, Penelope and Stephen C. Levinson
  1978 Universals of Language Usage: Politeness Phenomena. In *Questions and Politeness: Strategies in Social Interaction*. Esther N. Goody, ed. Pp. 56–311. Cambridge: Cambridge University Press.
Bruner, Edward M.
  1986 Ethnography as Narrative. In *The Anthropology of Experience*. Victor Turner and Edward M. Bruner, eds. Pp. 139–155. Urbana: University of Illinois Press.
Bruner, Jerome, C. Roy, and N. Ratner
  1982 The Beginnings of Request. In *Children's Language*, Vol. 3. K. E. Nelson, ed. Pp. 91–138. New York: Gardner Press.
Burgos-Debray, Elisabeth (Ed.)
  1984 *I, Rigoberta Menchu: An Indian Woman in Guatemala*. London: Verso Editions.
Burman, Sandra and Pamela Reynolds (Eds.)
  1986 *Growing Up in a Divided Society: The Contexts of Childhood in South Africa*. Johannesburg: Ravan Press.
Button, Graham, Paul Drew, and John Heritage (Eds.)
  1986 *Human Studies: Special Issue*. Dordrecht, the Netherlands: Martinus Nijhoff.
Button, Graham and John R. Lee (Eds.)
  1987 *Talk and Social Organisation*. Clevedon, England: Multilingual Matters.
Campbell, J. K.
  1964 *Honour, Family, and Patronage: A Study of Institutions and Moral Values in a Greek Mountain Community*. Oxford: Clarendon Press.
Caplow, Theodore
  1968 *Two against One: Coalitions in Triads*. Englewood Cliffs, N.J.: Prentice-Hall.
Cazden, Courtney B.
  1976 The Neglected Situation in Child Language Research and Education. In *Rethinking Childhood: Perspectives on Development and Society*. Arlene Skolnick, ed. Pp. 149–167. Boston: Little, Brown and Co..
Cazden, Courtney, Martha Cox, David Dickerson, Zina Steinberg, and Carolyn Stone
  1979 "You All Gonna Hafta Listen": Peer Teaching in a Primary Classroom. In *Minnesota Symposia on Child Psychology*, Vol. 12. W. Collins, ed. Pp. 183–231. Hillsdale, N.J.: Lawrence Erlbaum Associates.
Cazden, Courtney, Vera John, and Dell Hymes (Eds.)
  1972 *The Functions of Language in the Classroom*. New York: Teachers College Press.
Chafe, Wallace
  1976 Givenness, Contrastiveness, Definiteness, Subjects, Topics, and Points of View. In *Subject and Topic*. Charles N. Li, ed. Pp. 25–56. New York: Academic Press.

Chance, M. R. A. and C. J. Jolly
  1970 *Social Groups of Monkeys, Apes, and Man*. London: Jonathan Cape.
Chomsky, Noam
  1965 *Aspects of the Theory of Syntax*. Cambridge: M. I. T. Press.
Cicourel, A.
  1974 *Cognitive Sociology*. New York: Free Press.
Cohn, Bernard S.
  1967 Some Notes on Law and Change in North India. In *Law and Warfare: Studies
    in the Anthropology of Conflict*. Paul Bohannan, ed. Pp. 139–159. Garden City,
    N.Y.: Natural History Press.
Cole, P. and J. L. Morgan
  1975 *Syntax and Semantics*, Vol. 3: *Speech Acts*. New York: Academic Press.
Coleman, James
  1961 *The Adolescent Society*. New York: Free Press.
Collier, Jane Fishburne
  1973 *Law and Social Change in Zinacantan*. Stanford: Stanford University Press.
Colson, Elizabeth
  1953 *The Makah Indians*. Manchester: Manchester University Press.
Cook-Gumperz, Jenny
  1981 Persuasive Talk: The Social Organization of Children's Talk. In *Ethnography
    and Language in Educational Settings*. Judith L. Green and Cynthia Wallat, eds.
    Pp. 25–50. Norwood, NJ: Ablex.
  1986a Caught in a Web of Words: Some Considerations on Language Socialization
    and Language Acquisition. In *Children's Worlds and Children's Language*. Jenny
    Cook-Gumperz, William A. Corsaro, and Jürgen Streeck, eds. Pp. 37–64. Ber-
    lin: Mouton de Gruyter.
Cook-Gumperz, Jenny (Ed.)
  1986b *The Social Construction of Literacy*. Cambridge: Cambridge University Press.
Cook-Gumperz, Jenny and William A. Corsaro
  1977 Social-Ecological Constraints on Children's Communicative Strategies. *So-
    ciology* 11:411–434.
  1986 Introduction. In *Children's Worlds and Children's Language*. Jenny Cook-Gum-
    perz, William A. Corsaro, and Jürgen Streeck, eds. Pp. 1–11. Berlin: Mouton
    de Gruyter.
Cook-Gumperz, Jenny, William A. Corsaro, and Jürgen Streeck (Eds.)
  1986 *Children's Worlds and Children's Language*. Berlin: Mouton de Gruyter.
Corsaro, William A.
  1977 The Clarification Request as a Feature of Adult Interactive Styles with Young
    Children. *Language in Society* 6:183–207.
  1979 Young Children's Conception of Status and Role. *Sociology of Education* 52:46–
    59.
  1981 Friendship in the Nursery School: Social Organization in a Peer Environ-
    ment. In *The Development of Children's Friendships*. Steven R. Asher and John
    M. Gottman, eds. Pp. 207–241. Cambridge: Cambridge University Press.
  1985 *Friendship and Peer Culture in the Early Years*. Norwood, N.J.: Ablex.
Corsaro, William A. and Thomas Rizzo
  1990 Disputes and Conflict Resolution among Nursery School Children in the
    U.S. and Italy. In *Conflict Talk*. Allen Grimshaw, ed. Pp. 21–66. Cambridge:
    Cambridge University Press.
Corsaro, William A. and Jürgen Streeck
  1986 Studying Children's Worlds: Methodological Issues. In *Children's Worlds and
    Children's Language*. Jenny Cook-Gumperz, William A. Corsaro, and Jürgen
    Streeck, eds. Pp. 13–35. Berlin: Mouton de Gruyter.

Corsaro, William A. and G. Tomlinson
  1980 Spontaneous Play and Social Learning in the Nursery School. In *Play and Culture*. H. Schwartzman, ed. Pp. 105–124. West Point, N.Y.: Leisure Press.
Coulter, Jeff
  1979 Elementary Properties of Argument Sequences. Paper presented at Conference on Ethnomethodology and Conversation Analysis, Boston University.
Cox, Bruce A.
  1970 What Is Hopi Gossip About? Information Management and Hopi Factions. *Man* 5:88–98.
Csikszentmihalyi, M. and R. Larson
  1984 *Being Adolescent: Conflict and Growth during the Teenage Years*. New York: Basic Books.
Cullen, J. M.
  1972 Some Principles of Animal Communication. In *Non-verbal Communication*. Robert A. Hinde, ed. Pp. 101–125. Cambridge: Cambridge University Press.
Damico, S. B.
  1975 Sexual Differences in the Responses of Elementary Pupils to Their Classroom. *Psychology in the Schools* 12:462–467.
Damon, William
  1977 *The Social World of the Child*. San Francisco: Jossey-Bass.
  1978 *Social Cognition: New Directions for Child Development*. San Francisco: Jossey-Bass.
  1983 The Nature of Social-Cognitive Change in the Developing Child. In *The Relationship between Social and Cognitive Development*. Willis F. Overton, ed. Pp. 103–141. Hillsdale, N.J.: Lawrence Erlbaum Associates.
Darnell, Regna
  1974 Correlates of Cree Narrative Performance. In *Explorations in the Ethnography of Speaking*. Richard Bauman and Joel Sherzer, eds. Pp. 315–336. Cambridge: Cambridge University Press.
Dawe, H. C.
  1934 An Analysis of Two Hundred Quarrels of Preschool Children. *Child Development* 5:139–157.
de Castro, Lucia Rabello
  1988 Aspects of Childcare in Single and Two-Parent Families of Lower Socioeconomic Status of an Urban Population. In *Growing into a Modern World: An International Interdisciplinary Conference on the Life and Development of Children in Modern Society*, Vol. 2. Karin Ekberg and Per Egil Mjaavatn, eds. Pp. 946–965. Trondheim, Norway: The Norwegian Centre for Child Research.
Dégh, Linda
  1969 *Storytelling in a Hungarian Peasant Community*. Bloomington: Indiana University Press.
Dégh, Linda and Andrew Vazsonyi
  1971 Legend and Belief. *Genre* 4:281–304.
Denzin, Norman K.
  1977 *Childhood Socialization*. San Francisco: Jossey-Bass.
  1982 The Significant Others of Young Children: Notes toward a Phenomenology of Childhood. In *The Social Life of Children in a Changing Society*. Kathryn M. Borman, ed. Pp. 29–46. Hillsdale, N.J.: Lawrence Erlbaum Associates.
Dillard, J. L.
  1972 *Black English*. New York: Random House.
Dobbert, M. L.
  1981 Designing Peaceful Societies. Paper presented at the Meeting of the American Anthropological Association, Los Angeles.

Dobbert, Marion Lundy and Betty Cooke
1985 Why Children Should Learn Through Other Children: Young Primates as Social Learners. Paper presented at the Meeting of the American Anthropological Association, Washington, D.C.

Dore, John
1977 "Oh Them Sheriff": A Pragmatic Analysis of Children's Responses to Questions. In *Child Discourse*. Susan Ervin-Tripp and Claudia Mitchell-Kernan, eds. Pp. 139–163. New York: Academic Press.
1978 Requestive Systems in Nursery School Conversations: Analysis of Talk in Its Social Context. In *Recent Advances in the Psychology of Language*. E. Campbell and P. Smith, eds. Pp. 271–292. New York: Plenum.

Dorson, Richard M.
1967 *American Negro Folktales*. Greenwich, Conn.: Fawcett Publications.

Dougherty, Molly
1978 *Becoming a Woman in Rural Black Culture*. New York: Holt, Rinehart and Winston.

Douvan, Elizabeth and Joseph Adelson
1966 *The Adolescent Experience*. New York: Wiley.

Duck, Steve and Robin Gilmour (Eds.)
1981 *Personal Relationships 2: Developing Personal Relationships*. London: Academic Press.

Dunn, Judy
1986 Growing Up in a Family World: Issues in the Study of Social Development in Young Children. In *Children of Social Worlds: Development in a Social Context*. Martin Richards and Paul Light, eds. Pp. 98–115. Cambridge, Mass.: Harvard University Press.

Duranti, Alessandro
1988 From Politics to Grammar: Tellings and Retellings in a Samoan *Fono*. Paper presented at the Invited Session on *Interactive Narrative and Transformations* at the Meeting of the American Anthropological Association, Phoenix.
in press Doing Things with Words: Conflict, Understanding and Change in a Samoan *Fono*. In *Disentangling: Conflict Discourse in the Pacific*. Karen Watson-Gegeo and Geoff White, eds. Stanford: Stanford University Press.

Dweck, Carol S.
1981 Social-Cognitive Processes in Children's Friendships. In *The Development of Children's Friendships*. Steven R. Asher and John M. Gottman, eds. Pp. 322–334. Cambridge: Cambridge University Press.

Eckert, Penelope
1988 Adolescent Social Structure and the Spread of Linguistic Change. *Language in Society* 17:183–207.

Edelman, C. O. and D. R. Omark
1973 Dominance Hierarchies in Young Children. *Social Science Information* 12:103–110.

Edelsky, Carole
1982 When She's/He's Got the Floor, We've/He's Got It. Paper presented at the 10th World Congress of Sociology, Mexico City.

Eder, Donna
1985 The Cycle of Popularity: Interpersonal Relations among Female Adolescents. *Sociology of Education* 58:154–165.
1988 Building Cohesion through Collaborative Narration. *Social Problems Quarterly* 51:225–235.
1990 Serious and Playful Disputes: Variation in Conflict Talk among Female Adolescents. In *Conflict Talk: Sociolinguistic Investigations of Arguments in Conversa-*

tions. Allen D. Grimshaw, ed. Pp. 67–84. Cambridge: Cambridge University Press.

Eder, Donna and Janet Enke
1988 Gossip as a Means for Strengthening Social Bonds: A Sociolinguistic Approach. Paper presented at the Meeting of the American Sociological Association, Atlanta.

Eder, Donna and Maureen T. Hallinan
1978 Sex Differences in Children's Friendships. *American Sociological Review* 43:237–250.

Eder, Donna and Stephanie Sanford
1986 The Development and Maintenance of Interactional Norms among Early Adolescents. In *Sociological Studies of Child Development,* Vol. 1. Patricia A. Adler and Peter Adler, eds. Pp. 283–300. Greenwich, Conn.: JAI Press Inc.

Eifermann, Rivka
1968 School Children's Games. Unpublished H. E. W. Office of Education, Bureau of Research, Final Report, Contract No. OE-6–21–010.

Eisenberg, Ann R. and Catherine Garvey
1981 Children's Use of Verbal Strategies in Resolving Conflicts. *Discourse Processes* 4:149–170.

Eisenstadt, S. N.
1956 *From Generation to Generation: Age Groups and Social Structure.* New York: Free Press of Glencoe.

Elkin, F. and G. Handel
1978 *The Child and Society,* 3rd ed. New York: Random House.

Ellis, S., B. Rogoff, and C. Cromer
1981 Research Reports: Age Segregation in Children's Social Interactions. *Developmental Psychology* 17:399–407.

Emerson, Robert
1969 *Judging Delinquents: Context and Process in Juvenile Court.* Chicago: Aldine.

Epstein, A. L.
1969 Gossip, Norms, and Social Network. In *Social Networks in Urban Situations.* J. Clyde Mitchell, ed. Pp. 117–127. Manchester: Manchester University Press.

Erickson, Frederick
1979 Talking Down: Some Cultural Sources of Miscommunication in Interracial Interviews. In *Nonverbal Communication: Applications and Cultural Implications.* Aaron Wolfgang, ed. Pp. 99–126. New York: Academic Press.

1982 Money Tree, Lasagna Bush, Salt and Pepper: Social Construction of Topical Cohesion in a Conversation among Italian-Americans. In *Analyzing Discourse: Text and Talk (Georgetown University Round Table on Languages and Linguistics 1981).* Deborah Tannen, ed. Pp. 43–70. Washington, D.C.: Georgetown University Press.

Erickson, Frederick and Gerald Mohatt
1982 Cultural Organization of Participation Structures in Two Classrooms of Indian Students. In *Doing the Ethnography of Schooling.* G. Spindler, ed. Pp. 132–174. New York: Holt, Rinehart and Winston.

Ervin-Tripp, Susan
1976 "Is Sybil There?": The Structure of Some American English Directives. *Language in Society* 5:25–67.

1982a Ask and It Shall Be Given to You: Children's Requests. In *Contemporary Perceptions of Language.* Heidi Byrnes, ed. Pp. 235–243. Washington, D.C.: Georgetown University Press.

1982b Structures of Control. In *Communicating in the Classroom.* Louise Cherry Wilkinson, ed. Pp. 27–47. New York: Academic Press.

Ervin-Tripp, Susan and Claudia Mitchell-Kernan
   1977 Introduction. In *Child Discourse*. Susan Ervin-Tripp and Claudia Mitchell-Kernan, eds. Pp. 1–26. New York: Academic Press.
Ervin-Tripp, Susan, Mary C. O'Connor, and Jarrett Rosenberg
   1984 Language and Power in the Family. In *Language and Power*. Cheris Kramarae, Muriel Schulz, and William O'Barr, eds. Pp. 116–135. Los Angeles: Sage.
Ervin-Tripp, Susan, Amy Strage, Martin Lampert, and Nancy Bell
   1987 Understanding Requests. *Linguistics* 25:107–143.
Feshbach, Norman and Gittelle Sones
   1971 Sex Differences in Adolescent Reactions toward Newcomers. *Developmental Psychology* 4:381–386.
Festinger, Leon
   1954 A Theory of Social Comparison Processes. *Human Relations* 7:117–140.
Fillion, Bryant, Carolyn Hedley, and Emily C. deMartino
   1987 *Home and School: Early Language and Reading*. Norwood, N.J.: Ablex.
Fine, Gary Alan
   1979 Small Groups and Culture Creation: The Idioculture of Little League Baseball Teams. *American Sociological Review* 44:733–745.
   1980 The Natural History of a Preadolescent Male Friendship Group. In *Friendship and Social Relations in Children*. Hugh C. Foot, Antony J. Chapman, and Jean R. Smith, eds. Pp. 293–320. New York: John Wiley and Sons.
   1981 Friends, Impression Management, and Preadolescent Behavior. In *The Development of Children's Friendships*. Steven R. Asher and John M. Gottman, eds. Pp. 29–52. Cambridge: Cambridge University Press.
Finnegan, Ruth
   1967 *Limba Stories and Story-telling*. Oxford: Clarendon Press.
Fishman, Pamela
   1978 Interaction: The Work Women Do. *Social Problems* 25:397–406.
Florio, Susan
   1978 Learning How to Go to School: An Ethnography of Interaction in a Kindergarten/First Grade Classroom. Unpublished Ph.D. Dissertation, Harvard University Graduate School of Education.
Folb, Edith
   1980 *Runnin' Down Some Lines*. Cambridge, Mass.: Harvard University Press.
Foley, Donald L.
   1950 The Use of Facilities in a Metropolis. *American Journal of Sociology* 56:238–246.
Foot, Hugh C., Antony J. Chapman, and Jean R. Smith
   1980 *Friendship and Social Relations in Children*. New York: John Wiley and Sons.
Fowler, Roger
   1985 Power. In *Handbook of Discourse Analysis*, Vol. 4: *Discourse Analysis in Society*. Teun A. van Dijk, ed. Pp. 61–82. London: Academic Press.
Frake, Charles O.
   1980 Author's Postscript. In *Language and Cultural Description*. Anwar S. Dil, ed. Pp. 333–336. Stanford: Stanford University Press.
Frankenberg, Ronald
   1957 *Village on the Border*. London: Cohen and West.
Fraser, Bruce and Winnie Nolen
   1981 The Association of Deference with Linguistic Form. *International Journal of the Sociology of Language* 27:93–109.
Garfinkel, Harold
   1967 *Studies in Ethnomethodology*. Englewood Cliffs, N.J.: Prentice-Hall.
Garfinkel, Harold and Harvey Sacks
   1970 On Formal Structures of Practical Actions. In *Theoretical Sociology*. J. D.

McKinney and E. A. Tiryakian, eds. Pp. 337–366. New York: Appleton-Century Crofts.

Garvey, Catherine
1974 Some Properties of Social Play. *Merrill-Palmer Quarterly* 20:163–180.
1975 Requests and Responses in Children's Speech. *Journal of Child Language* 2:41–63.
1977 *Play*. Cambridge, Mass.: Harvard University Press.
1984 *Children's Talk*. Cambridge, Mass.: Harvard University Press.

Genishi, Celia and Marianna di Paolo
1982 Learning through Argument in a Preschool. In *Communicating in the Classroom*. Louise Cherry Wilkinson, ed. Pp. 49–68. New York: Academic Press.

Georges, Robert A.
1969 Towards an Understanding of Storytelling Events. *Journal of American Folklore* 89:313–328.

Gilligan, Carol
1982 *In a Different Voice: Psychological Theory and Women's Development*. Cambridge, Mass.: Harvard University Press.
1987 Moral Orientation and Moral Development. In *Women and Moral Theory*. Eva Feder Kittay and Diana T. Meyers, eds. Pp. 19–33. Totowa, N.J.: Rowman and Littlefield.

Gilmore, David
1978 Varieties of Gossip in a Spanish Rural Community. *Ethnology* 17:89–99.

Gilmore, Perry and Allan A. Glatthorn (Eds.)
1982 *Children in and out of School: Ethnography and Education*. Washington, D.C.: Center for Applied Linguistics.

Glassner, Barry
1976 Kid Society. *Urban Education* 11:5–21.

Glazer, Mark
1976 On Verbal Dueling among Turkish Boys. *Journal of American Folklore* 89:87–89.

Gleason, Jean Berko and Esther Blank Greif
1983 Men's Speech to Young Children. In *Language, Gender, and Society*. Barrie Thorne, Cheris Kramarae, and Nancy Henley, eds. Pp. 140–150. Rowley, Mass.: Newbury House.

Gluckman, Max
1955 *The Judicial Process among the Barotse of Northern Rhodesia*. Glencoe: The Free Press.
1963 Gossip and Scandal. *Current Anthropology* 4:307–315.
1968 Psychological, Sociological, and Anthropological Explanations of Witchcraft and Gossip: A Clarification. *Man* 3:20–34.

Goffman, Erving
1953 Communication Conduct in an Island Community. Unpublished Ph.D. Dissertation, Department of Sociology, University of Chicago.
1959 *The Presentation of Self in Everyday Life*. New York: Doubleday.
1961a *Asylums: Essays on the Social Situation of Mental Patients and Other Inmates*. Garden City, N.Y.: Anchor Books, Doubleday.
1961b *Encounters: Two Studies in the Sociology of Interaction*. Indianapolis: Bobbs-Merrill.
1963 *Behavior in Public Places: Notes on the Social Organization of Gatherings*. New York: Free Press.
1964 The Neglected Situation. In *The Ethnography of Communication*. John J. Gumperz and Dell Hymes, eds. *American Anthropologist* 66, 6, pt. II:133–136.
1967 *Interaction Ritual: Essays on Face-to-Face Behavior*. Garden City, N.Y.: Doubleday.

1971 *Relations in Public: Microstudies of the Public Order.* New York: Basic Books.
1974 *Frame Analysis: An Essay on the Organization of Experience.* New York: Harper and Row.
1977 The Arrangement between the Sexes. *Theory and Society* 4:301–331.
1981 *Forms of Talk.* Philadelphia: University of Pennsylvania Press.
1983 The Interaction Order. *American Sociological Review* 48:1–17.
Goldman, Lawrence
1986 Review of *Dangerous Words: Language and Politics in the Pacific.* Donald Lawrence Brenneis and Fred R. Myers, eds. *American Ethnologist* 13:404–405.
Goodenough, Ward H.
1964 Cultural Anthropology and Linguistics. In *Language in Culture and Society: A Reader in Linguistics and Anthropology.* Dell Hymes, ed. Pp. 36–39. New York: Harper and Row.
1965 Rethinking "Status" and "Role": Toward a General Model of the Cultural Organization of Social Relationships. In *The Relevance of Models for Social Anthropology.* Michael Banton, ed. Pp. 1–24. London: Tavistock.
1981 *Culture, Language, and Society,* 2nd ed. Menlo Park: Benjamin Cummings.
Goodman, M. E.
1970 *The Culture of Childhood.* New York: Teachers College Press.
Goodwin, Charles
1981 *Conversational Organization: Interaction between Speakers and Hearers.* New York: Academic Press.
1984 Notes on Story Structure and the Organization of Participation. In *Structures of Social Action.* Max Atkinson and John Heritage, eds. Pp. 225–246. Cambridge: Cambridge University Press.
1986 Audience Diversity, Participation, and Interpretation. *Text* 6(3):283–316.
Goodwin, Charles and Alessandro Duranti
in press Rethinking Context: An Introduction. In *Rethinking Context: Language as an Interactive Process.* Alessandro Duranti and Charles Goodwin, eds. Cambridge: Cambridge University Press.
Goodwin, Charles and Marjorie Harness Goodwin
1987 Concurrent Operations on Talk: Notes on the Interactive Organization of Assessments. *IPrA Papers in Pragmatics* 1, No.1:1–52.
1990 Interstitial Argument. In *Conflict Talk.* Allen Grimshaw, ed. Pp. 85–117. Cambridge: Cambridge University Press.
Goodwin, Marjorie Harness
1980a "He-Said-She-Said": Formal Cultural Procedures for the Construction of a Gossip Dispute Activity. *American Ethnologist* 7:674–695.
1980b Processes of Mutual Monitoring Implicated in the Production of Description Sequences. *Sociological Inquiry* 50:303–317.
1980c Directive/Response Speech Sequences in Girls' and Boys' Task Activities. In *Women and Language in Literature and Society.* Sally McConnell-Ginet, Ruth Borker, and Nelly Furman, eds. Pp. 157–173. New York: Praeger.
1985a Byplay: The Framing of Collaborative Collusion. Paper presented at the Invited Session on *Framing Discourse: Public and Private in Language and Society* at the Meeting of the American Anthropological Association, Washington, D.C.
1985b The Serious Side of Jump Rope: Conversational Practices and Social Organization in the Frame of Play. *Journal of American Folklore* 98:315–330.
Goodwin, Marjorie Harness and Charles Goodwin
1986 Gesture and Coparticipation in the Activity of Searching for a Word. *Semiotica* 62(1/2):51–75.
1987 Children's Arguing. In *Language, Gender, and Sex in Comparative Perspective.*

Susan Philips, Susan Steele and Christine Tanz, eds. Pp. 200–248. Cambridge: Cambridge University Press.

Gordon, David and Susan Ervin-Tripp
1984 The Structure of Children's Requests. In *The Acquisition of Communicative Competence*. Richard L. Schiefelbusch and Joanne Pickar, eds. Pp. 295–321. Baltimore: University Park Press.

Gordon, David and George Lakoff
1971 Conversational Postulates. *Papers from the Seventh Regional Meeting of the Chicago Linguistic Society*:63–84.

Gossen, Gary H.
1974 To Speak with a Heated Heart: Chamula Canons of Style and Good Performance. In *Explorations in the Ethnography of Speaking*. Richard Bauman and Joel Sherzer, eds. Pp. 389–413. Cambridge: Cambridge University Press.
1976 Verbal Dueling in Chamula. In *Speech Play: Research and Resources for the Study of Linguistic Creativity*. B. Kirshenblatt-Gimblett, ed. Pp. 121–148. Philadelphia: University of Pennsylvania Press.

Gottman, John M. and Jennifer T. Parkhurst
1980 A Developmental Theory of Friendship and Acquaintanceship Processes. In *Development of Cognition, Affect, and Social Relations: The Minnesota Symposia on Child Psychology*, Vol. 13. W. Andrew Collins, ed. Pp. 197–254. Hillsdale, N.J.: Lawrence Erlbaum Associates.

Grant, Linda
1984 Black Females' "Place" in Desegrated Classrooms. *Sociology of Education* 57:98–111.

Green, E. H.
1933a Friendship and Quarrels among Preschool Children. *Child Development* 4:237–252.
1933b Group Play and Quarrelling among Preschool Children. *Child Development* 4:302–307.

Green, Judith and Cynthia Wallat (Eds.)
1981 *Ethnography and Language in Educational Settings*. Norwood, N.J.: Ablex.

Grice, H. P.
1975 Logic and Conversation. In *Syntax and Semantics*, Vol. 3: *Speech Acts*. P. Cole and J. L. Morgan, eds. Pp. 41–58. New York: Academic Press.

Griffin, Peg and Roger W. Shuy
1978 *Children's Functional Language and Education in the Early Years*. Arlington, Va.: Center for Applied Linguistics.

Grimshaw, Allen (Ed.)
1990 *Conflict Talk*. Cambridge: Cambridge University Press.

Gulliver, P. H.
1969a Dispute Settlement without Courts: The Ndendeuli of Southern Tanzania. In *Law in Culture and Society*. Laura Nader, ed. Pp. 24–68. Chicago: Aldine.
1969b Introduction to Case Studies in Non-Western Societies. In *Law in Culture and Society*. Laura Nader, ed. Pp. 11–23. Chicago: Aldine.
1979 *Disputes and Negotiations: A Cross-Cultural Perspective*. New York: Academic Press.

Gumperz, John J.
1972 Introduction. In *Directions in Sociolinguistics: The Ethnography of Communication*. John J. Gumperz and Dell Hymes, eds. Pp. 1–25. New York: Holt, Rinehart and Winston.
1981 Conversational Inference and Classroom Learning. In *Ethnography and Language in Educational Settings*. Judith Green and Cynthia Wallat, eds. Pp. 3–23. Norwood, N.J.: Ablex.
1982 *Discourse Strategies*. New York: Cambridge University Press.

Gumperz, John J. and Dell Hymes (Eds.)
  1972 *Directions in Sociolinguistics: The Ethnography of Communication*. New York: Holt, Rinehart and Winston.
Gunter, Richard
  1974 *Sentences in Dialogue*. Columbia, S.C.: Hornbeam Press.
Halliday, M. A. K.
  1975 *Learning How to Mean*. London: Edward Arnold.
Halliday, M. A. K. and Rugaiya Hasan
  1976 *Cohesion in English*. London: Longman.
Hallinan, Maureen T.
  1979 Structural Effects on Children's Friendships and Cliques. *Social Psychological Quarterly* 42:43–54.
  1980 Patterns of Cliquing among Youth. In *Friendship and Social Relations in Children*. H. C. Foot, A. J. Chapman, and J. R. Smith, eds. Pp. 321–341. New York: John Wiley and Sons, Ltd.
Handel, Gerald (Ed.)
  1988 *Childhood Socialization*. New York: Aldine de Gruyter.
Hanks, William F.
  in press(a) Metalanguage and Pragmatics of Deixis. In *Reflexive Language*. J. Lucy, ed. Cambridge: Cambridge University Press.
  in press(b) *Referential Practice: A Study in the Social Basis of Language and Experience in Maya Culture*. Chicago: University of Chicago Press.
Hannerz, Ulf
  1967 Gossip Networks and Culture in a Black American Ghetto. *Ethnos* 32:35–60.
  1969 *Soulside: Inquiries into Ghetto Culture and Community*. New York: Columbia University Press.
Harkness, Sara and Charles M. Super
  1985 The Cultural Context of Gender Segregation in Children's Peer Groups. *Child Development* 56:219–224.
Harré, Rom
  1974 The Conditions for a Social Psychology of Childhood. In *The Integration of a Child into a Social World*. Martin P. M. Richards, ed. Pp. 245–262. Cambridge: Cambridge University Press.
Harris, Clement
  1974 *Hennage: A Social System in Miniature*. New York: Holt, Rinehart and Winston.
Hart, R. A.
  1979 *Children's Experience of Place*. New York: Irvington Press.
Hartup, Willard W.
  1978 Children and Their Friends. In *Issues in Childhood Social Development*. Harry McGurk, ed. Pp. 130–170. London: Methuen.
  1980 Toward a Social Psychology of Childhood: Trends and Issues. In *Development of Cognition, Affect, and Social Relations*. W. Andrew Collins, ed. Pp. 273–279. Hillsdale, N.J.: Lawrence Erlbaum Associates.
  1983 Peer Relationships. In *Handbook of Child Psychology*, Vol. 3: *Socialization, Personality, and Social Development*. P. H. Mussen, ed. Pp. 103–196. New York: Wiley.
Haviland, John Beard
  1977 *Gossip, Reputation, and Knowledge in Zinacantan*. Chicago: University of Chicago Press.
  1986 "Con Buenos Chiles": Talk, Targets, and Teasing in Zinacantan. *Text* 6(3) (Special Issue entitled "The Audience as Co-author" edited by A. Duranti and D. Brenneis): 249–282.
  1989 Sure, Sure: Evidence and Affect. *Text* 9:27–68.

Heath, Christian
1986 *Body Movement and Speech in Medical Interaction*. Cambridge: Cambridge University Press.
Heath, Shirley Brice
1983 *Ways with Words: Language, Life, and Work in Communities and Classrooms*. Cambridge: Cambridge University Press.
Heritage, John C.
1984a *Garfinkel and Ethnomethodology*. Cambridge: Polity Press.
1984b A Change-of-State Token and Aspects of Its Sequential Placement. In *Structures of Social Action*. J. Maxwell Atkinson and John Heritage, eds. Pp. 299–345. Cambridge: Cambridge University Press.
1985 Recent Developments in Conversation Analysis. *Sociolinguistics Newsletter* 15, No.1:1–19.
Heritage, John C. and J. Maxwell Atkinson
1984 Introduction. In *Structures of Social Action*. J. Maxwell Atkinson and John Heritage, eds. Pp. 1–16. Cambridge: Cambridge University Press.
Hollos, Marida and William Beeman
1978 The Development of Directives among Norwegian and Hungarian Children. *Language in Society* 7:345–356.
Holmes, Dick
1984 Explicit-Implicit Address. *Journal of Pragmatics* 8:311–320.
Homans, G. C.
1950 *The Human Group*. New York: Harcourt.
Honko, Lauri
1964 Memorates and the Study of Folk Beliefs. *Journal of the Folklore Institute* 1:5–19.
Hotchkiss, J. C.
1967 Children and Conduct in a Ladino Community of Chiapas, Mexico. *American Anthropologist* 69:711–718.
House, Juliane and Gabrielle Kasper
1981 Politeness Markers in English and German. In *Conversational Routine*. F. Coulmas, ed. Pp. 157–185. The Hague: Mouton.
Hughes, Linda A.
1983 Beyond the Rules of the Game: Girls' Gaming at a Friends' School. Unpublished Ph.D. Dissertation, University of Pennsylvania, Graduate School of Education.
1988 "But That's Not *Really* Mean": Competing in a Cooperative Mode. *Sex Roles* 19:669–687.
in press The Study of Children's Gaming. In *A Handbook of Children's Folklore*. Brian Sutton-Smith, Jay Mechling, and Thomas Johnson, eds. Washington, D.C.: Smithsonian Institution Press.
Hymes, Dell H.
1962 The Ethnography of Speaking. In *Anthropology and Human Behavior*. Thomas Gladwin and William C. Sturtevant, eds. Pp. 13–53. Washington, D.C.: Anthropological Society of Washington.
1972 The Contribution of Folklore to Sociolinguistic Research. In *Towards New Perspectives in Folklore*. Américo Paredes and Richard Bauman, eds. Pp. 42–50. Austin: University of Texas Press.
1974 *Foundations in Sociolinguistics: An Ethnographic Approach*. Philadelphia: University of Pennsylvania Press.
1986 Discourse: Scope without Depth. *International Journal of the Sociology of Language* 13:49–89.
Jakobson, Roman
1966 Grammatical Parallelism and Its Russian Facet. *Language* 42:399–429.
1968 Poetry of Grammar and Grammar of Poetry. *Lingua* 21:597–609.

James, S. L.
  1975 The Effect of Listener and Situation on the Politeness of Preschool Children's
  Directive Speech. Unpublished Ph.D. Dissertation, University of Wisconsin.
Jefferson, Gail
  1972 Side Sequences. In *Studies in Social Interaction*. David Sudnow, ed. Pp. 294–
  338. New York: Free Press.
  1973 A Case of Precision Timing in Ordinary Conversation: Overlapped Tag-
  Positioned Address Terms in Closing Sequences. *Semiotica* 9:47–96.
  1978 Sequential Aspects of Storytelling in Conversation. In *Studies in the Organization of Conversational Interaction*. Jim Schenkein, ed. Pp. 219–248. New York:
  Academic Press.
  1979 A Technique for Inviting Laughter and Its Subsequent Acceptance/Decli-
  nation. In *Everyday Language: Studies in Ethnomethodology*. George Psathas, ed.
  Pp. 79–96. New York: Irvington Publishers.
  1984 On the Organization of Laughter in Talk about Troubles. In *Structures of
  Social Action*. J. Maxwell Atkinson and John Heritage, eds. Pp. 346–369. Cam-
  bridge: Cambridge University Press.
  1987 Exposed and Embedded Corrections. In *Talk and Social Organisation*. Graham
  Button and John R. E. Lee, eds. Pp. 86–100. Clevedon, England: Multilingual
  Matters Ltd.
Jefferson, Gail and Jim Schenkein
  1978 Some Sequential Negotiations in Conversation: Unexpanded and Expanded
  Versions of Projected Action Sequences. In *Studies in the Organization of Con-
  versational Interaction*. Jim Schenkein, ed. Pp. 155–172. New York: Academic
  Press.
Jenkins, Mercilee MacIntyre
  1984 The Story Is in the Telling: A Cooperative Style of Conversation among
  Women. In *Gewalt durch Sprache: Die Vergewaltingung von Frauen in Gesprachen*.
  Senta Tromel-Plotz, ed. Pp. 333–353. Frankfurt, Germany: Fischer Taschen-
  buch Verlag.
Jordan, Brigitte and Lucy Suchman
  1987 Interactional Troubles in Survey Interviews. Paper presented in the session
  Cognitive Aspects of Surveys, 1987 American Statistical Association Meetings,
  August 19, 1987, San Francisco.
Kalčik, Susan
  1975 " . . . Like Anne's Gynecologist or the Time I Was Almost Raped": Personal
  Narratives in Women's Rap Groups. *Journal of American Folklore* 88:3–11.
Katriel, Tamar
  1985 *Brogez*: Ritual and Strategy in Israeli Children's Conflicts. *Language in Society*
  14:467–490.
Keenan, Elinor Ochs
  1974 Conversational Competence in Children. *Journal of Child Language* 1:163–183.
  1977 Making It Last: Uses of Repetition in Children's Discourse. In *Child Discourse*.
  Susan Ervin-Tripp and Claudia Mitchell-Kernan, eds. Pp. 125–138. New York:
  Academic Press.
  1983 Evolving Discourse: The Next Step. In *Acquiring Conversational Competence*.
  Elinor Ochs and Bambi B. Schieffelin, eds. Pp. 40–49. Boston: Routledge and
  Kegan Paul.
Keenan, Elinor Ochs and Ewan Klein
  1975 Coherency in Children's Discourse. *Journal of Psycholinguistic Research* 4:365–
  380.
Keiser, R. Lincoln
  1969 *The Vice Lords: Warriors of the Streets*. New York: Holt, Rinehart and Winston.

Keller-Cohen, Deborah, Karen Cayo Chalmer, and Jane E. Remler
1979 The Development of Discourse Negation in the Nonnative Child. In *Developmental Pragmatics*. Elinor Ochs and Bambi B. Schieffelin, eds. Pp. 305–322. New York: Academic Press.

Kendon, Adam
1985 Behavioural Foundations for the Process of Frame Attunement in Face-to-Face Interaction. In *Discovery Strategies in the Psychology of Action*. Gerry Ginsburg et al., ed. Pp. 229–253. London: Academic Press.

Kerber, Linda K. et al.
1986 On *In a Different Voice*: An Interdisciplinary Forum. *Signs: Journal of Women in Culture and Society* 11:304–333.

Kernan, Keith T.
1977 Semantic and Expressive Elaboration in Children's Narratives. In *Child Discourse*. Susan Ervin-Tripp and Claudia Mitchell-Kernan, eds. Pp. 91–102. New York: Academic Press.

Kirsh, Barbara
1983 The Use of Directives as Indication of Status among Preschool Children. In *Developmental Issues in Discourse*. Jonathan Fine and Roy O. Freedle, eds. Pp. 269–290. Norwood, N.J.: Ablex.

Kirshenblatt-Gimblett, Barbara
1974 A Parable in Context. In *Folklore: Performance and Communication*. Dan Ben-Amos and Kenneth S. Goldstein, eds. Pp. 105–130. The Hague: Mouton.

Knapp, Mary and Herbert Knapp
1976 *One Potato, Two Potato: The Secret Education of American Children*. New York: Norton.

Kochman, Thomas
1970 Toward an Ethnography of Black American Speech Behavior. In *Afro-American Anthropology*. Norman E. Whitten, Jr. and John F. Szwed, eds. Pp. 145–162. New York: Free Press.
1972 Toward an Ethnography of Black American Speech Behavior. In *Rappin' and Stylin' Out: Communication in Urban Black America*. Thomas Kochman, ed. Pp. 241–264. Chicago: University of Illinois Press.
1981 *Black and White: Styles in Conflict*. Chicago: University of Chicago Press.
1983 The Boundary between Play and Nonplay in Black Verbal Dueling. *Language in Society* 12:329–337.

Kohlberg, L.
1984 *The Psychology of Moral Development*. San Francisco: Harper and Row.

Konner, M.
1975 Relations among Infants and Juveniles in Comparative Perspective. In *Friendship and Peer Relations*. M. Lewis and L. A. Rosenblum, eds. Pp. 99–129. New York: Wiley.

Kramarae, Cheris
1981 *Women and Men Speaking: Frameworks for Analysis*. Rowley, Mass.: Newbury House.

Kurth, Suzanne B.
1970 Friendships and Friendly Relations. In *Friendships and Friendly Relations*. George J. McCall, ed. Pp. 136–170. Chicago: Aldine.

Labov, William
1970 *The Study of Nonstandard English*. Champaign, Ill.: National Council of Teachers.
1972a *Language in the Inner City: Studies in the Black English Vernacular*. Philadelphia: University of Pennsylvania Press.
1972b *Sociolinguistic Patterns*. Philadelphia: University of Pennsylvania Press.
1974 The Art of Sounding and Signifying. In *Language in Its Social Setting*. William

W. Gage, ed. Pp. 84–116. Washington, D.C.: Anthropological Society of Washington.

1982 Speech Actions and Reactions in Personal Narrative. In *Georgetown University Round Table on Languages and Linguistics 1981: Analyzing Discourse: Text and Talk.* Deborah Tannen, ed. Pp. 219–247. Washington, D.C.: Georgetown University Press.

Labov, William, P. Cohen, C. Robins, and J. Lewis

1968 *A Study of the Nonstandard English of Negro and Puerto Rican Speakers in New York City.* Report of Cooperative Research Project 3288. Mimeograph. New York: Columbia University.

Labov, William and David Fanshel

1977 *Therapeutic Discourse: Psychotherapy as Conversation.* New York: Academic Press.

Labov, William and Joshua Waletzky

1968 Narrative Analysis. In *A Study of the Nonstandard English of Negro and Puerto Rican Speakers in New York City.* William Labov, P. Cohen, C. Robins, and J. Lewis, eds. Pp. 286–338. New York: Columbia University.

Ladd, D. Robert Jr.

1980 *The Structure of Intonational Meaning: Evidence from English.* Bloomington: Indiana University Press.

Ladd, Gary W., Craig H. Hart, Emily M. Wadsworth, and Beckie S. Golter

1988 Preschoolers' Peer Networks in Nonschool Settings: Relationship to Family Characteristics and School Adjustment. In *Social Networks of Children, Adolescents, and College Students.* Suzanne Salzinger, John Antrobus, and Muriel Hammer, eds. Pp. 61–92. Hillsdale, N.J.: Lawrence Erlbaum Associates.

Ladner, J. A.

1971 *Tomorrow's Tomorrow: The Black Woman.* New York: Anchor Books.

LaFontaine, Jean

1986 An Anthropological Perspective on Children in Social Worlds. In *Children of Social Worlds: Development in a Social Context.* Martin Richards and Paul Light, eds. Pp. 10–30. Cambridge, Mass.: Harvard University Press.

La Gaipa, John J.

1981 Children's Friendships. In *Personal Relationships 2: Developing Personal Relationships.* Steve Duck and Robin Gilmour, eds. Pp. 161–185. London: Academic Press.

Lakoff, George

1968 *Counterparts, or the Problem of Reference in Transformational Grammar.* Bloomington: Indiana University, Linguistics Club.

Lakoff, Robin

1973 Language and Women's Place. *Language in Society* 2:45–80.

1975 *Language and Women's Place.* New York: Harper.

1977 What You Can Do with Words: Politeness, Pragmatics, and Performatives. In *Proceedings of the Texas Conference on Performatives, Presuppositions, and Implicatures.* A. Rogers, B. Wall, and J. Murphy, eds. Arlington, Va.: Center for Applied Linguistics.

Lave, Jean

1988 *Cognition in Practice.* Cambridge: Cambridge University Press.

Lave, Jean, Michael Murtaugh, and Olivia de la Rocha

1984 The Dialectic of Arithmetic in Grocery Shopping. In *Everyday Cognition: Its Development in Social Context.* Barbara Rogoff and Jean Lave, eds. Pp. 67–94. Cambridge, Mass.: Harvard University Press.

Leary, James P.

1976 Fists and Foul Mouths: Fights and Fight Stories in Contemporary Rural American Bars. *Journal of American Folklore* 89:27–39.

Lee, Richard Borshay
  1986 Eating Christmas in the Kalahari. In *Anthropology 86/87: Annual Editions*. Elvio Angeloni, ed. Pp. 17–20. Guilford, Conn.: Dushkin. [Reprinted from *Natural History*, 1969.]
Lein, Laura and Donald Brenneis
  1978 Children's Disputes in Three Speech Communities. *Language in Society* 7:299–323.
Lemann, Nicholas
  1986 The Origins of the Underclass. *The Atlantic Monthly* 257:31–55; 258:54–68.
Leont'ev, A. N.
  1981 The Problem of Activity in Psychology. In *The Concept of Activity in Soviet Psychology*. James V. Wertsch, ed. Pp. 37–71. Armonk, N.Y.: M. E. Sharpe.
Lever, Janet Rae
  1974 Games Children Play: Sex Differences and the Development of Role Skills. Unpublished Ph.D. Dissertation, Department of Sociology, Yale University.
  1976 Sex Differences in the Games Children Play. *Social Problems* 23:478–487.
  1978 Sex Differences in the Complexity of Children's Play and Games. *American Sociological Review* 43:471–483.
Levinson, Stephen C.
  1979 Activity Types and Language. *Linguistics* 17:365–399.
  1983 *Pragmatics*. Cambridge: Cambridge University Press.
  1986 Putting Linguistics on a Proper Footing: Explorations in Goffman's Concepts of Participation. Paper presented to the conference "Erving Goffman: An Interdisciplinary Appreciation," York, England, July 1986.
Lévi-Strauss, Claude
  1963 *Structural Anthropology*. New York: Basic Books.
Lewis, D.
  1975 The Black Family: Socialization and Sex Roles. *Phylon* 36:221–237.
Lewis, M. and L. Rosenblum
  1975 *Friendship and Peer Relations*. New York: Wiley.
Lieberman, Kenneth
  1985 *Understanding Interaction in Central Australia: An Ethnomethodological Study of Australian Aboriginal People*. Boston: Routledge and Kegan Paul.
Lubin, David and David Forbes
  1984 Children's Reasoning and Peer Relations. In *Everyday Cognition: Its Development in Social Context*. Barbara Rogoff and Jean Lave, eds. Pp. 220–237. Cambridge, Mass.: Harvard University Press.
Lucy, John A. and Suzanne Gaskins
  1989 Language Diversity and the Development of Thought. Paper presented at the Meeting of the American Anthropological Association, Washington, D.C.
Lyons, John
  1977 *Semantics*. Cambridge: Cambridge University Press.
McAdoo, H. P.
  1983 *Extended Family Support of Single Black Mothers*. Columbia, Md.: Columbia Research Systems.
McCall, George J.
  1970 The Social Organization of Relationships. In *Social Relationships*. George McCall, ed. Pp. 30–34. Chicago: Aldine.
McCarl, Robert S.
  1976 Smokejumper Initiation: Ritualized Communication in a Modern Occupation. *Journal of American Folklore* 89:49–80.
  1980 Occupational Folklife: An Examination of the Expressive Aspects of Work Culture with Particular Reference to Fire Fighters. Ph.D. Dissertation, Department of Folklore, Memorial University of Newfoundland.

Maccoby, Eleanor Emmons
    1986 Social Groupings in Childhood: Their Relationship to Prosocial and Anti-
    social Behavior in Boys and Girls. In *Development of Antisocial and Prosocial
    Behavior: Theories, Research, and Issues*. D. Olweus, J. Block, and M. Radke-
    Yarrow, eds. Pp. 263–284. San Diego: Academic Press.
Maccoby, Eleanor Emmons and Carol Nagy Jacklin
    1974 *The Psychology of Sex Differences*. Stanford: Stanford University Press.
    1987 Gender Segregation in Childhood. *Advances in Child Development and Behavior*
    20:239–287.
McConnell-Ginet, Sally
    1980 Linguistics and the Feminist Challenge. In *Women and Language in Literature
    and Society*. Sally McConnell-Ginet, Ruth Borker, and Nelly Furman, eds. Pp.
    3–25. New York: Praeger.
    1983 Review of *Language, Sex, and Gender: Does "la Difference" Make a Difference?*
    edited by Judith Orasanu, Mariam K. Slater, and Leonore Loeb Adler and
    Sexist Language: A Modern Philosophical Analysis, edited by Mary Vetterling-
    Braggin. *Language* 59:373–391.
McDermott, Raymond P.
    1976 Kids Make Sense: An Ethnographic Account of the Interactional Manage-
    ment of Success and Failure of One First-Grade Classroom. Unpublished Ph.D.
    Dissertation. Stanford University.
McDermott, Raymond P. and Kenneth Gospodinoff
    1979 Social Contexts for Ethnic Borders and School Failure. In *Nonverbal Behavior:
    Applications and Cultural Implications*. A. Wolfgang, ed. Pp. 175–196. New York:
    Academic Press.
McDermott, Raymond P., Kenneth Gospodinoff, and Jeffrey Aron
    1978 Criteria for an Ethnographically Adequate Description of Concerted Activi-
    ties and Their Contexts. *Semiotica* 24:245–275.
McGhee, Z.
    1900 A Study in the Play Life of Some South Carolina Children. *Pedagogical Seminar*
    7:459–491.
McGurk, Harry (Ed.)
    1978 *Issues in Childhood Social Development*. London: Methuen.
McLaughlin, Margaret L.
    1984 *Conversation: How Talk Is Organized*. Beverly Hills: Sage Publications.
McLoyd, Vonnie C., Shirley Aisha Ray, and Gwendolyn Etter-Lewis
    1985 Being and Becoming: The Interface of Language and Family Role Knowledge
    in the Pretend Play of Young African American Girls. In *Play, Language, and
    Stories: The Development of Children's Literate Behavior*. Lee Galda and Anthony
    D. Pellegrini, eds. Pp. 29–43. Norwood, N.J.: Ablex.
McRobbie, Angela and Jenny Garber
    1976 Girls and Subcultures. In *Resistance through Rituals: Youth Subcultures in Post-
    war Britain*. Stuart Hall and Tony Jefferson, eds. Pp. 209–222. London: Hutch-
    inson and Co.
McTear, Michael F.
    1980 Getting It Done: The Development of Children's Abilities to Negotiate Re-
    quest Sequences in Peer Interaction. *Belfast Working Papers in Language and
    Linguistics* 4:1–29.
Malinowski, Bronislaw
    1959 The Problem of Meaning in Primitive Languages. In *The Meaning of Meaning*.
    C. K. Ogden and I. A. Richards, eds. Pp. 296–336. New York: Harcourt, Brace
    and World [1923].
    1973 The Group and Individual in Functional Analysis. In *High Points in Anthro-*

pology. Paul Bohanan and Mark Glazer, eds. Pp. 275–293. New York: Alfred A. Knopf. [Reprinted from *American Journal of Sociology* 44, 1939.]

Maltz, Daniel N. and Ruth A. Borker
  1983 A Cultural Approach to Male-Female Miscommunication. In *Communication, Language, and Social Identity*. John J. Gumperz, ed. Pp. 196–216. Cambridge: Cambridge University Press.

Maynard, Douglas W.
  1984 *Inside Plea Bargaining: The Language of Negotiation*. New York: Plenum.
  1985a On The Functions of Social Conflict among Children. *American Sociological Review* 50:207–223.
  1985b How Children Start Arguments. *Language in Society* 14:1–29.
  1986a The Development of Argumentative Skills among Children. In *Sociological Studies of Child Development* Vol. 1. Patricia A. Adler and Peter Adler, eds. Pp. 233–258. Greenwich, Conn.: JAI Press.
  1986b Offering and Soliciting Collaboration in Multi-Party Disputes Among Children (and Other Humans). *Human Studies* 9:261–285.

Mead, George H.
  1934 *Mind, Self, and Society*. Chicago: University of Chicago Press.
  1973 The Art and Technology of Field Work. In *A Handbook of Method in Cultural Anthropology*. Raoul Naroll and Ronald Cohen, eds. Pp. 246–265. New York: Columbia University Press.

Medrich, Elliott A., Judith Roizen, Victor Rubin, and Stuart Buckley
  1982 *The Serious Business of Growing Up: A Study of Children's Lives outside School*. Berkeley: University of California Press.

Mehan, Hugh
  1979 *Learning Lessons*. Cambridge, Mass.: Harvard University Press.
  1985 The Structure of Classroom Discourse. In *Handbook of Discourse Analysis*, Vol. 3: *Discourse and Dialogue*. Teun A. van Dijk, ed. Pp. 119–131. London: Academic Press.

Meyers, Diana T. and Eva Feder Kittay
  1987 Introduction. In *Women and Moral Theory*. Eva Feder Kittay and Diana T. Meyers, eds. Pp. 3–16. Totowa, N.J.: Rowman and Littlefield.

Michaels, Sarah
  1981 "Sharing Time": Children's Narrative Styles and Differential Access to Literacy. *Language in Society* 10:423–442.

Milan, W.
  1976 The Influence of Sex and Age Factors in the Selection of Polite Expressions: A Sample from Puerto Rican Spanish. *La Revista Bilingue* 3:99–121.

Mishler, Elliot G.
  1986 *Research Interviewing: Context and Narrative*. Cambridge, Mass.: Harvard University Press.

Mitchell, J. Clyde
  1966 Theoretical Orientations in African Urban Studies. In *The Social Anthropology of Complex Societies*. Michael Banton, ed. Pp. 37–68. London: Tavistock.
  1974 Social Networks. In *Annual Reviews*, Vol. 3. Bernard J. Siegel, Alan R. Beals, and Stephen A. Tyler, eds. Pp. 201–227. Palo Alto: Annual Reviews, Inc.

Mitchell-Kernan, Claudia
  1971 Language Behavior in a Black Urban Community. Monographs of the Language Behavior Laboratory, No. 2, University of California, Berkeley.
  1972 Signifying and Marking: Two Afro-American Speech Acts. In *Directions in Sociolinguistics: The Ethnography of Communication*. John J. Gumperz and Dell Hymes, eds. Pp. 161–179. New York: Holt, Rinehart and Winston.

Mitchell-Kernan, Claudia and Keith T. Kernan
  1977 Pragmatics of Directive Choice among Children. In *Child Discourse*. Susan

Ervin-Tripp and Claudia Mitchell-Kernan, eds. Pp. 189–208. New York: Academic Press.

Moerman, Michael
1988 *Talking Culture: Ethnography and Conversation Analysis*. Philadelphia: University of Pennsylvania Press.

Moerman, Michael and Harvey Sacks
1988 On "Understanding" in the Analysis of Natural Conversation. In *Talking Culture: Ethnography and Conversation Analysis*. Michael Moerman, ed. Pp. 180–186. Philadelphia: University of Pennsylvania Press.

Moshin, Nadeem
1988 Child Labour in Slums: A Barrier to Children's Growth. In *Growing into a Modern World: An Interdisciplinary Conference on the Life and Development of Children in Modern Society*. Karin Ekberg and Per Egil Mjaavatn, eds. Pp. 735–743. Trondheim: The Norwegian Centre for Child Research.

Nader, Laura
1969 Styles of Court Procedure: To Make the Balance. In *Law in Culture and Society*. Laura Nader, ed. Pp. 69–91. Chicago: Aldine.

Nader, Laura and Harry F. Todd (Eds.)
1978 *The Disputing Process: Law in Ten Societies*. New York: Columbia University Press.

Nelson, Katherine
1981 Social Cognition in Script Framework. In *Social Cognitive Development: Frontiers and Possible Futures*. John H. Flavell and Lee Ross, eds. Pp. 97–118. Cambridge: Cambridge University Press.

Newman, Denis
1978 Ownership and Permission among Nursery School Children. In *The Development of Social Understanding*. Joseph Glick and K. Alison Clarke-Stewart, eds. Pp. 213–249. New York: Gardner Press.

Ochs, Elinor
1988 *Culture and Language Development: Language Acquisition and Language Socialization in a Samoan Village*. Cambridge: Cambridge University Press.
1989 Indexing Gender. Ms.

Ochs, Elinor and Bambi B. Schieffelin
1983 *Acquiring Conversational Competence*. Boston: Routledge and Kegan Paul.

Ochs, Elinor, Ruth Smith, and Carolyn Taylor
1989 Detective Stories at Dinnertime: Problem-Solving through Co-narration. *Cultural Dynamics* 2:238–257.

Ochs, Elinor, Carolyn Taylor, Dina Rudolph, and Ruth Smith
1989 Narrative Activity as a Medium for Theory-Building. Ms.

Omark, Donald R., F. F. Strayer, and Daniel G. Freedman (Eds.)
1980 *Dominance Relations: An Ethological View of Human Conflict and Social Interaction*. New York: Garland STPM Press.

Opie, Iona and Peter Opie
1969 *Children's Games in Street and Playground*. Oxford: Clarendon Press.

Ortner, Sherry B.
1974 Is Female to Male as Nature Is to Culture? In *Woman, Culture, and Society*. Michelle Z. Rosaldo and Louise L. Lamphere, eds. Pp. 67–88. Stanford: Stanford University Press.

Oswald, Hans, Lothar Krappman, Irene Chowdhuri, and Maria von Salisch
1985 Gaps and Bridges: Interactions between Girls and Boys in Elementary School. Paper presented at the Eighth Biennial Meeting of the International Society for the Study of Behavioral Development, Tours, France.

Overing, J.
1986 Men Control Women? The "Catch 22" in the Analysis of Gender. *International Journal of Moral and Social Studies* 1:135–156.

Overton, Willis F.
  1983 *The Relationship between Social and Cognitive Development*. Hillsdale, N.J.: Lawrence Erlbaum Associates.
Paine, Robert
  1967 What Is Gossip About: An Alternative Hypothesis. *Man* 2:278–285.
Parsons, E. C.
  1966 *Mitla, Town of the Souls*. Chicago: University of Chicago Press.
Pepler, Debra, Carl Corter, and Rona Abramovitch
  1982 Social Relations among Children: Comparison of Sibling and Peer Interaction. In *Peer Relationships and Social Skills in Childhood*. Kenneth H. Rubin and Hildy S. Ross, eds. Pp. 209–227. New York: Springer-Verlag.
Philips, Susan U.
  1972 Participant Structures and Communicative Competence: Warm Springs Children in Community and Classroom. In *Functions of Language in the Classroom*. C. B. Cazden, V. P. John, and D. Hymes, eds. Pp. 370–394. New York: Columbia Teachers Press.
  1980 Sex Differences and Language. In *Annual Review of Anthropology 9*. Bernard Siegel, Alan R. Beals, and Stephen A. Tyler, eds. Pp. 523–544. Palo Alto: Annual Reviews, Inc.
Piaget, Jean
  1926 *The Language and Thought of the Child*. London: Kegan, Paul, Trench, Trubner and Co.
  1965 *The Moral Judgment of the Child (1932)*. New York: Free Press.
Pike, Kenneth L.
  1973 Sociolinguistic Evaluation of Alternative Mathematical Models: English Pronouns. *Language* 29:121–160.
Pitcher, E. and L. Schultz
  1983 *Boys and Girls at Play: The Development of Sex Roles*. New York: Praeger.
Polanyi, Livia
  1979 So What's the Point? *Semiotica* 25:207–241.
  1985 *Telling the American Story: A Structural and Cultural Analysis of Conversational Storytelling*. Norwood, N.J.: Ablex.
Pomerantz, Anita
  1975 Second Assessments: A Study of Some Features of Agreements/Disagreements. Unpublished Ph.D. Dissertation, Division of Social Sciences, University of California, Irvine.
  1978 Compliment Reponses: Notes on the Co-operation of Multiple Constraints. In *Studies in the Organization of Conversational Interaction*. J. Schenkein, ed. Pp. 79–112. New York: Academic Press.
  1984 Agreeing and Disagreeing with Assessments: Some Features of Preferred/Dispreferred Turn Shapes. In *Structures of Social Action: Studies in Conversation Analysis*. J. Maxwell Atkinson and John Heritage, eds. Pp. 57–101. Cambridge: Cambridge University Press.
  1987 An Information-Seeking Strategy: Straight-Way Offering a Legitimate Reason as a Best Guess. Ms.
Pratt, Mary Louise
  1977 *Toward a Speech Act Theory of Literary Discourse*. Bloomington: Indiana University Press.
Prince, Gerald
  1980 Introduction to the Study of the Narratee. In *Reader-Response Criticism: From Formalism to Post-structuralism*. Jane P. Tompkins, ed. Pp. 7–25. Baltimore: Johns Hopkins University Press.
Propp, Vladimir
  1968 *The Morphology of the Folktale*. Austin: University of Texas Press (2nd edition, Translated by T. Scott).

Radcliffe-Brown, A. R.
  1973 On Social Structure. In *High Points in Anthropology*. Paul Bohannan and Mark Glazer, eds. Pp. 304–316. New York: Alfred A. Knopf.
Reisman, Karl
  1970 Cultural and Linguistic Ambiguity in a West Indian Village. In *Afro-American Anthropology: Contemporary Perspectives*. Norman E Whitten, Jr. and John F. Szwed, eds. Pp. 129–144. New York: Free Press.
  1974a Contrapuntal Conversations in an Antiguan Village. In *Explorations in the Ethnography of Speaking*. Richard Bauman and Joel Sherzer, eds. Pp. 110–124. Cambridge: Cambridge University Press.
  1974b Noise and Order. In *Language in Its Social Setting*. William W. Gage, ed. Pp. 56–73. Washington D.C.: The Anthropological Society of Washington.
Reynolds, Pamela
  1988 The Double Strategy of Children in South Africa. In *Growing into a Modern World: An International Interdisciplinary Conference on the Life and Development of Children in Modern Society*, Vol. 3. Karin Ekberg and Per Egil Mjaavatn, eds. Pp. 1124–1165. Trondheim: The Norwegian Centre for Child Research.
Richards, Martin P. M. (Ed.)
  1974 *The Integration of a Child into a Social World*. Cambridge: Cambridge University Press.
Rintell, Ellen
  1981 Sociolinguistic Variation and Pragmatic Ability. *International Journal of the Sociology of Language* 27:11–34.
Robinson, John A.
  1981 Personal Narratives Reconsidered. *Journal of American Folklore* 94:58–85.
Rogoff, Barbara
  1984 Introduction: Thinking and Learning in Social Context. In *Everyday Cognition: Its Development in Social Context*. Barbara Rogoff and Jean Lave, eds. Pp. 1–8. Cambridge, Mass.: Harvard University Press.
Rosaldo, Michelle Z.
  1974 Woman, Culture, and Society: A Theoretical Overview. In *Woman, Culture, and Society*. Michelle Z. Rosaldo and Louise L. Lamphere, eds. Pp. 17–42. Stanford: Stanford University Press.
Rose, Dan
  1987 *Black American Street Life: South Philadelphia, 1969–1971*. Philadelphia: University of Pennsylvania Press.
Rubin, Kenneth H. and Hildy S. Ross
  1982 Introduction: Some Reflections on the State of the Art: The Study of Peer Relationships and Social Skills. In *Peer Relationships and Social Skills in Childhood*. Kenneth H. Rubin and Hildy S. Ross, eds. Pp. 1–8. New York: Springer-Verlag.
Rubin, Zick
  1980 *Children's Friendships*. Cambridge: Harvard University Press.
Sachs, Jacqueline
  1987 Preschool Boys' and Girls' Language Use in Pretend Play. In *Language, Gender, and Sex in Comparative Perspective*. Susan Philips, Susan Steele, and Christine Tanz, eds. Pp. 178–188. Cambridge, Mass.: Cambridge University Press.
Sacks, Harvey
  1963 Sociological Description. *Berkeley Journal of Sociology* 8:1–16.
  1967 Unpublished class lectures.
  1970 Unpublished class lectures.
  1972 On the Analyzability of Stories by Children. In *Directions in Sociolinguistics: The Ethnography of Communication*. John J. Gumperz and Dell Hymes, eds. Pp. 325–345. New York: Holt, Rinehart and Winston.
  1973 On Some Puns with Some Intimations. In *Report of the Twenty-third Annual*

Round Table Meeting on Linguistics and Language Studies. Roger W. Shuy, ed. Pp. 135–144. Washington, D.C.: Georgetown University Press.

1974 An Analysis of the Course of a Joke's Telling in Conversation. In *Explorations in the Ethnography of Speaking*. Richard Bauman and Joel Sherzer, eds. Pp. 337–353. Cambridge: Cambridge University Press.

1978 Some Technical Considerations of a Dirty Joke. In *Studies in the Organization of Conversational Interaction*. Jim Schenkein, ed. Pp. 249–269. New York: Academic Press.

1984 Notes on Methodology. In *Structures of Social Action*. J. Maxwell Atkinson and John Heritage, eds. Pp. 21–27. Cambridge: Cambridge University Press.

1987 On the Preferences for Agreement and Contiguity in Sequences in Conversation. In *Talk and Social Organisation*. Graham Button and John R. E. Lee, eds. Pp. 54–69. Clevedon, England: Multilingual Matters.

Sacks, Harvey, Emanuel A. Schegloff, and Gail Jefferson
1974 A Simplest Systematics for the Organization of Turn-Taking for Conversation. *Language* 50:696–735.

Salzinger, Suzanne, John Antrobus, and Muriel Hammer (Eds.)
1988 *Social Networks of Children, Adolescents, and College Students*. Hillsdale, N.J.: Lawrence Erlbaum Associates.

Saussure, Ferdinand de
1985 The Linguistic Sign. In *Semiotics: An Introductory Anthology*. Robert E. Innis, ed. Pp. 28–46. Bloomington: Indiana University Press.

Savasta, M. L. and Brian Sutton-Smith
1979 Sex Differences in Play and Power. In *Die Dialektik des Spiels*. Brian Sutton-Smith, ed. Pp. 143–150. Schorndoff: Holtman.

Savin-Williams, Richard
1980 Social Interactions of Adolescent Females in Natural Groups. In *Friendship and Social Relations in Children*. Hugh C. Foot, Antony J. Chapman, and Jean R. Smith, eds. Pp. 343–364. New York: John Wiley and Sons Ltd.

Schegloff, Emanuel A.
1968 Sequencing in Conversational Openings. *American Anthropologist* 70:1075–1095.

1972 Notes on a Conversational Practice: Formulating Place. In *Studies in Social Interaction*. David Sudnow, ed. Pp. 75–119. New York: Free Press.

1984 On Some Questions and Ambiguities in Conversation. In *Structures of Social Action*. J. Maxwell Atkinson and John Heritage, eds. Pp. 28–52. Cambridge: Cambridge University Press.

Schegloff, Emanuel A., Gail Jefferson, and Harvey Sacks
1977 The Preference for Self-Correction in the Organization of Repair in Conversation. *Language* 53:361–382.

Schegloff, Emanuel A. and Harvey Sacks
1973 Opening Up Closings. *Semiotica* 8:289–327.

Schenkein, Jim
1978 *Studies in the Organization of Conversational Organization*. New York: Academic Press.

Schieffelin, Bambi B.
1981 Talking Like Birds: Sound Play in a Cultural Perspective. In *The Paradoxes of Play*. J. Loy, ed. Pp. 177–184. New York: Leisure Press.

Schiffrin, Deborah
1980 Meta-talk: Organizational and Evaluative Brackets in Discourse. *Sociological Inquiry* 50:199–236.

1984 Jewish Argument as Sociability. *Language in Society* 13:311–335.

Schildkrout, Enid
1978 Roles of Children in Urban Kano. In *Sex and Age as Principles of Social Differentiation*. J. S. LaFontaine, ed. Pp. 109–137. New York: Academic Press.

Schofield, Janet Ward
    1981 Complementary and Conflicting Identities: Images and Interaction in an Interracial School. In *The Development of Children's Friendships*. Steven R. Asher and John M. Gottman, eds. Pp. 53–90. Cambridge: Cambridge University Press.
Schwartzman, Helen B.
    1978 *Transformations: The Anthropology of Children's Play*. New York: Plenum.
Scollon, Ron and Suzanne B. K. Scollon
    1980 Literacy as Focussed Interaction. *Quarterly Newsletter of the Laboratory of Comparative Human Cognition* 22(2):26–29.
Scribner, Sylvia (Ed.)
    1984 Cognitive Studies of Work. *The Quarterly Newsletter of the Laboratory of Comparative Human Cognition* 6 ns. 1–2:1–4.
Searle, John R.
    1969 *Speech Acts*. London: Cambridge University Press.
Selman, Robert L.
    1973 A Structural Analysis of the Ability to Take Another's Social Perspective: Stages in the Development of Role-taking Ability. Paper presented at the Meeting of the Society for Research in Child Development, Philadelphia.
    1980 *The Growth of Interpersonal Understanding*. New York: Academic Press.
    1981 The Child as a Friendship Philosopher. In *The Development of Children's Friendships*. Steven R. Asher and John M. Gottman, eds. Pp. 242–272. Cambridge: Cambridge University Press.
Selman, R. L. and D. F. Byrne
    1974 A Structural-Developmental Analysis of Levels of Role-Taking in Middle Childhood. *Child Development* 45:803–806.
Shantz, Carolyn Uhlinger
    1975 The Development of Social Cognition. In *Review of Child Development Research*, Vol. 5. E. Mavis Hetherington, ed. Pp. 257–323. Chicago: University of Chicago Press.
    1983 Social Cognition. In *Handbook of Child Psychology*, 4th ed., Vol. III: *Cognitive Development*. Paul H. Mussen, ed. Pp. 495–555. New York: John Wiley and Sons.
    1987a Conflicts between Children. *Child Development* 58:283–305.
    1987b The Promises and Perils of Social Conflict. Paper presented for discussion at the Symposium "Conflicts between Children: Opportunities and Dangers for Development" at the Meeting of the Society for Research in Child Development, Baltimore, Md.
Shatz, Marilyn
    1983 Communication. In *Handbook of Child Psychology*, 4th ed., Vol. III: *Cognitive Development*. Paul H. Mussen, ed. Pp. 841–889. New York: John Wiley and Sons.
Shatz, M. and R. Gelman
    1973 The Development of Communication Skills: Modifications in the Speech of Young Children as a Function of Listener. Monographs of the Society for Research in Child Development, 38, No. 152.
Sheldon, Amy
    1989 Sociolinguistic Challenges to Self-Assertion and How Very Young Girls Meet Them. Paper presented at the Women in America Conference, Georgetown University.
Sherif, Muzafer and Carolyn W. Sherif
    1953 *Groups in Harmony and Tension*. New York: Harper and Row.
Sherzer, Joel
    1980 Tellings and Retellings: An Aspect of Cuna Indian Narrative. Paper pre-

sented at the Annual Meeting of the Semiotic Society of America, Bloomington, Indiana.

1987 A Discourse-Centered Approach to Language and Culture. *American Anthropologist* 89:295–309.

Shields, M. M.

1981 Parent-Child Relationships in the Middle Years of Childhood. In *Personal Relationships 2: Developing Personal Relationships*. Steve Duck and Robin Gilmour, eds. Pp. 141–159. London: Academic Press.

Shuman, Amy

1986 *Storytelling Rights: The Uses of Oral and Written Texts by Urban Adolescents*. Cambridge: Cambridge University Press.

Simmel, Georg

1902 The Number of Members as Determining the Sociological Form of the Group. *American Journal of Sociology* 8:158–196.

1950 *The Sociology of Georg Simmel*. Translated by Kurt Wolff. Glencoe, Ill.: Free Press.

Skolnick, Arlene

1976 *Rethinking Childhood: Perspectives on Development and Society*. Boston: Little, Brown and Co.

Smith, Barbara Herrnstein

1980 Afterthoughts on Narrative. *Critical Inquiry* 7:213–236.

Speier, Matthew

1973 *How to Observe Face-to-Face Communication: A Sociological Introduction*. Pacific Palisades, Calif.: Goodyear.

1976 The Adult Ideological Viewpoint in Studies of Childhood. In *Rethinking Childhood: Perspectives on Development and Society*. Arlene Skolnick, ed. Pp. 168–186. Boston: Little, Brown and Company.

Spindler, George (Ed.)

1982 *Doing the Ethnography of Schooling: Educational Anthropology in Action*. New York: Holt, Rinehart and Winston.

Stack, Carol

1974 *All Our Kin: Strategies for Survival in a Black Community*. New York: Harper and Row.

Stahl, Sandra S. K.

1977 The Personal Narrative as Folklore. *Journal of the Folklore Institute* 14:9–30.

Stone, Carolyn R. and Robert L. Selman

1982 A Structural Approach to Research on the Development of Interpersonal Behavior among Grade School Children. In *Peer Relationships and Social Skills in Childhood*. Kenneth H. Rubin and Hildy S. Ross, eds. Pp. 163–183. New York: Springer-Verlag.

Strayer, F. F.

1980 Social Ecology of the Preschool Peer Group. In *Development of Cognition Affect and Social Relations*. W. Andrew Collins, ed. Pp. 165–196. Hillsdale, N.J.: Lawrence Erlbaum Associates.

Strayer, F. F. and Janet Strayer

1980 Preschool Conflict and the Assessment of Social Dominance. In *Dominance Relations: An Ethological View of Human Conflict and Social Interaction*. Donald R. Omark, F. F. Strayer, and Daniel G. Freedman, eds. Pp. 137–157. New York: Garland STPM Press.

Streeck, Jürgen

1983 *Social Order in Child Communication. A Study in Microethnography. Pragmatics and Beyond 4*. Amsterdam: Benjamins, BV.

Sullivan, H. S.

1953 *The Interpersonal Theory of Psychiatry*. New York: Norton.

Suthinee, Santaputra
 1988 Growing Up in Thai Society. In *Growing into a Modern World: Proceedings from an International Interdisciplinary Conference on the Life and Development of Children in Modern Society*. Karin Ekberg and Per Egil Mjaavatn, eds. Pp. 897–907. Trondheim: The Norwegian Centre for Child Research.
Suttles, G. D.
 1968 *The Social Order of the Slum*. Chicago: University of Chicago Press.
 1975 Community Design: The Search for Participation in a Metropolitan Society. In *Metropolitan America in Contemporary Perspective*. Amos H. Hawley and Vincent P. Rock, eds. Pp. 235–298. New York: John Wiley.
Sutton-Smith, Brian
 1953 Seasonal Games. *Western Folklore* 12:186–193.
 1968 The Folk Games of the Children. In *Our Living Traditions: An Introduction to American Folklore*. T. P. Coffin, ed. Pp. 179–191. New York: Basic Books.
 1979 The Play of Girls. In *Becoming Female*. Claire B. Kopp and Martha Kirkpatrick, eds. Pp. 229–257. New York: Plenum.
 1982 A Performance Theory of Peer Relationships. In *The Social Life of Children in a Changing Society*. Kathryn M. Borman, ed. Pp. 65–77. Hillsdale, N.J.: Lawrence Erlbaum Associates.
 1985 Ambivalence in Toyland. *Natural History* 94:6–10.
Sutton-Smith, Brian and B. Rosenberg
 1971 Sixty Years of Historical Change in the Game Preferences of American Children. In *Child's Play*. R. E. Herron and Brian Sutton-Smith, eds. Pp. 119–126. New York: John Wiley and Sons, Inc.
Sutton-Smith, Brian, B. G. Rosenberg, and E. F. Morgan, Jr.
 1963 Development of Sex Differences in Play Choices during Preadolescence. *Child Development* 34:119–126.
Szwed, John
 1966 Gossip, Drinking, and Social Control: Consensus and Communication in a Newfoundland Parish. *Ethnology* 5:434–441.
Tannen, Deborah
 1979 What's in a Frame? In *New Directions in Discourse Processing*. Roy Freedle, ed. Pp. 137–181. Norwood, N.J.: Ablex.
 1981 New York Jewish Conversational Style. *International Journal of the Sociology of Language* 30:131–149.
 1982 The Oral/Literate Continuum in Discourse. In *Spoken and Written Language: Exploring Orality and Literacy*. Deborah Tannen, ed. Pp. 1–16. Norwood, N.J.: Ablex.
 1984 *Conversational Style*. Norwood, N.J.: Ablex.
Teraski, Alene
 1976 Pre-announcement Sequences in Conversation. Social Science Working Paper 99. Mimeograph. Irvine: University of California.
Thorne, Barrie
 1986 Girls and Boys Together . . . but Mostly Apart: Gender Arrangements in Elementary School. In *Relationships and Development*. William W. Hartup and Zick Rubin, eds. Pp. 167–184. Hillsdale, N.J.: Lawrence Erlbaum Associates.
 1987a Re-visioning Women and Social Change: Where Are the Children? *Gender and Society* 1:85–109.
 1987b Crossing the Gender Divide: What "Tomboys" Can Teach Us about Processes of Gender Separation among Children. Paper presented at the Conference "Ethnographic Approaches to Children's Worlds and Peer Culture," Trondheim, Norway.
Thorne, Barrie and Nancy Henley
 1975 *Language and Sex: Difference and Dominance*. Rowley, Mass.: Newbury House.

Thorne, Barrie, Cheris Kramarae, and Nancy Henley
   1983 *Language, Gender, and Society.* Rowley, Mass.: Newbury House.
Thorne, Barrie and Zella Luria
   1986 Sexuality and Gender in Children's Daily Worlds. *Social Problems* 33:176–190.
Tuma, N. B. and M. T. Hallinan
   1979 The Effects of Sex, Race, and Achievement on Schoolchildren's Friendships. *Social Forces* 5:111–130.
Turner, Victor W.
   1980 The Anthropology of Experience. Paper presented at the 79th Annual Meeting of the American Anthropological Association, Washington, D.C.
   1986 Dewey, Dilthey, and Drama: An Essay in the Anthropology of Experience. In *The Anthropology of Experience.* Victor W. Turner and Edward M. Bruner, eds. Pp. 33–44. Urbana: University of Illinois Press.
Vaughn, Brian E. and Everett Waters
   1980 Social Organization among Preschool Peers. In *Dominance Relations: An Ethological View of Human Conflict and Social Interaction.* Donald R. Omark, F. F. Strayer, and Daniel G. Freedman, eds. Pp. 359–379. New York: Garland STPM Press.
Vinacke, W. Edgar and Abe Arkoff
   1957 An Experimental Study of Coalitions in Triads. *American Sociological Review* 22:406–414.
Vološinov, V. N.
   1971 Reported Speech. In *Readings in Russian Poetics: Formalist and Structuralist Views.* Ladislav Matejka and Krystyna Pomorska, eds. Pp. 149–175. Cambridge, Mass.: MIT. Press.
   1973 *Marxism and the Philosophy of Language.* Translated by Ladislav Matejka and I. R. Titunik. New York: Seminar Press. (First Published 1929 and 1930).
Von Glascoe, Christine A.
   1980 The Work of Playing "Redlight". In *Play and Culture: 1978 Proceedings of the Association for the Anthropological Study of Play.* Helen B. Schwartzman, ed. Pp. 228–231. West Point, N.Y.: Leisure Press.
Vuchinich, Samuel
   1984 Sequencing and Social Structure in Family Conflict. *Social Psychology Quarterly* 47:217–234.
Vygotsky, L. S.
   1962 *Thought and Language.* Cambridge, Mass.: MIT Press.
   1978 *Mind in Society.* Cambridge, Mass.: Harvard University Press.
   1981 The Genesis of Higher Mental Functions. In *The Concept of Activity in Soviet Psychology.* James V. Wertsch, ed. Pp. 144–188. Armonk, N.Y.: M. E. Sharpe.
Waldrop, Mary F. and Charles F. Halverson
   1975 Intensive and Extensive Peer Behavior: Longitudinal and Cross-Sectional Analyses. *Child Development* 46:19–26.
Walters, Joel
   1980 Strategies for Requesting in Spanish and English. *Language Learning* 29:277–293.
Watson, Karen Ann
   1973 A Rhetorical and Sociolinguistic Model for the Analysis of Narrative. *American Anthropologist* 75:243–264.
Watson-Gegeo, Karen Ann and Stephen T. Boggs
   1977 From Verbal Play to Talk Story: The Role of Routines in Speech Events among Hawaiian Children. In *Child Discourse.* Susan Ervin-Tripp and Claudia Mitchell-Kernan, eds. Pp. 67–90. New York: Academic Press.

Watson-Gegeo, Karen Ann and David Gegeo
　1989 Learning to Think Straight: Language, Culture and Cognitive Development in Kwara'Ae. Paper presented at the Meeting of the American Anthropological Association, Washington, D.C.

Werner, Oswald and Joann Fenton
　1973 Method and Theory in Ethnoscience or Ethnoepistemology. In *A Handbook of Method in Cultural Anthropology*. Raoul Naroll and Ronald Cohen, eds. Pp. 537–578. New York: Columbia University Press.

Wertsch, James V.
　1981 The Concept of Activity in Soviet Psychology: An Introduction. In *The Concept of Activity in Soviet Psychology*. J. V. Wertsch, ed. Pp. 3–36. Armonk, N.Y.: M. E. Sharpe.
　1985a *Vygotsky and the Social Formation of Mind*. Cambridge, Mass.: Harvard University Press.

Wertsch, James V. (Ed.)
　1985b *Culture, Communication, and Cognition: Vygotskian Perspectives*. Cambridge: Cambridge University Press.

West, Candace
　1979 Against Our Will: Male Interruptions of Females in Cross-Sex Conversation. *Annals of the New York Academy of Sciences* 327:81–97.
　1990 Not Just "Doctors' Orders": Collaborative Speech Sequences in Patients' Encounters with Women Physicians. *Discourse and Society* 1:85–112.

West, Candace and Don H. Zimmerman
　1985 Gender, Language, and Discourse. In *Handbook of Discourse Analysis*, Vol. 4. Teun A. van Dijk, ed. Pp. 103–124. London: Academic Press.

White, Sheldon H. and Alexander W. Siegel
　1984 Cognitive Development in Time and Space. In *Everyday Cognition: Its Development in Social Context*. Barbara Rogoff and Jean Lave, eds. Pp. 238–277. Cambridge, Mass.: Harvard University Press.

Whiting, Beatrice and Carolyn Pope Edwards
　1973 A Cross-Cultural Analysis of Sex Differences in the Behavior of Children Aged Three through Eleven. *Journal of Social Psychology* 91:171–188.

Whiting, J. W. M. and B. Whiting
　1973 Altruistic and Egoistic Behavior in Six Cultures. In *Cultural Illness and Health: Essays in Human Adaptation*. L. Nader and T. W. Maretzki, eds. Pp. 56–66. Washington, D.C.: American Anthropological Association.

Whyte, William Foote
　1943 *Street Corner Society*. Chicago: University of Chicago Press.

Wierzbicka, Anna
　1985 Different Languages, Different Speech Acts. *Journal of Pragmatics* 9:145–178.

Wilkinson, Louise Cherry
　1982 *Communicating in the Classroom*. New York: Academic Press.
　1984 Classroom Status from a Sociolinguistic Perspective. In *The Development of Oral and Written Language in Social Contexts*. Anthony Pellegrini and Thomas Yawkey, eds. Pp. 145–153. Norwood, N.J.: Ablex.

Wilson, Peter J.
　1974 Filcher of Good Names: An Inquiry into Anthropology and Gossip. *Man* 9:93–102.

Wittgenstein, Ludwig
　1958 *Philosophical Investigations*. Edited by G. E. M. Anscombe and R. Rhees, translated by G. E. M. Anscombe. 2nd ed. Oxford: Blackwell.

Wolfe, Tom
　1987 *The Bonfire of the Vanities*. New York: Bantam Books.

Wolfson, Nessa
  1978 A Feature of Performed Narrative: The Conversational Historical Present. *Language in Society* 7:215–237.
Women for Guatemala
  1987 Guatemala's Children: An Overview. *The Voice of Guatemalan Women, Ch' Abuj Ri Ixoc* Spring issue: 1–12.
Wood, B. and R. Gardner
  1980 How Children "Get Their Way": Directives in Communication. *Communication Education* 29:264–272.
Wootton, A. J.
  1981 The Management of Grantings and Rejections by Parents in Request Sequences. *Semiotica* 37:59–89.
  1984 Some Aspects of Children's Use of "Please" in Request Sequences. In *Interpretive Sociolinguistics*. Peter Auer and Aldo di Luzio, eds. Pp. 147–162. Tübingen: Gunter Narr Verlag.
  1986 Rules in Action: Orderly Features of Actions That Formulate Rules. In *Children's Worlds and Children's Language*. William Corsaro, Jenny Cook-Gumperz, and Jürgen Streeck, eds. Pp. 147–168. The Hague: Mouton.
Wulff, Helena
  1988 *Twenty Girls: Growing Up, Ethnicity, and Excitement in a South London Microculture*. Stockholm: University of Stockholm.
Yaeger, Malcah
  1974 Speech Styles and Pitch Contours on Negatives. JASA 55, Supplement 543.
Yaeger-Dror, Malcah
  1985 Intonational Prominence on Negatives in English. *Language and Speech* 28:197–230.
Yaeger-Dror, Malcah and E. Sister
  1987 "Scuse me, waitaminute!": Directive Use in Israeli Hebrew. *Linguistics* 25:1127–1163.
Yanagisako, Sylvia Junko and Jane Fishburne Collier
  1987 Toward a Unified Analysis of Gender and Kinship. In *Gender and Kinship: Essays Toward a Unified Analysis*. Jane Fishburne Collier and Sylvia Junko Yanagisako, eds. Pp. 14–50. Stanford: Stanford University Press.
Yawkey, Thomas D. and Thomas J. Miller
  1984 The Language of Social Play in Young Children. In *The Development of Oral and Written Language in Social Contexts*. Anthony Pellegrini and Thomas Yawkey, eds. Pp. 95–103. Norwood, N.J.: Ablex.
Yngvesson, Barbara
  1976 Responses to Grievance Behavior: Extended Cases in a Fishing Community. *American Ethnologist* 3:353–373.
Young, Virginia H.
  1970 Family and Childhood in a Southern Negro Community. *American Anthropologist* 72:269–288.
Youniss, James
  1978 The Nature of Social Development: A Conceptual Discussion of Cognition. In *Issues in Childhood Social Development*. Harry McGurk, ed. Pp. 203–227. London: Methuen.
  1980 *Parents and Peers in Social Development: A Sullivan-Piaget Perspective*. Chicago: University of Chicago Press.
Youniss, J. and J. A. Volpe
  1978 A Relational Analysis of Children's Friendships. In *New Directions for Child Development: Social Cognition*. W. Damon, ed. San Francisco: Jossey-Bass.
Zahn-Waxler, Carolyn, Ronald Iannotti, and Michael Chapman
  1982 Peers and Prosocial Development. In *Peer Relationships and Social Skills in*

Childhood. Kenneth H. Rubin and Hildy S. Ross, eds. Pp. 133–162. New York: Springer-Verlag.

Zigler, E. and I. L. Child

1969 Socialization. In *The Handbook of Social Psychology*, 2nd ed., Vol. 3. G. Lindzey and E. Aronson, eds. Pp. 450–589. Reading, Mass.: Addison-Wesley.

Zimmerman, Don H. and Candace West (Eds.)

1980 *Sociological Inquiry: Special Double Issue on Language and Social Interaction*.

Name Index

Abrahams, Roger D., 43, 185, 188, 191, 219, 237, 259, 284, 285, 313n.41, 320n.18, 325nn.12, 15, 327n.11
Abramovitch, Rona, 12, 311n.18, 317n.14
Adelson, Joseph, 48
Adger, Carolyn Temple, 143, 188, 308n.11, 319n.6, 322n.44
Adler, Patricia A., 308nn.14, 15
Adler, Peter, 308nn.14, 15
Agar, Michael, 22
Alanen, Leena, 283, 308n.14
Allen, Donald E., 141
Almirol, Edwin B., 191, 324nn.20, 21
Ambert, Annie-Marie, 308n.14
Andersen, Elaine Slosberg, 17, 68, 127, 308n.11
Antrobus, John, 309n.1
Arkoff, Abe, 48
Aron, Jeffrey, 308n.11
Aschenbrenner, J., 318nn.15, 16
Asher, Steven R., 308n.14
Atkinson, J. Maxwell, 7, 73, 307n.4
Austin, J. L., 63, 65, 66

Babcock, Barbara A., 237
Bailey, F. G., 286
Bakhtin, Mikhail M., 229, 245
Baratz, Joan C., 285
Barker, R. G., 310n.15
Barrios de Chungara, Domitila, 21
Barth, Fredrik, 47
Bartz, K. W., 125
Bateson, Gregory, 326n.10
Baugh, John, 285
Bauman, Richard, 188, 237, 320nn.18, 29, 325nn.6, 12, 16
Baumrind, D., 125
Bearison, D. J., 16
Becker, Judith, 65, 66, 68, 69, 70, 72, 327n.4
Beeman, William, 72
Bell, Nancy, 72
Bellinger, David C., 125, 317nn.10, 12, 13
Ben-Amos, Dan, 237, 307n.5, 325n.12
Bereiter, Carl, 327n.14
Berentzen, Sigurd, 37, 46, 133, 135, 136, 307n.8, 308n.14, 309n.1, 312n.32, 313n.40, 315nn.1, 5, 318nn.15, 19, 20, 325n.17
Bergmann, Jörg, 7
Berndt, Thomas J., 17, 310nn.8, 16, 311n.27, 312n.32
Bernstein, Basil, 327n.14
Besnier, Niko, 7
Best, Raphaela, 43, 46, 49, 313nn.42, 46
Bilmes, Jack, 279
Binzen, Peter, 31

Bloome, David, 307n.11
Blum-Kulka, Shoshana, 68, 72, 317nn.2, 4
Boas, Franz, 3
Boggs, Stephen T., 143, 188, 237, 319nn.3, 8, 320n.24, 321nn.32, 33
Bogoch, Bryna, 72
Borker, Ruth A., 53, 136, 137, 318n.1
Brady, Margaret K., 38, 237, 325n.12
Brecht, Richard D., 212
Bremme, Donald W., 307n.11
Brenneis, Donald, 7, 10, 17, 143, 144, 188, 308n.11, 318n.2, 319n.13, 320n.23, 321nn.33, 35, 322nn.40, 41, 323n.13, 324n.3
Briggs, Charles, 237, 274
Brown, Penelope, 68, 70, 117, 120, 136, 141, 315n.9, 317n.2, 318n.1
Bruner, Edward M., 65, 279
Buckley, Stuart, 35, 310n.9, 11, 17, 311n.20
Burgos-Debray, Elisabeth, 21
Burman, Sandra, 21
Button, Graham, 307n.4
Byrne, D. F., 309n.20

Campbell, J. K., 191
Caplow, Theodore, 48, 323n.14
Cazden, Courtney B., 68, 100, 307n.11, 309n.18
Chafe, Wallace, 198
Chagnon, N., 325n.10
Chalmer, Karen Cayo, 320n.22
Chance, M. R. A., 102
Chapman, Antony J., 308nn.13, 14
Chapman, Michael, 317n.10
Child, I. L., 13
Chomsky, Noam, 3, 287
Chowdhuri, Irene, 311n.27, 314n.57
Cicourel, Aaron, 308n.14
Cohen, P., 18, 285, 327n.14
Cohn, Bernard S., 156
Cole, P., 314n.3
Coleman, James, 43
Collier, Jane Fishburne, 156, 327n.8
Colson, Elizabeth, 191, 322n.2
Cook-Gumperz, Jenny, 12, 68, 188, 307n.11, 308nn.11, 14, 317n.5, 322n.38, 327n.3
Cooke, Betty, 310n.12
Corsaro, William A., 23, 68, 127, 129, 143, 188, 307n.11, 308nn.11, 14, 309n.19, 312nn.37, 39, 318n.17, 319nn.5, 6, 10, 327n.3
Corter, Carl, 12, 311n.18, 317n.14
Coulter, Jeff, 320n.23
Cox, Bruce A., 191
Cox, Martha, 68, 100,
Cromer, C., 21, 311nn.18, 27, 312n.31

Csikszentmihalyi, M., 311n.23
Cullen, J. M., 1

Damico, S. B., 314n.55
Damon, William, 15, 17, 308n.14
Danet, Brenda, 72
Darnell, Regna, 325n.15
Dawe, H. C., 319n.1
de Castro, Lucia Rabello, 21
de Fornel, Michel, 314n.1
Dégh, Linda, 325n.12
de la Rocha, Olivia, 309nn.17, 21
deMartino, Emily C., 308n.11
Denzin, Norman K., 308nn.13, 14
Dillard, J. L., 285
diPaolo, Marianna, 143, 144, 188, 312n.39,
    319n.3, 320nn.20, 22, 322n.43
Dobbert, M. L., 310n.12, 312n.36
Dore, John, 66, 308n.11
Dorson, Richard M., 259
Dougherty, Molly, 310n.17
Douvan, Elizabeth, 48
Drew, Paul, 307n.4
Duck, Steve, 308n.14
Dunn, Judy, 12, 21
Duranti, Alessandro, 10, 237, 315n.6, 318n.2,
    324n.3
Dweck, Carol S., 49, 53

Eckert, Penelope, 307n.9
Eckhardt, Rosalind, 38
Edelman, C. O., 49
Edelsky, Carole, 237
Eder, Donna, 7, 39, 43, 46, 48, 49, 133, 137,
    188, 237, 327nn.9, 10
Edwards, Carolyn Pope, 49, 310n.18, 313n.42
Eifermann, Rivka, 39, 313n.44
Eisenberg, Ann R., 143, 163, 188, 197, 308n.11,
    319nn.3, 4, 320n.22
Eisenstadt, S. N., 312n.31
Elkin, F., 308n.14
Ellis, S., 21, 311nn.18, 27, 312n.31
Emerson, Robert, 201, 323n.12
Engelmann, Siegfried, 327n.14
Enke, Janet, 7
Epstein, A. L., 191
Erickson, Frederick, 10, 12, 307n.11, 308n.11
Ervin-Tripp, Susan, 11, 66, 68, 69, 70, 71, 72,
    73, 78, 80, 106, 127, 308n.11, 315n.13,
    318n.17, 319n.3
Etter-Lewis, Gwendolyn, 125, 318nn.15, 16,
    17

Fanshel, David, 16, 65, 66, 67, 68, 69, 78, 92,
    141, 177, 231, 314n.1, 317n.4, 320n.21
Fenton, Joann, 274
Feshbach, Norman, 48
Festinger, Leon, 312n.38
Fillion, Bryant, 308n.11
Fine, Gary Alan, 308n.14, 310n.16, 312n.39

Finnegan, Ruth, 325n.12
Fishman, Pamela, 237
Florio, Susan, 308n.11
Folb, Edith, 285
Foley, Donald L., 311n.20
Foot, Hugh C., 308nn.13, 14
Forbes, David, 308n.14
Fowler, Roger, 314n.3
Frake, Charles O., 287
Frankenberg, Ronald, 191
Fraser, Bruce, 72
Freedman, Daniel G., 17

Garber, Jenny, 11
Gardner, R., 68, 72
Garfinkel, Harold, 1, 4, 15, 221
Garvey, Catherine, 68, 127, 143, 163, 188, 197,
    308nn.11, 12, 315n.13, 316n.15, 319nn.3, 4,
    320nn.22, 23
Gegeo, David, 12
Gelman, R., 308n.12
Genishi, Celia, 143, 144, 188, 312n.39, 319n.3,
    320nn.20, 22, 322n.43
Georges, Robert, A., 237, 325n.12
Gerson, Rimona, 72
Gilligan, Carol, 49, 134, 137, 219, 284,
    324n.18, 327nn.6, 7
Gilmore, David, 191
Gilmore, Perry, 308n.11
Gilmour, Robin, 308n.14
Glassner, Barry, 308n.14
Glatthorn, Allan A., 308n.11
Glazer, Mark, 322n.41
Gleason, Jean Berko, 125, 317nn.10, 11, 12,
    13
Gluckman, Max, 191, 251, 263
Goffman, Erving, 2, 8, 10, 15, 22, 40, 49, 73,
    74, 80, 84, 89, 93, 122, 123, 141, 142, 157,
    185, 198, 207, 223, 230, 231, 232, 233, 234,
    235, 237, 245, 246, 260, 263, 267, 279,
    314n.4, 319n.11, 323n.11, 325n.9
Goldman, Lawrence, 7
Golter, Beckie S., 21, 326n.2
Goodenough, Ward H., 7, 8, 9, 285, 323n.7
Goodman, M. E., 308n.14
Goodwin, Charles, 10, 19, 23, 213, 236, 237,
    244, 307n.4, 315nn.6, 4, 6, 316nn.16, 17,
    324n.3, 326n.5
Goodwin, Marjorie Harness, 19, 134, 213,
    237, 246, 284, 315nn.4, 6, 316nn.16, 17,
    320n.26, 326n.5
Gordon, David, 66, 106, 318n.17
Gospodinoff, Kenneth, 12, 308n.11
Gossen, Gary H., 322n.41
Gottman, John M., 17, 308n.14
Grant, Linda, 314n.55, 317n.9
Green, E. H., 319n.1, 322n.45
Green, Judith, 308n.11
Greif, Esther Blank, 125, 317n.11
Grice, H. P., 66

Griffin, Peg, 308n.11
Grimshaw, Allen, 318n.2
Gulliver, P. H., 156
Gumperz, John J., 8, 22, 23, 122, 307n.7
Gunter, Richard, 147
Guy, Rebecca F., 141

Halliday, M. A. K., 145, 150, 153, 308n.12, 323n.6, 327n.14
Hallinan, Maureen T., 39, 48, 49, 133, 137, 308n.14, 310n.16, 311n.27, 314n.54
Halverson, Charles F., 39, 48, 137
Hammer, Muriel, 309n.1
Handel, Gerald, 308n.14
Hanks, William F., 10, 89, 91, 315n.8
Hannerz, Ulf, 29, 185, 188, 191, 284
Harkness, Sara, 21, 311n.27
Harré, Rom, 13
Harris, Clement, 191
Hart, Craig H., 21, 326n.2
Hart, R. A., 310n.15
Hartup, Willard W., 12, 38, 39, 43, 49, 308n.14, 311n.27, 312n.36
Hasan, Rugaiya, 145, 150, 153, 323n.6, 327n.14
Haviland, John Beard, 7, 191, 307n.6, 319n.16, 324n.3
Heath, Christian, 10, 307n.4
Heath, Shirley Brice, 38, 308n.12, 310n.11, 312n.33
Hedley, Carolyn, 308n.11
Henley, Nancy, 117, 318n.1
Heritage, John C., 3, 5, 7, 73, 307nn.3, 4
Hollos, Marida, 72
Holmes, Dick, 326n.2
Homans, G. C., 310n.16
Honko, Lauri, 326n.9
Hotchkiss, J. C., 191
House, Juliane, 72
Hughes, Linda A., 43, 134, 188, 314n.53, 318n.21, 323n.15, 324n.19
Hymes, Dell H., 22, 23, 237, 307n.11, 309n.3

Iannotti, Ronald, 317n.10

Jacklin, Carol Nagy, 21, 49, 285
Jakobson, Roman, 177
James, S. L., 68
Jefferson, Gail, 6, 16, 25, 146, 157, 160, 212, 236, 237, 246, 307nn.2, 4, 319n.14, 323n.7, 324n.3, 326n.1
Jenkins, Mercilee MacIntyre, 237
John, Vera, 307n.11
Jolly, C. J., 102
Jordan, Brigitte, 274

Kalčik, Susan, 284
Kasper, Gabrielle, 72
Katriel, Tamar, 223, 320nn.20, 27, 324n.20, 326n.1

Keenan, Elinor Ochs, 12, 321n.31
Keiser, R. Lincoln, 37
Keller-Cohen, Deborah, 320n.22
Kendon, Adam, 10
Kerber, Linda K., 327nn.6, 7
Kernan, Keith T., 17, 68, 105, 127, 237, 308n.11, 313n.49, 318n.3
Kirsh, Barbara, 72
Kirshenblatt-Gimblett, Barbara, 237
Kittay, Eva Feder, 327n.6
Klein, Ewan, 12, 321n.31
Knapp, Herbert, 311n.26, 313n.45
Knapp, Mary, 311n.26, 313n.45
Kochman, Thomas, 142, 149, 185, 188, 258, 259, 267, 285, 313nn.41, 51, 324n.16
Kohlberg, L., 324n.18
Konner, M., 12, 39
Kramarae, Cheris, 117, 318n.1
Krappman, Lothar, 311n.27, 314n.57
Kurth, Suzanne B., 310n.16

Labov, William, 11, 16, 18, 29, 65, 66, 67, 68, 69, 78, 92, 141, 177, 185, 199, 229, 231, 232, 234, 235, 237, 279, 285, 314n.1, 317n.4, 320nn.19, 21, 322n.39, 324nn.4, 5, 325n.6, 326nn.6, 8, 327n.14
Ladd, D. Robert Jr., 147, 151, 181, 321n.37
Ladd, Gary W., 21, 326n.2
Ladner, J. A., 318n.15
LaFontaine, Jean, 3, 11, 283, 308n.14
La Gaipa, John J., 13, 17
Lakoff, George, 66, 274
Lakoff, Robin, 117, 125, 141, 318n.1
Lampert, Martin, 72
Lando, B., 311n.18
Larson, R., 311n.23
Lave, Jean, 3, 8, 14, 17, 309nn.17, 21
Leary, James P., 325n.12
Lee, John R., 307n.4
Lee, Richard Borshay, 46, 47
Lein, Laura, 17, 143, 144, 188, 308n.11, 319n.13, 320n.23, 321nn.33, 35, 322n.40, 323n.13
Lemann, Nicholas, 29
Leont'ev, A. N., 14
Lever, Janet Rae, 39, 42, 48, 49, 133, 134, 137, 219, 309n.8, 311nn.19, 22, 23, 24, 312nn.30, 35, 313nn.44, 46, 315n.2
Levin, E. S., 125
Levinson, Stephen C., 2, 8, 10, 66, 68, 70, 81, 120, 141, 235, 307nn.3, 4, 315n.9, 317n.2
Lévi-Strauss, Claude, 229, 234
Lewis, D., 318n.16
Lewis, J., 18, 285
Lewis, M., 308nn.13, 14
Lieberman, Kenneth, 325n.11
Lubin, David, 308n.14
Luria, Zella, 49, 133, 314n.56
Lyons, John, 315n.12

McAdoo, H. P., 318n.15
McCall, George J., 17
McCarl, Robert S., 237
Maccoby, Eleanor Emmons, 21, 49, 285
McConnell-Ginet, Sally, 318n.1
McDermott, Raymond P., 12, 308n.11
McGhee, Z., 311n.22
McGurk, Harry, 308n.14
McLaughlin, Margaret L., 141
McLoyd, Vonnie C., 125, 318nn.15, 16, 17
McRobbie, Angela, 11
McTear, Michael F., 66, 316n.15
Malinowski, Bronislaw, 7, 11, 286
Maltz, Daniel N., 53, 136, 137, 318n.1
Maynard, Douglas W., 143, 144, 157, 158, 188, 197, 241, 307n.4, 308n.11, 312n.39, 319nn.2, 4, 8, 320nn.24, 27, 28
Mead, George H., 308n.14
Mead, Margaret, 235, 309n.2
Medrich, Elliott A., 35, 310nn.9, 11, 17, 311n.20
Mehan, Hugh, 12, 308n.11, 316n.14
Meyers, Diana T., 327n.6
Michaels, Sarah, 308n.11
Milan, W., 72
Miller, Thomas J., 307n.10
Mishler, Elliot G., 237, 274, 324n.1
Mitchell, J. Clyde, 20
Mitchell-Kernan, Claudia, 11, 17, 68, 105, 127, 185, 258, 259, 267, 285, 308n.11, 313n.49, 318n.3
Moerman, Michael, 5, 224, 326n.1
Mohatt, Gerald, 308n.11
Morgan, E. F., 311n.21, 312n.30
Morgan, J. L., 314n.3
Moshin, Nadeem, 21
Murtaugh, Michael, 309nn.17, 21

Nader, Laura, 156, 192, 223, 322n.3
Nelson, Katherine, 16
Newman, Denis, 15
Nolen, Winnie, 72

Ochs, Elinor, 8, 9, 237, 321n.31
O'Connor, Mary C., 72
Olshtain, Elite, 68, 72, 317nn.2, 4
Omark, D. R., 49
Omark, Donald R., 17
Opie, Iona, 38, 311n.20, 312n.28
Opie, Peter, 38, 311n.20, 312n.28
Ortner, Sherry B., 285
Oswald, Hans, 311n.27, 314n.57
Overing, J., 285, 327n.8
Overton, Willis F., 308n.14

Paine, Robert, 191
Parkhurst, Jennifer T., 17
Parsons, E. C., 326n.3
Pepler, Debra, 12, 317n.14
Philips, Susan U., 308n.11, 318n.1

Piaget, Jean, 11, 13, 134, 159, 188, 189, 219, 283, 308n.14, 319n.1, 320n.22, 327n.5
Pike, Kenneth L., 323n.8
Pitcher, E., 318n.15
Polanyi, Livia, 237, 325n.6
Pomerantz, Anita, 40, 69, 144, 146, 152, 315n.6, 319nn.9, 15, 320n.23
Pratt, Mary Louise, 237, 325n.6
Prince, Gerald, 325nn.7, 8
Propp, Vladimir, 232

Radcliffe-Brown, A. R., 3, 287
Ratner, N., 65
Ray, Shirley Aisha, 125, 318nn.15, 16, 17
Reisman, Karl, 188, 285, 313n.41
Remler, Jane E., 320n.22
Reynolds, Pamela, 21
Richards, Martin P. M., 283, 308n.14
Rintell, Ellen, 72
Rizzo, Thomas, 143, 188, 308n.11, 309n.19, 319nn.5, 6, 10
Robins, C., 18, 285, 327n.14
Robinson, John A., 325n.6
Rogoff, Barbara, 14, 21, 311nn.18, 27, 312n.31
Roizen, Judith, 35, 310nn.9, 11, 17, 311n.20
Rosaldo, Michelle Z., 284
Rose, Dan, 33, 142, 310n.10, 313n.50, 314n.58, 322n.1, 324nn.22, 23, 326nn.4, 7
Rosenberg, B., 311n.21, 312n.30
Rosenberg, Jarrett, 72
Rosenblum L., 308nn.13, 14
Ross, Hildy S., 308n.14
Roy, C., 65
Rubin, Kenneth H., 308n.14
Rubin, Victor, 35, 310nn.9, 11, 17, 311n.20
Rubin, Zick, 16, 308nn.13, 14, 311n.25, 322n.45
Rudolph, Dina, 237

Sachs, Jacqueline, 127
Sacks, Harvey, 4, 5, 6, 7, 8, 16, 25, 82, 91, 93, 146, 157, 177, 198, 200, 212, 216, 224, 234, 235, 236, 251, 261, 279, 307nn.2, 4, 314n.59, 319n.7, 320n.17, 326nn.1, 3, 4, 2, 327n.13
Salzinger, Suzanne, 309n.1
Sanford, Stephanie, 43, 327n.10
Sapir, Edward, 3
Saussure, Ferdinand de, 3, 8
Savasta, M. L., 42, 48
Savin-Williams, Richard, 11, 37, 48, 308n.14
Schegloff, Emanuel A., 6, 16, 23, 25, 66, 82, 89, 90, 146, 157, 200, 212, 216, 307nn.2, 3, 4, 315n.8, 326n.1
Schenkein, Jim, 160, 307n.4
Schieffelin, Bambi B., 12, 321n.31
Schiffrin, Deborah, 72, 237, 322n.38
Schildkrout, Enid, 21
Schofield, Janet Ward, 49, 313n.47
Schultz, L., 318n.15
Schwartzman, Helen B., 308n.11

Scollon, Ron, 237
Scollon, Suzanne B. K., 237
Scribner, Sylvia, 309nn.17, 21
Searle, John R., 66, 314n.3
Selman, Robert L., 17, 123, 308n.14, 309n.20, 316n.13, 317n.7
Shantz, Carolyn Uhlinger, 15, 16, 17, 141, 308n.14, 309n.20, 322n.45
Shatz, Marilyn, 308nn.12, 13
Sheldon, Amy, 143
Sherif, Carolyn W., 312n.37
Sherif, Muzafer, 312n.37
Sherzer, Joel, 237, 286
Shields, M. M., 16, 17
Shuman, Amy, 7, 12, 309n.3, 327n.12
Shuy, Roger W., 285, 308n.11
Siegel, Alexander W., 308n.16
Simmel, Georg, 1, 48
Sister, E., 70
Skolnick, Arline, 308n.14
Smith, Barbara Hernstein, 324n.4, 325n.14
Smith, Jean R., 308nn.13, 14
Smith, Ruth, 237
Sones, Gittelle, 48
Speier, Matthew, 16, 308n.14
Spindler, George, 308n.11
Stack, Carol, 318n.15, 327n.7
Stahl, Sandra S. K., 237
Steinberg, Zina, 68, 100
Stone, Carolyn R., 68, 100, 123, 308n.14, 316n.13, 317n.7
Strage, Amy, 72
Strayer, F. F., 17, 103, 312n.38
Strayer, Janet, 103
Streeck, Jürgen, 308n.14, 327n.3
Suchman, Lucy, 274
Sullivan, H. S., 308n.14
Super, Charles M., 21, 311n.27
Suthinee, Santaputra, 21
Suttles, G. D., 37, 311n.20
Sutton-Smith, Brian, 12, 33, 37, 42, 48, 137, 308n.14, 311n.21, 312nn.29, 30
Szwed, John, 191

Tannen, Deborah, 72, 237, 325n.6
Taylor, Carolyn, 237
Terasaki, Alene, 198
Thorne, Barrie, 21, 43, 49, 53, 117, 133, 136, 285, 308n.14, 314n.56, 318n.1, 327n.3
Todd, Harry F., 156, 192, 223, 322n.3
Tomlinson, G., 307n.11
Tuma, N. B., 314n.54
Turner, Victor W., 190, 225, 239, 324nn.24, 2

Vaughn, Brian E., 102
Vazsonyi, Andrew, 325n.12
Viezzer, Moema, 21
Vinacke, W. Edgar, 48
Vološinov, V. N., 80, 90, 93, 201, 232, 245, 267, 279, 319n.11, 321n.36
Volpe, J. A., 17, 308n.14
Von Glascoe, Christine A., 324n.19
von Salisch, Maria, 311n.27, 314n.57
Vuchinich, Samuel, 188
Vygotsky, L. S., 8, 13, 14, 15, 308n.14

Wadsworth, Emily M., 21, 326n.2
Waldrop, Mary F., 39, 48, 137
Waletzky, Joshua, 231, 235, 237
Wallat, Cynthia, 308n.11
Walters, Joel, 72
Waters, Everett, 102
Watson, Karen Ann, 234, 237, 325n.6
Watson-Gegeo, Karen Ann, 12, 237
Werner, Oswald, 274
Wertsch, James V., 8, 13, 14
West, Candace, 117, 307n.4, 317n.3, 318n.1
White, Sheldon H., 308n.16
Whiting, Beatrice, 49, 310n.18, 313n.42, 322n.45
Whiting, J. W. M., 322n.45
Whyte, William Foote, 37
Wierzbicka, Anna, 72
Wilkinson, Louise Cherry, 308n.11
Wilson, Peter J., 322n.2
Wittgenstein, Ludwig, 81
Wolfe, Tom, 315n.10
Wolfson, Nessa, 237
Women for Guatemala, 21
Wood, B., 68, 72
Wootton, A. J., 66, 316n.15
Wright, H. F., 310n.15
Wulff, Helena, 327n.10

Yaeger, Malcah, 151
Yaeger-Dror, Malcah, 70, 72, 151
Yanagisako, Sylvia Junko, 327n.8
Yawkey, Thomas D., 307n.10
Yngvesson, Barbara, 156
Young, Virginia H., 318n.16
Youniss, James, 17, 189, 308n.14, 322n.45, 327n.5

Zahn-Waxler, Carolyn, 317n.10
Zigler, E., 13
Zimmerman, Don H., 307n.4, 318n.1

Subject Index

Accusations
directs 200–01
he-said-she-said, 190, 194–202
alternative formats, 199
as context-creating, 195, 224
as embedded structures, 224
as first pair parts, 200, 202
as framing devices, 195–97, 199,
as "reported speech," 201–02
face-saving nature, 202–03, 224
four-stage, 202–05
indirect speech, 203, 208
information states of participants, 198
third (intermediary) parties, 196–97, 199,
201–03, 224
triadic nature, 197, 205, 323n.8
warrants, 201–02
Activities, as basic unit of cultural analysis,
8–9
importance across disciplines, 8
situated activity systems, 8, 19
speech events, 8, 307n.7
Activity theory, 13–14
Agreement, preference for, 144–45
cross-cultural studies, 319n.16
intonation, 146
other-initiated repair, 146
Alliance formation, 48, 133–34, 201
among boys, 248
among girls, 42, 45–49, 135–36
coalitions in friendship, 47
cross-cultural, 318n.20
exclusiveness, 48, 133–34
Argument types
primitive argument, 159
quarrel, 159
See also Conflict, Counters, He-said-she-
said, Opposition sequencing

Basing, 118, 154–55
Black English Vernacular, 18, 29, 327n.14
Bragging
and boys' social organization, 40–41
avoidance among adults, 40
contrasted with boasting, 313n.41
cross-cultural studies, 313n.42
gender differences in, 46
in boys' games, 40–42

Change-of-state token, 157, 213
Child language studies
alternative psychological perspectives,
307n.10

classroom, 308n.11
experimental studies, 308n.12
language acquisition, 12–13
need for naturalistic studies, 309nn.18, 19,
20, 327n.4
preschool focus, 12–13,
Children's activities, 35–39
care giving and ethnicity, 317n.9, 318n.16
child care, 36, 38, 125–26, 137, 312nn.33,
34, 36
chores, 36, 310n.18, 311n.19
clubs, 33, 311nn.24, 25
gender differences in, 35–39,
jobs, 36
play, 36–39
pretend play, 126–34, 308n.11, 318n.15
spatial organization of play, 35–36, 310n.11
task activity, 75–77, 109
See also Comparisons, Conflict, Directives,
He-said-she-said
Classroom interaction research, 12, 307n.11
Comparisons, 39–46
across gender groups, 49–53
age as a variable, 312n.39
boys', 39–42, 313n.48
class differences, 313n.46
cross-age, 51
cross-cultural parallels, 46, 135–36, 313n.40
features of hierarchy, 312n.38
gender differences, 44–46, 313n.44
gender group boundary marking, 49–51
girls', 42–46, 313nn.44, 46, 47, 49
in the African-American community,
313nn.50, 51
younger children's, 322n.43
Conflict
adult intervention, 144, 156
"adversarial talk," 141, 143
affective alignment, 142, 163
alignment in, 158, 165
alliances, 165
and deferential interaction, 141
and developmental research, 188–89
and role-play data, 144, 323n.13
as aggressive behavior, 141, 322n.45
as political activity, 142, 144, 157, 165, 219
as social construction, 142
as theater, 142
character contests, 142, 188
conflict resolution, 143, 157. See also Dispute process types
"contest" element among females, 219
cooperative production of meaning, 189
cross-cultural research, 188, 320n.27,
322n.44, 324n.20

definitions, 143, 319nn.2, 3, 8
dyadic v. multiparty, 143, 197–98, 223
frame switching, 168–77
highlighting opposition, 145, 162–63, 319nn.6, 7, 8
multiparty, 158
proof strategies, 165–70
  logical paradox, 169–70, 256
  witnesses, 166–67
psychological interpretations, 141,
psychological studies, 143, 197, 319nn.1, 5
relationship to gender, 188
sequencing strategies, 158–77
See also Dispute process types, He-said-she-said, Opposition sequencing, Opposition turns
Conversation
as a resource for organizing social life, 4, 7
sequential organization, 6
Conversation analysis
and analysis of culture, 7–8, 287
and cognitive anthropology, 7, 274
and ethnographic practice, 7, 274, 279
and interview techniques, 6, 23, 274, 279
distinguished from linguistics, 5
methodology, 4–8, 22–23, 274, 287, 307n3, 327n.13
proof procedures, 6
research reviews, 307nn.3, 4
Counters
next moves in arguments, 240–41
next moves to directives, 105, 116, 121–23, 130

Developmental research in psychology
as needing to investigate social world, 308n.16
as paradigm for study of children, 308n.15
friendship studies, 17
problems with interview procedures, 17, 309n.20
social cognition, 15–16
social skills, 16
Directives, 63–137
address terms in, 84–88, 315n.9
  insult terms, 84–85, 105, 319n.12
  "man," 86–88, 99, 315n.10
  personal names, 86–87
adult/child, 123–26
affective valences, 87, 106
aggravation, 67–70, 78–80, 106
aggravation and syntactic shape, 80–84
animations of cited figures, 81, 84, 89–90
as activity systems, 88
as alignment displays, 73–74, 85–88, 95–99, 107–08
as dramaturgical structure, 91, 108
as dynamic fields of action, 89, 108
as social comparisons, 63, 97, 105, 318n.3

as social control mechanisms, 67–69, 78, 102, 105–06, 131,314n.3
as social frames, 70–72, 314n.4
asymmetry
  and aggravation, 81
  and social imposition, 79, 97
  in "playing house" frame among girls, 127–32
  in speaker/addressee roles, 95, 106–08
  in teacher/novice roles, 99–102, 122–23
  stage manager position in "house," 131–34
bald imperatives, 78–79, 84, 106, 117–21, 123–24
boys' accounts
  egocentric needs of speaker, 97–99
  needs of the activity, 98–99, 104, 106
  pejorative assessments of recipient, 79, 83
  rights and duties, 92, 105
character ties, 88–90
class and ethnic differences, 125
context-influenced, 72–74, 85, 317n.13
cross-cultural research, 72
definition, 63, 65
format tying, 92
formulating space, 82–83, 89
gender differences, 64, 84, 109–11, 113, 116–17, 135–37, 317nn.3, 10, 11
girls' accounts
  benefits for recipient, 112, 121–22, 125, 128
  needs of the activity, 112–13
honorifics, 85–86
hypothetical scene construction, 91–92
in play frames, 126–35
indirection and mitigation, 69–70
leadership roles, 107, 130–32, 318n.19
marked forms of girls, 118
maximum efficiency constraint, 120
mitigation, 67–70, 118, 317nn.2, 4
modal constructions
  as mitigators, 317n.4
  boys as suppliants, 95
  girls' proposals for action, 111
need statements, 68, 69, 98, 315n.13
negotiation of relationships, 107, 133–34
next moves in directive sequences
  boys', 103–07
  girls', 113–16
  in "house" frame, 129–30
participant depictions, 79–81
political nature of, 94, 97, 106–07,
preconditions, 92
pronouns
  depicting participants, 80–81, 110–111, 317n.5
  lumping participants, 110, 316n.1
  partitioning participants, 94–96
requests, 95, 106, 129

Directives (*Cont'd*)
  role complementarity, 107, 135
  scene transformations, 91–93
  sequential environments, 66, 73, 82–84,
    316n.15
  situated within activities, 81–84, 118–22,
    136–37
  social imposition and aggravation, 78
  speech act theory models, 65–66, 81, 103
  symmetry
    avoiding differentiation or social impo-
      sition, 115–17
    in speaker/addressee roles, 110–12
    in type of directive usage, 113–15, 318n.17
    teacher/novice role among girls, 123
  syntactic shape and social imposition, 67–
    70, 78–79, 110–11
  time structure, 110, 117
  typologies, 68
Dispute process types
  brogez, 223, 324n.20
  conflict resolution, 143, 157
  degradation ceremony, 221–22
  mediation, 156, 223, 320n.20
  negotiation, 192
  noncompromise in children's disputes, 157,
    188, 192, 223, 319n.6
  ostracism, 118, 190, 221–23
  remedial exchanges, 157, 214–15
  ridicule, 222
  settlement, 156, 322n.3
  stalemate, 215–18
  withdrawal, 218
  See also Conflict, He-said-she-said

Ethnicity, 188, 285, 307n.1, 317n.15, 318n.16
Everyday cognition, 14, 309nn.17, 21
Exclusion, 48, 83, 89, 94, 222, 264

Fieldwork, 22–24
  children's perceptions of ethnographer, 24
  field site, 29–35
  methodology, 22–24, 283
  observation v. participant observation, 23
  recording techniques, 19, 22
Format tying, 177–85
  as a template for sequencing, 184
  cross-cultural, 321nn.32, 33, 322nn.40, 41
  embedding, 180, 181, 224, 242
  escalations, 180, 321n.35
  parallelism, 185, 320n.29
  realigning participation, 179, 180
  relationship to ritual insult, 185–88
  repetition, 179
Frame analysis
  animating present and nonpresent parties
    in stories as a political move, 260, 262–
    67, 278
  animations of cited figures in directives, 81,
    84, 89–90

character animation in stories, 232–33,
  244–46, 249–50
Goffman's perspective outlined, 232–34
he-said-she-said accusations as framing devices, 10, 195–99
See also Participation frameworks, Story
  transformations, Transformations
Friendships
  among girls, 45–49, 52, 137
  cross-gender, 49–52
  exclusiveness in, 51

Games
  and social organization, 39–42
  competitions, 40–42, 76
  conflict during, 134, 136, 312n.35, 324n.19
  cycles, 37, 42, 75
  dialogue games, 38, 312n.28
  jump rope, 42–43, 313n.45
  skelly, 37, 311n.26
  younger children's repertoire, 38
Gender roles
  boys' comparisons, 39–42
  cross-cultural studies, 307n.8
  girl/boy interaction, 49–52
  girls' and boys' dispute stories compared,
    278–79
  girls' comparisons, 42–46
  girls' skill in argumentation 48, 188, 224–
    25, 284
  girls' use of bald imperatives, 117
  in achieving social organization, 136–37
  in alliance formation, 48
  in children's directives, 64, 84, 97–99, 109–
    11, 113, 116–17, 122, 135–37, 317nn.3,
    10, 11
  in children's responsibilities, 36, 38, 125–
    26, 137, 312nn.33, 34, 36
  in children's talk, 9, 284–85, 318n.1
  in instructor role, 99–102, 122–23
  in play, 36–39, 134, 311nn.20, 21, 22, 23,
    312n.30
  See also Gendered behavior, models of
Gendered behavior, models of
  "arrangement between the sexes," 49
  "different voice," 64, 136, 284, 327nn.6, 7
  male domination, 117
  Maple Street children's, 49–52
  public and private, 284–85, 327n.8
  reviews of literature, 318n.1
  "separate worlds" model, 53, 136
  women as "more polite," 117
  women as unconcerned with legalistic de-
    bate, 219
Gossip
  among black adults, 324n.23
  ethnographic research, 7, 191, 307n.6,
    327n.12
  targets of, 263, 324n.21
  See also He-said-she-said

He-said-she-said
  accusations, 190, 195–202
  adult forms, 322n.1
  affect displays, 211, 219, 224
  as "social drama," 190, 203, 213, 225
  as character contest, 190, 219, 224
  as political process, 190, 219, 223
  as vernacular legal process, 219, 223
  closings, 214–18
    aphorisms as topic bounding, 216
    avoidance, 218
    stalemate, 215–18
  degradation ceremony, 221–22
  fights, 208
  focusing topic, 213, 219
  fourth-stage transformations, 202–05
  frame transformation, 211, 214
  "getting something straight," 200, 217
  jealousy, 220, 223
  keying, 215, 218, 223
  multiparty participation, 209–10
  offenses, 199, 323n.10
  ostracism, 190, 221–23, 225
  participation framework, 190, 195, 203,
    213, 224, 259–60
  responses
    counters, 202
    as face-saving, 208, 224, 323n.15
    counteraccusations, 201, 202, 209, 211,
      323n.12
    denials, 200, 205–09, 323n.11, 324n.16
    recontextualizations, 207–08
  righteous indignation, 224, 286
  stages, 197, 203
  "swagging," 217–18, 274
  talk about absent parties, 199
  third-party participation, 191, 202, 214,
    223, 224
  trajectory, 209–13
  "two against one" alignments, 201–02, 223,
    323n.14
  See also Accusations
Human interaction
  and social behavior, 1–2
  as integrating language, culture, and social
    organization, 2
  interest for social anthropologists, 5–6
Hypothetical event construction
  in arguments, 171–73
  in directives, 91–93
  in stories, 250–51

Indirect speech acts, 66–70
Instigating
  as political process, 258, 263, 267
  definitions, 258–59
  "indirection" in, 267
Instigating stories
  alignment and affect, 265, 267
  animation of "cited figures," 263–66

  as recruiting devices, 276–77
  audience response as "getting involved,"
    261
  coimplicating listeners, 260–62, 267
  commitments as accountable actions, 273–
    74
  compared to boys' dispute stories, 278–79
  cross-cultural comparisons, 326n.1, 326n.4
  differentiated recipient response, 267–71
  eliciting a commitment to confront, 265–67
  enactments as idealized versions, 274
  enactments of possible worlds, 274
  extended example, 299–305
  features, 262
  recipient design, 262–63
  relationship of present parties to story
    characters, 263–66
  righteous indignation, 267
  selective reporting, 274–75, 278–79, 324n.4
  strategic interaction, 267
  talk about absent parties, 262
  within larger realms of action, 267, 278–79
Insults. *See* Pejorative person descriptors,
  Ritual insults
Intonation
  adult and child disagreement contrasted,
    151, 320n.21
  as contextualization cue, 122–23, 136
  in directives, 88, 99
  in opposition moves, 146–47, 151, 162, 181,
    319n.13, 321n.37, 322n.38
  in predisagreements, 146

Language
  as a constitutive feature of social action, 4,
    286
  as an autonomous formal system, 3
  as reflective v. constitutive of social order,
    286
  See also Intonation, Metaphorical speech,
    Opposition turns, Parallelism, Pronouns,
    Sound play
Legal anthropology, 156
  See also Conflict, Dispute process types,
    He-said-she-said

Maps of neighborhood, 31, 34
Material culture
  as basis for comparison, 41, 44, 45
  boys', 37, 75–76
  clothing and ethnicity, 313n.50
  girls', 36, 109
  resource allocation and social organization,
    315n.5
Metaphorical speech, 170–77

Occasion-specific identities, 195, 203, 204,
  205, 236, 323n.7
Opposition sequencing, 158–77
  age differences, 320n.24

Opposition sequencing (*Cont'd*)
  extended series, 160–63
  justifications, 163–65, 320n.24
  recycling positions, 154–63, 320nn.22, 23
  replacement, 145, 161, 181–82
  rounds, 184, 240–42
  substitution, 161, 182
Opposition turns, 143–56
  affective valences, 146–47, 181
  alignment displays in, 149, 152
  as social portraits, 149–50, 155
  categorizations, 154–56
  challenges, 147
  character constructions, 146–49
  disagreements, 151–53
  disclaimers, 153–54
  distinct from other-initiated repair, 146
  indirect responses, 153–55
  intensifiers, 149
  intonation, 146–47, 151, 162, 181, 319n.13,
    321n.37, 322n.38
  language play, 179
  partial repetition, 145–46, 149, 154, 319n.10
  participation frameworks, 152, 156, 241
  person descriptors, 148–50, 162
  polarity, 145, 159, 181
  relationship to repair, 144–48, 157
  returns, 152–53, 180
  rhythm, 319n.12
  substitutions, 150–51
  turn shape, 145–47
  wit assessment in counter moves, 149, 180

Parallelism, 177
Participation frameworks
  in directives, 85, 88
  in he-said-she-said disputes, 190, 195, 203,
    213, 224
  in return and exchange moves, 152, 240–
    42, 244, 319n.15
  in stories, 239, 244, 245
Peer group
  and linguistic study, 11
  as an institution for learning, 11, 326n.1
  as locus for study of language, 11–13,
    307n.9
  compared with sibling systems, 317n.14
  cross-cultural differences, 21, 310n.18,
    311n.27, 327n.10
  importance in development, 308n.14
  Maple Street group composition, 289–90
  mixed gender interaction, 12, 21, 38,
    311n.27
  multiage interaction, 12, 21, 38–39, 137,
    312n.31
  neglect of female peer group studies, 11–
    12
  neighborhood as setting for interaction,
    20–21, 33

  proximity, 35, 310n.16
  reasons unstudied, 308n.13
Pejorative person descriptors (insult terms)
  in directives, 84–88
  in opposition sequences, 148–50
Play preferences
  and social organization, 39–42
  age differences, 36–39
  cross-cultural studies, 315n.1
  gender differences, 36–39, 311nn.21, 22,
    23, 312n.30
  multi-age preferences of girls, 39
Politeness and language structure
  in directives, 68–70
  pragmatic organization of, 141
Pragmatics, 177
Pronouns
  in directives
    deictics animating characters and recipi-
      ents, 80
    possessives creating character ties, 88–92
    possessives indexing social information,
      96
    possessives partitioning participants, 94–
      96
  in opposition sequences, 179–81
  in stories, 325n.9

Reported speech, 201, 232
Reporting as social construction, 274–75, 279,
  325nn.10, 14
  See also Instigating
Righteous indignation, 224, 267, 286
Ritual insult, 185–88
  and opposition sequences, 188
  as format tying, 186–88
  as transformation in alignment framework,
    187
  attributes cited, 322n.39
  extended sequence, 291–93
  girls' competence, 188
  in taunting, 221–22
  research, 185
  wit assessment, 185

School settings, 12, 21, 144, 189, 284
Signifying, 259
Social class
  and children's responses to imperatives,
    129
  and girls' criteria for comparison, 43
  and living arrangements, 309n.7, 310n.10,
    11
  and mother/child directives, 125
  and neighborhoods, 309nn.3, 5
  and peer learning possibilities, 310n.12
  and play patterns, 20, 33, 35, 39, 309n.8,
    310n.9
  similarities in girls' notions of conceit, 46

working-class features of Maple Street, 21
29–33
Social organization among children
age-group boundaries, 35, 51, 310n.15
age-heterogeneous groups, 312n.31
and leadership, 107
asymmetrical arrangements, 77, 129–32,
135
gender boundary marking, 49–51
gender differences, 109, 113, 134–37,
310nn.17, 18, 312n.32
inter-ethnic group interaction, 314n.55
mixed-gender friendships, 311n.27,
314nn.54, 56, 57
networks, 309n.1
same-age clusters, 12, 21, 34–35, 38, 311n.27
same-gender clusters, 34–35, 311n.27,
312n.32, 314n.59
shifting hierarchies among boys, 41–42, 46,
75, 312n.37, 316n.16
social differentiation among girls, 42–46,
134–35
spatial positioning and social inclusion, 82–
83, 89
structure of attention, 102
team organization, 76, 82, 314n.53, 315n.2,
318n.21
territoriality as a resource, 77
within games, 134, 318n.21
Social perspective taking, 317n.7
Social science partitioning, 2–4
Socialization, 13, 283, 327n.3
Sound play
among young children, 321n.31
in dispute, 174, 176, 182–83
Sounding, 185, 320n.19
Speech act theory
problems with treatment of discourse phenomena, 177, 179
theoretical perspectives, 177, 314n.2
Stories
animation of characters, 245, 248–50
as conversational anchor, 250, 252
as recruiting devices, 246–48, 256, 276–77
as strategic interaction, 256, 277
as vernacular theatrical performance, 230,
239, 246, 324n.2
audience, 230, 244, 246–48, 324n.3, 325n.12
conarration, 237, 244
counters, 248–56
cycled stories, 252–55
differentiated participation, 247, 248–50
elliptical processes, 326n.3

evaluation, 245, 246, 247, 250, 324n.6
extended stories in disputes, 295–98
hypothetical stories, 250–51, 253
internal structure, 231, 237, 246–56
intertextuality, 246, 249
invitations to laugh during, 246, 249
participation frameworks, 239, 244, 248,
325n.8
quoted talk as refrain, 249–50, 251
second stories, 91, 93, 251, 252
See also Instigating stories
Stories, perspectives on
across disciplines, 324n.1
conversation analysis, 229
embedded within conversation and interaction, 234
emergent structures, 236
motive power, 236, 278, 326n.2
multiunit turn, 235, 243
participation structures, 236
prefaces, 236
segments, 236,
ethnography of speaking, 229, 237
folklore, 229, 232, 237, 325n.12
Goffman, 229, 230
footing, 245
frame analysis, 232–33, 245, 260
participation structure, 233
Labov, 229, 231–32
definition of narrative, 231
evaluation, 232
internal structure, 231
Story transformations
hypothetical stories, 250–51, 253, 276–78
preplayings, 271–74
replayings, 274–75

Terms of address
honorifics, 85–86
insult terms, 84–85, 105, 319n.12
"man," 86–88, 99, 315n.10
personal names, 86–87
Texts, relevance for anthropological research,
7, 287, 307n.5,
Transcription, 25–26
Transformations
in genre during dispute, 243–44, 246, 248,
256–57
next moves in arguments, 177–85,
next moves in directives, 91–93
next moves in stories, 250–51, 253, 271–78
Tying techniques, 177